Discourse on Leadership

T0331116

In a wide-ranging and provocative new study, Bert A. Spector provides a critical analysis of past and present theories of leadership. Spector asserts that our perception of leadership influences who we vote for, who we hire and promote, and ultimately to whom we choose grant our authority. Focusing on leadership in discourse, the book sets out to explore how the notion of leadership has been articulated, studied, and debated by academics, but also by practitioners, journalists, and others who seek to influence the thoughts of others. Paying particular attention to the social, economic, political, intellectual, and historical forces that have helped shape the discussion, *Discourse on Leadership* offers an insightful historiography of leadership as a concept and how our understanding of it continues to evolve.

BERT A. SPECTOR (PhD, American History) is Associate Professor of International Business and Management at Northeastern University's D'Amore-McKim School of Business. His research interests include organizational change, leadership, business model innovation, and management history. His articles have appeared in *Leadership, Management & Organizational History* and the *Harvard Business Review*. He is the author/co-author of seven previous books, including *The Critical Path to Corporate Renewal* which received the Johnson, Smith, and Knisely Award for New Perspectives on Executive Leadership. He has been a visiting professor at MIT's Sloan School of Management and INSEAD.

Discourse on Leadership

A Critical Appraisal

Bert A. Spector
Northeastern University, Boston

CAMBRIDGE
UNIVERSITY PRESS

CAMBRIDGE
UNIVERSITY PRESS

University Printing House, Cambridge CB2 8BS, United Kingdom

Cambridge University Press is part of the University of Cambridge.

It furthers the University's mission by disseminating knowledge in the pursuit of education, learning and research at the highest international levels of excellence.

www.cambridge.org
Information on this title: www.cambridge.org/9781107049789

First published 2016

A catalogue record for this publication is available from the British Library

Library of Congress Cataloging in Publication data
Spector, Bert, author.
Discourse on leadership : a critical appraisal / Bert A. Spector.
New York : Cambridge University Press, 2016.
Includes bibliographical references and index.
LCCN 2016026750   ISBN 9781107049789 (hardback)
LCSH: Leadership.   Leadership – Research.
LCC HD57.7.S69444   2016   DDC 303.3/4 – dc23
LC record available at https://lccn.loc.gov/2016026750

ISBN 978-1-107-04978-9 Hardback

To
Maureen
Kayte & Tess

Contents

Acknowledgments

It is always wise to start acknowledgments by recognizing the invaluable contributions of those closest to you. In the D'Amore-McKim School of Business at Northeastern University in Boston, my gratitude (and apologies for being a constant source of pestering!) to Nick Athanassiou, Allan Bird, Paula Caligiuri, Len Glick, Harry Lane, Jeanne McNett, Donald Margotta, Joe Raelin, and Christian Thoroughgood. At the larger university, my thanks to James Dendy (Snell Library), Maureen Kelleher (Sociology), Stephen Nathanson (Philosophy), and Kathrin Zippel (Sociology). I also want to thank Lori Lefkovitz and Tim Cresswell of the Northeastern University's Humanities Center as well as the 2014–2105 Humanities Fellows with whom I shared a productive and insight-producing year. Beyond Northeastern, my appreciation for the contributions of Françoise Chevalier (HEC-Paris), David Collinson (Lancaster University Management School), Keith Grint (University of Warwick Business School), Barbara Kellerman (Harvard University Kennedy School of Government), Deborah Kolb (Simmons College and the Harvard Law School Program on Negotiations), Karen Ward Mahar (Siena College), Albert Mills (Saint Mary's University), Andrew Pettigrew (University of Oxford Said Business School), José Santos (INSEAD), Günter Stahl (Vienna University of Economics and Business), and Dennis Tourish (Royal Holloway University of London and *Leadership*). Finally, my thanks to the two professors who served as mentors in my training as a historian: Richard Kirkendall and David Thelen.

Prologue: A Discussion without End and the Nature of This Inquiry

The central premise of *Discourse on Leadership* can be stated simply: ideas have consequences. They help shape how we view and interact with our world and are reciprocally shaped by the world. Based on that premise, I set out to study the *idea* of leadership. Our perception of leadership – what it is and should be – impacts who we vote for, who we hire and promote, and to whom we grant authority. Who do we turn to in times of turmoil and uncertainty? What are our expectations from those we designate as leaders? Our answers are shaped in significant measure by our understanding of the concept of leadership.

This is *not* a book about leadership in practice. There are no "how-to" lessons here; no frameworks for helping readers become more effective, more authentic, more transformative, more charismatic, or more extraordinary.

What I set out to explore was leadership in discourse: how the concept of leadership has been articulated, studied, and debated by academics as well as practitioners, journalists, and those who sought to influence the thoughts of others. My underlying assumption is that discourse generally and leadership discourse in particular is – and here I quote from Keith Grint – "not so much a reflection of material reality but a construction of it, a particular way of representing the world through language and practice."[1] I sought to understand the ways in which our construction of leadership has evolved over the years; paying particular attention to the social, economic, political, intellectual, and other historical forces that have shaped the discussion. *Discourse on Leadership* brings the discipline of history and the particular concerns of intellectual history to the subject.

Any appraisal of discourse that selects leadership as its focal interest faces an immediate challenge: the topic is broad and the literature is vast. Ralph Stogdill's massive survey of leadership research published first in 1974 famously offered over 6,000 citations. And this was before James MacGregor Burns' seminal 1978 *Leadership* revitalized interest in the field. The journals *Leadership* and *Leadership Quarterly* added to

1

the accumulation of knowledge and the richness of discourse. There is a lot, in other words, to cover. For *Discourse on Leadership*, I focused on business organizations as a key arena of activity where understanding and analysis is articulated, debated, and regularly reshaped. I tried not to be overly rigid in that focus, however.

Anyone who has ventured into the field knows that leadership is a broadly interdisciplinary topic. Burns' landmark book approached the subject from the political science perspective. His formulation of transformational leadership, in turn, gave rise to a robust inquiry into leadership as it unfolded within managerial and organizational research. In order to reflect that interdisciplinary spirit, I ventured beyond business into the fields of history, political science, communications, mathematics, sociology, psychology, law, philosophy, cognitive science, literary criticism, economics, anthropology, biology, and even fiction (F. Scott Fitzgerald makes a cameo appearance in Chapter 7). Nonetheless, I always returned to the question: how is leadership conceived within the context of a business organization?

Within that setting, I paid particular attention to *executive* leadership; that is, leadership as exercised by individuals who sit atop an organizational hierarchy. This was not an automatic or obvious choice. There was a time, largely before the publication of Burns' *Leadership*, when the discourse leaned heavily on behaviors of individuals within small groups and actions taken by supervisors of shop floor workers. The 6,000 plus citations in Stogdill's handbook were full of titles such as *The Foreman on the Assembly Line*, "Supervisory Attitudes toward the Legitimacy of Influencing Subordinates," and "Emergent Leadership in Small, Decision-Making Groups." Burns, who had previously penned an acclaimed biography of Franklin Roosevelt, focused on "the statesmen who moved and shook the world."[2] In doing so, he called attention to leadership of large institutions.

Analysis of small-group leadership continued. But a great deal of attention and an overwhelming amount of popular interest concentrated on those folks at the top: executives who could employ hierarchical power in order to achieve results. After the 1984 publication of the best-selling CEO memoir *Iacocca* (it was the best-selling nonfiction book in the United States for two years running), fascination with top executives and their apparent capacity for miraculous turnaround dominated the popular mind and shaped academic inquiry. Although leadership unfolds at multiple levels of an organization, I am offering a focus on the top.

To undertake this critical examination of the leadership discourse, I followed the literature trail wherever it took me. There were some constraints to that journey imposed by issues of translation and accessibility.

The literature has been largely, though by no means exclusively, framed by U.S.-based scholars, publishers, and journals, which became a dominant voice as the discourse evolved in the years after the Second World War.[3] A more critical approach to management, organizational, and leadership studies paid close attention to issues of ideology, power, conflicting interests, and competing constructions of performance, while raising questions of epistemology generally absent from traditional social science work. That discourse took root largely but by no means exclusively outside of the United States. I paid close attention to this contribution as well.

I place my work here firmly in the category of history, specifically intellectual history. The point of reference for my approach is John Higham's classic definition of intellectual history as the history of thought. Specifically, intellectual historians ask how and why ideas occur when they do.[4] I abide by Drew Maciag's suggestion that *intellectual* be construed broadly to embrace "such persons [who] produced writing, speeches, sermons, and other *textual* material intended for public consumption."[5] There will be references to scholarly articles and books, but also to newspaper pieces, television appearances, and blogs. As a scholar of U.S. history, my analysis of the discourse occurs largely within the context of that country.

The primary medium through which historians work is narrative. So, I have constructed a story line. Although I review a vast scope of leadership literature, this is not a systematic survey of all of the key writings and categorizations of the field. There are articles and reviews aplenty that have done this quite well. What I am proposing, instead, is a history of the discourse. Therefore, I will turn to the questions posed by Hayden White. "What does it mean to *think historically*, and what are the unique characteristics of a specifically *historical method* of inquiry?"[6]

The Special Problem of Reading the Past

Why should historians, at the outset of their work, even bother to consider the nature of history writing rather than simply getting on with it?[7] The reasons are numerous and persuasive. Stating the author's theory of knowledge informs the reader. How are statements and conclusions contained in the writing to be understood? What stance did the author take toward sources in constructing the interpretation?

Historical writing always involves two separate but interrelated levels of interaction: one between historians and readers, and the other between historians operating in their present tense and the primary object of study situated somewhere in their past tense. These two interactions are related.

The nature of the second discourse – between present and past – should be made clear to enable a transparent dialogue between the author and the reader.

My position is that history – and I am referring here to the output of a historian's work – is *a narrative that is set in the past and offers the opportunity for critical perspective on the present*. With that definition as a base, I can parse the individual components, starting with the *past*.

The Past as "Absent Reality"

Whatever level of interest the historian may have in the present – and worthwhile historical writing always offers a perspective on the present – the primary focus is unequivocally set in the past. The object of the historian's study, noted White, can only be "the sum total of all the *events* (including the interconnections between them) that happened in 'the past.'"[8] That last set of quote marks around "the past" suggests that we are about to enter a territory demanding special and careful consideration.

The discipline of history, wrote M.C. Lemon, "is defined essentially in terms of this special problem requiring knowledge of the past."[9] So, what is the "special problem"? To what extent is that challenge different from the one that faces, say, laboratory scientists where the subject of study can be immediately observed and even recreated? To answer that, we need to start with a consideration of the nature of time.[10]

Historians have a specialized task, which is to construct a memory of the past, first for themselves and then to be offered to others. The most salient point about the past, and the one that endows the study of the past with its special challenges, is that it does not exist. It *did* exist – at least in terms of people, place, and events – but it *does* not currently. It is, in Allan Megill's phrase, an "absent reality."[11]

The past, then, is not experienced in the present; it is recalled in the present. That act of recall does not occur in a vacuum. There is both a personal and a social context to memory. Just as individuals situate and support their own memory, so does the current social context apply a filter to what they "remember."[12] For that reason, it is especially significant to examine the filters on which historians rely in order to interpret the past.

One filter is created by the artifacts, typically recorded documents, which provide the historian with primary sources.[13] To study artifacts from the past is not to experience the past. Artifacts, rather, are "standing proxies" for a time that no longer exists.[14] These proxies are tangible and shareable, but they do not provide an absolute and uncontestable mirror image of the past.

The second filter is provided by the historian who responds to the tangible traces of the past and relates "findings" to the reader. Historians see the past through one set of clues, then apply the process of selection, highlighting some documents while relegating others to the background in order to create a second set of filters built on their own values.[15]

Historians, in other words, do not mirror the past so much as they act upon it. They construct a version of the past in order to reveal themes, interactions, and meanings.[16] Patricia Ewick and Susan Silbey added that, in order to perform that task, the scholar engages in "some form of selective appropriation of past events and characters."[17] The findings presented by the historian do not duplicate or mirror the past. That inability to duplicate the past – I'm not saying *difficulty* but rather *impossibility* – brings us squarely into the debate of how to understand that reconstitution of the past, a reconstruction that unfolds through the structure of narrative.

Narrative Representations

To understand the process by which we engage the past, we can start with the distinction between description and representation, both of which make up key components of any narrative.

Description and representation are different concepts. That was the insight of Frank Ankersmit.[18] The example he used for understanding *description* was the statement, "This cat is black." What makes that statement descriptive is that it references a thing that exists outside of the consciousness of the historian, in this case, a particular cat: *this* cat and not any other cat. Historical description can and should be documented with references to a thing. As a reader, I can view the object myself and ask: Is that cat really black? Perhaps it is deep navy blue or a subtle shade of gray? Hold on a moment, I notice a tinge of green that all previous historians have missed. Differences can and will occur in description, but there is always reference to a tangible object.

Ankersmit offered "the Renaissance is the birth of modernity" as a statement of *representation*. There is no tangible thing here, no cat to examine independently of the historian. "Renaissance," "modernity," and the metaphor of birth are all abstractions. In other words, the reference here is between these constructs and not a thing but another abstraction. We expect historians to tell us how and why they arrived at this particular representation. But we, as readers, doubt – or at least should doubt – that this is the only way to represent the past. As historians, we know that other representations are possible and may be equally plausible.

Now, to leave Ankersmit and turn to my own work, I can be descriptive and note that, in 1978, political scientist James MacGregor Burns published a book on leadership in which he posited a distinction between "transactional" and "transforming" leaders. I can also describe the subsequent management authors who referenced Burns' book and his formulation. This is description. I offer citations which point to tangible objects, particular publications by Noel Tichy and Bernard Bass, for instance. The reader can look at the same things I looked at – the primary artifacts I cite as evidence – and make a determination concerning the validity of my description.

On the other hand, statements such as "transformational leadership created a significant turning point in management dialogue on leadership" and "transformational leadership gained popularity because of the economic turmoil of the late 1970s" are both representations. They are statements made up entirely of abstractions. My intention is not to convince you that these representations are the only possible way to see the past. Rather, my goal is to have you come away thinking that my representations are plausible, coherent, and worth considering. That is the posture I assume throughout *Discourse on Leadership*.

While building on both description and representation, historical narratives contain three core elements:[19]

- *Continuity* creates the boundaries for the story. In the case of *Discourse on Leadership*, the continuity is provided by the focus on expressed ideas concerning leadership in business organizations. Without continuity, there is no story.
- *Change* is equally vital to the construction of a narrative. If the expressed ideas about leadership in 1990 were precisely the same as they were in the 1980s or 1900, there is no historical narrative, just stasis.
- Change occurs through *agency*, which recognizes that the key actors in the narrative – those who have written about leadership – made choices that influenced the plot.

Narrative, in other words, is not a simple stimulus → response connection. Rather, it presents the historian's argument about interconnections, choices, and consequences.

In order to locate continuity, change, and agency, historians apply coherence and meaning to a period of time past. That is the point at which historians, along with their training, social theories, and ideologies both explicit and tacit, do the work of constructing narrative and writing history.[20] Here, we reach another vital junction in our consideration of the nature of narrative construction.

Are historians revealing a coherent narrative as it existed in the past? Or are they imposing a narrative – the process is referred to as *emplotment* – on the past that never really existed? If you accept Henri-Irénée

Marrou's view of the past as "infinitely complex," something as "obscure, confused, multiform, and unintelligible" as the present, then you must conclude that the answer is emplotment, which grows out of the interaction between the historian's imagination in the present and the representation of the past.[21]

My own theory of historical writing, and the underlying perspective of *Discourse on Leadership*, falls within the deconstructionist view advocated by Michel Foucault, Hayden White, Alun Munslow, and others.[22] To appreciate that perspective, we can start with a contrary view, a positivist theory of historical work offered by Richard Evans, a leading scholar of Nazi Germany.

A *Narrative, Not* The *Narrative*

In offering a "defense of history," Evans proclaimed, "I will look humbly at the past, and say despite them all: it really happened, and we really can, if we are very scrupulous and careful and self-critical, find out how it happened and reach some tenable though always less than final conclusions about what it all meant."[23] He claimed to be addressing *all* history, but he wasn't. He was standing up for a traditional, positivist approach as the only history.

The notion of positivist history is straightforward: a single narrative existed in the past. The task of the historian is, through painstaking and rigorous accumulation, to uncover that narrative. This was the approach taken by the great and influential business history scholar, Alfred Chandler. By amassing enough data and reviewing enough documents, he believed he could arrive at the truth about how American business institutions evolved.[24]

These positivist historians envisioned themselves following what J.H. Hexter referred to as the "reality rule," the commitment to first discover and then reveal "the reality of what happened in the past."[25] The historical narrative can, and should, strive to achieve a mirror image of the past, the argument went, rendering the past in such a way that is as clear and understandable to readers today as it was to those who lived it.[26]

But ask yourself: is the present in which you live really clear and understandable? Does a clear and coherent story line actually exist? And if it is not, what are the chances that it will be rendered clear and understandable to future generations of historians with unequivocal accuracy? Deconstructionist critics of the reality rule mounted a frontal assault on the traditional or positivist approach being advocated by Evans.

Historians who insisted they had discovered "the reality of what happened in the past" were guilty, in Foucault's view, of "transcendental narcissism."[27] The narcissism to which Foucault referred resided in the claim by the positivist historians – not such a humble claim after all – that with the benefit of both temporal distance and strict adherence to academic rigor, they could divine meaning in an obscure, confused, and infinitely complex past and present it "as it actually happened."[28]

Foucault, along with a host of others – prominently Hayden White, Frank Ankersmit, Louis Mink, Keith Jenkins, Roland Barthes, Alun Munslow, and Albert Mills – insisted that Richard Evans got it wrong. No single, coherent, uncontestable narrative existed in the past. Therefore, none could be constructed in the present. Denying the positivists' assertion that the story is there, waiting to be discovered, Munslow insisted that the goal of the historian is to offer "a plausible and therefore quite acceptable" narrative without claiming it to be *only possible* narrative.[29] Once we embrace the argument that no single reconstruction of the past can be taken as definitive, we as readers can judge narratives on the basis of *plausibility*.

Deconstructionists dismissed the notion that historians exist independently of the history they are writing. They rejected one of the most fundamental premises of the "science" of history: that objectivity is desirable or even possible. The positivist approach maintained that by removing the historian and the values brought to the inquiry, the result would be superior history. Just the opposite was true, wrote Ankersmit. The application of one's values to the historical inquiry "will often be a useful or even indispensable guide on our difficult way to historical truth."[30]

It may seem at this point that the deconstructionist position on history borders on fiction writing.[31] And yes, there was something to the comparison of history to fiction in the deconstructionist view. In fact, that comparison was embraced proudly and openly. Louis Mink was one of the most forceful advocates of the position that history and fiction have much in common as modes of understanding.

Like fiction, history offers readers an "encounter with otherness," resulting in the capacity to share experiences across time.[32] To be effective, the writing of both fiction and history depends on the author's skills and subtlety in imagining stories.[33] In that regard, agreed Munslow, history *is* much like fiction, "an exercise in creative imagination."[34] There is, he and Keith Jenkins wrote, "*no* story, *no* narrative, *no* emplotment or argument in the past per se." Because the past "has in it neither rhyme nor reason," the historian must deploy imagination to offer both rhyme and reason.[35] True detachment is both impossible and undesirable.

The historian is not a blank slate but rather an *agent of imagination*; trained in the appropriate techniques, required to make specific reference to verifiable artifacts of the past (description) and then expected to deploy imagination to produce a – not the – narrative (representation).

This is not to say that history and fiction are interchangeable. History, Mink wrote, "is obligated to rest upon evidence of the occurrence in real space and time of what it describes and insofar as it must grow out of a critical assessment of the received materials of history, including the analysis and interpretations of other historians."[36] Fiction has no such obligation. White agreed: "Events have to be taken as given; they are certainly not constructed by the historian" as they might well be by the fiction writer.[37] And Munslow offered his view of what distinguishes good from bad history:

Hopefully, the narrative in a deconstructionist essay will be coherent and sensible, but it will not be epistemologically self-assured . . . For every history that aims to get at the past as it really happened, there is always another version, which, like the first, is by definition another fiction. As to what constitutes good history, then, it is that it is self-reflexive enough to acknowledge its limits, especially aware that the writing of history is far more precarious and speculative than empiricists usually admit.

Claims of scientifically certifiable truths may be comforting to readers; they are not, however, possible.

"It is probably best," Munslow concluded, "to view historical narratives as propositions about how we *might* represent a past reality, suggestions of *possible* correspondence rather than *the* correspondence." In the realm of science, a proposition represents but the preliminary step on the path to constructing empirical indicators that can then be used to develop testable hypotheses. In the realm of history, such controlled testing is impossible. One can work only to offer alternative propositions. That is why history writing, in the words of Dutch historian Pieter Geyl, is "a discussion without end."[38]

A Critical Perspective

A critical perspective on the present should not be interpreted in a reductionist manner as mere didacticism. Writing intellectual history in the 1930s, Arthur O. Lovejoy concluded his study with a chapter entitled, "The Outcome of the History and Its Moral."[39] Today, insistence of proclaiming a moral would be condemned, and rightly so, as didactic, smacking of arrogance and dogmatism, lacking in the very propositional tentativeness that characterizes deconstructionist history.[40]

The output of historians' work involves an engagement with both the past and the present.[41] It does not follow, however, that the assumption of a critical perspective amounts to teaching a lesson (a moral). Rather, it offers a platform for a diagnostic re-examination followed by learning.

The opportunity for insights offered by the past – by the historian's view of the past – can and should provide perspective on the present. That opportunity is placed in the hands of the reader, not imposed by the historian on the reader.[42]

In their call for a new management and organizational history that would overcome the "morbidity" of traditional approaches, Michael Rowlinson and colleagues suggested that a critical perspective could help explain how the "present order has been constructed," a vital, even necessary first step in the process of reconsideration, change, and improvement.[43] My hope and intention is for this critical examination of the idea of leadership in business organizations to avoid such morbidity and open opportunities to consider paths forward beyond the overuse, misuse, and abuse of the concept.

Management authors – and here I mean academics, consultants, and practitioners alike – often use history, or at least its trappings, to position their findings and advocate for their conclusions. This is not a critical perspective. Their primary focus is on the present; on *their* present. Their use of history includes none of the tools or discipline of history. Their approach to the past and their application of the past to the present are fundamentally flawed.

Embellished Reminiscence

Join me in visiting a piece of "history" employed by a prominent leadership scholar in setting up his argument.[44]

Business organizations today, the writer insisted, are being forced "to reconsider traditional strategies, policies, and routine methods of doing business. As a result, thousands and thousands of managers and executives are being asked to develop new products, new distribution channels, new marketing methods, new manufacturing processes, new financing strategies, and much more. And literally millions of people are being called upon to implement those new ideas." These new pressures of adapting to "an environment of uncertainty caused by intense competitive activity, and then getting others, often many others, to accept a new way of doing things" are placing demands on managers that simply did not exist in the relatively tranquil decades of recent memory.[45]

What assumptions would you make about when this observation was written? Furthermore, to what relatively tranquil decades of the recent past was the author referring?

John Kotter used these words in his introduction to a 1988 leadership book. His thesis was that the unprecedented environmental complexity of the 1980s demanded something more than mere management; it required true leadership. And the relatively calm decades to which he referred were the 1950s, 1960s, and early 1970s. Kotter may be the only scholar *ever* to refer to the 1960s as relatively calm. Despite the popular saying that if you remember the Sixties, you weren't there, I remember. They weren't calm.[46]

It is not my intention simply to expose an instance of a misappropriation of the past on the part of a single author.[47] Rather, I call attention to a more general tendency in management literature to treat the past ahistorically. When we assume that the present is a time of unprecedented turbulence in comparison to a tranquil past, we constrain our capacity to learn from the past. Corporate executives have always lived under unprecedented environmental turbulence. To assume that those leaders, as well as the writers who were contemporaneously participating in the leadership discourse, were reacting not to turbulence but tranquility is to misread the past and distort our narrative reconstruction. Yet, this kind of distortion occurs all-too-regularly in management writing.

There are really two interrelated phenomena at play. The first is an assertion that the times in which we live are exceptionally turbulent. The second is an attribution of tranquility in comparison to the present. The first I refer to as *presentism,* and the second I label the *tranquility fallacy*.[48] Both run deeply and broadly through leadership discourse, serving to distort our understanding of the past and limit our analysis of the present.

Let's agree rather quickly to the absurdity of the claim that the 1960s represented a period of calm. But how about conducting a reality check on the 1950s in the United States, the Eisenhower era? Did American managers of the 1950s look out of their windows, read their newspapers, and see tranquility? Or did they instead experience turbulence?

For anyone who would care to treat the past on its own terms rather than from a presentist's perspective, there is plentiful evidence that folks experienced the 1950s as a period of not just turbulence but *unprecedented* turbulence. For example, the constant fear of nuclear annihilation. Or the upending challenge of the burgeoning civil rights movement. The American economy was certainly growing, but it was also changing dramatically.

Karen Mahar found evidence that executives themselves – her study focused on managers within General Electric – faced a steady erosion of their sense of self-efficacy during the decade. Among the causes were the massive changes taking place in the strategies and structure of American business in the 1950s.[49] To round out the picture of how managers experienced the 1950s, let me conclude with an end-of-the-decade piece by Melvin Anshen.

Anshen's 1959 focus was squarely on technological innovation. "It is becoming commonplace," he wrote, "to observe that we are living on the verge of a revolution in the technology of business administration."[50] Note first "commonplace" and then the phrase, *on the verge of a revolution*. This does not suggest tranquility. In particular, the application of computers in the service of managerial decision making – and, remember, this was 1959 – constituted "a radical transformation in the sphere of management equal in magnitude and significance to the changes in production wrought by the great Industrial Revolution."

In understanding how managers respond to their environment, the important question is not "how do we scholars in retrospect define that environment?" but "how did managers *at the time* perceive their environment?" The goal of the historian, noted C. Behan McCullagh, is to represent the past "in the context of what they take to have been the circumstances of its origin"; that is, how people experienced their own time.[51]

In his sweeping history of pre-World War I Europe, Philipp Blom critiqued presentism by contrasting the typical view of the era with the reality as experienced by the people who lived it. The period before the outbreak of war is regularly depicted as the calm before the storm, regarded "as idyllic," as a "beautiful, intact society about to be shattered by the forces driving it inexorably towards disaster."[52] But for contemporaries, the reality was dramatically different:

To most people who lived around 1900, this nostalgic view with its emphasis on solidity and grace would have come as a surprise. Their experience of this period was as yet unembellished by reminiscence. It was more raw and marked by fascinations and fears much closer to our own time.[53]

Management writers may feel that the advantage of perspective provides them with the ability to proclaim the past as a period of calm, predictable tranquility. But this is embellished reminiscence, a distortion of the past. A golden rule for historians is to understand the past on its own terms.[54] Most managers in the past experienced something very different from calm, predictable tranquility.

Getting On with It

Now that I have offered for your consideration my assumptions about the task of writing history and constructing a narrative; it's time to get on with it. This will not be a straightforward time-line narrative, first *A*, then *B*, followed by *C*. I do start at the "beginning," at what I consider to be the first modern leadership theory. From there, I pick up of significant themes that weave their way through the discourse. The epilogue presents a chronologically ordered time line.

The narrative that I construct reveals a long-standing tension between the desire to place an individual center stage in organizational life and the recognition that complex environmental dynamics help shape events. It recognizes the ongoing need to find order in the organization while simultaneously responding to a dynamic world roiled by constant upheavals in technology, markets, stakeholder expectations, and competition. It is a conversation that celebrates the independent agency of nonleaders in helping to guide organizations, and at the same time worries about the potential for both disobedient disruption and toxic obedience. It is a discourse that belatedly recognized the persistence of bias and continues to debate the matter of how to move past that prejudice. The discourse on leadership wrestles fitfully and uncomfortably with the centrality of power and ideology. And it is a dialogue that often builds on an important analytic tool, Weber's ideal types, and then distorts the purpose, meaning, and utility of that tool.

Before diving into the text, let me make one style point. Because I am focusing on leadership discourse, my database is composed of the words of others. In order to render those words as accurately as possible, I have neither added nor removed any emphasis that was not provided in the original work. Thus, all the words inside quote marks that are italicized here were emphasized – either through italics or underlining – in the original.

NOTES

1 Keith Grint, *The Arts of Leadership* (Oxford: Oxford University Press, 2000), 25.
2 This quote is from an assessment of Burns' work offered in Bernard M. Bass, "A Seminal Shift: The Impact of James Burns' *Leadership*," *Leadership Quarterly* 4 (1993), 375–6.
3 Morgen Witzel does a particularly important job of tracing the non-U.S., non-Western branches of management thought in *A History of Management Thought* (London: Routledge, 2012). Witzel has been one of the most engaging and imaginative historians operating in the field of management. His work frequently challenges received wisdom concerning the evolution of management thought.
4 John Higham, "American Intellectual History: A Critical Appraisal," *American Quarterly* 13 (1961), 219–33.
5 Drew Maciag, "When Ideas Had Consequences – Or, Whatever Happened to Intellectual History?" *Reviews in American History* 39 (2011), 744.
6 Hayden White, *Metahistory: The Historical Imagination in Nineteenth-Century Europe* (Baltimore: John Hopkins University Press, 1973), 1.

7   This is a paraphrase of Alun Munslow, "Why Should Historians Write about the Nature of History (Rather Than Just Do It)?" *Rethinking History* 11 (December 2007), 613.

8   Hayden White, "Response to Arthur Marwick," *Journal of Contemporary History* 30 (April 1995), 238.

9   M.C. Lemon, *The Discipline of History and the History of Thought* (London: Routledge, 1995), 7.

10 There is a well-developed philosophy of time, known as "presentism." My brief discussion is based on John Bigelow, "Presentism and Properties," *Philosophical Perspectives* 10 (1996), 35–52; Roderick Chisholm, "Referring to Things That No Longer Exists," *Philosophical Perspectives* 4 (1990), 545–56; Neil McKinnon and John Bigelow, "Presentism, and Speaking of the Dead," *Philosophical Studies* 160 (2012), 253–63; Francesco Orillia, "Dynamic Events and Presentism," *Philosophical Studies* 160 (2012), 407–14; and Bradford Snow, "Experience and the Passage of Time," *Philosophical Perspectives* 25 (2011), 359–87.

11 Allan Megill, "Five Questions on Intellectual History," *Rethinking History: The Journal of Theory and Practice* 15 (2011), 498.

12 On the social context of memories, see Eviater Zerubavel, "Social Memories: Steps to a Sociology of the Past," *Qualitative Sociology* 19 (1996), 283–99. On the usefulness of shared memory as a source of social glue, see Jeffrey K. Olick, *The Politics of Regret: On Collective Memory and Historical Responsibility* (New York: Routledge, 2007).

13 Historians can also fruitfully utilize the tools of archeology to investigate remnants of the past. Doyne Dawson, "The Origins of War: Biological and Anthropological Theories," *History and Theory* 35 (February 1996), 1–28; Robin Fleming, "Writing Biography at the Edge of History," *American Historical Review* 114 (June 2009), 606–14.

14 McKinnon and Bigelow, "Presentism, and Speaking of the Dead," 255.

15 William H. Dray, *Philosophy of History* (Englewood Cliffs: Prentice-Hall, 1964).

16 Gabrielle Durepos and Albert J. Mills, "Actor-Network Theory, ANTi-History and Critical Organizational Historiography," *Organization* 19 (2011), 1–19.

17 Patricia Ewick and Susan Silbey, "Subversive Stories and Hegemonic Tales: Toward a Sociology of Narrative," *Law & Society Review* 29 (1995), 197–226.

18 Frank Ankersmit, *Historical Representation* (Stanford: Stanford University Press, 2001). This is quite similar to Danto's construction of factual and conceptual evidence. Arthur C. Danto, *Analytical Philosophy of History* (Cambridge: Cambridge University Press, 1965).

19 Lemon, *The Discipline of History*.

20 Alun Munslow, "Where Does History Come From?" *History Today* 52 (March 2002), 18.

21 Henri-Irénée Marrou, *The Meaning of History* (Baltimore: Helicon, 1966), 40.

22 For a concise overview of the historiography debate, see Marc Trachtenberg, *The Craft of International History: A Guide to Method* (Princeton: Princeton

University Press, 2006). I don't hold to his conclusion that deconstructionist history allows, even justifies political "bias." I maintain, rather, that "bias" – at least as understood as the particular worldview of the historian – is a natural outcome of all historical undertakings, traditional history as well as deconstructionist history. Take Arthur Schlesinger, Jr., a paragon of traditional history and a wonderful constructor of narrative. His take on the presidency of Andrew Jackson almost precisely mirrored his own New Deal liberalism. You may agree or disagree with Schlesinger (and plenty of Jacksonian historians have disagreed), but (a) that bias doesn't detract in any way from the contribution his book makes and (b) bias is not limited to any one approach. See Arthur M. Schlesinger, Jr., *The Age of Jackson* (Boston: Little, Brown, 1945). For a sharply contrasting view of Jackson's presidency, see Ronald Takaki, *A Different Mirror: A History of Multicultural America* (Boston: Little, Brown, 1993).

23   Richard L. Evans, *In Defense of History* (New York: Norton, 1999), 253.
24   For an appreciative overview of Chandler's methodology, see Thomas K. McCraw, "Introduction: The Intellectual Odyssey of Alfred D. Chandler," in McCraw, ed., *The Essential Alfred Chandler: Essays Toward a Historical Theory of Big Business* (Boston: Harvard Business School Press, 1988), 1–21.
25   J.H. Hexter, "The Rhetoric of History," *History and Theory* 6 (1967), 4–5.
26   Alexander Lyon Macfie, "A Possible (Common-Sense) Defense of (My) History: A Response to Keith Jenkins," *Rethinking History* 13 (September 2009), 345–55. The article specifically references and responds to a previous article by Keith Jenkins in which he wrote: "I hold the view . . . that whilst the 'world' is 'out there' *meanings* are not; that whilst the world is 'out there' *truths* are not." Keith Jenkins, "'Nobody Does It Better': Radical History and Hayden White," *Rethinking History* 12 (March 2008), 60.
27   Michel Foucault, *The Archaeology of Knowledge* (New York: Pantheon, 1972), 203.
28   This is a quote from Arthur Marwick, *The Nature of History* (London: Macmillan, 1970), 15. Marwick famously delivered a 1993 talk at the Open University in which he adopted the purposefully intemperate title, "Metahistory Is Bunk, History Is Essential." He and Hayden White engaged in a contentious debate on the pages of the *Journal of Contemporary History*. See Arthur Marwick, "Two Approaches to Historical Study: The Metaphysical (Including 'Postmodernism') and the Historical," *Journal of Contemporary History* 30 (January 1995), 5–35, and White, "Response to Arthur Marwick," 233–46. Marwick's title is, in my reading, inconsistent. He starts by arguing that there are "two approaches to historical study." Following the colon, however, he insists that only one approach – the one he is advocating – can be said to be "historical."
29   Alun Munslow, *Deconstructing History* (London: Routledge, 2006), 13.
30   Ankersmit, *Historical Representation*, 77.
31   Keith Jenkins went so far as to refer to history as "past-tensed fictions." In her extended obituary of Jenkins, Beverley Southgate admitted that, "in his repudiation of history and of the past itself Keith may have been more 'extreme' than many historical theorists," although he was not without

support. Keith Jenkins, *At the Limits of History: Essays on Theory and Practice* (London: Routledge, 2009), 151; Beverley Southgate, "Replacing the Past with Disobedience," *Rethinking History: The Journal of Theory and Practice* 17 (2013), 224.

32 Steven G. Smith, "Historical Meaningfulness in Shared Action," *History and Theory* 48 (February 2009), 16.

33 Louis O. Mink, "History and Fiction as Models of Comprehension," *New Literary History* 1 (Spring 1970), 541–56.

34 Munslow, *Deconstructing History*, 99.

35 Keith Jenkins and Alun Munslow, "Introduction" in *The Nature of History Reader* (London: Routledge, 2004), 12.

36 Mink, "History and Fiction," 545.

37 White, "Response to Arthur Marwick," 238–9.

38 Geyl is quoted in Ankersmit, *Historical Representation*, 50.

39 Arthur O. Lovejoy, *The Great Chain of Being: Study of the History of an Idea* (Cambridge: Harvard University Press, 1936). In his survey of intellectual history in the United States, David Hollinger refers to this book as the most influential in fueling a history of ideas. David A. Hollinger, "The MVHR, the JAH, and Intellectual History," in Richard S. Kirkendall, ed., *The Organization of American Historians and the Writing and Teaching of American History* (New York: Oxford University Press, 2011), 148.

40 Charles Repp, "What's Wrong with Didacticism?" *British Journal of Aesthetics* 52 (2012), 271–86.

41 *And* the future, Alun Munslow adds. *The Routledge Companion to Historical Studies* (London: Routledge, 2000).

42 This is where popular historian Doris Kearns Goodwin went astray in my view. After her hugely entertaining and insightful examination of Abraham Lincoln hit the best-seller lists, Goodwin offered "leadership lessons" for contemporary corporate executives to be gleaned from Lincoln. Demonstrating her capacity to employ management jargon, she noted, "What Lincoln had, it seems to me, is an extraordinary amount of emotional intelligence." The notion that the Presidency of Abraham Lincoln could offer such clear lessons for others to follow is, at best, ahistorical, and at worst a form of didacticism. See Doris Kearns Goodwin, *A Team of Rivals: The Political Genius of Abraham Lincoln* (New York: Simon & Schuster, 2005) and "Leadership Lessons from Abraham Lincoln," *Harvard Business Review* 87 (April 2009), 44–45.

43 Michael Rowlinson et al., "Critical Management and Organizational History," in *The Oxford Handbook of Critical Management Studies* (New York: Oxford University Press, 2011), 287.

44 I present this argument in greater depth in Bert A. Spector, "Using History Ahistorically: Presentism and the Tranquility Fallacy," *Management & Organizational History* 9 (2014), 305–13.

45 John P. Kotter, *The Leadership Factor* (New York: Free Press, 1988), 9.

46 Kotter should know better. According to his Wikipedia biography, Kotter was an undergraduate student at MIT throughout the late 1960s. MIT was such a hotbed of student and faculty antiwar protests – often focusing on the university's participation in government-sponsored defense research – that

it became the university most represented on President Nixon's "enemies" list.

47 I thank Phil Scranton for this "misappropriation of history" phrase.

48 Charles Booth and Michael Rawlinson define "presentism" as the phenomenon of reporting a research finding "as if it had occurred in a decontextualized, extended present." Throughout the book, I will be using presentism in a different, though I believe highly complementary, sense. Booth and Rowlinson, "Management and Organizational History: Prospects," *Management and Organizational History* 1 (2006), 6. Bruce Kuklick added his own definition of the term – "interpreting the past in terms applicable to the present" – which is a bit closer to my own and also complementary. Kuklick, "Myth and Symbol in American Studies," *American Quarterly* 24 (October 1972), 441.

49 Karen W. Mahar, "'Definitely a Man's Man': Executive Culture at General Electric, 1945–1960," a paper presented at the annual meeting for Business History Conference, Columbus, Ohio, March 21–23, 2013.

50 Melvin Anshen, "The Manager and the Black Box," *Harvard Business Review* 37 (1959), 85.

51 C. Behan McCullagh, "What Do Historians Argue About?" *History and Theory* 43 (February 2004), 21.

52 This is the era dramatized in the early seasons of ITV's *Downton Abbey* series.

53 Philipp Blom, *The Vertigo Years: Europe, 1900–1914* (New York: Basic Books, 2008), 1–2.

54 Alun Munslow, "Managing the Past," in Patricia Genoe McLaren et al., eds., *The Routledge Companion to Management and Organizational History* (London: Routledge, 2015), 131.

1 The Great Man and the Beginning of Contemporary Discourse

The roots of contemporary leadership discourse can be traced back to a series of six public lectures delivered in Victorian London in 1840. That was the setting for Scottish philosopher Thomas Carlyle's articulation of the Great Man Theory, his assertion that certain individuals, certain *men*, were gifts from God placed on earth to provide the "lightning" needed to uplift human existence. There were intellectual precursors to Carlyle's views, to be sure: Sun Tzu and Plato, among them. Still, any consideration of leadership – what it is and is not – rests on the shoulders of Carlyle and his view of how world history has unfolded.

Contemporary leadership theorists may reject the Great Man – in truth, virtually all do – or they may simply ignore Carlyle. Plus, it isn't much of a theory, at least not a theory about how to lead. It is more a view of the world, a notion of how history unfolds, a call for recognition and humble obedience, even subservience, to the most able man.

And there's that *man* element. To say this is a gendered view of leadership, an assertion that the movers and shakers of world history have always been and will always be men, is more than a slight understatement. We like to think we have moved beyond that gender bias, although perhaps not as far as we believe.

For many leadership theorists, Carlyle is an anachronism, an unwelcomed reminder of a nonscientific past. Contemporary surveys occasionally mention Carlyle's Great Man Theory before moving on to more rigorous academic categories: traits, behaviors, contingencies, and so forth.[1] The Great Man theory does not fit into the "rigorous scholarly theory and research" that makes up the contemporary canon of leadership discourse.[2] A "trait approach" emphasizing the extraordinary attributes that set effective leaders apart from less effective ones can be seen as a more recent echo of the Great Man.[3] Trait theory too is often dismissed as unsatisfying, misleading, or both.[4]

Writing in the early 20th century, Sigmund Freud offered his own spin on the great man. For Freud, the great man, an uncapitalized construct, was articulated not as a moral *proscription* for how followers should react, but rather as an analytic *description* of the elemental forces that lead people to seek heroes. There is a direct narrative line that can be drawn from Carlyle's Great Man to Sigmund Freud's father figure and then to the present-day veneration of corporate saviors and the "great" CEO.

Find the Ablest Man

In the spring of 1840, Carlyle delivered his lectures on the role played by heroes in shaping the arc of history. The following year those lectures were brought together in a single volume entitled *On Heroes, Hero-Worship, and the Heroic in History*. The Great Man theory was born.

Carlyle's voice in those lectures is unquestionably off-putting to the contemporary ear. There is the obvious gender bias of his formulation, a rendering of his reading of history as unfolding through the efforts of dominant males combined with what Keith Grint referred to as the prevalent Victorian conviction that leadership was "irredeemably masculine."[5] There is the deep religiosity of his language, a reflection of the strict Calvinist upbringing provided by his parents who expected him to become a preacher.[6] And perhaps most distinctly, there is his admonition that "our" job, those of us not divinely designated, is to recognize the Great Man, lift him to a position of prominence, and then obey. A "sick" world would thus be healed through subservience to God's chosen one.[7]

A Discourse Undertaken

In a period of crisis and upheaval – the aftermath of the French Revolution and Napoleonic wars and the accelerating pace of industrialization – Carlyle looked for a source of strength, direction, wisdom, and uplift. Those reassurances were no longer provided by the Church, which in Carlyle's view had become a discredited shepherd. Moving away from Calvinism involved a commensurate break with his father, so parental authority seemed as unreliable as Church hierarchy.[8] Carlyle's quest led him to the Great Man: an individual of this earth but unmistakably sent by God.

Already a well-known intellectual on his way to becoming "the most widely read and most greatly admired social philosopher of his time," Carlyle fought off his discomfort with public speaking in order to earn the significant fees associated with lecturing.[9] He opened the talks on heroes by explaining his intent. "We have undertaken to discourse here for a little on the Great Men," he explained to his audience, "their manner of appearance in our world's business, how they have shaped themselves in the world's history, what ideas men found of them, what work they did – on Heroes."[10] Carlyle labored to demonstrate how "the great man, with his free force direct out of God's own hand" shaped the world.[11]

Given his loss of faith in the Church and his dismay over the revolutions that had spread across Europe, Carlyle wondered about authority. Who had it? Under what claims was it to be held? Who would exercise it in the future? From Carlyle's vantage, wrote Chris Vanden Bossche, "it appeared not only that authority had shifted, but that the transcendental grounds for it had been undermined."[12] So, if old platforms for authority were passing, what would replace them? In *On Heroes*, Carlyle provided his answer: the "Able-man," an individual who has been "sent by God" to have "a divine right over me."[13]

Looking back at the French Revolution, Carlyle laid the responsibility for the collapse of the *Ancien Régime* squarely on the shoulders of its inept royal head, Louis XVI.[14] Louis was a far-from-able man, and revolutions occur, insisted Carlyle, when "you have put a too *Un*able Man at the head of affairs!"[15] Societies bedeviled by the lack of an Able Man at their helm had one core responsibility: find him, and:

raise *him* to the supreme place, and loyally reverence him; you have a perfect government for that country; no ballot box, Parliamentary eloquence, voting, constitution-building, or other machinery whatsoever can improve it a whit. It is the perfect state; an ideal country. The Ablest Man; he means also the truest-hearted, justest, the Noblest Man: what he *tells us to do* must be precisely the wisest, fittest, that we could anywhere or anyhow learn; – the thing which it will in all ways behoove us, with right loyal thankfulness, and nothing doubting, to do![16]

Locating an Able-man and having the multitudes agree that this *was* the Able-man, however, was no easy matter. "That we knew in some tolerable measure how to find him, and that all men were ready to acknowledge his divine right when found: that is precisely the healing which a sick world is everywhere, in the ages, seeking after!"[17] Carlyle was offering as much an argument for how the world worked as a theory of leadership. Great men were sent by God to be heroes and these heroes became leaders through the righteous process of hero-worship.

Perhaps no statement found in the lectures is more frequently quoted than what follows from the opening of *On Heroes*:

For, as I take it, Universal History, the history of what man has accomplished in this world, is at bottom the History of the Great Men who have worked here. They were the leaders of men, these great ones, the modelers, planners, and in a wide sense creators, of whatever the general mass of men contrived to do or attain; all things that we see standing accomplished in the world are properly the outer material result, the practical realization and embodiment, of Thoughts that dwelt in the Great Men sent into the world: the soul of the whole world's history, it may justly be considered, were the history of these.[18]

The goal of the lectures, then, was explicitly pedantic: to convince listeners to "bow down submissive before great men," an act which would allow the worshiper to "feel himself to be more noble and blessed."[19]

Carlyle's great men were an eclectic group: prophets, poets, priests, men of letters, and kings. That Shakespeare was as much a great man as Oliver Cromwell and Martin Luther may seem like something of a surprise. After all, what did the Bard lead? But to Carlyle, "all the greatness of man" came out decisively in Shakespeare. "That Shakespeare is the chief of all Poets hitherto; the greatest intellect who, in our recorded world, has left record of himself in the way of Literature. I know no such a power of vision, faculty of thought, if we take all the characters of it, in any other man."[20] "Nature" had offered Shakespeare to the world and Nature was pleased with the result.

Still, it was the final lecture, "The Hero as King," that carried the greatest weight for Carlyle and cemented the connection between heroes and leaders. It was "the last form of Heroism," he wrote, "that which we call Kingship":

The Commander over Men he to whose will our wills are to be subordinated, and loyally surrender themselves, and find their welfare in doing so, may be reckoned the most important of the Great Men. He is practically the *summary* for us of *all* the various figures of Heroism; Priest, Teacher, whatsoever of earthly or of spiritual dignity we can fancy to reside in a man, embodies itself here, to *command* over us, furnish us with constraint practical teaching, tell us for the day and hour what we are to *do*.[21]

It was this amalgam Great Man who should be raised to "the supreme place." Carlyle admitted indifference to the process of such elevation. It was the fact of elevation and the resultant worshipful voluntary subjugation that would lead to "the perfect state; an ideal country."[22]

Carlyle's view of history as working through the deeds of great men, or conversely through the absence of such a hero, did not go uncontested among his contemporaries. Ideas, at least important ones, seldom do. In *On Heroes*, Carlyle rejected any critique:

He [the Great Man] was the 'creature of the Time,' they say; the Time called him forth, the Time did everything, he did nothing – but what we the little critic could have done too! This seems to me but melancholy work. The Times call forth? Alas, we have known Times *call* loudly enough for their great man; but not find him when they called! He was not there; Providence had not sent him; the Time, *calling* its loudest, had to go down to confusion and wreck because he would not come when called ... His word is the wise healing word which we all can believe in. All blazes round him now, when he has once struck on it, into fire like his own.[23]

Critics of the Great Man theory, Carlyle maintained, belittled themselves through their egregious misreading of how the world works.

It is impossible to miss the stern proselytizing, the righteous indignation, and the reproachful tone of these words. No surprise that Carlyle's work found particular favor among the rising acolytes of 20th century Italian fascism and German Nazism.[24] Carlyle with his Great Man Theory was called upon to add a "veneer of respectability" to "the fascists, who were delighted to find their ideas proclaimed in eloquent words by the great Victorian."[25]

Modernists generally and rationalists in particular harbor a deep unease with hero-worship. Carlyle's preaching – that is the best word for it – is easy to resist or ignore on scientific, moral, and political grounds. The formulation of a great man holding sway over the rest of us nonetheless continues to resonate. In the world of business, the search for a hero to "save" failing companies exerts considerable appeal.

Nancy Koehn argued that the upward spiral of CEO pay following the well-publicized executive misdeeds that helped trigger the recession of 2007–2008 could be attributed directly to this ongoing belief in the "Great Man."[26] Driven by a "quasi-religious belief" in the power and influence of an individual hero, board members and investors regularly search for "saviors."[27] Occasionally, that savior is a woman, but the search remains active. Boards hire, and then frequently dismiss CEOs, both male and female, always on the lookout for the latest savior.

So why the enduring appeal? Sigmund Freud had an explanation.

A Primal Drive

It's hard to conceive of two individuals as existing in such sharp contrast as Thomas Carlyle and Sigmund Freud. One was a man of God, the other of science. One was a sermonizer, the other an analyzer. Yet both proposed their own version of a great man theory and his – always *his* – role in history.

By the time of the 1937 publication of his *Moses and Monotheism*, a revisionist study of the great Hebrew hero and savior, Freud had established a worldwide psychoanalytic movement.[28] In search of analytic rigor to aid his and others' clinical assessment of patients, Freud delved into the unconscious working of the mind. Over time, intellectual curiosity led him to a broader perspective, seeking to illuminate a linkage between individual psychology and group dynamics, religious belief, and the structure of history. Although the study of Moses represented his most fully realized view of the hero role in history, his notion of the great man (I am using small letters rather than capitals because it is meant to be descriptive in Freud's case) can be traced to earlier works, most specifically his 1921 *Group Psychology and the Analysis of the Ego.*

For Freud, the need for a single, special leader was primal, arising from the drive for dependency and even love. He opened his reasoning by situating the individual within a larger collective: a tribe, a clan, or a family. This was the unit that proscribed the psychological world of individuals. Freud reflected the gender biases of the Victorian era as much as did Carlyle. He placed the father as the central figure in the family unit.

On a personal level, Freud's focus emerged from his personal struggle with his own father.[29] According to Samuel Slipp, a complex interaction of forces – "losses of important early childhood attachment figures; unconscious conflicts with his mother, who appeared to be seductive, aggressive, intrusive, and exploitive; his mother's own frustrations as a person and her constricted social role; and anti-Semitism, which contributed to his father's economic failure and Freud's own professional difficulties" – compounded Freud's gender biases and his search for a father figure.[30] Some of the authors of classic mid-20th-century feminist books, Simone de Beauvoir and Betty Friedan, for example, chastised Freud explicitly for what they held to be his oppressive position, based on age-old attitudes, concerning women.[31] As Carlyle did decades earlier, Freud both reflected and reinforced the prevailing gender attitudes of his time.

For Freud, group membership conveyed many obvious benefits to individual members, including safety and security. However, by following a single leader, group members tend to bend their thinking "in the direction of the approximation to the other individuals in the group."[32] Group members would opt for conformity while sacrificing individuality.

Freud selected two institutions to offer illustrative examples of this attraction: the Catholic Church and the military. Christ for the Church and the commander-in-chief for the military were both father figures, loved by group members and thought to love all followers within the group equally. Those assumptions were based on the basic process of identification. This was, for Freud, the earliest expression of an emotional tie with another person: particularly the son identifying with the father. "A little boy will exhibit a special interest in his father; he would like to grow up like him and be like him, and take his place everywhere."[33] Identification with a father figure was a natural, even inevitable form of emotional attachment.

For Freud, the leader was always male; a *father* figure. Charles Strozier and Daniel Offer explained that "Freud always examines the unfolding of the Oedipus complex" – this being the primary source of conflict within the family – "from the boy's point of view, adding only parenthetically that the analogue of the boy's conflicts occurs in girls."[34] Carlyle's gendered view derived from his reading of world history as unfolding through the actions of men; for Freud, it derived from the assumed role of the father as head of the family.

In Freud's treatment of Moses, we can see his most complete statement of the role of the male hero-leader in human society. Writing in the *American Journal of Psychoanalysis*, Jerome Appelbaum suggested that Freud had spent a lifetime obsessing with the story of Moses as a consequence of his unresolved, troubled relationship with his father.[35] That obsession with a father figure recurred throughout his work.

Freud's Moses story departed in dramatic ways from that found in the Old Testament. Rather than being a Jewish son sent floating down the Nile, he was an Egyptian born into royalty. His later struggle with Pharaoh was, in this narrative, a struggle – perhaps symbolic but maybe not – with his "real" father. Moses emerged as a hero by rebelling against this father, killing him "in some guise or another."[36]

Monotheism, which Moses institutionalized among the Hebrews, represented for Freud the triumph of the father figure, the single male deity who could serve as the organizing totem for his followers. Moses was the great man, with monotheism representing the institutionalization of the single male authority figure.

Thus, we have a significant refinement of the desire and drive for a great man to lead us. Throughout history, Freud noted, "the great majority of people have a strong need for authority which they can admire."[37] Freud replaced Carlyle's belief in divine intervention with individual psychology, family dynamics, and psychosexual drives. He nonetheless located what he felt was a recurring human desire for a single, male hero. This father figure satisfied a primal need for protection and love.

Freud addressed many of the same matters taken up by Carlyle, most particularly the source and role of authority in human existence. Carlyle and Freud make an odd couple, but they were co-authors of a broadly conceived great man theory (see Table 1.1). There were also significant differences.

For Carlyle, dependence on the Great Man offered nothing but uplift: all upside. For Freud, dependency inevitably led to a marked reduction in intellectual engagement on the part of group members. Part of this dynamic created a pathway to passivity and dependence.[38] It was also a view that was echoed in the concept known as "groupthink," which involved placing a higher value on group membership than on individual autonomy. For Freud, the presence of a strong, attractive individual leader exacerbated the tendency to submerge the individual into the

Table 1.1 *Comparing the Contributions of Carlyle and Freud*

Carlyle	Great Man Theory	Freud
Great men were sent by God to be heroes and these heroes became leaders through the righteous process of hero-worship	*Core of theory*	Humans have a primal need for a father figure to whom they offer dependence and love in return for protection and reciprocated love
God	*Source of authority*	Position in family
Male – by virtue of history	*Gender*	Male – by virtue of patriarchal family structure
Respect	*Exchange with followers*	Love
Loyal reverence	*Role of followers*	Submission
Not recognizing great man	*Inherent danger*	Mistreatment by great man
Uplift	*Outcome of obedience*	Reduced autonomy of group members

group. Group members provided the leader with love and expected that love to be reciprocated equally.[39]

In Freud's view, the great man was "the father that lives in each of us from his childhood days for the same father whom the hero of legend boosts of having overcome." The "picture of the father," then, included the "decisiveness of thought, the strength of will, the self-reliance and independence of the great man" as well as "his divine conviction of doing the right thing which may pass into ruthlessness." The great man will be admired, trusted, and followed. However, "one cannot help but being afraid of him."[40]

That final note – "one cannot help but being afraid of him" – marked a distinction with the jubilant tone so prevalent in Carlyle. And Freud did not stop with that warning. By admiring a leader unconditionally, followers were submitting to authority. In so doing, followers rendered themselves vulnerable. Submission enabled an authority figure who "dominates and sometimes even ill-treats them."[41] Writing on the cusp of World War II (Freud left Vienna for London the year prior to the publication of *Moses and Monotheism*), Freud's warning was tangible and immediate.[42]

A Fully Relevant Construct

Scholarship in post-World War II America slowly but unmistakably moved away from a focus on individuals – Great Men and father figures alike – as the sole movers and shakers of events. Walter Nord and Suzy Fox noted that trend in the domain of psychology, traditionally a field concerned with the individual and "the quest to uncover the essential properties and universal features of the typical human being." Their study of published psychology research suggested that a reorientation had occurred. The tendency, although far from universal, was to move "from viewing individuals independently of context, to consideration of interplay between individuals and their contexts."[43]

That movement, unexpected though it may be in the field of psychology (an "under-recognized" shift according to Nord and Fox), was fundamental to a number of other fields long before the postwar era. In one of the early direct rebukes to Carlyle, Herbert Spencer presented a core sociological view of unfolding of events as being shaped more by context than by the efforts of individuals, no matter how great they might be.

Spencer was influenced by newly emergent theories of evolution: Darwin of course, but more specifically the work of French biologist Jean-Baptiste Lamarck. Spencer offered his own *Principles of Biology* (1864) with its notion of "survival of the fittest." His thoughts were also shaped by the ongoing work of French philosopher Auguste Comte who published a series of books between 1830 and 1842 under the general title, *The Course in Positive Philosophy*. Spencer became a founding voice in the field of sociology.[44] In his 1873 *Study of Sociology*, a founding text in the evolution of sociological inquiry, Spencer took direct aim at Carlyle's Great Man theory.

The great man must always be considered and understood in terms of the times in which he lived. "Even if we were to grant the absurd supposition that the genesis of the great man does not depend on the antecedents furnished by the society he is born in," Spencer wrote, "there would still be the quite sufficient facts that he is powerless in the absence of the material and mental accumulations which his society inherits from the past, and that he is powerless in the absence of the co-existing population, character, intelligence, and social arrangements."[45] Great men, if and when they did appear, were products of social and historical forces rather than gifts bestowed on human civilization by God.

That view, that the individual leader was a product of larger forces was not unique to sociology. We can find evidence of it in history writing as well. Historical biographer Allan Nevins was fond of quoting from a letter by Abraham Lincoln. In April 1864, Lincoln wrote to a lawyer friend in a contemplative mood. This was an especially ripe moment for introspection, with the president awaiting a Senate vote for the Thirteenth Amendment ending slavery. Lincoln was humble. "I claim not to have controlled events," he observed, "but confess plainly that events have controlled me."[46] Lincoln may have been expressing a bit too much humility.[47] He was, after all, the consensus selection by historians as the single most influential figure in American history.[48] Nonetheless, he recognized the larger forces that served to shape events and control outcomes.[49]

In the next century, Martin Luther King appeared to offer new evidence of the decisive role that an individual could play in shaping events. But beware of overascribing causation to the efforts of an individual, no matter how special or prominent that individual. That was a caution offered by historians.

When the *Journal of American History* devoted a special issue to the impact of King on the civil rights movement of the 1950s and 1960s, special issue editor Nathan Irvin Huggins took pains to distance himself from attribution of causation to individual actions alone. "He was only one man in a movement; although a very prominent one." We can be sure, Huggins added, that *some* of what occurred in the 1960s "would have occurred without any given individual, Martin Luther King included." He added, "No one is more troubled than I am by Great Man approaches to historical events."[50]

The disinclination to place any individuals, regardless of their capabilities, prominence, and appeal, at the center of analysis found some support among some management scholars. In a 1977 *Academy of Management Review* article, Jeffrey Pfeffer echoed the caution of sociologists and historians. Sure, we like to believe that individuals can triumph over "a complex set of interactions," noted Pfeffer.[51] It is a comforting illusion and seems to make solutions relatively easy. Look for better leaders. But causes were far more complex and solutions far more difficult to achieve.

That stream was picked up by James Meindl and colleagues when they wrote about the "romance of leadership." In a 1985 *Administrative Science Quarterly* article, Meindl and colleagues noted the degree to which organizations and the public obsess over and celebrate individual leadership. But that is a simple, even simplistic way for people to understand complex interactions.[52]

How and why do organizations, groups, even societies and nations succeed or fail? People often attribute success or failure of institutions (or any other social groups) to the actions of individuals. It is easy to understand the appeal of such an attribution. According to Freud, it is primal, basic to our search for a father figure/protector. In a chaotic, complex world, it seems to uphold individual agency: the capacity of one person within a social setting to take independent actions and make autonomous decisions that matter.[53] And humans, according to evolutionary psychologists, are natural followers.

"At the dawn of human history, more than two million years ago," wrote Mark van Vugt and Anjana Anuja, "in the hostile environment of the African savannah, there was safety in numbers. Individuals who possessed the cognitive ability for followership thrived better than those lacking it." Studies of human attachment have argued that infants come into the world biologically preprogrammed to form attachments to authority figures, an impulse which Freud laid to a longing for parental authority.[54] We are all born to follow.

The manner in which people interpret their world figures into the elevation of the individual. We construct narratives and tell stories. Inherent in that mode of knowledge construction is a kind of hero's journey, either a romantic drama of "the hero's transcendence of the world" – here I am quoting from Hayden White – or a comedic/tragic plot in which the hero falls.[55] Those stories have a common theme: an individual protagonist resides at the core.

It is not much of a mystery to appreciate why corporate executives cling to a kind of great person theory. Eric Guthey and colleagues noted a trend, dating back to the later 19th century, for business executives to construct a narrative in which "they can remain floating in mid-air by virtue of their own innate skills and exemplary characteristics." CEOs take pains to claim authorship of great successes for their companies, while blaming failures on outside forces: unfair foreign competition, crippling state regulation, world economic trends, and even bad weather.[56]

By romanticizing their own role in the company's success, CEOs seek to enhance their self-esteem. With adulation comes prestige, power, and control.[57] CEOs seek to assure others – shareholders (both current and potential future investors), board members, fellow executives, and employees at all levels – that their leadership is worthy of followership; that they are indeed great men and women.

Corporations construct a context intended explicitly to reinforce that heroic great person image: public ceremonies, elaborate executive searches, ceremonial inaugurations, and the granting of elaborate symbols and perquisites. "If leaders are chosen by using a random number table," Jeffrey Pfeffer reasoned, "persons are less likely to believe in their effects than if there is an elaborate search or selection process followed by an elaborate ceremony signifying the changing of control." Additionally, "if the leader has a variety of perquisites and symbols that distinguish him or her from the rest of the organization," the perception of worthiness, of greatness, is enhanced.[58]

There are great people, heroes worthy being admired, exalted, and followed. In its circular logic – leaders must be important because we act as if they are important which we do because, well, they must be important –

the celebration of the heroic leader becomes self-reinforcing even without being empirically demonstrated. And when the organization fails, when performance disappoints, the route to correction is clear: find a new leader.

Looking Backward/Looking Forward

All the rigorous scholarly research and theorizing we may undertake cannot diminish the human striving to locate heroic leaders. People seek a narrative structure that brings legitimacy to abstractions, offers coherence in response to apparent chaos, and asserts human agency in the face of seemingly unmanageable complexity. This is not entirely rational. It may, in fact, be the opposite. The search may also be delusional and self-defeating. The Great Man Theory, more fully understood, helps our appreciation of what James Meindl and associates referred to as the lofty elevation of a concept of leadership by imbuing it with "mystery and near mysticism."[59]

Neither Carlyle not Freud paid much attention to what, precisely, their great man did in order to influence followers and shape history. What are the behaviors that allow leaders to be effective? Is there a universal answer to the behavioral question or are effective behaviors contingent on the particular context in which leaders – and followers – find themselves?

NOTES

1 See, for example, Raul Maloş, "The Most Important Leadership Theories," *Annals of Economic Studies* (January 2012), 413–20.
2 David V. Day et al., "Advances in Leader and Leadership Development: A Review of 25 Years of Research and Theory," *Leadership Quarterly* 25 (2014), 64.
3 Peter G. Northouse, *Leadership: Theory and Practice* (Los Angeles: Sage, 2010).
4 Gary Yukl, "Managerial Leadership: A Review of Theory and Research," *Journal of Management* 15 (1989): 251–89.
5 Grint, "A History of Leadership," in Alan Bryman et al., eds., *The SAGE Handbook of Leadership* (Los Angeles: Sage, 2011), 8.
6 Chris R.V. Bossche, *Carlyle and the Search for Authority* (Columbus: Ohio State University Press, 1991).
7 Thomas Carlyle, *On Heroes, Hero-Worship, and the Heroic in History* (New Haven: Yale University Press, 1841/2013).
8 Bossche, *Carlyle and the Search for Authority*.
9 J. Salwyn Schapiro, "Thomas Carlyle, Prophet of Fascism," *Journal of Modern History* 17 (1945), 99.
10 Carlyle, *On Heroes*, 16.

11 Ibid., 29. In his book, the Great Man is sometimes capitalized, sometimes not.

12 Bossche, *Carlyle and the Search for Authority*.

13 Ibid.

14 Carlyle had written a massive three-volume history of the French Revolution that is said to have served as a primary source for Charles Dickens' *A Tale of Two Cities*, published twenty-two years later.

15 Carlyle, *On Heroes*, 162.

16 Ibid.

17 Ibid., 163–4.

18 Ibid., 21.

19 Ibid., 31.

20 Ibid., 95.

21 Ibid., 162.

22 Ibid.

23 Ibid., 29.

24 Schapiro, "Thomas Carlyle, Prophet of Fascism"; Alan Steinweis, "Hitler and Carlyle's 'Historical Greatness,'" *History Today* 45 (1995), 33–39. Keith Grint offered the following assessment of the relationship between Carlyle, Nazism, and Hitler: "Despite Carlyle's virulent anti-Semitism, he was not a particular favorite author of Hitler's, though the model for Carlyle's 'great' leader was also Hitler's: Frederick the Great. [Joseph] Goebbels (Hitler's propaganda chief) read sections of Carlyle's biography to Hitler in the last month of the war in a vain attempt to boost the Führer's collapsing morale . . . if there was ever a 'great' leader – though the term 'great' is a misnomer here if it implies anything positive – to fit Carlyle's 'great-leaders-of-history' approach to leadership, Hitler is one such leader." Grint, *The Arts of Leadership*, 290.

25 Schapiro, "Thomas Carlyle, Prophet of Fascism," 114.

26 Nancy F. Koehn, "Great Men, Great Pay? Why CEO Compensation Is Sky High," accessed at www.washingtonpost.com/opinions/great-men-great-pay-why-ceo-compensation-is-sky-high/2014/06/12.

27 Rakesh Khurana, "The Curse of the Superstar CEO," *Harvard Business Review* 80 (September 2002), 2–8.

28 Barbara Kellerman discussed Freud's analysis in terms of followership in *Followership: How Followers are Creating Change and Changing Leaders* (Boston: Harvard Business School Press, 2008).

29 Charles B. Strozier and Daniel Offer, "Freud and His Followers," in Strozier et al., eds., *The Leader: Psychological Essays* (New York: Springer, 2011), 25.

30 Samuel Slipp, *The Freudian Mystique: Freud, Women, and Feminism* (New York: New York University Press, 1993), 1.

31 Simone de Beauvoir, *The Second Sex* (New York: Knopf, 1962); and Betty Friedan, *The Feminine Mystique* (New York: Norton, 1963). Freud's emphasis on female "hysteria" attracted special condemnation. For a review of the extensive debate, see Mari Jo Buhle, *Feminism and Its Discontents: A Century of Struggle with Psychoanalysis* (Cambridge: Harvard University Press, 1998).

32 Sigmund Freud, *Group Psychology and the Analysis of the Ego* (New York: Liveright Publishing, 1921/1967), 20.

33 Ibid., 37.

34 Strozier and Offer, "Freud and His Followers," 28.
35 Jerome Appelbaum, "Father and Son: Freud Revisits His Oedipus Complex in *Moses and Monotheism*," *American Journal of Psychoanalysis* 72 (2012), 166–84.
36 Strozier and Offer, "Freud and His Followers," 28.
37 Sigmund Freud, *Moses and Monotheism* (New York: Vantage, 1937/1967), 111. For an appreciative assessment of this work, Freud's final book, see Richard J. Bernstein, *Freud and the Legacy of Moses* (Cambridge: Cambridge University Press, 1998). Bernstein places *Moses and Monotheism* in the context of Freud's late-in-life attempt to determine the meaning of his own Jewishness.
38 Deborah Frieze and Margaret Wheatley, "It's Time for the Heroes to Go Home," *Leader to Leader* 62 (2011), 27–32; Blair McPherson, "No More Heroes," *Human Resource Management International Digest* 16 (2008), 6–9.
39 This was Freud, so, yes, that attraction was in part sexual; a libidinous attraction to the father-figure/leader. On "groupthink," see Irving L. Janis, *Victims of Groupthink: A Psychological Study of Foreign Policy Decisions and Fiascos* (Boston: Houghton Mifflin, 1972); William H. Whyte, "Groupthink," *Fortune* (March 1952): 114–17, 142, 146.
40 Freud, *Moses and Monotheism*, 170.
41 Ibid., 111.
42 Freud's leave-taking was sanctioned by the Nazi regime. The government insisted that he sign a statement saying that he had not been molested in any way and that he had been able to continue with his scientific work. Freud signed, and then added with clear and brutal sarcasm: "I can most highly recommend the Gestapo to everyone." Mark Edmundson, "Defender of the Faith?" *New York Times Sunday Magazine*, Sept. 9, 2007, accessed at www.nytimes.com/2007/09/09/magazine/09wwln-lede-t.html?pagewanted= all&_r=0.
43 Walter R. Nord and Suzy Fox, "The Individual in Organizational Studies: The Great Disappearing Act?" in Stewart Clegg and Cynthia Hardy, eds., *Studying Organization: Theory and Method* (Thousand Oaks: Sage, 1999), 142.
44 John David Yeadon, *Herbert Spencer: The Evolution of a Sociologist* (New York: Basic Books, 1971).
45 Herbert Spencer, *The Study of Sociology* (Ann Arbor: University of Michigan Press, 1873/1961), 31.
46 Abraham Lincoln, letter to Albert G. Hodges, April 1864, accessed at www.abrahamlincolnonline.org/lincoln/speeches/hodges.htm.
47 A 2012 Steven Spielberg movie covering the events of this same month showed no similar humility toward Lincoln's role as a prime mover. See H.K. Bush, "What Historians Think about Spielberg's *Lincoln*," *Cineaste* 38 (Spring 2013), 13–19.
48 A poll of historians crowned Lincoln with that distinction. The *Atlantic Magazine*, the poll's sponsor, noted, "He saved the Union, freed the slaves, and presided over America's second founding." I like to think that the historians who participated in the poll would have been at least a bit embarrassed by that overattribution of individual causation. Lincoln himself certainly

would have been. Accessed at www.theatlantic.com/magazine/archive/2006/12/the-100-most-influential-figures-in-american-history/305384.

49   Munslow noted that historians tend to avoid explicit discussions of the concept of causation. Munslow, *The Routledge Companion*, 37–43. For excellent discussions on the distinction between conditions and causation in historical writing, see Raymond Martin, "Causes, Conditions, and Causal Importance," *History and Theory* 21 (February 1982), 53–74; Elizar Weinryb, "The Justification of a Causal Thesis: An Analysis of the Controversies over the Theses of Pirenne, Turner, and Weber," *History and Theory* 14 (February 1975), 32–56.

50   Nathan Irvin Huggins, "Martin Luther King, Jr.: Charisma and Leadership," *Journal of American History* 74 (September 1987), 477–8.

51   Jeffrey Pfeffer, "The Ambiguity of Leadership," *Academy of Management Review* 2 (1977), 109.

52   James R. Meindl et al., "The Romance of Leadership," *Administrative Science Quarterly* 30 (1985), 78. See also Judy Gray and Iain L. Densten, "How Leaders Woo Followers in the Romance of Leadership," *Applied Psychology: An International Review* 56 (2007), 558–81; Clara Kulich et al., "Where Is the Romance for Women Leaders? The Effects of Gender on Leadership Attributions and Performance-Based Pay," *Applied Psychology: An International Review* 56 (2007), 582–601; James R. Meindl and Sanford B. Ehrlich, "The Romance of Leadership and the Evaluation of Organizational Performance," *Academy of Management Journal* 30 (1987), 91–109.

53   For a discussion of the concept of agency as well as definitional debates, see Mustafa Emirbayer and Ann Mische, "What Is Agency?" *American Journal of Sociology* 103 (January 1998), 962–1023.

54   John Bowlby, *Attachment and Loss* (New York: Basic Books, 1969); Micha Popper, "Toward a Theory of Followership," *Review of General Psychology* 15 (2011), 29–36; Mark van Vugt and Anjana Ahuja, *Naturally Selected: Why Some People Lead, Others Follow, and Why It Matters* (New York: Harper, 2011), 22.

55   White, *Metahistory*, 8–9.

56   Eric Guthey et al., *Demystifying Business Celebrity* (London: Routledge, 2010), 41; Barry M. Staw et al., "The Justification of Organizational Performance," *Administrative Science Quarterly* 28 (1985), 582–600; Gerald R. Salancik and James R. Meindl, "Corporate Attributions as Strategic Illusions of Management Control," *Administrative Science Quarterly* 29 (1984), 238–54; Gray and Densten, "How Leaders Woo Followers in the Romance of Leadership," 558–81; Michelle C. Bligh et al., "Romancing Leadership: Past, Present, and Future," *Leadership Quarterly* 22 (2011), 1058–77.

57   William J. Goode, *The Celebration of Heroes: Prestige as a Social Control System* (Berkeley: University of California Press, 1978).

58   Pfeffer, "Ambiguity of Leadership," 109.

59   Meindl et al., "The Romance of Leadership," 78.

2 More Who than Do and the Trait versus Behavior Debate

In his insightful 1967 *Organizations in Action*, James Thompson noted that all organizations exist in a state of constant tension between control and autonomy, stasis and change, unity of direction, and responsiveness to external dynamism.[1] To survive, organizations need to create a stable, unified system that remains responsive to a dynamic environment. The task of organizational leaders, then, is to achieve, maintain, and – when needed – adjust the requisite tension among these contrary forces.

But what, specifically, do leaders do in order to meet that goal?

Perhaps we can divine an understanding of the specifics involved in enacting the leadership role by reading the memoirs of leaders themselves. This is the forum for leaders of all sorts – successful executives (say, Meg Whitman), organizational innovators (Ricardo Semler), media moguls (Oprah Winfrey), serial failures (Carly Fiorina), flamboyant entrepreneurs (Richard Branson), cigar-chomping tough guys (Lee Iacocca), generals (Colin Powell), diplomats (Colin Powell again), sports coaches (Mike Krzyzewski), and even the occasional best-selling pastor (John C. Maxwell) – to tell you what they did and what you can do.[2] Some of these offerings may be interesting, perhaps even inspiring. For the most part, however, their secrets turn out to be obvious boilerplate prescriptions of dubious worth and questionable applicability.

In fact, the question of what it is, precisely, that leaders do has received relatively little attention in the discourse. To Carlyle, leaders shape history; to Freud, leaders offer love and protection. In management discourse, analysis of what leaders do frequently takes the form of searching for broad organizational role categories. Leaders plan, align, anticipate, motivate, monitor, and reward. Then the discussion quickly veers into a question of who leaders are, what traits they bring to bear on their job.

In late 2001, the editors of the *Harvard Business Review* assembled a panel of corporate CEOs with the goal of answering just that question. The opening gambit was to ask each participant to identify "the three most important tasks of a leader."[3] The notion that "leaders" as a general

33

construct have proscribed tasks is a bit of a fiction. The question was really about the role of a corporate CEO.

Perhaps tripping over this implicit conflation of "leader" and "CEO," the responses were mostly at the level of broad role definitions. "The first thing a leader has to do is set the vision for the organization," said one. Another insisted that a leader must develop "a conceptual, strategic ability to sense what's going on in the outside world as well as inside the organization." Taking what he thought was a "somewhat different direction," a third ignored roles, instead suggesting that, first and foremost, a leader needed to "have a sense of the inexorability of tomorrow."[4]

Looking for congruence in the responses, the (unnamed) *Review* editor suggested common themes. "*The first would be the necessity of formulating and communicating a vision for the organization. Then comes the need to add value to the enterprise. And the final theme is the organizational imperative to motivate followers.*"[5] Identifying "themes" isn't quite the same as enunciating just what it is that leaders do, the stated aim of the roundtable.

Twelve years after that panel, a group of consultants took to the pages of the *Review* to offer their own read on the tasks of "strategic leadership." Strategic leadership as a field purposely conflated the CEO and leadership roles. Strategic leaders, according to H. Igor Ansoff, developed "the future growth and profitability potential of the firm."[6] The three strategy consultants offered a set of categories of strategic leaders' roles. They *anticipate* trends and opportunities in an uncertain world. They *challenge* the status quo within their organizations. They *interpret* complex information. They *decide* and then *align* the internal elements of their organizations with those decisions. Finally, they *learn* from others: about themselves and about their organization.[7] Thus, the authors managed to suggest useful domains of leadership activities. But what about specifics?

It is quite possible that no segment of society has given more thought to the specifics of just what it is that leaders do than has the military. Because the armed forces have contributed in varied and significant ways to the discourse on leadership, it is worthwhile to focus there.

The Warrior Model of Leadership

Even while acknowledging that the military has paid concerted attention to leadership over the years, I hasten to add that attention does not necessarily translate into useful specificity. To illustrate, I can turn to a 2006 field manual published by the U.S. Army.

What does an army leader do, the manual asked? Well, they "lead," they "develop," and they "achieve."[8] Not so insightful.

After offering a few tautologies – leadership involves "leading others" and "leading by example" – the manual adds communicating and exerting influence "beyond the chain of command." Preparing oneself, creating a "positive" environment, and "developing others" all contribute to the leader's task.

Not all of the manual's explanations of the leader's role are quite so banal. Placing the "greater good" of the organization and the "mission first" couples with "empowering subordinates" to learn more and perform better, and engaging subordinates in a process of reviewing actions in order to "discover for themselves what happened, why it happened, how to sustain strengths, and how to improve on weaknesses." That process of diagnosis and criticism, known in the military as an after-action review, is indeed a specific and powerful activity that leaders can engage in with followers, although the effectiveness of such an intervention depends on the willingness of all parties to engage equally in both advocacy and inquiry. Finally, character and personal bearing are suggested as attributes that allow individuals to be effective leaders.[9]

Whatever it is that leaders do, the military has long been convinced that they make the difference between success and failure. "In military affairs," Tolstoy famously wrote in *War and Peace*, "the strength of an army is the product of its mass and some unknown x." That "unknown x" – the spirit of the troops, their willingness to obey, skill to execute, and commitment to victory – flowed directly, Tolstoy believed, from what it was that their leaders did.

There is nothing like war to focus attention on leadership. Keith Grint noted the centrality of a war context – dating back to Sun Tzu's *The Art of War* – in shaping leadership discourse.[10] A "warrior model of leadership" – that's a term applied by David Nice – traditionally defined military attitudes and assumptions.[11] Fundamental to that warrior model was the conviction that the requirements of leadership were shaped by the contingencies of war.[12] Danger was ever-present, success a matter of life and death, and "unswerving obedience" a critical element of effectiveness.[13]

The task of a warrior leader was to mold a fighting force capable of victory. Soldiers should be trained in short- or close-order drill in order to ensure that they would perform "without any conscious mental activity" and instinctively demonstrate "*unhesitating obedience to the will of your leader.*"[14] That theme of leaders producing obedience recurs throughout the discourse on the warrior model.

In the midst of World War II, a U.S. naval officer, Arthur A. Ageton, attempted to define leadership with particular reference to serving as a naval commander. "In any command," he wrote, "a leader will always be the one who goes before his followers to show them the way he wishes them to proceed, and he will be followed by others in conduct and opinion only as far and as well as he succeeds in endowing them with his spirit by his sincere interest in their welfare and by his superior example and precept."[15]

The ideal leader/follower relationship unfolds in a way to ensure that the followers "will execute his will, comply with his demands . . . learn his wishes, and carry out his orders cheerfully, willingly, and even blindly." How different is Ageton's ideal leader from Thomas Carlyle's 19th-century Great Man? Recall Carlyle's plea that followers "bow down submissive before great men."[16] The enduring appeal of Carlyle's theory was apparently hard to shake.

Unlike Carlyle, however, Ageton seemed at least a bit conflicted regarding submission. Later in the book, for instance, he insisted: "The Navy does not want blind, unreasoning loyalty. Rather, what is desired is a reasoned and intelligent execution of orders." What the navy did want was followers who were "ready to jump at a word from you, whether they think you are right or wrong." Ageton may have been somewhat conflicted about the notion of obedience, but he mainly came down on the *obey-my-orders-right-or-wrong* side of the leadership equation.[17]

Ageton spoke from his own personal vantage point embedded high up in the ranks. That was useful but certainly not the whole story. Why not ask frontline solders to examine critically their own leaders and do so in the middle of a real shooting war? But who would be audacious enough to propose such an undertaking? The answer, perhaps not so surprisingly, was a sociologist. What is surprising, shocking really, is that the military agreed.

Ask the Warriors Themselves

From his position as director of the professional staff of the War Department's Information and Education Division, University of Chicago-trained sociologist Samuel Stouffer hatched a plan. His team would conduct an attitude survey of American soldiers deployed overseas. During World War II, no less, Stouffer's training in techniques of statistical data gathering and analysis led him to assert his capacity to "provide a base of factual knowledge which would help the Director of the Army Information and Education Division in his administrative and policy decisions."[18] The announced justification was to help the War Department plan for the end-of-war necessity of reintroducing millions of soldiers to civilian life.

Stouffer and his team would conduct large-scale opinion surveys of American troops covering a wide range of attitudes, including attitudes toward officers. The results of that survey, made available to the public four years after the war ended, offered candid insights into the attitudes that helped shape a future generation of men. The existence of such a survey was rather remarkable, all the more so for how close it came to being vetoed by civilian – not military – authorities.

On first being informed of the request, Secretary of War Henry Stimson said no. Anonymous opinion, he argued, whether positive or negative, "is destructive in its effect on a military organization where accepted responsibility on the part of every individual is fundamental. It is therefore directed that because of their anonymous nature, polls will not be permitted among the personnel of the army of the United States."[19]

It took the top military brass, particularly Chief of Staff George Marshall and Supreme Allied Commander Dwight Eisenhower, to overturn that civilian resistance. Eisenhower was famously insistent on open dialogue. "I have no sympathy with anyone, whatever his station," he lectured a mixed military and civilian audience on the eve of D-Day, "who will not brook criticism."[20] He saw no reason to stop a poll.

What came across loud-and-clear in the response of troops was the expectation that military officers behave in ways consistent with a notion of fairness. Those officers rated most highly were praised for exhibiting an interest in the men and their needs and for being "helpful" to those men while recognizing their abilities.

Unsurprisingly, the survey surfaced a number of complaints about officers, particularly in their treatment of the frontline grunts of the war. Most notable were concerns that officers assumed privileges denied to the troops. Here's a typical observation offered by a survey respondent:

The officers on this command are the most selfish egotistical people I've ever come across. They never think of the men but get very angry when things do not go right for themselves. A good illustration is the incident where the officers' club was built before the hospital. Another example of the officers' selfishness occurs practically daily in the PX [Post Exchange]. They are allowed to enter the PX at all hours for the ridiculous reason that it is beneath them to wait their turn to get served. After all, we do belong to the greatest democracy the world has ever known, but you would never know it after being stationed in the Persian Gulf Service Command.[21]

Left unexamined was the performance question. Put aside what the troops liked or disliked in their officers. Did leaders who took advantage of uneven access to "food, liquor, and women" mold an effective or ineffective fighting force? That was never asked, let alone answered.

A False Analogy

Despite the temptation to analogize business and war, it is presumptuous to draw a direct parallel between military leadership at a time of war and leadership in business organizations.[22] The stakes are not parallel. The demands for obedience have a different relationship to success. Dwight Eisenhower launched the D-Day invasion in June 1944 knowing with certainty that a significant percentage of the first-wave troops would be killed. The soldiers themselves, after landing on the beach, had no option but to charge directly into a deadly curtain of German fire. And when Eisenhower toured the Ohrdruf concentration camp the following April, he witnessed the profound stakes of war and victory.[23] Even stipulating the cutthroat nature of competition and the centrality of business to people's lives and livelihood, this is *not* analogous to business competition.

Still, two facts make this attention to the state of military discourse coming out of World War II relevant. First, the men who served in the war would soon inhabit the offices of corporate America during a period of explosive postwar growth. And second, a remarkable amount of research conducted on leadership in the ensuing Cold War years grew out of military funding. That was particularly true of psychological inquiry that focused on the personal dynamics of leadership. "Virtually all psychological research" conducted in the early Cold War years, wrote Ellen Herman, "had military applications." With the weaponization of psychology, the field exploded, and with it, the study of the psychology of leadership.[24]

Searching for the Holy Grail

Writing in 1947, Professor Cecil Gibb noted the tendency among psychologists to think of leadership as a personality attribute of the individual, a trait "that some persons possess and others do not." That belief led to a search for "persons who have this trait well developed." Find a person with the right traits – traits being understood as a person's "general characteristics, including capacities, motives, or patterns of behavior" that might be inherited, acquired, or some combination of the two – and you have the right leader.[25] Leadership, in the trait view, becomes an assertion of personality, a "property of individuals," noted David Knights and Majella O'Leary, and "not that of social groups or institutions."[26]

Gibb himself was highly dubious of that trait approach. "Leadership is not an attribute of the personality," he insisted.[27] He was joined a year later by the eminent leadership scholar, Ralph Stogdill. After surveying the available research on traits, Stogdill concluded that "a person does not become a leader by the possession of some combination of traits."[28] Stogdill was part of a research team examining leadership behaviors. This skepticism about traits, however, was not widely shared.

Walter Palmer, in a 1974 *Personnel Psychology* article, noted a near-obsessive search among psychologists for a definitive cluster of leadership traits. "A single, unique style of management of guaranteed effectiveness has been the Holy Grail of personality and management researchers for many years," he suggested.[29] As expected, the origins of that psychological pursuit can be traced to the military.

Decisiveness and High Heels

Prior to World War I, the U.S. Army gave surprisingly little organized and disciplined thought to leadership. Richard Faulkner ascribed that lack of attention to a number of fundamental assumptions made by and about military personnel. Leadership was thought to be a matter of breeding, combined with a *noblesse oblige* notion of paternalism. In military thinking, "officer" and "leader" were taken to be interchangeable. Officers were simply assumed to be leaders, and military leaders were officers.

"The army of the World War I era had no set doctrine to define, codify, or explain the organization's view on leadership," Faulkner noted.[30] Instead, the military relied largely on a "proper education" plus a battery of rigorous physical tests and recommendations from current officers and well-connected sponsors to produce individuals capable of the leadership that would add the Unknown X.

The buildup that followed the United States' 1917 entry into the First World War (known to contemporaries as the "Great War" or the "War that will End War") demanded some degree of rigor. There was just too much pressure being applied to the recruitment of "manpower" and the selection and training of officers.

The field of Industrial Psychology was then in its infancy, born with the 1913 publication of Hugo Munsterberg's *Psychology and Industrial Efficiency*.[31] With the declaration of war, the urgency to apply that science to the demands of the military was recognized by practicing psychologists. The President of the American Psychological Association created a Committee on the Psychological Examination of Recruits that went on to recommend the mental examination of every soldier entering the military.

The traditional method of selecting officers proved to be a bottleneck to the explosive growth of the military. Because intelligence was assumed to be a core trait of effective leadership, the army turned to intelligence testing as a way of screening for high potential officers. French psychologist Alfred Binet along with colleague Théodore Simon first published a pioneering intelligence test in 1908, followed in 1916 by efforts from William Stern and Lewis Terman at Stanford University to develop a measure of intelligence known as intelligence quotient (IQ).[32] Terman's tests were made available to the military and eventually administered to over 80,000 men.[33] The goal was to search for leadership potential in a much broader swath of the population than had previously been considered.

With attention focused mainly on leadership traits, a 1917 New York University study conducted by Paul and Edith Mulhall Achilles moved beyond IQ tests to look at critical "character qualities." Enoch Gowin had developed a number of "traits" that he argued could be used to judge "executive ability": integrity, initiative, perseverance, health, aggressiveness, organizing abilities, and judgment among them.[34] How would veteran military officers rate these traits? Overall, there was consensus. Yes, these were the key traits of effective officers.[35]

The two decades following Armistice Day proved to be less a period of peace than a buildup to a second massive war.[36] Although the civilian armies of the United States stood down, the slow rise of a new military threat loomed in Germany. Attention to the psychology of military leadership may have lagged in the United States, but it blossomed in a nation racked by difficult economic times, deeply held resentments, and frenzied hatreds. German universities became the center of psychology research, with particular focus on "personality" and "character."[37]

In the mid-1930s – Hitler had, by then, declared his political philosophy in *Mein Kampf*, claimed the role of Führer and Reich Chancellor, tripled the size of the army, and ordered military conscription – Germany established a central psychological laboratory in Berlin with over one hundred psychologists. A 1937 law required that the military develop a cadre of Ph.D. trained psychologists, the main task of which was to select future officers. The work of those psychologists led to a set of "special aptitudes" for officers.

Although "automobile and tank driving" (skills) and a "marching orientation" (perhaps a trait?) were included among the desired factors, the focus was on intelligence, an ability to use "will power" – defined as planning, attention, clear thinking under physical and emotional stress, energy, perseverance, and willingness to try "with all one's might" – the capacity to command people, and "expressive movements" in speech, facial expression, hand gestures, and penmanship.[38]

By this point, the German army was administering aptitude tests and paying considerable attention to the conditioning of soldiers to specific tasks and demands. When it came to the special qualities of leadership, however, greater attention was paid to the "whole personality." German psychologists emphasized the innate nature of leadership qualities. Leadership traits were inherited, invariably influenced by "racial" factors.[39]

With the entry of the United States into the Second World War, intense psychological interest in the dynamics of leadership resumed. A group of psychologists at the University of Illinois, for instance, created a course and authored an accompanying textbook designed to prepare civilian students to serve as military officers. "The need for practical psychological training in the handling of men in military situations," wrote Leon Pennington and H.W. Case, "has been increasingly evident since the beginning of the war."[40] Convinced that military leadership would account for the difference between "the freedoms or serfdom of the people," Pennington's team analyzed leadership.[41]

As was typical of the focus on individual leaders, the attraction of *who* outweighed the appeal of *do*. Pennington's group zeroed in on the "traits" that would allow leaders to supply the Unknown X. "Decisiveness," "force and aggressiveness," "tact," "energy," and "humanity" were listed. So was appearance. And for those not sufficiently tall to strike a commanding pose, the writers had a simple suggestion: wear "higher heels."[42]

This may strike you as a mixture of the sublime and the ridiculous. Did Tolstoy have high-heeled shoes in mind when he hailed the significance of the Unknown X? Still, as risible as the particular suggestion may seem, there is something refreshing about the Americans' democratic approach to assuming the mantle of leadership in contrast to the hereditary racism of the Nazi model. Not blessed with the genetic predisposition to grow to a commanding height? No problem. Just buy platform shoes.

With the defeat of Nazi Germany and Fascist Italy, an American model of what Grint thought of as rational individualism turned attention back to the trait question.[43] Consideration settled momentarily on authoritarianism as a trait to be avoided in a leader. Theodor Adorno's *Authoritarian Personality* suggested that a particular constellation of personality traits could shape a "potentially fascistic individual" who would "readily accept fascism if it should become a strong or respectable social movement."[44] His F-Scale test was used by the military to weed out officer candidates, although how widely or effectively is not apparent.[45]

The influence of Adorno's work waned quickly. The study was attacked for its methodological flaws. Ideological opposition to its insistence that fascism was a real possibility in the United States further hampered acceptance.[46] Additionally, the F-Scale was conceived in reactive, negative terms: a filter to apply in order to avoid potential mistakes. Although it was systemic, it was not holistic, taking into account only a portion – albeit a highly dangerous and volatile portion – of the person. Psychologists found a more comforting home in the work that was being offered on general personality traits.

Starting as early as Gordon Allport's work in the 1930s, psychologists had been advocating the use of everyday language to describe an individual's personality. Together with Henry Odbert, Allport identified "generalized and personalized determining tendencies" that constituted "consistent and stable modes of an individual's adjustment to his environment." As researchers expanded and contracted the list of potential personality variables, Ernest Tupes and Raymond Christal in 1961 settled on "five relatively strong and recurrent factors and nothing more of any consequence." The Big Five typology – which ultimately included openness to experience, conscientiousness, extraversion, agreeableness, and neuroticism (referred to in combination by the acronym OCEAN) – was said to provide the basic building blocks of an individual's personality.[47]

The emergence of this positive and holistic statement of an individual's personality offered psychologists a safe haven from authoritarianism and its accompanying assumption of the possibility of a native fascism in the United States (ironically, given that this was the height of the postwar Red Scare). Within the leadership domain, the greatest interest settled on extraversion (outgoing and energetic qualities) and agreeableness (friendly and compassionate qualities). Interest, however, did not translate into satisfying and replicable conclusions.

Leadership discourse eventually turned away from the personality "Big Five," preferring instead drive, self-confidence, leadership motivation (meaning that leaders were people who want to be leaders), honesty and integrity, cognitive abilities, and knowledge of the business.[48] Psychologist Daniel Goleman added "emotional intelligence" with its components of social awareness, self-management, and empathy.[49] Even so, the degree to which these or *any* personality characteristics could be associated with effective leadership remained unsettled.

From Traits to Skills

The notion of traits never disappeared entirely from the discussion. Popular press articles continued to focus on individual characteristics and the alleged impact of leader personality on profitability.[50] As late as 2005, Anthony Mayo and Nitin Nohria could write in the *Harvard Business Review* that leaders were different from the rest of us because they possessed "an almost uncanny ability to understand the context they live in."[51] The commitment of the *Review* to the notion that leaders were different and special was perhaps unsurprising. The idea may well have held great appeal to its executive readers. But there is no doubt that trait theory carried with it a hint of innateness. It should not be a surprise, therefore, to find disquiet with any theory that attributed outstanding leadership to inborn traits.

Writing in what was then named the *Journal of the Academy of Management*, Michael Mescon, Dean of the Georgia State University business school, insisted that there existed no specific cluster of traits that "universally distinguished the leader from the non-leader." Individuals "are not innately endowed with certain traits which make them leaders any more than individuals are born physicians, lawyers, or educators."[52]

A robust study of skills and how skills related to specific task requirements had coalesced around what became known as the human engineering movement. Once again, the military offered a welcoming environment. During and immediately after World War II, military psychologists saw in human engineering a methodology to advance the proper matching of person and task. The initial attention was on the need to match personal skills with the technological requirements of a job. The Office of Naval Research established a Human Engineering Section in order to, according to its director, address problems that "seem to arise whenever man is confronted with technological advances." Citing the time studies of Frederick Taylor and the motion studies of Frank and Lillian Gilbreth, Leonard Mead set his sights on "that endeavor which seeks to match human beings with human beings so that their combined output will be comfortable, safe, and more efficient."[53]

In a 1955 article, Robert Katz urged that business executives turn their attention away from traits altogether and concentrate instead on skills. A search for the "ideal executive" should ask not "what good executives *are* (their innate traits and characteristics)." Rather, the search should focus "on what they *do* (the kinds of skills which they exhibit in carrying out their jobs effectively)."[54] Katz joined a long line of scholars in confusing behaviors (what they do) with skills (their capabilities).

Like so many other leadership writers, Katz sought to locate universalities. What skills would apply to *all* leaders under *all* circumstances? This was an absurd quest based on a grandiose conceit. By focusing solely on the qualities of individuals, it also represented a profound misunderstanding of the dynamics of leadership and the causes of performance in complex organizations.

U.S.-based corporations including General Electric, AT&T, and Standard Oil pioneered the creation of internal psychology research units built to scientifically match skills and jobs.[55] As attention shifted from placing individuals in technical jobs to the identification and development of executive talent, assessments focused on a mixture of personality traits (testing for "dogmatism," a slight reworking of authoritarianism that avoided the ideologically ripe term *fascism*), intellectual skills (vocabulary, comprehension, even math), and occasionally problem-solving attributes judged by observing individuals in role-playing situations.[56]

Whether referred to as skills or competencies, this approach to understanding leadership represented a fragmented, nonsystemic attempt to identify universality. The competency model broke leadership into "independent components without seeing it as an integrated whole," wrote Richard Bolden and Jonathan Gosling. In challenging the "competency paradigm," Brigid Carroll and colleagues argued against depicting individuals "as acting and performing in isolation from others and context." The idea that individuals could achieve outstanding performance for their organizations "by adopting the same generic prescribed behaviors rather than being cognizant and compensatory where one is stronger and weaker" was nonsense.[57]

Both sets of authors also called attention to the lack of situational sensitivity inherent in the skills/competency approach. A large body of literature emerged simultaneously with the skills paradigm that urged scholars to stop seeking universals and start focusing on leadership enactment in particular circumstances.[58] Situational leadership suggested that effectiveness derived from the degree of congruence between how leaders enacted their roles – made decisions, interacted with followers, and so forth – and the situation in which they found themselves. The "maturity" of the group being led, the type of decisions being made, even the preferred style of the individual leaders were all considered to be critical contingencies.

Situational and contingency theories invited their own critical appraisal. Keith Grint located important distinctions between the two. Contingency theory suggests that different leaders will be more suited to particular environments, while situational leadership argues that individual leaders can and should adapt their own styles depending on the context.[59] Still, both assumed a scientifically verifiable, uncontested "situation" to which leaders respond.

How individual leaders read, interpret, and respond to the "situation" is a contestable rather than self-apparent matter. "The environment is not some objective variable that determines a response," insisted Grint, "but rather an 'issue' to be constituted into a whole variety of 'problems' or 'irrelevancies.'"[60] Leaders engage in the active construction of just what the environment is and how to respond most effectively. How an environment is understood should be seen not as an independent variable to leader actions but rather as an organic activity of leadership.

Behavioral Approaches

Skills and competencies may be similar concepts, but what about skills and behaviors? Although the two would seem to be quite different, it isn't always easy to distinguish within the literature. In 1982, for instance, Richard Boyatzis identified five clusters of behavioral competencies associated with above-average managerial performance: goal and action management, leadership, human resource management, focus on others, and directing subordinates.[61] But what, exactly, is a behavioral competency? A behavior? A competency? A competency that enables a particular behavior? The answer is not always clear.

In addressing the question of leadership behavior, writers have been negligent in not defining with any degree of precision what they mean by *behavior*. Behaviors – and let's stick to human behaviors for purposes of this discussion – can be understood as bodily motions (or conscious lack of motion) undertaken intentionally.[62] There are, as might be expected, ongoing disputes about the meaning of intentionality, but I will adhere to the classic understanding offered by Talcott Parsons and Edward Shills. A behavior is an intentional action when it is "oriented to the attainment of ends or goals in situations."[63]

Orthogonal Dimensions

A group of researchers at Ohio State University under the direction of Carroll Shartle attempted to identify the role of leaders in business and the behaviors needed to enact those roles. Leadership, for the researchers, was a behavior that was enacted by an individual in order to direct the activities of a group "toward a shared goal."[64] Shartle had developed his interest in job analysis during the Second World War, helping the military create the *Dictionary of Occupational Titles*.[65] His wartime work did not afford him an opportunity to study executives, but that was where he turned his attention after arriving at Ohio State following the war.

Shartle's research project was part of an explosion of interest in social science research in the United States following World War II. Mark Solovey's review of the post-World War II social science movement noted a dramatic and unprecedented growth in interest, as well as a gradual assumption of academic leadership by U.S. colleges, universities, and research centers.[66]

Fueled by generous grants from the U.S. federal government, most typically from the Department of Defense, social sciences were "bound up with the ideological and practical requirements of the Cold War." Believing, wrote Theodore Porter, that "a strong economy and a healthy population were vital to national security," social scientists sought to define a haven of neutrality that relied on claims of pure science to shield them from the ideological battles both within the United States and on a global stage.[67]

As social scientists increasingly became professionalized, they tended to abandon a search for fundamental theory, turning instead to the pursuit of "continuity, codification, convergence, and cumulation."[68] That critique was offered in 1970 by Alvin Gouldner in his enormous examination of the "coming crisis of western sociology." Industry leaders, in turn, found it increasingly expedient and safe to turn to social sciences for help with matters of coordination, control, and productivity.

The expansion of both the breadth and depth of corporations in the United States following the Second World War led a number of executives to search for tools within the social science fields of psychology, sociology, and anthropology. Organizations that had relied heavily on physical science research – often in the chemical, electrical equipment, and aircraft industries – turned increasingly to social sciences.

As human relations found its way into corporate personnel departments, social scientists enthusiastically enlisted as "servants of power." That colorful and critical phrase, offered by Loren Baritz in a 1960 book, implied a none-too-subtle caveat. "Managers did not make use of social science out of a sense of social responsibility," Baritz noted, "but out of a recognized need to attack age-old problems of costs and worker loyalty with new weapons designed to fit the needs and problems of the twentieth century."[69] This tripartite alliance between the social scientists, the state, and corporate institutions was knowingly and, for the most part, uncritically embraced.[70]

Indeed, much of the work at Ohio State relied on both military funding and industry support. Ralph Stogdill initiated fieldwork with the support of the Office of Naval Research. Graduate students, including Bernard Bass, Karl Weick, and Bob House, conducted much of the original testing on the behavioral questionnaire within the Air Force and at International Harvester.[71] Seeking focus on the enacted behaviors of individuals, the research group asked subordinates to classify the actual behaviors of their leaders.[72] How often does he – and it was always "he" – do "personal favors for group members," "criticize poor work," "emphasize the meeting of deadlines."

As is apparent, these questions called on subjective evaluations on the part of subordinates. Interpretation was built into the next step as well. The researchers identified two principal dimensions: "initiating structure" and "consideration"; the first relating to task performance, and the second to the well-being of employees.

Although later descriptions of the research suggested that these two categories were proposed by the respondents themselves or were derived empirically from a factor analysis of the responses, neither was quite the case. As Edwin Fleishman wrote, the mass of responses from the survey were reviewed and classified by a panel of "expert judges" (the quote marks supplied by Fleishman) into "nine a priori 'dimensions' of leadership behavior." As a next step, researchers assigned specific behaviors, say "origination of new ideas or practices," to a specific dimension; in that case, initiation. Subsequent analysis by the researchers placed factors into the two "major" categories: initiating and consideration.[73]

Shartle and colleagues made the assumption that the two dimensions – focusing on getting the job done and caring about how the individuals performing the job felt about their work and environment – were apparently separable dimensions of leadership behavior; that is, both leaders and followers held a mutual understanding that they were separate, and could all agree as to which behaviors reflected which dimension. That was a stretch.

Think of bosses doing personal favors for group members, or explaining their actions to subordinates. These were classified as behaviors indicative of high consideration. Bosses who criticized poor work and emphasized meeting job deadlines were demonstrating what the researchers called initiating structure. Leaders could be strong or weak on either dimension because the dimensions were orthogonally independent.

The act of interpreting the motive behind an individual's behavior requires attribution. In this case, the researchers were classifying behaviors into these two categories: consideration and initiating structure. Why, for instance, does the boss do personal favors for subordinates? Can we really assume that *all* subordinates will *always* interpret "doing favors" as an act of consideration rather than an attempt to influence task performance? Of course not. And how did the researchers at Ohio State know that criticizing a subordinate's work performance was always taken by subordinates to be a behavior lacking in consideration? Perhaps subordinates interpreted this criticism as an act of consideration.

Building on their questionable assumptions and attributions, and maintaining that leadership represented an assertion of individual intent, the researchers determined that the "ideal leader" was someone who was "high" (that is, strong) on both dimensions. The interaction between the ideal leader and performance outcomes was assumed.

University of Michigan researchers developed a similar categorization of leader behaviors. They labeled the two dimensions "production orientation" and "employee orientation." Additionally, Robert Blake popularized a managerial grid that posited attention to production and attention to people as the two key, orthogonally related variables of effective behavior.[74] These were useful abstractions, offering an opportunity for further dialogue, debate, and analysis. But they were presented as empirical realities, not abstractions.

Codifying the Roles

Roles are not behaviors. Rather, they are social expectations imposed through a set of rules and definitions associated with the occupancy of a prescribed position.[75] "Mother" and "father" are role designations, as are "CEO" and "Divisional Vice President." Conceptually, behaviors *must* be separated from roles to acknowledge that no two individuals are likely to enact the same role in the same way.

Modern analysis of managerial roles dates back to the earliest years of the 20th century. But there is no reason to stop there. Morgen Witzel noted a trend toward "standardization and routine in administration" as far back as Medieval Europe.[76] The focus of attention was on political entities and religious orders.[77]

Attempting to come to terms with the newly emergent industrial organizations in the late 19th–early 20th century, the chief engineer at the Midvale Steel Works in Philadelphia endeavored to apply his mechanical training to broader theoretical questions. What was the best way, the most *scientific* way, for industrial firms to operate? And what were the implications for management roles?

In his 1911 book, *The Principles of Scientific Management*, Frederick Winslow Turner laid out four management roles, which he labeled as duties.[78] The first two involved the development of scientifically defined work elements, and then the proper placement and training of the "men" within those positions. Taylor then urged managers to "heartily cooperate with the men" as a way of ensuring that work was being done in accordance with the "science" of maximum efficiency. Finally, management should "take over all work for which they are better fitted than the workers." Responsibilities that had been left to the workmen in the past, a remnant of the preindustrial craft system, must be assumed by management to allow workers to concentrate on the performance of specific tasks. The "old" ways of doing things, renounced by Taylor as the "rule-of-thumb" method, needed to be scrubbed from efficient, scientifically run companies.[79]

Taylor's admonitions to management, along with other early management theorists – most notably Henri Fayol and his fourteen general principles for management articulated in his 1914 *General and Industrial Administration* – were not responses to already existent institutional expectations; they were attempts to create expectations. Although published in 1914, Fayol's book remained obscure outside of France until the publication of an English translation in 1949.

By the 1970s, management roles had become well proscribed in business. Henry Mintzberg positioned himself not as a prophet – here's what managers should do – but as an observer. His 1973 *Nature of Managerial Work* started with observations of what managers did and then induced roles. With his focus on roles, Mintzberg's goal was to arrive at a science of management.

"What kinds of activities does the manager perform?" Mintzberg asked. From his research, he would infer a set of "basic roles" along with three broad role categories: *informational* (managing by information), *interpersonal* (managing through people), and *decisional* (managing through action) roles.[80] Mintzberg's study clinically zeroed in on the daily lives of five CEOs.

Mintzberg purposefully placed his analysis within management literature rather than focusing on the view from the top. "The liberty is taken of referring to these finding as descriptive of managerial, as opposed to chief executive, work," he explained. "This is done because many of the findings are supported by studies of other types of managers."[81] The question remained: what did leadership look like at the top? How did the possession of hierarchical authority and responsibility impact the enactment of leadership?

A View of and from the Top

Was there ever a time when business executives did not think strategically? Haven't business leaders always needed to apply some notion of how to compete in the future? Yes, answered H. Igor Ansoff, but... Most planning for the future involved management by extrapolation: do more of what has worked, less of what hasn't. This was a dose of presentism and the tranquility fallacy from one of the founders of strategic management, relying as it did on his insistence that *only* in the 1990s did "environmental turbulence" become "discontinuous and novel."[82]

Morgen Witzel found ample evidence that "business leaders before modern times" were analyzing risks and making strategic decisions.[83] Additionally, attention to systemic thinking in what might broadly be defined as political philosophy, can be traced back to Chinese (Han Fei), Greek (Hesiod), and Islamic (Al-Farabi) thinkers. The writings of Nicoló

Machiavelli, especially *The Prince* (1513), had a "profound and lasting effect" on Western approaches to the role of leaders in taking advantage of strategic opportunities when they unfolded, added Witzel.[84]

The advent of strategic management in business is often associated with Ansoff's 1979 *Strategic Management* as well as two books by Michael Porter: *Competitive Strategy* (1980) and *Competitive Advantage* (1985).[85] Walter Kiechel made a compelling case, however, that the transformation to formal strategic thinking in corporate America occurred with the 1963 creation of the Boston Consulting Group (BCG).

Thinking and Behaving Strategically

Bruce Henderson, a former Westinghouse executive and Arthur D. Little consultant, founded BCG in order to provide a framework for executives to put together in a systematic way "all the elements that determined their corporate fate, in particular, the three C's central to any good strategy: the company's costs relative to other companies; the definition of the markets the company served – its customers, in other words – and its positioning vis-à-vis competitors."[86]

Henderson's interest was mainly in analytics, most notably the BCG growth-share matrix for evaluating a corporation's portfolio of business holdings. This is the "dog" (low market share – low growth), "cash cow" (high market share – low growth), "question mark" (low market share – high growth), and "star" (high market share – high growth) categorization with which every business student is familiar. Henderson's goal was to move corporations beyond intuitive and traditional approaches to planning for the future and toward concepts and techniques that would be "logical and tightly reasoned."[87]

In 1963, Henderson's colleague Seymour Tilles published two articles that, for the first time, drew out the leadership implications of strategic management. For Tilles, strategy was really a "simple" matter: "a set of goals and major policies" intended to indicate "what the company as a whole is trying to *achieve* and to *become*."[88] The real challenges lie in implementation. In order to think and *act* strategically, general managers needed to rise above the clichéd definitions of how they did their jobs. This was prior to the 1980s fashion of separating management from leadership and reflected the sense that it was the general manager who stood as the accountable overseer of the performance of a (separable) business unit. To act strategically required these general managers to take a "systems approach" to their job.

"The basic notion of a system," Tilles explained, "is simply that it is a set of interrelated parts." The strategic leader's task was to define the company as a system: "How do things as a company all fit together."[89] Not a simple task, Tilles admitted.

A science of systemic thinking emerged decades earlier, in the 1940s, when a group of like-minded mathematicians coalesced in England during World War II around the government's request for help in managing the complexities of the military. After the war, American mathematician Norbert Wiener gathered a group, including W. Ross Ashby, Stafford Beer, Alan Turing, and Margaret Mead, to develop a body of knowledge on what they labeled "cybernetics": a science of systems.[90] The intention of the science, according to Ashby, was to provide "effective methods for the study, and control, of systems that are intrinsically extremely complex."[91] The human brain seemed to be the most prominent and obvious target for that inquiry.

The brain is indeed a prototypical complex system, made up of multiple elements continuously sending and receiving signals both internally and from a dynamic external environment. That isn't a bad description of a complex business organization: multiple elements continuously sending and receiving signals both from each other and from a dynamic external environment. That connection between the brain and the business organization was made explicitly by British theorist Stafford Beer.

In his 1957 *Cybernetics and Management*, Beer offered what he referred to as a "most important" distinction between a "deterministic" system in which components of the system interact in "a perfectly predictable way," and a "probabilistic" system in which "no precisely detailed prediction can be given."[92] After offering a topology of system complexity from simple to extremely complex, he presented examples of probabilistic, extremely complex systems: the brain, the economy, and *the company*.

Business organizations may well be systems, but most managers, Tilles observed, treated them instead as conglomerations of individual parts. Their working assumption was that as long as the constituent components – the various functions and units that made up the business – hummed along smoothly, the business would thrive. Not so. Those components needed to be integrated in a manner that met the needs of the business' customers. And the integration task did not end there. There were external "groups" – what would twenty years later be called "stakeholders" – that needed to be thought of as part and parcel of an integrated organizational system.[93]

Strategic leaders, in Tilles' view, needed to get their heads out of the company, stop concentrating so relentlessly on internal measures like profit, market share, and return on investment, and take into account the external environment. A slew of external groups – shareholders, to be sure, but also employees, consumers, competitors, suppliers, creditors, as well as the host community and the nation – all have a stake in judging the performance of the firm. The general manager "should never be concerned with a *single* objective." Rather, he "must be concerned with a *set* of objectives; and thus the trade-off of one good against another is a critical aspect of his responsibility."

With his attention on managers, Tilles was something of an exception. For the most part, strategy theorists followed Henderson's example. Michael Porter, with his training in industrial organization economics, assumed that appropriate economic analysis would lead to appropriate decisions. "There was no attention to managers," noted Donald Hambrick. Managers "were presumed to be fully capable of figuring all this neat economic stuff and arriving at the 'right' strategic solution." Hambrick's faculty colleagues joked "that you could always tell if a [teaching] case had been written by Mike Porter" because "it didn't have any people in it."[94] To counter that overly analytic tendency, Hambrick focused his own research on the strategic role of top managers, referred to as "upper echelons." His stated goal was to put "top managers back in the strategy picture."[95]

Leadership focuses on building a relationship with followers. Strategic leadership involved relational activity, but also selecting and developing executives, composing and molding the top management team, and paying attention to the symbolic meaning of their own actions and behaviors.[96] Writing with Sidney Finkelstein, Hambrick suggested that CEOs operated in two domains. The first, referred to as substantive, involved securing and allocating resources and making decisions concerning the product-market arena in which the firm intended to compete. The second domain was more symbolic, recognizing that the communication style, personal demeanor, and behaviors of the CEO all communicated an image both internally and externally.[97]

Not all writers were quite so enamored with the idea of connecting the role of top management to strategy. Henry Mintzberg frequently and insistently made the point that the notion of strategy was built on a fundamental contradiction, or at least a tension. Strategy, he noted, was a concept "rooted in stability." Strategic leaders calculated a path to the future based on the assumption that the future "can be made knowable, or at least controllable."[98] Managers, especially when faced with the inevitable time pressures that come with the job, "tend to favor action over reflection."[99]

As comforting as the assumption of control may be, Mintzberg insisted that it was fallacious. The future is, ultimately, unknowable. That did not suggest to Mintzberg that strategy was a waste of effort or, worse, a delusion of control in an uncontrollable environment. Rather, it was an exercise that required intuition and creativity on the part of strategic leaders. Engaging constituents in a journey rather than calculating a specific plan allows for a flexible, responsive strategy to emerge. The key for effective strategic leaders was not to be completely calculating or totally intuitive, but rather to walk on two feet: "one deliberate, the other emergent."[100]

Perhaps the best insight into the unfolding role of CEO as strategic leader came not from academia but from a thoughtful practitioner. If you return to the list of leadership memoirs offered at the beginning of this chapter, you may notice one significant title missing, one that should be considered independently. Alfred Sloan's *My Years with General Motors* appeared in 1964 and became the first best seller offered by a corporate executive.[101]

Giving Alfred Sloan the Last Word

Although lacking the language of systems thinking and strategic leadership, Sloan brought to his stewardship of General Motors, starting in the 1920s, an approach to thinking systemically about his organization. He did not need the science of cybernetics to tell him that the company was a complex system in need of direction.

My Years with General Motors was not strictly a memoir. Although Sloan offered some personal biography, he declined to allow any shred of human warmth to seep through the pages.[102] But for a chance to understand how an executive understood his strategic role, the book is unparalleled. Furthermore, without intending any "universal principles of management," Sloan offered his own insights, defining the chief executive role as he saw it.[103]

Sloan's insights were formulated shortly after arriving at GM in 1918. That was when William Durant purchased Sloan's United Motor Services, installing the young businessman as a vice president of GM. Durant ran what can be described as a "loose ship," offering little oversight or coordination of the GM's many divisions. After replacing Durant at the top, Sloan worked to create a strategically aligned General Motors characterized by "decentralization with coordinated control."[104]

Just how Sloan enacted his role, or at least his version of it, was on full display in the book. Even before taking the reins at GM, he sought to gain an understanding of the business and revenue models for the company, a matter in which Durant had little apparent interest. "The important thing was that no one knew how much was being contributed – plus or minus – by each division to the common good of the corporation. And because no one knew where the efficiencies and inefficiencies lay, there was no objective basis for the allocation of new investment."[105]

Once he replaced Durant at the top, Sloan worked to ensure that he and his top team developed what he referred to as a "concept of the industry."[106] Executives, he believed, should first look at and then respond to the world outside of their own business. Given that he was running one of the first multibusiness corporations in the world, Sloan insisted on a principle of organization that trended "toward a happy medium . . . between the extremes of pure centralization and pure decentralization."[107]

Divisional performance goals needed to be consistent with a satisfactory long-run return on investment. Each product line, from Chevrolet to Cadillac was provided with a market position that ranged from a $450 selling point for Chevy to a $3500 price point for Cadillac:

> Having thus separated out a set of related price classes, we set forth an intricate strategy which can be summarized as follows: We proposed in general that General Motors should place its cars at the top of each price range and make them of such quality that they would attract sales from below that price, selling those to customers who would see the price advantage in a car of close to the quality of the higher-priced competition. This amounted to quality competition against cars below a given price tag, and price competition against cars above that price.[108]

Each division would overlap slightly with the ones above and below (except for Cadillac, which was at the top of the price/quality hierarchy, and Chevrolet, which was at the base).

Perhaps Sloan's most impressive accomplishment was structuring GM in a way consistent with his operational philosophy. Divisions were provided with high levels of autonomy, including their own functional support areas. Each division would be a profit center. In order to achieve coordination, he structured multiple layers of coordinating committees, staffing those committees with both corporate staff (himself included) and divisional representation. By providing voice to the divisions in creating corporate policies, Sloan ensured that "experienced automobile men" were integrated into all corporate decisions.[109]

Sloan's contribution to strategic leadership is far-reaching and significant. As a result, a number of leadership writers idealized Sloan and his contributions. Warren Bennis, for one, labeled him a great leader and complained about the lack of such meaningful leadership in the 1980s.[110] That is a mistake: Sloan should not be glorified.

Anyone reading Sloan's memoir in search of a defense or even an acknowledgment of his oft-times ruthless competitiveness, his vitriolic opposition to the New Deal and labor unions, or his oversight of the company's helpful participation in Germany's war buildup will be disappointed.[111] And it must be acknowledged that immediately after his retirement, the company he built so carefully and successfully for thirty years began its long descent toward bankruptcy.

What Sloan can be understood is an individual who thought systematically about his role as head of a giant corporation and who articulated the significant roles – designer, coordinator, planner, even organizational philosopher – he played in that position.

Looking Backward/Looking Forward

With its tendency to focus on individual causation in understanding organizational dynamics, leadership discourse often focused on traits, skills, roles, and behaviors of individuals designated to be leaders. The hope was that some set or mixture of one or more elements could be identified that provided insight into just what it was that made individuals effective leaders. Executives have been eager to publish their own view of what made them so successful.

The military led the way in more rigorous exploration, even to the point of allowing a sociologist to ask soldiers at the front line during a war to discuss the behaviors they most appreciated in their immediate commanders. But, despite intense attention and massive effort put into what one critic dismissed as a search for the Holy Grail, definitive results remained elusive.

Individuals do help shape the behaviors of others. When those individuals have access to organizational levers of power, that capacity to influence others is enhanced. For that reason, the concept of power and its intersection between leaders and followers must be considered in relationship to the discourse of leadership.

NOTES

1 James B. Thompson, *Organizations in Action: Social Science Bases of Administrative Theory* (New York: McGraw-Hill, 1967).

2 Richard Branson, *Losing My Virginity: How I Survived, Had Fun, and Made a Fortune Doing Business My Way* (New York: Crown, 2011); Carly Fiorina, *Tough Choices: A Memoir* (New York: Portfolio, 2006); Lee Iacocca and William Novak, *Iacocca: An Autobiography* (New York: Bantam Books, 1984); Mike Krzyzewski and Donald T. Phillips, *Leading with the Heart: Coach K's Successful Strategies for Basketball, Business, and Life* (New York: Warner Books, 2000); John C. Maxwell, *The 21 Irrefutable Laws of Leadership: Follow Them and People Will Follow You* (Nashville: Thomas Nelson, 1998); Colin Powell, *It Worked for Me: In Life and Leadership* (New York:

Harper, 2012); Ricardo Semler, *Maverick: The Success Story behind the World's Most Unusual Workplace* (New York: Warner Books, 1993); Meg Whitman and Joan Hamilton, *The Power of Many: Values for Success in Business and Life* (New York: Crown, 2010); Oprah Winfrey and Joan Barthel, *Oprah* (New York: Knopf, 1998).

3 "All in a Day's Work: A Roundtable with Raymond Gilmartin, Frances Hesselbein, Frederick Smith, Lionel Tiger, Cynthia Tragge-Lakra, and Abraham Zaleznik," *Harvard Business Review* 79 (December 2001), 55–66. Zaleznik, a Harvard Business School professor who studied leadership, was the only non-CEO in the group.

4 Ibid.

5 Ibid., 56–57.

6 H. Igor Ansoff, "Conceptual Underpinnings of Systematic Strategic Management," *European Journal of Operational Research* 19 (1985), 2.

7 Paul J.H. Schoemaker et al., "Strategic Leadership: The Essential Skills," *Harvard Business Review* 91 (January–February 2013), 131–4. There are dozens, most likely hundreds, of taxonomies of general leadership behaviors. Edwin Fleishman and colleagues surveyed the then-current state of such offerings in "Taxonomic Effects in the Description of Leader Behavior: A Synthesis and Functional Interpretation," *Leadership Quarterly* 2 (1991), 245–87. I feature the Schoemaker et al. categorization because of its appearance in the *Harvard Business Review* and its contrast to the earlier panel discussion. These taxonomies typically confuse the constructs of roles and behaviors.

8 Department of the Army, *Army Leadership: Competent, Confident, Agile (Field Manual 22-100)* (Washington, D.C.: Department of the Army, 2006), 2–4.

9 Ibid., 1–1, 1–3. Along with Michael Beer, I analyzed the power of organizational diagnosis in Beer and Spector, "Organizational Diagnosis: Its Role in Organizational Learning," *Journal of Counseling and Development* 71 (1993), 642–50.

10 Grint, "A History of Leadership."

11 David C. Nice, "The Warrior Model of Leadership: Classic Perspective and Contemporary Relevance," *Leadership Quarterly* 9 (1998), 321–33.

12 John Keegan, *A History of Warfare* (New York: Knopf, 1993); Leonard Wong et al., "Military Leadership: A Context-Specific Review," *Leadership Quarterly* 22 (2003), 657–92.

13 Grint, *The Arts of Leadership*, 17.

14 Training manuals quoted in Richard S. Faulkner, *The School of Hard Knocks: Combat Leadership in the American Expeditionary Forces* (College Station: Texas A&M University Press, 2012), 12.

15 Arthur A. Ageton, *Naval Leadership and the American Bluejacket* (New York: McGraw-Hill, 1944), 1.

16 Carlyle, *On Heroes*, 31.

17 Ageton, *Naval Leadership*, 10, 17.

18 Samuel A. Stouffer et al., *The American Soldier: Adjustment during Army Life*, Vol. 1 (Princeton: Princeton University Press, 1949), ix.

19 Ibid., 12.

20 Eisenhower is quoted in Rick Atkinson, *The Guns at Last Light: The War in Western Europe, 1944–1945* (New York: Henry Holt, 2013), 6.

21 Stouffer et al., *The American Soldier*, 370.

22 For an example of just such an analogy, see Mark B. Fuller, "Business as War," *Fast Company* (undated), accessed at www.fastcompany.com/55076/business-war, 1993.

23 Video of Eisenhower's second visit to the camp can be seen at www.youtube.com/watch?v=Sh3uqAasdKU.

24 Ellen Herman, *The Romance of American Psychology: Political Culture in the Age of Experts* (Berkeley: University of California Press, 1995), 127. On the weaponization of psychology and its explosive growth during the early Cold War years, see Donald S. Napoli, *Architects of Adjustment: The History of the Psychological Profession in the United States* (Port Washington: Kennikat Press, 1981). The weaponization of psychology continued for decades. In 2015, the American Psychological Association admitted that several of its leaders had worked with the U.S. military to shape abusive interrogation techniques – i.e., torture – to be used on war-on-terror prisoners. As two psychiatrists writing for the *Los Angeles Times* observed, "The APA's relationship with military intelligence dates back to its contributions in critical areas such as aptitude assessment and teamwork during World War I and II. After the 9/11 attacks, the APA sought to become an indispensable source of psychological expertise for counter-terrorism efforts at the Pentagon and CIA." In August 2015, the APA Council of Representatives voted to prohibit psychologists from participating in national security interrogations. Roy Eidelson and Jean Maria Arrigo, "How the American Psychological Association Lost Its Way," *Los Angeles Times*, July 30, 2015, accessed at www.latimes.com/opinion/op-ed/la-oe-arrigo-psychologists-apa-report-20150729-story.html; and www.apa.org/news/press/statements/interogations for the APA's official statement.

25 That definition of traits is from Shelley A. Kirkpatrick and Edwin A. Locke, "Leadership: Do Traits Matter?" *Academy of Management Executive* 5 (1991), 48.

26 David Knights and Majella O'Leary, "Leadership, Ethics and Responsibility to the Other," *Journal of Business Ethics* 67 (2006), 129.

27 Cecil A. Gibb, "The Principles and Traits of Leadership," *Journal of Abnormal and Social Psychology* 42 (1947), 267.

28 Ralph Stogdill, "Personal Factors Associated with Leadership: A Survey of the Literature," *Journal of Psychology* 25 (1948), 35–71.

29 Walter J. Palmer, "Management Effectiveness as a Function of Personality Traits of the Manager," *Personnel Psychology* 27 (1974), 283.

30 Faulkner, *School of Hard Knocks*, 9.

31 Hugo Munsterberg, *Psychology and Industrial Efficiency* (Boston: Houghton-Mifflin, 1913). That estimation of the book's seminal role is from Graham Richards, *Putting Psychology in Its Place: Critical Historical Perspectives* (London: Routledge, 2000).

32 Theta H. Wolf, "The Emergence of Binet's Concepts and Measurement of Intelligence: A Case History of the Creative Process, Part II," *Journal of the History of the Behavioral Sciences* 5 (1969), 207–37.

33 Reported in Lewis M. Terman, "The Use of Intelligence Tests in the Army," *Psychological Bulletin* 15 (1918), 177–87.

34 Enoch B. Gowin, *Selection and Training of the Business Executive* (New York: Macmillan, 1918).

35 Paul S. Achilles and Edith Mulhall Achilles, "Estimates of the Military Value of Certain Character Qualities," *Journal of Applied Psychology* 1 (1917), 305–16.

36 Historian Philipp Blom made the point that contemporaries were well aware that massive war might well erupt again. See *Fracture: Life and Culture in the West, 1918–1938* (New York: Basic Books, 2015).

37 My review of German psychology and the military buildup is based on L.H. Ansbacher, "German Military Psychology," *Psychology Bulletin* 38 (1941), 370–92; Ladislas Farago, *German Psychological Warfare* (New York: G.P. Putnam's Sons, 1942); J.B. Maller, "Studies in Character and Personality in German Psychological Literature," *Psychological Bulletin* 30 (1933), 209–32; Frederick Wyatt and Hans Lukas Teuber, "German Psychology under the Nazi System: 1933–1940," *Psychological Review* 51 (1944), 229–47; and Robert M. Yerkes, "Man-Power and Military Effectiveness: The Case for Human Engineering," *Journal of Consulting Psychology* 5 (1941), 205–9.

38 Ansbacher, "German Military Psychology," 380.

39 Ibid.

40 Leon Alfred Pennington and H.W. Case, "A Course in Military Psychology," *Psychological Bulletin* 39 (1942), 377.

41 Leon Alfred Pennington and Romeyn B. Hough, Jr., *The Psychology of Military Leadership* (New York: Prentice-Hall, 1943), 101.

42 Ibid., 118.

43 Grint, "A History of Leadership," in *Sage Handbook of Leadership*.

44 Adorno, *Authoritarian Personality*, 1.

45 Edwin P. Hollander, "Authoritarianism and Leadership Choice in a Military Setting," *Journal of Abnormal and Social Psychology* 49 (1954), 365–70.

46 John Levi Martin, "The Authoritarian Personality, 50 Years Later: What Questions Are There for Political Psychology?" *Political Psychology* 22 (2001), 1–26; Martin Roiser and Carla Willing, "The Strange Death of the Authoritarian Personality: 50 Years of Psychological and Political Debate," *History of the Human Sciences* 15 (2002), 71–96.

47 Gordon W. Allport and Henry S. Odbert, "Trait Names: A Psycho-Lexical Study," *Psychological Monograph* 47 (1936), 1–171; Ernest Tupes and Raymond Christal, *Recurrent Personality Factors Based on Trait Ratings* (Washington, D.C.: United States Air Force, 1961). For an assessment of the surprisingly convoluted development of the personality factor model, see John M. Digman, "Personality Structure: Emergence of the Five-Factor Model," *Annual Review of Psychology* 41 (1990), 417–40. Neuroticism, which is decidedly *not* everyday language, is defined as a tendency to experience unpleasant emotions such as anger, anxiety, depression, and vulnerability easily.

48 Kirkpatrick and Locke, "Leadership: Do Traits Matter?"

49 Daniel Goleman et al., *Primal Leadership: Realizing the Power of Emotional Intelligence* (Boston: Harvard Business School Press, 2002).

50 David R. Hannah and Christopher D. Zatzick, "An Examination of Leader Portrayals in the U.S. Business Press following the Landmark Scandals of the Early 21ˢᵗ Century," *Journal of Business Ethics* 79 (2008), 361–77.

51 Anthony J. Mayo and Nitin Nohria, "Zeitgeist Leadership," *Harvard Business Review* 83 (October 2005), 45.

52 Michael H. Mescon, "The Dynamics of Industrial Leadership," *Journal of the Academy of Management* 1 (1958), 14.

53 Leonard C. Mead, "A Program of Human Engineering," *Personnel Psychology* 1 (1948), 304–6.

54 Robert L. Katz, "Skills of an Effective Administrator," *Harvard Business Review* 33 (January–February 1955), 33–34.

55 Laura L. Koppes, *Historical Perspectives in Industrial and Organizational Psychology* (Mahwah, NJ: Lawrence Erlbaum Associates, 2007).

56 Douglas W. Bray and Donald L. Grant, "The Assessment Center in the Management of Potential for Business Management," *Psychological Monographs* 80 (1966), 1–27; D.J. Hardesty and W.S. Jones, "Characteristics of Judged High Potential Management Personnel – The Operations of an Industrial Assessment Center," *Personnel Psychology* 21 (1968), 85–98.

57 Richard Bolden and Jonathan Gosling, "Leadership Competencies: Time to Change the Tune?" *Leadership* 2 (2006), 150; Brigid Carroll et al., "Leadership as Practice: Challenging the Competency Paradigm," *Leadership* 4 (2008), 365.

58 See, for example, Fred E. Fiedler, *A Theory of Leadership Effectiveness* (New York: McGraw-Hill, 1967); Paul Hersey and Kenneth Blanchard, "Life-cycle Theory of Leadership," *Training and Development Journal* 23 (1969), 26–34; Robert J. House, "A Path-Goal Theory of Leader Effectiveness," *Administrative Science Quarterly* 16 (September 1971), 321–39; Warren H. Schmidt and Robert Tannenbaum, "Management of Differences," *Harvard Business Review* 38 (1960), 107–15; Robert Tannenbaum and Fred Massarik, "Leadership: A Frame of Reference," *Management Science* 4 (1957), 1–19; Robert Tannenbaum and Warren H. Schmidt, "How to Choose a Leadership Pattern," *Harvard Business Review* 36 (March–April 1958), 85–101; Victor H. Vroom and Philip Yetton, *Leadership and Decision Making* (Pittsburgh: University of Pittsburgh Press, 1973).

59 Grint, *The Arts of Leadership*.

60 Keith Grint, "Problems, Problems, Problems: The Social Construction of 'Leadership,'" *Human Relations* 58 (2005), 1470. In this thoughtful article, Grint does not dismiss contingency theory entirely. Rather, he suggests a topology by which leaders construct environmental problems – simple, wicked, and critical – and the expected response of leaders.

61 Richard E. Boyatzis, *The Competent Manager: A Model for Effective Performance* (New York: Wiley, 1982).

62 Many behavioralists will dissent from even that understanding. They typically disassociate the movement that constitutes manifest behavior from intention or any other mental process. Further, human behavior is awarded no favored status. The original "behavioralist manifesto," published by John Watson in 1913, refused to privilege human over any other animal behavior, insisting the behavioralist "recognizes no dividing line between man

and brute." For an analysis of behavioralism as a search for the "physics of behavior," see Norman Malcolm, *Problems of Mind: Descartes to Wittgenstein* (New York: Harper, 1971). The Watson quote is from "Psychology as the Behavioralist Views It," *Psychological Review* 20 (1913), 158.

63 Talcott Parsons and Edward Shils, *Toward a General Theory of Action* (Cambridge: Harvard University Press, 1951/1962). For some psychologists, this definition conflates a distinction between "behavior" and "action." Lawrence Mohr, for example, referred to a *behavior* as an intentional bodily motion and an *action* as a set of behaviors that could be interpreted as trying to achieve or do something. Lawrence Mohr, *The Causes of Human Behavior: Implications for Theory and Method in the Social Sciences* (Ann Arbor: University of Michigan Press, 1996).

64 John K. Hemphill and Alvin E. Coons, "Development of the Leader Behavior Description Questionnaire," in Ralph M. Stogdill and Alvin E. Coons, eds., *Leader Behavior: Its Description and Measurement* (Columbus: Ohio State University Bureau of Business Research, 1957), 7.

65 Shartle reviews his own background as well as that of the Ohio State program in "Early Years of the Ohio State University Leadership Studies," *Journal of Management* 5 (1979), 127–34. For an example of his wartime contribution, see Carroll L. Shartle and Beatrice J. Dvorak, "Organizational Analysis Activities in the War Manpower Commission," *Psychological Bulletin* 40 (1943), 701–13.

66 The rise of Nazism and wartime destruction in Europe played no small part in the emergence of the United States as "the world's leader in the social sciences," according to Solovey. Mark Solovey, "Cold War Social Science: Specter, Reality, or Useful Concept?" in Mark Solovey and Hamilton Cravens, eds., *Cold War Social Science: Knowledge Production, Liberal Democracy, and Human Nature* (New York: Palgrave, 2012), 2. In his study of the "Americanization" of the social sciences following World War II, David Paul Haney acknowledged the continued and considerable influence of European thinkers but insisted that the interpretation of those ideas became embedded and institutionalized through a small number of U.S.-based universities. See *The Americanization of Social Science: Intellectuals and Public Responsibility in the Postwar United States* (Philadelphia: Temple University Press, 2008).

67 Theodore M. Porter, "Positioning Social Science in Cold War America," in Solovey and Cravens, eds., *Cold War Social Science*, ix–xi.

68 Alvin W. Gouldner, *The Coming Crisis of Western Sociology* (New York: Basic Books, 1970), 17.

69 Loren Baritz, *The Servants of Power: A History of the Use of Social Science in American Industry* (Middletown: Wesleyan University Press, 1960), 198.

70 Porter, "Positioning Social Science," xiii. Baritz, a historian with an interest in the social use of knowledge, was certainly a contemporaneous critic. That alliance was subjected to far more introspection and criticism during the Vietnam era, notes Porter. The above-cited book by Gouldner is a prime example.

71 Edwin A. Fleishman, "The Description of Supervisory Behavior," *Journal of Applied Psychology* 37 (February 1953), 1–6.

72 Shartle, "Early Years," 132.

73 Hemphill and Coons, "Development of the Leader Behavior Description Questionnaire," 10–11; Fleishman, "The Description of Supervisory Behavior," 1.

74 Robert R. Blake, *The Managerial Grid: Key Orientations for Achieving Production through People* (Houston: Gulf Publishing, 1964); David Bowers and Stanley Seashore, "Predicting Organizational Effectiveness with a Four-Factor Theory of Leadership," *Administrative Science Quarterly* 11 (1966), 238–63; Dorwin Cartright and Alvin F. Zander, *Group Dynamics Research and Theory* (Evanston: Row, Peterson, 1960); Rensis Likert, *New Patterns of Management* (New York: McGraw-Hill, 1961).

75 Edwin J. Thomas and Bruce J. Biddle, "The Nature and History of Role Theory," in Bruce J. Biddle and Edwin J. Thomas, eds., *Role Theory: Concepts and Research* (New York: Wiley, 1966), 3–19.

76 Witzel, *A History of Management Thought*, 41.

77 Michael Clanchy, *From Memory to Written Record: England, 1066–1307* (Oxford: Blackwell, 1993); Katja Rost et al., "The Corporate Governance of Benedictine Abbeys: What Can Stock Companies Learn from Monasteries?" *Journal of Management History* 16 (2010), 90–115; and Morgen Witzel, "Monks and Multinationals: Business Models of the Middle Ages," *European Business Forum* 18 (Summer 2004), 74–76.

78 Frederick Taylor's evolving theories of Scientific Management can be traced through *A Piece-Rate System* (New York: American Society of Mechanical Engineers, 1895); *Shop Management* (New York: Harper & Brothers, 1903); and *The Principles of Scientific Management* (New York: Harper & Brothers, 1911). For an excellent overview of Taylor and his work, see Robert Kanigel, *The One Best Way: Frederick Winslow Taylor and the Enigma of Efficiency* (New York: Viking, 1997).

79 Taylor, *The Principles of Scientific Management*, 20.

80 For a more detailed discussion of his structured observation methodology, see Henry Mintzberg, "Structured Observation as a Method to Study Managerial Work," *Journal of Management Studies* 7 (February 1970), 87–104. For follow-up research that largely validated Mintzberg's findings, see Lance B. Kurke and Howard E. Aldrich, "Mintzberg Was Right! A Replication and Extension of *The Nature of Managerial Work*," *Management Science* 29 (August 1983), 975–84.

81 Henry Mintzberg, "Managerial Work: Analysis from Observation," *Management Science* 18 (1971), 99.

82 Ansoff, "Conceptual Underpinnings," 4.

83 Morgen Witzel, *Builders and Dreamers: The Making and Meaning of Management* (London: Financial Times Prentice-Hall, 2002).

84 Witzel, *A History of Management Thought*, 19–31, 65; Morgen Witzel, "The Leadership Philosophy of Han Fei," *Asia Pacific Business Review* 18 (2012), 489–503. Witzel does not deny the rather troubling ethics of Machiavelli's assertion in *The Prince* that "the end justifies the means."

85 H. Igor Ansoff, *Strategic Management* (New York: Wiley, 1979); Michael E. Porter, *Competitive Strategy: Techniques for Analyzing Industries and Competitors* (New York: Free Press, 1980) and *Competitive Advantage: Creating and*

Sustaining Superior Advantage (New York: Free Press, 1985). Porter's first book dealt primarily with industry analysis and introduced the well-known Five Forces framework. The second book focused more on internal company dynamics. In 1987 Porter turned his attention to corporate strategy and its distinction from competitive or business strategy. See "From Competitive Advantage to Corporate Strategy," *Harvard Business Review* 65 (May–June 1987), 43–50.

86 Walter Kiechel III, *The Lords of Strategy: The Secret Intellectual History of the New Corporate World* (Boston: Harvard Business Press, 2010), xii.

87 Bruce D. Henderson, *Henderson on Corporate Strategy* (Cambridge: Abt Books, 1979), 4.

88 Seymour Tilles, "How to Evaluate Corporate Strategy," *Harvard Business Review* 41 (July–August 1963), 112.

89 Seymour Tilles, "The Manager's Job: A Systems Approach," *Harvard Business Review* 41 (January–February 1963), 73–81.

90 Stafford Beer, *Cybernetics and Management* (London: English University Press, 1957), 1–4.

91 W. Ross Ashby, *An Introduction to Cybernetics* (New York: Wiley, 1956), 5–6.

92 Beer, *Cybernetics and Management*, 12.

93 R. Edward Freeman introduced the formal concept of stakeholders in 1984. Freeman, *Strategic Management: A Stakeholder Approach* (Boston: Pitman, 1984).

94 Hambrick is quoted in Albert A. Cannella, "Upper Echelons: Donald Hambrick on Executives and Strategy," *Academy of Management Executive* 15 (2001), 37.

95 Donald C. Hambrick, "Putting Top Managers Back in the Strategy Picture," *Strategic Management Journal* 10 (1989), 5–15.

96 Ibid., 6.

97 Donald Hambrick and Sydney Finkelstein, "Managerial Discretion: A Bridge between Polar Views of Organizations," in Larry L. Cummings and Barry M. Staw, eds., *Research in Organizational Behavior* 9 (Greenwich: JAI Press, 1987), 372.

98 Henry Mintzberg, "The Strategy Concept II: Another Look at Why Organizations Need Strategies," *California Management Review* 30 (Fall 1987), 29.

99 Henry Mintzberg, "The Fall and Rise of Strategic Planning," *Harvard Business Review* 72 (January–February 1994), 112.

100 Henry Mintzberg and James A. Waters, "Of Strategies, Deliberate and Emergent," *Strategic Management Journal* 6 (1985), 271.

101 Alfred P. Sloan, *My Years with General Motors* (New York: Doubleday, 1963/1990). The complex interaction between Sloan and his ghostwriter, John McDonald, is chronicled in McDonald, *A Ghost's Memoir: The Making of Alfred P. Sloan's My Years with General Motors* (Boston: MIT Press, 2003). Alfred Chandler served as a researcher for the book, so it was not devoid of academic influence. In another fascinating twist, Chandler was a descendant of the du Pont family. It was the du Ponts, as major investors in the early General Motors, who forced the resignation of William Durant, replacing him with Alfred Sloan. See Ernest Dale, "Contributions to Administration

by Alfred P. Sloan, Jr., and GM," *Administrative Science Quarterly* 10 (September 1967), 32–62.

102 That's the evaluation, with which I concur, offered by David Vogel, "The Books That Shaped the Public's View of Business," *Business & Society Review* 6 (Summer 1973), 58–63.

103 Sloan is quoted in "McKinsey-Academy Book Awards," *Academy of Management Journal* 8 (June 1965), 155.

104 Sloan, *My Years with General Motors*, 169.

105 Ibid., 48.

106 Ibid., 58.

107 Ibid., 67.

108 Ibid.

109 Ibid., 62.

110 Warren Bennis, *Why Leaders Can't Lead: The Unconscious Conspiracy Continues* (San Francisco: Jossey-Bass, 1989), 63.

111 For a more complete view, see David Farber, *Sloan Rules: Alfred P. Sloan and the Triumph of General Motors* (Chicago: University of Chicago Press, 2002). GM operated a subsidiary unit, Opal, in Germany in the years leading up to World War II. For an account of that period, see Henry Ashby Turner Jr., *General Motors and the Nazis: The Struggle for Control of Opel, Europe's Biggest Carmaker* (New Haven: Yale University Press, 2005).

Whistling in the Dark and the Insertion of
Power between Followers and Leaders

"Leadership can only occur if there is followership," wrote Mary Uhl-
Bien and colleagues. Absent "followers and following behaviors there is
no leadership."[1]

That statement seems pretty straightforward. Yet, like so much else
in this field, the leader/follower formulation and the mediating role of
power in defining that relationship has provoked analysis, debate, and
disagreement.

We obviously need to consider followers as well as leaders and their
combined impact on group outcomes. But who are the prime movers in
this interaction? Keith Grint has identified a process by which followers
ascribe extraordinary attributes to leaders in order to relieve themselves
of responsibilities, even anxieties.[2] Leaders, in turn, construct a community of followers, bound together by shared ideals, a love for the
leader, or perhaps even a sense of shared emotion rooted in some mixture of honor, greed, and distrust of the other. Leaders engage in acts of
imagination, envisioning an appealing future and persuading followers to
commit.[3]

But it is fair to wonder: do we have to accept as a universal truth
the assertion that leaders are *pro*active power wielders and followers are
*re*active adherents? Or, can we gain greater insight into the dynamics of
organizational life by considering that followers can, occasionally at least,
be the proactive element in the dyadic relationship?

Perhaps we could avoid that pro- and reactive polarity altogether.
Aren't organizational dynamics more complex than a simple *action* →
reaction formulation? Let's think, rather, of leaders and followers as co-
creators of the organization, engaging in what Dennis Tourish called a
"dialectic nexus of fluid relationships."[4] Every organizational member
plays an important role in a dynamic interactive process of identifying, achieving, and maintaining a desired state. In this view, leadership
unfolds in a way that is, according to Joseph Raelin, concurrent, collective, and collaborative.[5] Interactions are best understood as multidirec-
tional rather than unidirectional, as simultaneous rather than sequential,

and as spontaneous rather than proscribed. Both leaders and followers are accountable for the outcomes of their mutually constructed efforts.

Furthermore, are leaders and followers really separate and distinguishable groups? In organizational life, leaders invariably are also followers. Supervisors report to general managers, divisional heads report to corporate executives, and the CEO reports to the Board of Directors. True, the CEO may also be the Board's chairperson.[6] Even so, given the dominance of the shareholder primacy ideology, board members are expected to follow the lead – or, at the very least, serve the interests of – shareholders. (This can go on-and-on: for example, small shareholders are forced to accept the dominance of institutional investors in defining shareholder interests.) No one has unchallenged power and everyone is a follower at some point.

It has also been argued that the very notion of a world made up of leaders and followers is passé and counterproductive, a dated and dangerous remnant of the bygone industrial era. That was the position taken by Joseph Rost with his insistence that the idea of followership was an "outmoded concept." Within that industrial paradigm, followers could never "participate in the leadership decision-making process authentically." Decision making remains "the leader's prerogative."[7] This construct, Rost insisted, is no longer applicable to 21st-century organizations.

In the industrial context, "follower" was a negative term, one denoting passivity and compliance, lagging behind decidedly more powerful, influential, and creative leaders.[8] Even when some degree of follower agency is granted, leaders need to "stay ahead" of those followers. There is no denying that many organizations still operate within that paradigm.[9] Rost's point, however, is that the subordination of followers and the accompanying separation of deciding from acting simply does not apply in a world of complex, interactive, iterative, and simultaneous decision making and action.

And what's the implication of attaching the suffix "ship" to the end of "follower"? The distinction drawn between "leader" and "leadership" is between the individual actor (*leader*) and the process (*leadership*) that exercises power in order to engage people in action. Once we accept that followers are implicated in any process of leadership, do we really need to establish a separate designation for them, something called *followership*?

These questions all address issues of agency and proactivity. Acknowledging followership and leadership as separate, albeit interdependent, domains opens the possibility of inquiry into *critical* followership, and the relation of both leaders and followers to the dynamics of power.

Power always plays a distinct role in the leader/follower interplay.[10] An asymmetry results when leadership is exercised within the context of hierarchy. Followers often know more than leaders about vital operational matters of the organization: about their customers, their core technologies, even their competitors. Leaders, in their positions atop corporate hierarchy, have greater power: over strategic direction, resource allocation, performance metrics, and the hiring and firing of lower level executives. Leaders and followers become more clearly delineated by power distribution. Thus, the asymmetry.

The heavy lifting around theories of power has been undertaken mainly by sociologists, political scientists, psychologists, and the occasional philosopher.[11] For them, power is an immense and immensely complex construct that demands continuous inquiry.

Discomfort with Power

Since the 1930s, discourse on leader power and follower obedience has been shaped and reshaped by historical forces. Consider the rise of Nazism, World War II, and the Cold War that followed. Not surprisingly, attempts to digest the meaning of the rise of totalitarian dictators – Hitler, Stalin, and Mao most prominently – led to both an interest in and mistrust of power as a "naked" force able to induce obedience and obliterate morality. Psychologists Stanley Milgram and Philip Zimbardo conducted highly visible experiments that seemed to demonstrate the capacity of power, even in the absence of coercion, to engender "bad" behavior.[12] Political scientist James MacGregor Burns sought a more positive, moral course by separating, albeit awkwardly and unconvincingly, power from leadership.

The economic crisis in the United States during the 1970s directed the conversation into two intersecting pathways of power. "Empowerment" and the opportunity for leaders to empower followers became a prominent concern in reaction to the press discovery of a supposedly new and widespread disease: "blue-collar blues" being the label applied to what was depicted as a sudden rise and spread of alienation, even hostility, among a new generation of hourly workers. If alienation was the problem, then empowerment, supposedly a form of power redistribution, was offered as the cure.

The ferocity of Japanese competition that accompanied the U.S. economic decline in the 1970s provided the second aspect of the power dimension. Attention zeroed in on a phenomenon labeled organizational culture. Culture and power were highly interdependent, although that interdependence often went unacknowledged. Culture exerts power over followers to the extent that it helps define the boundaries in which actions must occur. Culture has the impact of sanctioning some behaviors – not by laws or rules but through the mechanism of social pressure and the expenditure of social capital – while labeling other behaviors as undesirable. And it is leaders – the organization's founders and successive executives – who define and institutionalize that culture.

Burns offered an explicit claim to a distinction between leadership and power in his 1978 *Leadership*. It was this book, more than any other single work, that shaped contemporary leadership discourse. Burns refocused attention away from leadership writ small with its focus on shop-floor supervision and small-group dynamics, to leadership writ large, with its attention to statesmen, movement leaders, and presidents. He presented a celebratory brief on behalf of the transforming potential of leadership.

Yet, Burns posed the question, "Why this preoccupation, this near-obsession with power?"[13] A perfectly reasonable response would be, "Because your book deals exclusively with powerful people, *defines leadership* through actions taken by powerful people." Reasonable, perhaps, but Burns would have had none of it.

Not all human interactions, he insisted, were "coercive and exploitive."[14] Right there, Burns offered insight into why he was so uncomfortable with power as an idea. Power, in Burns' view, was "coercive and exploitive." He used the term "naked power wielding" as a virtual synonym for power in order to reinforce that negative view.[15] Burns claimed to appreciate the reasons for the "obsession" with power on the part of political scientists: the concern among his contemporaries for the power exercised by mid 20th-century tyrants. But it was time to go further and dig deeper.

With the counterexamples of people he sought to memorialize as true leaders – Franklin Roosevelt, Mahatma Gandhi, and Martin Luther King most prominently – Burns held that it was time to see beyond exercises in naked power. We should understand leadership, yes, as "an aspect of power," he argued, but also as "a separate and vital process in itself."[16] That contradiction – *part of* but *separate from* – bespoke his intense unease.

But why the discomfort? Why did Burns insist on distancing leadership from power? The explanation likely lies in one name: Adolf Hitler. It is hard to overstate the impact that exposure to Hitler and horrors of the Holocaust had on an entire generation of social scientists. Burns intended to separate leadership from whatever it was that Hitler had done.

Hitler, Burns insisted, exercised power, no doubt about it. But that was not leadership, and no one should confuse the two. Because "Hitler's

Ghost" – that was Barbara Kellerman's striking label – hovered over so much of post-World War II discourse, it would be useful to explore the particular impact on the field of leadership.[17]

The "Hitler Question"

Burns told an anecdote concerning teaching leadership that throws light on his analysis. In an attempt to enliven his classes, Burns often posed what he called the "old chestnut" question: "Was Adolf Hitler a leader?"[18] The issue being raised was not so much about the nature of Hitler and his rule of Germany. It was intended, instead, to provoke inquiry into the nature of leadership.

Let us allow Burns to elaborate:

The last time I tried this, in an honors class, a woman student vehemently answered 'YES.' Evil though he was, she declared, he mirrored the hopes and hates of the German people, he won elections, and he fulfilled his promises by changing Germany along the lines his followers wanted – so how could he not be called a leader? She had the class all but convinced and almost had me too. Almost.

It was not, of course, that she was in any way pro-Hitler, who stands as perhaps the most universally detested man in all of human history. The problem is confusion not about Hitler but about the essence of leadership. Is leadership a neutral thing, a mechanical process or power available equally to a Hitler and a Gandhi? Or should it be defined as a *good* thing?

For Burns, this question was readily answered. Leadership, in his view, was good; that is, virtuous and ethical, helping people and institutions achieve such "lofty principles as order, liberty, equality (including brotherhood and sisterhood), justice, and the pursuit of happiness."

Although Hitler was definitely a powerful agent who ruled Germany, that did not make him a leader in the sense that Burns meant the term:

Clearly he could not be described as virtuous or ethical except by Nazi standards. His own "higher" vision was to restore order in the increasingly turbulent Germany of the early 1930s and then create a "Greater Germany" that would dominate Europe if not the world. In fact he left his country in defeat and devastation, so he was a terrible failure measured even by his own standards. If we test him instead by Enlightenment values of liberty and equality, he was a fanatical enemy of both. Nor did Hitler achieve another of what I call transforming values, one that perhaps embodies the others; he failed – utterly – to create for the people of Germany lasting, meaningful opportunities for the pursuit of happiness.

Burns' straightforward response to the Hitler Question, then, was this: "Hitler ruled the German people, but he did not lead them."[19]

Hitler was powerful and evil. But leadership, to Burns, was by definition good and morally uplifting, conforming to Enlightenment values.[20] Rather than celebrate the potential of power to be exercised on behalf of "good" outcomes, Burns insisted on separating power and leadership. Distance must be inserted and preserved.

There is another perspective, one articulated by the student who asked Burns the question in the first place. Leaders are individuals who exert power and influence the behavior of others. They can use that power to achieve either bad or good ends, or some combination. These leaders get other people to go along, to follow. Inspiration is part of that appeal, but fear and coercion can also be part of the mix as well. Remember Freud's admonition that the great man's conviction that he is doing the right thing "may pass into ruthlessness." For that reason, "one cannot help but being afraid of him."[21]

As Barbara Kellerman argued, to label Hitler a "power wielder" rather than a leader was to separate two inseparable concepts. She described an instance when the "old chestnut" question was posed to her by an audience member:

In a talk I once gave to the New Haven Jewish community, I referred to Hitler as a bad leader. The words were hardly out of my mouth when a member of the audience rose to differ. 'Hitler may have been bad, as in ethically bad,' he said. 'But he was a good leader in that he was very effective.'

"The man was right." Here she was breaking from Burns:

Given the ideology of National Socialism and the particulars of the Nazi agenda from 1933 to 1941 (when Germany made the mistake of invading the Soviet Union), Hitler's political and military strategies were nearly impeccable. Moreover, even between 1941 and 1945 – the period leading up to Germany's defeat, at least one of Hitler's most cherished objectives, the annihilation of European Jewry, was realized with astonishing efficiency.[22]

"Hitler's ghost," she insisted, hung over all post-World War II discussions of leadership.[23]

A number of scholars have parted ways with the "tacit alliance" among theoreticians, practitioners, researchers and educators, consultants and trainers that has removed not just Hitler but the very concept of Hitler from the leadership conversation; Kellerman and Keith Grint most prominently.[24] The discussion wasn't really about Hitler, anyway, Kellerman maintained. "Hitler is a metaphor – for the dark side of who we are and what we do," Kellerman noted. "Since we cannot grasp good without grasping bad, the bottom line is clear: to learn leadership without learning Hitler is to whistle in the dark."[25]

The Nature of Power

Leadership is a human relationship, a connection among two or more people. That relationship is typically characterized as leader and follower. Power is a mediating force in those relations.[26]

For all the complexity that they attach to the concept, political scientists start their exploration of the nature of power with a simple statement of causation: "*A* has power over *B* to the extent that he can get *B* to do something he would not otherwise do."[27] This is, undoubtedly, an oversimplification of an endlessly complex concept, but it's a good place to start. Power resides in the capacity of one or more individuals to impact the behavior of others. It is a force without which leaders simply cannot lead.[28]

If all leadership involves the exercise of power, can we make the reverse statement as well; that all exercises in power amount to leadership? On this point, there is no consensus. Burns answered unequivocally no. Given his discomfort with power, that was to be expected. "Leadership shares with power the central function of achieving purpose," he agreed. "But the reach and domain of leadership are, in the short range at least, more limited than those of power. Leaders do not obliterate followers' motives though they may arouse certain motives and ignore others."[29] This separation was based on Burns' negative, power-is-what-people-like-Hitler-and-Stalin-do view.

The other side of the debate is the position that yes, the exercise of power does amount to leadership. "If one member [of a group] has power over another," argued John R.P. French, Jr., and Richard Snyder, "then he has some degree of leadership."[30] These authors, and many others, rejected the exclusively negative view of power. Power can "obliterate followers' motives" when it was absolute; but it need not be so.

Power is neutral and ubiquitous in social relations. "Every social action is an exercise in power," wrote sociologist Amos Hawley in 1963, "every social equation is a power equation, and every social group and system is an organization of power."[31] To suggest that leadership and power are separable, then, is nonsense.

When we consider leadership within the context of a corporation, we can see the mutual dependence of leadership and power more clearly. That point was made by sociologist Rosabeth Moss Kanter in her 1977 study of an American corporation. Ostensibly focused on gender roles, *Men and Women of the Corporation* revealed what Kanter maintained was a tendency of bureaucracies to render powerless all participants, including managers.[32]

The bureaucratic nature of the large corporation worked to disperse power, undermining the capacity of anyone inside to amass resources and get something done. Individuals who were capable of rising above the erosion of power inherent in a bureaucracy became what she termed leaders. And it was, in Kanter's view, precisely this accumulation of power within the bureaucracy that attracted followers. Thus, not only does leadership require power, but also the accumulation of power in large bureaucratic organizations amounts to leadership.

To counter the insistence that any exercise of power obliterates followers' motivation, theorists have asserted that power only exists in the accompaniment of both choice and difference. Absent choice there is no exercise in power. That is, B must have the capacity to follow or reject A. Absent choice there is only domination. Furthermore, there cannot be consensus. If there is total consensus, no power will be exerted because none is called for.[33]

And what about resistance? "Because the exercise of power presumes a free subject," wrote Stewart Clegg, and because there are differences among followers, power will always encounter "resistance."[34] That is, in many ways, precisely what power does: allows the individual with less power to resist and enables the individual with more power to attempt to overcome that resistance.[35]

Confronting Obedience

For most social scientists in the first decades after the end of the war, Hitler's ghost shaped views of power with its potential to induce blind obedience. The question to be addressed was how and why a leader, in this case Hitler, was able to command such a high level of obedience directed toward such a monstrous end.[36] Social philosopher Dwight Macdonald warned that society had more to fear from the person who obeys the law than from the person who disobeys.[37]

Although not explicitly a study of German obedience, Yale University psychologist Stanley Milgram's experiments unfolded in the long shadow of the Holocaust.[38] Memories of World War II were very much in evidence in Milgram's motivation. He admitted to being haunted by the ability of Hitler to achieve obedience from Germans. "These inhumane policies may have originated in the mind of a single person," Milgram noted, "but they could only be carried out on a massive scale if a very large number of persons obeyed orders."[39]

Was obedience a contextually specific phenomenon, Milgram wondered? Or was it more widespread, perhaps even a phenomenon that could be repeated in the United States? The conclusion he drew from his Yale experiments was deeply disturbing.

Milgram began by asking students and colleagues to make a prediction. Think of an experiment, he said, in which a subject is instructed by a laboratory technician to inflict hard, physical pain on another person. Would the subject comply? Now, imagine a situation where the maximum punishment was administered through the activation of a gauge clearly labeled, "Danger: Severe Shock." How many would go along even to that extreme? Now, remember, there would be no physical force applied to the subject, just stern demands for compliance from an authority figure in a lab coat. Subjects had a choice, Milgram insisted. They were free to resist, call off their participation in the experiment, and leave the lab.[40]

Thinking (hoping?) that this could not happen here, predictions of obedience – that is, what percentage of subjects would obey up to the maximum impact of the punishment – ranged from 0.125 percent to 1.2 percent. Only a few, it was assumed, would comply with such a dangerous, potentially fatal order.

Then, the experiment, which involved considerable playacting and no actual physical punishment, unfolded. The subject was misled into thinking that he (and, yes, all subjects were male) was part of an investigation intended to study the effects of punishment on memory. The "victim," actually a trained confederate of Milgram's team, was hidden from sight but not from sound. A lab technician told the subject to administer increasingly harsh electric "shocks" up to and including the ultimate level. The playacting victim let out audible shrieks of pain and pleas to halt the experiment.[41]

The results, first reported in 1961, showed that instead of the predicted 0.125–1.2 percent range of obedience, the actual figure turned out to be 65 percent of subjects who were willing to go to the extreme level of punishment. Subsequent criticisms of Milgram's methodology and related questions about the validity of his findings should be acknowledged.[42] Still, the reported results suggested a devastating appreciation of the relationship between power and obedience. Milgram's findings seemed to demonstrate that obedience was not so difficult to achieve.[43]

Controversial though Milgram's conclusions were, they were part of a profound questioning of the role of followers in both responding to and influencing the acts of leaders. Ira Chaleff sought to chart a more positive path. Followers bore a responsibility, a moral responsibility, to be "shapers" rather than "implementers." Courageous followers – those with the courage to assume responsibility for themselves and their organization and to challenge leaders when leader actions violate their own sense of right and effective – were co-contributors with those leaders to the operations and outcomes of their organization. Followers do not "orbit" around leaders, he insisted. Rather, both "orbit around purpose."[44] Perhaps it would be possible for leaders and followers to share power for the achievement of a common purpose.

Power at the Heart of Leadership

For Michel Foucault, power but not dominance could be used for positive outcomes. In *Discipline and Punish*, he described how power was a force for the "humanization" of institutions like prisons. The exercise of power, which is a "complex social action," can invest people who do not have it with power:

We should admit rather that power produces knowledge (and not simply by encouraging it because it serves power or by applying it because it is useful); that power and knowledge directly imply one another; that there is no power relationship without the correlative constitution of a field of knowledge, nor any knowledge that does not presuppose and constitute at the same time power relations.[45]

Power coexists with knowledge, in Foucault's view. That mixture of power with knowledge can act as a countervailing force as "an opposition against secrecy, deformation, and mystifying representations imposed on people."[46] Power is not a force that obliterates human agency; dominance does. Power can lead to empowerment. And it was in the 1980s that managerial attention turned to empowerment as a "cure" – or at least an antidote – for powerlessness and alienation.

The notion of employee alienation from work has drawn the attention of observers as varied as Karl Marx, Emile Durkheim, and Herbert Marcuse.[47] Marx defined alienation as the separation of wage laborers from their work and from themselves. Durkheim argued in *Division of Labor* (1893) that major extensions in the division of labor led to increased anomie. For Marx, alienation was specific to the wage laborer. In his 1973 essay, "On the Philosophical Foundation of the Concept of Labor in Economics," Marcuse suggested that alienation was a function of labor generally and of technology more specifically.

It is unclear if many managers or leadership writers were attuned to the work of Marx, Durkheim, or Marcuse (none, judging by the lack of citations). However, in the early 1970s, events conspired to insert labor alienation into mainstream management discourse. A 1972 strike at General Motors' modern assembly plant in Lordstown, Ohio, triggered this growing concern, especially when the "legend" emerged – that was how

James O'Toole characterized contemporaneous press coverage – that the Lordstown strike represented something new and different in the American workforce, demanding a unique response from management.[48]

Opened in rural Ohio in 1966, the Lordstown plant was heralded as the world's most "efficient" – that is, speediest – auto assembly plant, churning out over one hundred Chevrolet Vegas an hour, compared to a company-wide average of fifty-five.[49] Despite these high hopes or, more likely, *because* of them, the atmosphere in the plant was marked by extreme levels of labor–management tension. "It was hard to find any positive single indicator of trust between the two parties," noted a GM manager. "The prevailing attitude was, 'We'll bury you unless you bury us first.'"[50]

Perhaps the Lordstown confrontation would have been dismissed as "merely" another case of labor–management tensions over assembly-line speedups, hyper-vigilant discipline, and fractured trust. That was the prevailing view until a reporter for the *New York Times* called attention to what he believed to be broader themes at play. "The outcome of the labor dispute in which the youngest local of the United Automobile Workers is confronting one of General Motors' toughest management teams could have wide repercussions for United States industry."[51]

After acknowledging the traditional roots of the tension in concerns with speedups and layoffs, the reporter highlighted the youthful rebelliousness of the workers. "I'm not going to run for anybody," one worker was quoted as saying. "There ain't anyone in that plant that is going to tell me to run."[52] Images of a youthful counterculture were reinforced with references to peace symbols (even among managers) and long hair at a time when peace signs and long hair symbolized a kind of youth-driven rebellion against traditional social arrangements.[53] The article even pictured workers gathering in the cafeteria to sing the old union song, "Solidarity Forever."[54]

Other press outlets picked up on and ran with the theme. "Unhappy Young Workers Called Threat to Output," warned the *Wall Street Journal*, while *Life Magazine* suggested, "Boredom Spells Trouble on the Line."[55] Even as the Lordstown story faded and peace returned to the plant, the term "blue-collar blues" spoke to "a downward spiral of income and self-esteem" among factory workers. "It is one of the most difficult social problems the country will face in the rest of the century," warned *Newsweek*, "and precious little is being done about it."[56] Professor Richard Walton brought the issue directly to the business world with a 1972 article, "How to Counter Alienation in the Plant."[57] Walton's suggested response: enhanced employee "voice." This was not empowerment, precisely, but rather the encouragement of "employee participation" on a "wide range of issues."[58]

Two organizational development consultants, Cynthia Scott and Dennis Jaffe, offered guidance to managers on how best to achieve employee empowerment. The goal was not empowerment for its own sake, not an ideological commitment to a just redistribution of authority within business organizations. Rather, empowerment was conceptualized as an antidote to employee alienation and resentment that would, the authors (and most other advocates) believed, lead to improved productivity and enhanced performance.[59] Theirs was a practitioner-oriented book in the most stereotypical sense: heavy on how-to's, lots of diagrams and self-questionnaires, lists designed to "check your style," and simplistic analysis.

Scott and Jaffe opened with a heavy dose of presentism: the business organization was "under attack" *as never before,* while employees were "demanding more meaning, more candor, and more fulfillment from their work."[60] Following these ahistorical claims of unprecedented challenge, the authors defined empowerment as "a fundamentally different way of working together."[61] Their list – and it was just that – provided the characteristics of an "empowered workplace." Some items focused on market awareness and responsiveness. Others made vague reference to the "content of the work." The only reference to power, and it was indirect, was their suggestion of "greater control over decisions about work."[62]

There was plenty of literature advocating empowerment, insisting that it was up to organizational leaders to empower employees. W. Warner Burke was an early advocate of the leader's responsibility to empower others. Likewise, Jay Conger proclaimed that the practice of "instilling a sense of power" sat at the heart of effective leadership.[63] Providing personal support and rewarding achievement "in visible and personal ways" was the route to "strengthening an individual's beliefs in his or her sense of power." These acts of empowerment, "the process of changing the internal beliefs of people," would foster "greater initiative and responsibility in subordinates' tasks."[64] The "employee empowerment era," with its reintegration of "thinking and doing" and its liberation of "the creative and innovative energies of employees," had begun.[65]

But that writing rarely included a serious consideration of the nature of power. What did the fad of empowerment have to do with power in organizations? And just what was meant by empowerment?

Conceptualizing Empowerment

In his 1999 analysis of the concept, Thomas Potterfield suggested that empowerment embodied "a belief in the basic dignity and worth of all human beings and in the power of ordinary people to participate more fully in making decisions that affect their lives."[66] Potterfield mistook a passing fad for a long-term movement:

Unlike many earlier attempts at participatory management, empowerment has really taken hold of the collective imaginations of corporate leaders and management theorists. In fact, empowerment theories and practices are among the most popular and influential concepts in the fields of organizational development and business management.[67]

Nonetheless, Potterfield had much insight to offer in understanding the concept.

The roots of empowerment could be traced as far back as the Protestant Reformation.[68] Protestant leaders Martin Luther and John Calvin, wrote Potterfield, "refocused the attention of many Christians away from the idea of salvation coming as a gift from God toward the idea of salvation as something that one earns" through their everyday lives.[69] European capitalism, which was complementary to Protestantism, "elevated the values of risk taking, planning one's future, and working with others who shared one's economic or social interests."[70]

Movements as diverse as Jeffersonian Democracy and Marxism expressed a belief in "the basic dignity and worth of all human beings and in the power of ordinary people to participate in making decisions that affect their lives."[71] Transcendental and existential philosophy emphasized the potential for and desirability of individual agency while the labor movement and liberation theory sought power through collective action.

In the 1960s and 1970s, empowerment emerged as a concept associated with social reform movements, possibly first being used as such in the title of the 1976 book, *Black Empowerment*, as a way to address the "powerlessness of black individuals, groups, and communities" arising through a process which denied both valued identities and access to valuable resources.[72] The phrase was an extension of the Black Power movement of the late 1960s most closely identified with Stokely Carmichael.[73]

But just how applicable was the concept of empowerment to business organizations? In truth, the meaning of the concept within a hierarchical business context was murky if not disingenuous. It should come as little surprise that a great deal of skepticism greeted attempts at empowerment. It had become a "vogue word" that encompassed many "*trivial*" schemes, including suggestion boxes. That was the critical conclusion of Tony Eccles, who added that although the term should not be taken as "a conscious hoax by senior managers," it was certainly a "self-deception in which responsibility is down-loaded onto less senior personnel."[74]

In one of the more insightful inquiries into empowerment, Cynthia Hardy and Sharon Leiba-O'Sullivan offered a hopeful reading, suggesting that at least some of the practices that constituted empowerment could result in positive experience for some individuals:

In other words, might not many of the practices of empowerment – those that grant autonomy, provide variety and challenge, relax formal controls, enhance the opportunity for personal initiative, generate an emotional attachment to collective goals – constitute subjects who believe themselves to be more highly valued, who feel more excitement and passion in their work, and who derive a more rewarding work experience?[75]

Efforts to increase employee participation in decision making can be seen as investing people who do not have it with their own power.

Although advocates claimed to be calling for the reallocation of power, there was little doubt that upper management retained final decision-making authority. "I did not find a single instance," wrote Potterfield, "where empowerment consultants were hired by factory workers."[76] It was, in his telling, a reform imposed on workers by management. Empowerment mechanisms could be granted by executives; they could also be taken away. In fact, the empowerment movement in U.S. industry often coincided with the so-called Southern Strategy pursued by General Motors and other large corporations to move operations to states with labor laws far more friendly to management than to unions.[77] Was that empowerment at all?

Empowerment advocates assumed mutuality of interests. That assumption was both vital and debatable. "If empowerment is embraced without a clear understanding of the mission and vision for the organization, and without the buy-in and commitment of those who are empowered toward achieving organizationally desirable goals," wrote Jeffrey Gandz and Frederick Bird, "then the shareholders have not been treated properly by management." Those who embrace empowerment "without exercising the requisite leadership bear considerable responsibility for the consequences."[78] For Gandz and Bird, the exercise of leadership demanded the articulation of "a clear understanding of the mission and vision for the organization." And what better tool for achieving that understanding than a single, strong organizational culture?

Cultural Framing and Leader Power

Of all the powers associated with leadership, at least for those willing to concede that leadership and power are indeed interconnected, the role of leaders in creating, maintaining, and/or changing an organizational culture may be the most prominent. The concept of organizational culture attracted considerable attention concurrently with the employee empowerment movement of the 1980s and 1990s. Both found nourishment in the same economic climate of the 1980s and were often seen as mutually reinforcing.

The rise of Japanese competition, most keenly felt in the United States automobile industry but also impacting steel, appliances, and other basic sectors, raised the question: what, exactly, were Japanese companies doing that allowed them to "beat" core American industries? *If Japan Can, Why Can't We?* was the title of a powerful and potentially disturbing 1980 NBC-TV documentary. A number of highly visible books – William Ouchi's *Theory Z* (1981) was the most popular, but there was also Ezra Vogel's *Japan as Number One* (1979) and Richard Pascale and Anthony Athos' *The Art of Japanese Management* (1981) – focused specific attention on Japanese culture.[79] Long-range perspectives, systemic thinking, attention to processes rather than individual effort, employee commitment to organizational goals, the capacity of individuals to "shut down the line" if quality problems arose, even morning exercises and group chanting of company songs were all said to contribute to the Japanese miracle.

The subtitles of these books – *Lessons for America, How American Business Can Meet the Japanese Challenge*, and *Applications for American Executives* – proclaimed the none-too-subtle theme. It was time for U.S. corporate leaders to start paying attention to this concept of culture. Two additional popular books – the phenomenally successful *In Search of Excellence* as well as Terrence Deal and Allan Kennedy's *Corporate Cultures* – offered some solace.[80] There *were* American corporations that remained world-class (IBM and Hewlett-Packard were frequently mentioned), and in all these cases, a strong homogeneous culture provided a key to their effectiveness.

Writing just before the explosion of interest in Japanese culture, Andrew Pettigrew issued an explicit call for the integration of sociological and anthropological insights into the study of organizations. After all, he wrote, "it is all too easy to forget the less rational and instrumental, the more expressive social tissue around us that gives those tasks meaning." It was culture, he argued, that offered "the system of such publically and collectively accepted meanings operating for a given group at a given time."[81]

Sociologists had for years urged the consideration of business organizations as social subcultures worthy of being studied:[82]

- Howard Becker insisted that "the problem of collective action, of how people manage to act together," lies at the "core" of the sociological discipline.[83]

- Both Elliott Jaques (on behalf of the Tavistock Institute of Human Relations) and Barry Turner called attention to the culture of subgroups within industrial settings.[84]
- Burton Clark drew attention to organizational myths – sagas; he called them – that offered a "collective understanding of unique accomplishment in a formally established group."[85]
- David Silverman suggested that an "organized pattern" of behavior could be found in any and all social units. That was, after all, a "basic tenet of sociology." A society's members were socialized to accept constraints that are imposed on its members. Referring to a predefined social reality rather than a culture, he argued that membership acceptance of that reality allowed individuals to believe they were behaving "naturally in the only way it is possible to act."[86]
- Erving Goffman's 1974 *Frame Analysis* emphasized the importance of adopting a schema of interpretation in order to organize experience and help explain "what is going on."[87] It is the frame, Goffman concluded, that transformed complex experience into meaning.[88]

The application of the cultural metaphor to business societies drew attention to the less rational, more symbolic elements of organizational life.[89]

Organizations require some agreed-to definition of purpose. Business organizations, after all, are not accidental or spontaneous gatherings of individuals. They are explicitly created, noted early culture theorist Edgar Schein, "because one or more individual perceived that the coordinated and concerted action of a number of people" could "accomplish something that individual action could not." The system of beliefs embedded in a culture "constitutes an agreement among members," added Stewart Ranson and colleagues, "that allows orderly action." Organized work would be impossible, continued V. Lynn Meek, "if people did not share some meanings, knowledge systems and symbols."[90]

Starting with Schein's 1985 *Organizational Culture and Leadership*, leaders came to be seen as the primary shapers of their company's culture. Schein started with founders – William Hewlett and David Packard were two prominent examples – who built their organizations not just around a new product idea but around their own values: their "assumptions about the nature of the world, the role that organizations play in that world, the nature of human nature, how truth is arrived at, and how to manage time and space."[91]

Once the founders departed, it was left to the successive leaders who purposefully leveraged organizational mechanisms – most particularly the allocation of rewards and status and the "criteria used for recruitment, selection, promotion, retirement, and excommunication" – to reinforce that culture.[92] Ongoing leader behaviors – how resources are allocated, how crises are responded to – further embedded cultural values.

The transformational and strategic leadership literature of the 1970s and 1980s picked up on that theme, agreeing that "the organization's culture develops in large part from its leadership."[93] It should be top management's "first priority" to build a "rich, engaging corporate purpose," more vital even than developing a "clear strategic plan" and erecting organizational structures and systems. It is through that sense of purpose that top leaders "establish and maintain a link between the company and each of its employees."[94]

Those who argued that leaders designed a firm's culture tended to overplay both the autonomy of the leader as well as the malleability of culture.[95] Leaders are as much a product of a culture as shapers of that culture.[96] "People do not leave their cultural perspectives at the gates of organizations," Albert Mills noted.[97] Culture was influenced by leaders but also reflected the larger culture in which the company operated.

Organizational culture became an increasingly popular mechanism by which leaders were urged to construct a framework for behaviors. After conducting a study of two companies said to have created and maintained "strong cultures" – Southwest Airlines and Nordstrom department stores – Jennifer Chatman and Sandra Eunyoung Cha heralded the capacity for culture to empower. "Unlike formal rules, policies, and procedures," they wrote, "culture empowers employees to think and act on their own in pursuit of strategic objectives, increasing their commitment to those goals."[98]

That may well be so, but how empowering was empowerment within a strong culture? In his study of the nature of power in international relations, Joseph Nye distinguished two types of power. Traditional or "hard" power depended on coercion, typically manifest through military might. A number of factors had rendered the exercise of hard power more unwieldy, costly, and ineffective. A second type of power – "soft" or "co-optive" – occurred when "one country gets other countries to *want* what it wants."[99]

Soft power, with its reliance in attraction and the appeal of shared values, helps shape the preferences of others:

If a state can make its power seem legitimate in the eyes of others, it will encounter less resistance to its wishes. If its culture and ideology are attractive, others will more willingly follow. If it can establish international norms consistent with its society, it is less likely to have change. If it can support institutions that make other states wish to channel or limit their activities in ways the dominant state prefers, it may be spared the costly exercise of coercive or hard power.[100]

It's an easy leap to depict culture, especially when combined with ideology, as a source of soft power relying on attraction and shared values.[101]

Strong performance cultures, for instance, may embrace market forces, infusing organizational systems with metrics derived from the external environment. Employees might well feel empowered to act more autonomously on behalf of the achievement of those metrics. But the context imposed by market forces is limiting. By drawing borders for autonomous action, in other words, culture may well empower while simultaneously maintaining existing power relationships.

And What about Charisma?

Charisma entered the leadership discourse through Max Weber. Although his writing on charisma as a source of authority occurred contemporaneously with Freud, it did not receive an English-language publication until after World War II. In considering multiple sources of authority, Weber noted an extraordinary, extra-worldly force located in what he termed "charisma." Weber contrasted charisma with more worldly sources of authority, or what Weber called "legitimate domination," such as traditional and legal authority. While those two sources were rooted in the temporal world, the essence of charisma involved a belief that the individual was uniquely and fundamentally wired into the ultimate force that determines order.[102] "Both rational and traditional authority are specifically forms of everyday routine control of action," argued Weber, "while the charismatic type is the direct antithesis of this."[103]

The charismatic grounds for authority resonated deeply with Carlyle's conception of the great man, resting as it did "on devotion to the exceptional sanctity, heroism, or exemplary character of an individual person, and of the normative patterns or order revealed or ordained by him." The individual is "obeyed" – that was Weber's term – by virtue of the "personal trust in his revelation, his heroism, or his exemplary qualities." And here, Weber added just a hint of qualification: "so far as they fall within the scope of the individual's belief in his charisma."[104]

Weber's concept of charismatic authority found its way into leadership discourse in the 1970s and 1980s. A 1977 article by Robert House argued for the relevance of charisma as a force of authority in formal organizations.[105] Bernard Bass agreed, asserting that charisma was "the most important component in the larger concept of transformational leadership."[106] That conflation of transformational and charismatic leadership became quite common in the leadership discourse.[107] Charisma was seen to be a formidable source of influence over followers.

Management consultants, over time, turned charisma into a kind of parlor trick that could be taught to executives. Olivia Fox Cabane's 2012 *The Charisma Myth* "exposed" the myth that charisma was something exceptional. I can teach you charm, persuasion, and a firm handshake, Cabane insisted. And thus, *anyone* can "master the art" of being charismatic.[108]

Granting power to leaders does not inherently disenfranchise followers. The discourse on followership proposed a role, even an obligation, for followers: critical nonobedience.

Favoring Critical Nonobedience

It was Robert E. Kelley who elevated *following* to a process distinct from leading. In a 1988 article he added *-ship* to the end of the word.[109] In order to appreciate the process of effective leadership, Kelley argued, we need to take into consideration not just the leader, but also the followers: the individuals who strive "without star billing" in "the pursuit of an organizational goal."[110] And just as there can be effective and ineffective leaders, there can be and are effective and ineffective followers.

Now we had arrived at a process of following, follower*ship*, which represented a separate, albeit interdependent construct. Followership, as opposed to the obedient act of following, was taken to add a measure of significance, even a sense of community that elevated followers onto a separate and co-equal level with leaders.[111]

Kelley offered a welcomed counterpart to a leader-centric view of organizational effectiveness. It was time, Kelley insisted, to stop viewing the world in terms of leaders, or even in terms of how followers view leaders. It could be, in fact – this was a point Kelley made in a follow-up 2008 piece – that leaders reflected followers far more than followers reflected leaders.

"We tend to think of leaders as the proactive 'cause' and followership as the reactive 'effect.'" But Kelley wondered what would happen if we reversed that thinking? "Are leadership attitudes, behaviors, and performance more the result of followership than the other way around?"[112] In this mirror image of the traditional leader-follow dichotomy, it was great followers who produced great leaders and, thus, great organizations. In that new formulation, followers assumed a responsibility – sometimes expressed in moral terms – to become proactive rather than reactive.

"The most capable followers in the world will fail if they gripe about their leaders but don't help them to improve," Ira Chaleff wrote in his 1997 *Courageous Followers*. "As a follower, I am working to sustain the courage it requires to be honest in my relations with leaders so I can tell them what they need to hear if they are to use their gifts effectively despite their inevitable human flaws."[113]

Chaleff acknowledged a kind of critical followership that awarded agency to those with less hierarchical power, opening the possibility of a wide range of responses. "The danger in the leader-follower relationship is the assumption that the leader's interpretation must dominate," Chaleff noted. "If this assumption exists on the part of either the leader or the follower, they are both at risk."[114]

What if dependency, cooperation, and loyalty were not immediately and automatically forthcoming? The capacity of employees to resist – to engage in what David Collinson and Stephen Ackroyd termed "oppositional" behavior – has been a concern of industrial theorists since the dawning of the industrial era.[115] Frederick Taylor recognized a rational bases for an employee to withhold effort, what he referred to as "soldiering." Maximum effort, early industrial workers believed (not without reason), could lead to a series of negative outcomes, including reducing employment and setting higher work standards.[116] For Taylor, the "fix" – aligning rewards and punishments with maximum output – was relatively simple to achieve. Nonetheless, reliance on rewards to shape obedient behavior regularly proves elusive, particularly given the unintended consequences of such interventions.

Carter Goodrich talked about the "frontiers of control"; a term he used to represent the contested organizational space in which multiple, even competing demands were played out.[117] Competing demands were an inevitable outcome of organizational life. In a Marxist class-conflict-based view of capitalism, oppressive modes of production created structural resistance. But even setting aside Marx, it was possible to suggest that inevitable tensions exist in the organizational need for order and control and an individual desire for autonomy.[118]

In his classic 1938 study of the functions of an executive, Chester Barnard insisted that for organizations to achieve their goals, individual members would be required, to some extent, to subordinate themselves to the collective. "*Organization results from the modification of individuals through control of or influence over these categories*," by which he meant purposes, desires, and "impulses of the moment."[119] Note his use of the word "modification" rather than, say, "denial" or "suppression." In Barnard's world, executives made deliberate, conscious decisions over how to achieve such modification. Individuals brought their own "*intention* and *meaning*" to the organization and thus chose whether to enter "into a specific cooperative system."[120]

Acceptance of a common set of organizational goals will never be universal. Inevitably, leaders and followers will struggle with each other.

Executives have one notion of how much autonomy, discretion, and freedom from direction can be granted to organizational members. Followers likely have another.[121] The struggle is inevitable and, potentially, positive.

A multiplicity of voices and diversity of perspectives can enrich internal dialogue and enhance organizational responsiveness. But it must be recognized that the field on which this struggle plays out is uneven. Executive leaders have more hierarchical power than individual followers. In attempting to seek some balance, unions can create a collective voice for followers. Individuals, however, are not without options.

In his 1970 *Exit, Voice, and Loyalty*, political economist Albert Hirschman noted that the "exit" option – if you are dissatisfied, then leave – is only occasionally realistic.[122] Not everyone can exit, or exit easily. When employees are loyal to a company and committed to its goals rather than frightened or coerced into staying, they are more likely to seek "voice." In that case, they can engage in activities perceived to be corrective. Recognition of agency for followers opens the possibility for a critical discourse among leaders and followers.

Acknowledging follower agency is often seen as problematic, certainly as challenging, by leaders. Executives highly value dependability, cooperation, and loyalty from their subordinates.[123] *You're either with us or against us.* Leaders may frame follower resistance in negative terms; it is a "bad thing" that expresses an irrational response to a dynamic and uncertain environment. In this view, employee resistance is quickly dismissed as invalid or disobedient. Noncompliance is repositioned as deviance, "voluntary behavior that violates significant organizational norms and in doing so threatens the well-being of an organization, its members, or both."[124] It is therefore a force to be overcome with the goal of getting everyone "on board." In fact, the very use of the term "resistance" carries with it pejorative implications.[125]

It should not be so.

Followers may engage in what Grint called as "Faustian pact" with leaders in which "leaders accumulate privileges of power and wealth or whatever is deemed appropriate at the expense of followers" in response to assuming responsibilities for performance outcomes.[126] But other terms are possible, even desirable.

When followers engage in critical nonobedience, the outcomes may be positive for the organization. Suzy Fox and Paul Spector noted a pro-organizational motive for the choice of role-enacting behaviors.[127] Followers may accept the espoused goals of the organization but believe that the leaders are either not fully competent to carry them out or fully committed to those espoused goals. A perceived gap between what leaders claim they seek in terms of organizational goals (their espoused values), and what their behaviors signal as their actual goals (their enacted values) can develop a deeply felt cynicism on the part of followers.[128]

Critical followership does not need to arise out of a lack of commitment to the organization and its goals. Leaders and followers can be allowed, even encouraged, to engage in a process that Melissa Carsten and Mary Uhl-Bien labeled "co-production" of leadership, both striving for improved organizational performance.[129] Co-production does not assume that leaders and followers have a common, friction-free notion of how to define that goal. Therefore, opposition to leadership may well provide an opportunity to learn, to adjust, and to recommit to shared goals. Followers become co-creators with leaders – not equally powerful but equally committed – to the achievement of those goals. This is at least the goal and the promise of followership as a separate and equal construct with leadership.

Looking Backward/Looking Forward

The "Hitler question" profoundly shaped the leadership discourse in the decades after World War II. What happened in Germany was not leadership, it was argued. Rather, it was some insane mixture of naked power, brute force, and blind obedience. To those who wanted to extol an exclusively positive construct of leadership – with James MacGregor Burns foremost among them – the segregation of leadership from power became an imperative. It simply had to be that folks such as Franklin Roosevelt, Mahatma Gandhi, and Martin Luther King represented an entirely separate plane of activity than did Hitler.

Subsequently, other scholars – Barbara Kellerman and Keith Grint among them –insisted on seeing the exercise of power as a necessary component of leadership. The counterargument is that to eliminate power from leadership discourse, even to relegate it to secondary status, seriously distorts our notion of what leadership is and how it operates within a social context. Leaders by definition have considerable power, and that power may be exercised for many reasons, good as well as ill.

But who gets to define "good"? All social entities proclaim, either explicitly or implicitly, what is held to be a good society. To appreciate the values embedded in such an understanding, we need to turn to the concept of ideology. Ideology refers to a widely shared and internally consistent belief system that provides a value-based lens through which adherents view, understand, and react to external events. Ideology can serve a functional role by providing "social cement" for a society; it may also lead to distortions, false consciousness, and the concealment of real interests.

In order to avoid an anemic conception of leadership, we need to consider the use of power as a method and the usefulness of ideology in defining the desired outcomes. Unfortunately, much of the discourse on leadership in the business arena has done just the opposite by ignoring power and denouncing ideology.

NOTES

1 Mary Uhl-Bien et al., "Followership Theory: A Review and Research Agenda," *Leadership Quarterly* 25 (2014), 83.
2 Keith Grint, "The Sacred in Leadership: Separation, Sacrifice and Silence," *Organization Studies* 31 (2010), 89–107.
3 Grint, *The Arts of Leadership*.
4 Dennis Tourish, *The Dark Side of Transformational Leadership: A Critical Perspective* (London: Routledge, 2013), 210.
5 Raelin adds "compassionate," which may be wishful thinking. Joseph A. Raelin, *Leaderful Organizations: How to Bring Out Leadership in Everyone* (San Francisco: Berrett-Koehler, 2003).
6 That is especially true in the United States. The 2008 Troubled Asset Relief Program required that all companies receiving government "bail out" money as a response to the Great Recession separate the two roles. That requirement suggests a belief that separating the CEO–board chair role represents good corporate governance. But it is not required for other public corporations. As of 2014 about half the companies in the *Fortune 500* list of publicly held corporations had split the roles.
7 Joseph Rost, "Followership: An Outmoded Concept," in Ronald E. Riggio et al., eds., *The Art of Followership: How Great Followers Create Great Leaders and Organizations* (San Francisco: Jossey-Bass, 2008), 55.
8 A number of scholars have noted the attribution of negativity to the term "follower." See, for example, Melissa K. Carsten et al., "Exploring Social Constructions of Followership: A Qualitative Study," *Leadership Quarterly* 21 (2010), 543–62; Brian Crossman and Joanna Crossman, "Conceptualizing Followership: A Review of the Literature," *Leadership* 7 (2011), 481–97; Robert Goffee and Gareth Jones, "Followership: It's Personal, Too," *Harvard Business Review* 79 (2001), 148; Colette B. Hoption et al., "Submitting to the Follower Label: Followership, Positive Affect and Extra-Role Behaviors," *Journal of Psychology* 220 (2012), 221–30; and Mary Uhl-Bien and Rajnandini Pillai, "The Romance of Leadership and the Social Construction of Followership," in Boas Shamir et al., eds., *Follower-Centered Perspectives on Leadership: A Tribute to the Memory of James R. Meindl* (Charlotte: Information Age Publishers, 2007), 187–210.
9 There are still contemporary versions of this argument. See, for example, Jan-Michael Ross and Dmitry Sharapov, "When the Leader Follows: Dethronement through Imitation," *Academy of Management Journal* 58 (June 2015), 658–79.

10 The uneasy relationship between the various schools of "leadership in the plural" and hierarchical power is discussed in Jean-Louis Denis et al., "Leadership in the Plural," *Academy of Management Annals* 6 (June 2012), 211–83.

11 For examples of management authors dealing with power, see S. Alexander Haslam et al., *The New Psychology of Leadership: Identity, Influence and Power* (New York: Psychology Press, 2011); John P. Kotter, *Power and Influence: Beyond Formal Authority* (New York: Press, 1985); Jeffrey Pfeffer, *Power in Organizations* (Marshfield: Pitman, 1981); Jeffrey Pfeffer, *Managing with Power: Politics and Influence in Organizations* (Boston: Harvard Business School Press, 1992); and Daan Van Knippenberg and Michael A. Hogg, eds., *Leadership and Power: Identity Processes in Groups and Organizations* (London: Sage, 2003).

12 Stanley Milgram, "Behavioral Study of Obedience," *Journal of Abnormal and Social Psychology* 67 (1963), 371–78; Philip G. Zimbardo and Ken Musen, *Quiet Rage: The Stanford Prison Study* (Stanford: Stanford University Press, 2003).

13 James MacGregor Burns, *Leadership* (New York: Harper, 1978), 9.

14 Ibid., 11.

15 Ibid., 19.

16 Ibid., 18.

17 Barbara Kellerman, "Hitler's Ghost: A Manifesto," in Barbara Kellerman and Larraine R. Matusak, eds., *Cutting Edge Leadership 2000* (College Park: Center for the Advanced Study of Leadership, 2000), 65–68.

18 The anecdote is from James MacGregor Burns, *Transforming Leadership: A New Pursuit of Happiness* (New York: Atlantic Monthly Press, 2003), 27–28.

19 Burns was not alone in this insistence that Hitler's actions did not qualify him as a leader. Political scientist Ronald Heifetz wrote, "Although dramatically mobilizing his society, both socially and economically, he did so primarily in the direction of avoiding tough realities. By providing illusions of grandeur, internal scapegoats, and external enemies, Hitler misdiagnosed Germany's ills and brought his nation to disaster. He exercised leadership no more than a charlatan practices medicine when providing fake remedies." Ronald A. Heifetz, *Leadership without Easy Answers* (Cambridge: Belknap Press, 1994), 24.

20 I think we can guess what Burns made of Wess Roberts' best seller: *The Leadership Secrets of Attila the Hun* (New York: Grand Central, 1989).

21 Freud, *Moses and Monotheism*, 170.

22 Barbara Kellerman, *Bad Leadership: What It Is, How It Happens, Why It Matters* (Boston: Harvard Business School Press, 2004), 29.

23 Kellerman, "Hitler's Ghost."

24 Grint offers a thoughtful and thorough assessment of Hitler as a leader in *The Arts of Leadership*, 289–358.

25 Kellerman, "Hitler's Ghost," 68.

26 The distinction, if such a distinction can be made, between "power" and "influence" is much debated. Jay Butler, for instance, sees power "as the superordinate concept under which authority and influence are subsumed."

Influence, in this view, "connotes informal procedures in contrast to formal ones and persuasion in contrast to order giving and receiving." David Bell suggests that power relies on extrinsic rewards and punishment while influence works to shape the behaviors of others without recourse to such sanctions. It is not uncommon to find the terms used as a single construct: power and influence. See David V.J. Bell, *Power, Influence, and Authority: An Essay in Political Linguistics* (New York: Oxford University Press, 1975); and Jay G. Butler, "On Power and Authority: An Exchange on Concepts," *American Sociological Review* 25 (October 1960), 731.

27 Robert A. Dahl, "The Concept of Power," *Behavioral Science* 2 (1957), 203.

28 Steven Lukes' "radical" view of power added that the exercise of power always moves people to take actions that oppose their own self-interest. The underlying concept of power is this: "*A* exercises power over *B* when *A* affects *B* in a manner contrary to *B*'s interests." See Lukes, *Power: A Radical View* (London: Palgrave Macmillan, 1974), 27.

29 Burns, *Leadership*, 18.

30 John R.P. French, Jr., and Richard Snyder. "Leadership and Interpersonal Power," in Dorwin Cartright, ed., *Studies in Social Power* (Ann Arbor: Institute for Social Research, 1959), 118.

31 Amos Hawley, "Community Power and Urban Renewal Success," *American Journal of Sociology* 68 (January 1963), 422.

32 Rosabeth Moss Kanter, *Men and Women of the Corporation* (New York: Basic Books, 1977).

33 This point in made in Michel Foucault, "The Subject and Power," *Critical History* 8 (Summer 1982), 777–95. Some theorists insist that power and domination are synonymous. "Power requires submission," wrote sociologist Robert Bierstedt in 1950. He preferred the term "influence" to designate a noncoercive impact on others. Robert Bierstedt, "An Analysis of Social Power," *American Sociological Review* 15 (December 1950), 731.

34 Stewart Clegg, "Theories of Power," *Theory, Culture & Society* 17 (2000), 144.

35 There is a robust field of study on "toxic" or "bad" leadership, attempting to understand why followers may opt to align with such leaders. The notion that leaders exercise power is fundamental to this stream of writing. See, for example, Barbara Kellerman, *Bad Leadership*; Manfred F.R. Kets de Vries, "The Spirit of Despotism: Understanding the Tyrant Within," *Human Relations* 59 (2006), 195–220; Jean Lipman-Blumen, *The Allure of Toxic Leaders: Why We Follow Destructive Bosses and Corrupt Politicians – And How We Can Survive Them* (New York: Oxford University Press, 2005); Art Padilla et al., "The Toxic Triangle: Destructive Leaders, Susceptible Followers and Conducive Environments," *Leadership Quarterly* 18 (2007), 176–94; Kathie L. Pelletier, "Leader Toxicity: An Empirical Investigation of Toxic Behavior and Rhetoric," *Leadership* 6 (2010), 373–89; Birgit Schyns and Jan Schilling, "How Bad Are the Effects of Bad Leaders? A Meta-Analysis of Destructive Leadership and Its Outcomes," *Leadership Quarterly* 24 (2013), 138–58; James B. Shaw et al., "A Method for Measuring Destructive Behavior and Identifying Types of Destructive Leaders in Organizations," *Leadership*

Quarterly 22 (2011): 575–90; Christian Thoroughgood et al., "The Susceptible Circle: Taxonomy of Followers Associated with Destructive Leadership,"
Leadership Quarterly 23 (2012), 897–917.

36   In his 1996 study, *Hitler's Willing Executioners*, Daniel Johan Goldhagen
     argued that "ordinary Germans" willingly, even enthusiastically supported
     Hitler and the execution of Jews "for the simple reason that, when it came
     to exterminating Jews," German citizens "did not *want* to say 'no.'" *Hitler's
     Willing Executioners: Ordinary Germans and the Holocaust* (New York: Knopf,
     1996), 14. Keith Grint added a cautionary note: "This does not mean that
     coercion was an insignificant element of Nazi control. Clearly, nothing could
     be further from the truth. However, the point I wish to make is that it was not
     just coercion that maintained Nazi control; collaboration, and collaboration
     above and beyond that required for self-preservation, was an axial principle
     upon which the Nazi behemoth rolled over European civilization and all but
     eliminated European Jews." Grint, *The Arts of Leadership*, 291–2.

37   Macdonald is cited in Zygmunt Bauman, *Modernity and the Holocaust* (Ithaca:
     Cornell University Press, 2000), 151.

38   James Waller noted that social scientists, for the most part, did not draw
     explicit attention to Holocaust studies until the 1960s. He explains this
     fifteen-year gap, in some part, by the Cold War preoccupation with the more
     immediate (albeit ideologically inflated) threat of the Soviet Union and the
     fear of nuclear war. James E. Waller, "The Social Sciences," in P. Hayes and
     J.K. Roth, eds., *The Oxford Handbook of Holocaust Studies* (New York: Oxford
     University Press, 2010), 667–79.

39   Milgram, "Behavioral Study of Obedience," 371. Milgram understood his
     findings to be consistent with Hannah Arendt's construct of the banality of
     evil. Jan De Vos, "From Milgram to Zimbardo: The Double Birth of Postwar
     Psychology/Psychologization," *History of the Human Sciences* 23 (2010), 156–
     75. Arendt set forth her controversial hypothesis that Nazism was often fueled
     by "average" people motivated less by ideology than by personal motives. See
     Arendt, *Eichmann in Jerusalem: Report on the Banality of Evil* (New York:
     Viking, 1963).

40   Well, maybe not quite as free as Milgram suggested. Dan McArthur noted,
     "When subjects asked to withdraw, they were told they *must* continue or
     that the experiment *demanded* that they continue and indeed that they *had
     no choice.*" Even though no overt coercion was used, MacArthur concluded,
     there was still psychological coercion. Dan McArthur, "Good Ethics Can
     Sometimes Mean Better Science: Research Ethics and the Milgram Experi-
     ments," *Science and Engineering Ethics* 15 (2009), 74.

41   The original film of the experiments can be viewed at www.youtube.com/
     watch?v=xOYLCy5PVgM.

42   For an overview of the Milgram studies, as well as a review of the criticisms
     of his methodology and ethics, see Thomas Blass, *The Man Who Shocked
     the World: The Life and Legacy of Stanley Milgram* (New York: Basic Books,
     2004).

43   Zygmunt Bauman suggested that contemporary social science has preferred
     to attack Milgram's methodology, which was certainly flawed, rather than to

accept and deal with the implications of his findings. Bauman, *Modernity and the Holocaust*.

44 Ira Chaleff, *The Courageous Follower: Standing Up To and For Our Leaders* (San Francisco: Barnett-Koehler, 1997), 13.

45 Michel Foucault, *Discipline and Punish: The Birth of the Prison* (New York: Vintage, 1979), 23, 27.

46 Foucault, "The Subject and Power," 781.

47 For an excellent review, see Marcello Musto, "Revisiting Marx's Concept of Alienation," *Socialism and Democracy* 24 (November 2010), 79–101.

48 James O'Toole, "Lordstown: Three Years Later," *Business and Society Review* 13 (Spring 1975), 65.

49 The Vega represented GM's ill-fated response to the small-car challenge being mounted by both German and Japanese imports. I owned one and loved it! I was not, however, in large company. Despite being named the 1971 *Motor Trend Car of the Year*, the model was plagued by high costs and low quality and taken out of production in 1977.

50 Quoted in James B. Treece, "The Mood at Lordstown Changed from Confrontation to Cooperation," *Automotive News* (October 31, 2011), 15.

51 Agis Salpukas, "Young Workers Disrupt Key GM Plant," *New York Times* (January 23, 1972), 1. Although not acknowledged specifically in the article, that tough management team was the result of the creation of a new General Motors Assembly Division, a consolidation of Fisher Body and final-assembly operations. Treece, "The Mood at Lordstown," 15.

52 Salpukas, "Young Workers," 31.

53 Salpukas suggested that the rebellion was directed as much against an unresponsive union as against GM management.

54 GM executives disputed the popular press interpretation of the so-called Lordstown Syndrome, insisting that other plants with workers younger than those in Ohio did not suffer the same turmoil. Plus, worker disputes, when they did occur, were said to be manifestations of traditional labor–management tensions. On management reactions, see Bert A. Spector and Paul Lawrence, "General Motors and the United Auto Workers," in Michael Beer et al., eds., *Human Resource Management: A General Manager's Perspective* (New York: Free Press, 1985), 683–710.

55 "Unhappy Young Workers Called Threat to Output," *Wall Street Journal*, September 12, 1972, 14; "Boredom Spells Trouble on the Line," *Life*, September 1972, 30.

56 Richard Manning and John McCormick, "The Blue-Collar Blues," *Newsweek* (June 4, 1984), 63.

57 Richard E. Walton, "How to Counter Alienation in the Plant," *Harvard Business Review* 50 (November–December 1972), 70–81.

58 Richard E. Walton, "From Control to Commitment in the Workplace," *Harvard Business Review* 63 (March–April 1985), 81.

59 Cynthia D. Scott and Dennis T. Jaffe, *Empowerment: Building a Committed Workforce* (London: Kogan Page, 1991).

60 Ibid., 13.

61 Ibid., 14.

62 Ibid.

63 W. Warner Burke, "Leadership as Empowering Others," in Suresh Srivastva, ed., *Executive Power: How Executives Influence People and Organizations* (San Francisco: Jossey-Bass, 1986), 51; Jay A. Conger, "Leadership: The Art of Empowering Others," *Academy of Management Executive* 3 (1989), 17.

64 Conger, "Leadership," 18–19.

65 Jeffrey Gandz, "The Employee Empowerment Era," *Business Quarterly* 52 (Autumn 1990), 74.

66 Thomas A. Potterfield, *The Business of Employee Empowerment: Democracy and Ideology in the Workplace* (Westport: Quorum Books, 1999), 41.

67 Ibid., 2.

68 Barbara Levy Simon, *The Empowerment Tradition in American Social Work: A History* (New York: Columbia University Press, 1994).

69 Potterfield, *The Business of Employee Empowerment*, 39.

70 Ibid., 40.

71 Ibid., 41.

72 Barbara B. Solomon, *Black Empowerment: Social Work in Oppressed Communities* (New York: Columbia University Press, 1976), 12.

73 Stokely Carmichael and Charles V. Hamilton, *Black Power: The Politics of Liberation in America* (New York: Vintage, 1967).

74 Tony Eccles, "The Deceptive Allure of Empowerment," *Long Range Planning* 26 (1993), 13, 17.

75 Cynthia Hardy and Sharon Leiba-O'Sullivan, "The Power behind Empowerment: Implications for Research and Practice," *Human Relations* 51 (1998), 467.

76 Perhaps not hired by factory workers exactly, but Paul Lawrence and I documented the agreement between GM and the UAW to jointly hire quality-of-work life consultants with the impetus provided by UAW leader Irving Bluestone. Spector and Lawrence, "General Motors and the United Auto Workers."

77 Company executives admitted to the reality of a Southern Strategy but argued that it was motivated by lower labor and operating costs and a desire to gain added political clout in a geographic area where the industry's influence had been weak. Union officials insisted that the Southern Strategy was driven by a desire to seek a "union-free environment." Spector and Lawrence, "General Motors and the United Auto Workers," 696–7.

78 Jeffrey Gandz and Frederick G. Bird, "The Ethics of Empowerment," *Journal of Business Ethics* 15 (1996), 387.

79 William Ouchi, *Theory Z: How American Business Can Meet the Japanese Challenge* (Reading: Addison-Wesley, 1981); Richard Tanner Pascale and Anthony G. Athos, *The Art of Japanese Management: Applications for American Executives* (New York: Simon & Schuster, 1981); Ezra F. Vogel, *Japan as Number One: Lessons for America* (Cambridge: Harvard University Press, 1979).

80 Terrence A. Deal and Allan A. Kennedy, *Corporate Cultures: The Rites and Rituals of Corporate Life* (Reading: Addison-Wesley, 1982); Thomas J. Peters

and Robert H. Waterman, *In Search of Excellence: Lessons from America's Best-Run Companies* (New York: Harper & Row, 1982).

81 Andrew M. Pettigrew, "On Studying Organizational Cultures," *Administrative Science Quarterly* 24 (December 1979), 574.

82 For a review of early inquiries into organizational culture, see Yvan Allaire and Mihaela E. Firsirotu, "Theories of Organizational Culture," *Organization Studies* 5 (1984), 193–226.

83 Howard S. Becker, "Culture: A Sociological View," *Yale Review* 71 (1982), 513. Becker, in fact, maintained that this was a core concern for *all* of social science.

84 Elliott Jaques, *The Changing Culture of a Factory: A Study of Authority and Participation in an Industrial Setting* (London: Tavistock Publications, 1951); Barry A. Turner, *Exploring the Industrial Subculture* (London: Macmillan, 1971).

85 Burton R. Clark, "The Organizational Saga in Higher Education," *Administrative Science Quarterly* 17 (June 1972), 178.

86 David Silverman, *The Theory of Organizations* (London: Heinemann, 1970).

87 Erving Goffman, *Frame Analysis: An Essay on the Organization of Experience* (Cambridge: Harvard University Press, 1974), 26.

88 Goffman took no note of the matter of what groups had the power to define the frame and, thus, establish the constraints. He wrote, in fact, that he made "no claim whatsoever to be talking about the core matters of sociology – social organization and social structure." He nonetheless recognized the potential for those controlling parties to fabricate meaning in a way to create "a false belief about what it is that is going on" and purposefully constrain others "in a construction that is clearly inimical to their private interests." Goffman, *Frame Analysis*, 13, 27, 103.

89 Gareth Morgan, *Images of Organization* (Beverly Hills: Sage, 1986).

90 Edgar H. Schein, *Organizational Culture and Leadership* (San Francisco: Jossey-Bass, 1985), 209; Stewart Ranson et al., "The Structuring of Organizational Structures," *Administrative Science Quarterly* 25 (March 1980), 5; V. Lynn Meek, "Organizational Culture: Origins and Weaknesses," *Organization Studies* 9 (1988), 467.

91 Schein, *Organizational Culture and Leadership*, 210.

92 Ibid., 225.

93 Bernard M. Bass and Bruce J. Avolio, "Transformational Leadership and Organizational Culture," *International Journal of Public Administration* 17 (March 1994), 541.

94 Christopher A. Bartlett and Sumantra Ghoshal, "Changing the Role of Top Management: Beyond Strategy to Purpose," *Harvard Business Review* 72 (November–December 1994), 79–88.

95 A point Edgar H. Schein himself made in *The Corporate Culture Survival Guide: Sense and Nonsense about Culture Change* (San Francisco: Jossey-Bass, 1999).

96 This point is made in Linda Smircich, "Concepts of Culture and Organizational Analysis," *Administrative Science Quarterly* 28 (1983), 339–58.

97 Albert J. Mills, "Organization, Gender, and Culture," in Albert Mills and Peta Tancreed, eds., *Gendering Organizational Analysis* (London: Sage, 1992), 98.

98 Jennifer A. Chatman and Sandra Eunyoung Cha, "Leading by Leveraging Culture," *California Management Review* 45 (Summer 2003), 23.

99 Joseph S. Nye, Jr., "Soft Power," *Foreign Policy* 80 (Autumn 1990), 166. A number of other dichotomous views of power have been suggested. Psychologist David McClelland, for instance, wrote about socialized (positive) power deployed on behalf of group goals, and personalized (negative) power deployed on behalf of self-aggrandizement. Another dichotomy referred to a distinction between an elitist view of power (power that was exercised by a relatively elite group) and a pluralist view of power (power that was exercised by an ever-shifting coalition of actors depending on the issues involved). Yet another, applied mainly to the study of Presidential power in America, related to a distinction between power that flowed from the office and power that was a function of the skills of the particular officeholder. Peter Bachrach and Morton S. Baratz, "Two Faces of Power," *American Political Science Review* 56 (December 1962), 947–52; David C. McClelland, *Power: The Inner Experience* (New York: Irvington Publishers, 1975); and Richard E. Neustadt, *Presidential Power: The Politics of Leadership* (New York: Wiley, 1960).

100 Nye, "Soft Power," 167.

101 In a follow-up analysis of the distinction, Nye proposed that the two types of power existed on a continuum or spectrum "from coercion to economic inducement to agenda setting to pure attraction." Joseph S. Nye, Jr., *Soft Power: The Means to Success in World Politics* (New York: Foreign Affairs, 2003), 7.

102 Adam B. Seligman, "Charisma and the Transformation of Grace in the Early Modern Era," *Social Research* 58, no. 3 (Fall 1991), 591–620.

103 Max Weber, *The Theory of Social and Economic Organizations* (New York: Oxford University Press, 1947), 361.

104 Max Weber, "Three Pure Types of Authority," in *Economy and Society* (Berkeley: University of California Press, 1978), 216.

105 Robert J. House, "A 1976 Theory of Charismatic Leadership," in J.G. Hunt and L.L. Larson, eds., *Leadership: The Cutting Edge* (Carbondale: University of Southern Illinois Press, 1977), 189–207.

106 Bernard M. Bass, "Leadership: Good, Better, Best," *Organizational Dynamics* 13 (Winter 1985), 34.

107 Susanne Braun et al., "Transformational Leadership, Job Satisfaction, and Team Performance: A Multilevel Mediation Model of Trust," *Leadership Quarterly* 24 (2013), 270–83; Adam M. Grant, "Leading with Meaning: Beneficiary Contact, Prosocial Impact, and the Performance Effects of Transformational Leadership," *Academy of Management Journal* 55 (2012), 458–76; Timothy A. Judge and Ronald F. Piccolo. "Transformational and Transactional Leadership: A Meta-analytic Test of Their Relative Validity," *Journal of Applied Psychology* 89 (2004), 755–68; Snjezana Kovjanic et al.,

"How Do Transformational Leaders Foster Positive Employee Outcomes? A Self-Determination-Based Analysis of Employees' Needs as Mediating Link," *Journal of Organizational Behavior* 33 (2012), 1031–52; Northouse, *Leadership*; Gary Yukl, *Leadership in Organizations*, 8th edition (Boston: Pearson, 2013).

108 Olivia Fox Cabane, *The Charisma Myth: How Anyone Can Master the Art and Science of Personal Magnetism* (New York: Portfolio, 2012).

109 The first usage of followership I could find was in Howard Wilson's 1971 *Industrial Management* article on "supervisory leadership." He drew attention to the degree to which "followership determines the effectiveness of the leader." Howard Wilson, "Changing Patterns of Supervisory Leadership," *Industrial Management* 13 (November 1971), 11.

110 Robert E. Kelley, "In Praise of Followers," *Harvard Business Review* 66 (November 1988), 144.

111 Goffee and Jones, "Followership: It's Personal, Too."

112 Robert E. Kelley, "Rethinking Followership," in Ronald E. Riggio et al., eds., *The Art of Followership*, 11.

113 Chaleff, *The Courageous Follower*, xix.

114 Ibid., 4–5.

115 David Collinson and Stephen Ackroyd, "Resistance, Misbehavior, and Dissent," in Stephen Ackroyd et al., eds., *Oxford Handbook of Work and Organization* (Oxford: Oxford University Press, 2005), 305–26. Another term that captures follower agency is "nonfollower behavior." This is used by Mary Uhl-Bien and colleagues to describe a situation when "one's leading attempts are not responded to with following behaviors. For example, nonfollowing can occur in formal hierarchical roles when a manager's leading behaviors are responded to with subordinates' resistance behaviors." This is nonfollower behavior only in situations when leaders define follower expectations narrowly and noncritically. Uhl-Bien et al., "Followership Theory," 99.

116 Kanigel, *The One Best Way*.

117 The term "frontiers of control" is from Carter Goodrich and cited in Stewart Clegg, "Organization and Control," *Administrative Science Quarterly* 26 (December 1981), 545.

118 This is the argument made by Linda L. Putnam et al., "Discourse and Resistance: Targets, Practices, and Consequences," *Management Communication Quarterly* 19 (August 2005), 5–18.

119 Barnard, *Functions of the Executive*, 17.

120 Ibid., 11, 17.

121 Clegg, "Organization and Control," 545. Peter Fleming and André Spicer noted the negative implications of the term "struggle" in *Contesting the Corporation: Struggle, Power, and Resistance in Organizations* (Cambridge: Cambridge University Press, 2007), 51.

122 Albert O. Hirschman, *Exit, Voice, and Loyalty: Responses to Decline in Firms, Organizations, and States* (Cambridge: Harvard University Press, 1970).

123 Augustine O. Agho, "Perspectives of Senior-Level Executives on Effective Followership and Leadership," *Journal of Leadership & Organizational Studies* 16 (November 2009), 159–66.

124 Sandra L. Robinson and Rebecca J. Bennett, "A Typology of Deviant Workplace Behaviors: A Multidimensional Scaling Study," *Academy of Management Journal* 38 (April 1995), 556.

125 Sandy Kristin Piderit, "Rethinking Resistance and Recognizing Ambivalence: A Multidimensional View of Attitudes toward an Organizational Change," *Academy of Management Review* 25 (2000), 783–94; Tony J. Watson, "Group Ideologies and Organizational Change," *Journal of Management Studies* 19 (1982), 259–75.

126 Grint, "The Sacred in Leadership," 99.

127 Suzy Fox, and Paul E. Spector, "A Model of Work Frustration-Aggression," Journal of Organizational *Behavior* 20 (1999), 915–31.

128 The espoused/enacted values dichotomy is from Chris Argyris and Donald A. Schön, *Organizational Learning: A Theory of Action Perspective* (Reading, MA: Addison-Wesley, 1978). On cynicism as a form of resistance, see Gideon Kunda, *Engineering Culture: Control and Commitment in a High-Tech Corporation* (Philadelphia: Temple University Press, 1992).

129 Melissa K. Carsten and Mary Uhl-Bien, "Ethical Followership: An Examination of Followership Beliefs and Crimes of Obedience," *Journal of Leadership and Organizational Studies* 20 (2013), 49–61.

4 The Sublime Myth and the Ideology of Purpose

In the world of public corporations, pragmatic leadership is virtually de rigueur.[1]

Business, after all, is about solving real-world problems, meeting challenges, and achieving results. The metrics used to delineate effective and ineffective performance, success and failure, are clear, objective, and indisputable. This is a setting with no room for and little patience with narrow, rigid ideology. The best leaders – that is, the most effective – take a hard, unblinkered look at the facts and respond appropriately. They work in a world brimming with scorecards and public accountings, and respond accordingly. To be sure, bad actors surface with alarming regularity. Still, even they are being pragmatic, although in a purely self-serving way.

This, at least, is the myth.

Two streams of academic research have recently emerged to bolster that myth. In one, Michael Mumford and colleagues distinguished between "pragmatic" and "ideological" leaders.[2] A 2007 *Leadership Quarterly* article named names: these are ideological leaders and these aren't.[3] Virtually all the names on the two lists came from historically significant national and/or political domains, but this was history absent rigor or discipline. To suggest, as the authors did, that W.E.B. Du Bois was ideological and Booker T. Washington was pragmatic is historical nonsense. Du Bois and Washington debated the appropriate response to racial segregation in late 19th century America, both offering visions for an idealized future and endorsing tactics for achieving these goals. Both were deeply ideological.[4]

There are only a few business leaders – J.P. Morgan, Lee Iacocca, Walt Disney, Katherine Graham, Alfred du Pont, and Roberto Goizueta among them – and they all are considered to be "non-ideological." The claim that the best business leaders are inherently pragmatic rather than ideological is thus reinforced.

In a second stream, Denise Rousseau, Jeffrey Pfeffer and others espoused the concept of "evidence-based management."[5] This supposedly new "paradigm" for decision making calls for facts, hard evidence, and logic to triumph over unsupported beliefs and assumptions. Human bias gives way to a scientific certainty about which all involved parties can agree, assuming of course that the involved parties are not "trapped by their beliefs and ideologies."[6] Again, the claim for the superiority of pragmatic leadership is maintained. Business has no place for ideology.[7]

The flaw in these assertions is this. All business is ideological, and therefore, *all business leadership is ideological*.

"Nonsense"

The terms "ideology" and "pragmatism" are often tossed about rather carelessly in order to highlight the supposed contrast between the two. Political theorist Svetozar Stojanović expressed a commonly held conception that ideologies are *distorted* reflections of reality: the "real world" as filtered through the biases of adherents. It is easy to spot the underlying epistemological assumption that Stojanović is making: an indisputable truth exists out there in the world just waiting to be discovered through the proper application of a nonideological, undistorted methodology.[8] Ideologues distort and pragmatists seek indisputable truth, reality as it "actually" is.

Not surprisingly, the conception of ideology attracts a wide array of negative adjectives: dogmatic, deceptive, manipulative, rigid, and doctrinaire among them. Pragmatists, conversely, are described as practical, realistic, sensible, hardheaded, and down-to-earth. There is no denying the normative stance embedded in that vocabulary: ideology is bad, pragmatism is good. Academics, in particular, distrust the notion of ideology, which is held to be a violation, even a denial, of scientific positivism. Argued legal scholar Jonathan Macey, academics deem ideology to be "abhorrently anti-intellectual."[9]

That anti-ideological/pro-pragmatic stance has been especially prominent in the United States. Americans tend to believe that ideology is something foreign and antithetical to their experience. Ideology is basically a European commodity; a bag of theoretical confusions (socialism, communism, fascism, and the like) that Americans left behind in the Old Country with their ancestors and with which they are happily unencumbered. However, the belief that Americans are hardheaded pragmatists, unaffected by ideologies as they deal with real-world problems is, insisted George Lodge, "nonsense."[10]

Nonsense it may be, but it is a powerful kind of nonsense.

American disdain of ideology, or at least of the *idea* of ideology, is perhaps understandable, forged as it was in the precariousness of the

American frontier, a vulnerability which demanded an immediate response for which the guiding principle was: will it work? Trappings of European society were shed and American character was formed at the juncture of settlement and frontier. This was the narrative reinforced by 19th-century historian Frederick Jackson Turner and his famous frontier thesis.[11] And many Americans accepted that story.

But not all. Large groups of those living in the new colonies – African slaves and British and German indentured servants, for instance – would undoubtedly dissent. Native Americans would certainly dispute the assertion that all responses to frontier challenges were simply pragmatic. And those Founding Fathers who penned the Declaration of Independence, fermented a revolution, and encoded rules of conduct in the U.S. Constitution, adhered to an ideology of patriarchy, individualism, private property, human bondage, and, although there was a considerable debate on this, limited government. To deny the Founding Fathers their ideology – as complex, contradictory, and nuanced as it was – is to view them myopically.

The concept of ideology is almost entirely absent from the prevailing leadership discourse except in the negative; calling attention to the far-more-desired notion of pragmatism. However, ideology sits, implicit and unacknowledged, within that discourse. It is important to unpack the concept and then compare it to pragmatism in order to ask: are they really bipolar concepts after all?

The European Roots of Ideology

The term "ideology" comes from 18th-century France. It was coined by Antoine Destutt de Tracy, manager of the newly founded *Institut de France*. De Tracy intended a neutral meaning as a science of ideas. Ideology represented something "very sensible," de Tracy insisted, "since it supposes nothing doubtful or unknown." It was, in fact, both positive and useful in that it took into account the "practical consequences" of knowledge.[12]

As we shall see, de Tracy's definition of ideology comes remarkably close to William James' conceptualization of pragmatism. So, how did the term ideology attract such a negative connotation as a distortion of reality? Why is it something that leaders are told to steer clear of if they want to be effective problem solvers and decision makers?

The shift away from a neutral definition of ideology occurred immediately, led by Napoleon. De Tracy and his cohorts, advocates of free expression and representative government, called for Napoleon to be unseated. The French emperor returned the favor by denouncing the avowedly liberal *idéologues*. By 1867, just over seven decades after de Tracy's coinage, the term was adopted by Friedrich Engels and Karl Marx to denote an expression of bourgeois class interests rather than a neutral science of ideas.

Marx viewed the defining tension of any and all societies as arising from class conflict. For Marx and Engels, ideological leaders promoted a false consciousness: a cloaking of real interests in an attempt by the ruling bourgeoisie to convince – deceive, really – the subordinate proletariat class to abandon their own betterment.[13] Class, power, ideology, and deception now became thoroughly intertwined; clearly a departure from the original intent of de Tracy.

Europeans defined and reshaped the concept of ideology. Pragmatism, a concept deeply rooted in American soil, rejected ideology altogether.

The American Roots of Pragmatism

For leaders to be pragmatic means what, exactly? The *Columbia Encyclopedia* defines pragmatism as a "method of philosophy" – note the use of the term *method* – "in which the truth of a proposition is measured by its correspondence with experimental results and by its practical outcome." Like de Tracy and the original *idéologues*, pragmatists had little use for speculation and debate on questions "that have no application and have no verifiable answers."[14] Pragmatists sought verifiable truth.

The founding of pragmatism is generally ascribed to American philosopher William James and a series of lectures delivered in 1907. In his second talk, James addressed what he referred to as the "pragmatic method." Practical consequences were basic to understanding the value of any and all ideas, he insisted. "What difference would it practically make if this notion rather than that notion was true?" he asked. "Whenever a dispute is serious, we ought to be able to show some practical difference that must follow from one side or the other's being right."[15]

For James, pragmatism was a method for identifying the "practical difference" of ideas. Pragmatism did not, he stated, "stand for any results. It is a method only."[16] This was a point James made often. Pragmatism "has no dogmas, and no doctrines save its method." No dogmas, no doctrines. The goal of the pragmatic method was to arrive at a usable and verifiable truth.

It is at this point, the insistence upon a material reality against which concepts can be tested, that pragmatism and ideology circle back on themselves and prove to be far less antithetical than might first be thought. Marx believed in the existence of an objective, discoverable reality, one that could be freed from bias and interpretation. William

James believed the same. Both pragmatists and ideologues maintained that there exists a reality that "actually is."

But truth is *not* the same to everyone. It is rather, in the colorful phrase of Friedrich Nietzsche, a "mobile army of metaphors, metonyms [a misleading figure of speech] and anthropomorphisms – in short, a sum of human relations."[17] No methodology or claim of truth can be considered nonideological. The definition of reality, even in its pragmatic sense, is a statement of ideology.

Rather than thinking about ideology solely in terms of false consciousness, it is more useful to start by defining ideology in its broadest sense to be a belief system. Not all belief systems are ideologies. What makes a belief system ideological is that it offers coherence and internal consistency. Nor are ideologies necessarily rigid. Some are, for sure. Fascism, for instance, presumes authoritarianism.[18] Pragmatism may be a perfect example of a less rigid ideology. Still, all claims of truth are inherently ideological in assumptions about a *preferred* world.[19] Pragmatists as well as ideologues claim a truth; in the case of pragmatists, the assertion is that they have discovered "the only road to parades"; a normative methodology for arriving at truth.

Let's bring this analysis back to leadership as exercised in a business setting. Recall James' admonition that pragmatism stands for method and not for any particular result. That description hardly applies to business leaders who indisputably work to achieve desired ends. The question to be asked is how to understand, define, and measure results. Who gets to determine the desired ends of the business? These questions place us firmly in the realm of leadership and corporate ideology.

Business Is Ideological as Are Its Leaders

There is no better place to start an examination of corporate ideology and leadership than with the following statement: "Stakeholders are total rubbish."

That proclamation emanated from Al Dunlap, then head of Scott Paper and one of the best-known U.S. business executives of the 1990s. Dunlap's intention was to denounce the notion that nonshareholders – customers, suppliers, employees, the host community – might have a legitimate stake in and a commensurate voice over the doings of the corporation. "It's the shareholders" – the owners of a company's stock – "who own the company," he insisted, and no one else.[20] That assertion – that shareholders "own" the public corporation – is an example of ideology. It is not a statement of indisputable fact, certainly not a scientifically verifiable law of nature. It is a statement of belief on the part of a corporate CEO, a leader who is stating as indisputable fact what he believed to be true and then acting upon it.

As Dunlap moved through a succession of corporations – Crown Zellerbach and Sunbeam, in addition to Scott – he placed the shareholder at the center of his universe. It was the sanctity of shareholders that was called upon to justify the slash-and-burn leadership tactics that earned him numerous sobriquets, including "Chainsaw Al" and "the meanest boss in America." The most important person in any company, he insisted "is the shareholder; not the CEO or the chairman of the board, and not the board of directors itself." Wall Street applauded that shareholder-first approach, even though Dunlap cloaked his corporate ideology in populist terms. "I'm not talking here about Wall Street fat cats," he insisted. "Working people and retired men and women have entrusted us with their 401 Ks [investment opportunities for employees, often in stocks, intended to build a retirement fund] and pension plans for their children's college tuition and their own long-term security."[21]

Steven Spinner, CEO of United Natural Foods, took a contrasting ideological position to Dunlap's. The goal of his company, he insisted, was to meet and exceed "the needs and expectations of all our stakeholders: our customers, associates, natural and specialty product consumers, suppliers, shareholders, communities, the environment, and the planet."[22] *This* was a statement of corporate ideology, no less than Dunlap's "stakeholders are total rubbish" premise.

Spinner was certainly justifying a system and supporting actions quite different from those pursued by Dunlap. Nonetheless, both examples bring us face-to-face with corporate leaders presenting their positions in terms of an ideology, expressing what Ingalill Holmberg and Lars Stannegård called "a hope, and suggestions of how to achieve the hoped for future"[23]

Ideology is a belief system called upon to justify a particular order, an arrangement of power and authority, rights and privileges, sanctioned and unsanctioned behavior, rewards and punishment.[24] Ideologies are used to validate the favoring of some groups over others; perhaps those in power, perhaps those seeking power. Ideology supports leader assertion of legitimacy, both for themselves and their goals.

Organizational hierarchy depends on a system-justifying ideology. The exercise of power by individuals and groups within the organization is embedded within a carefully constructed ideology of legitimacy. Ideology can justify the exercise of power by those who have power, and resistance by those who do not.[25] All businesses are steeped in ideology, and claims of legitimacy within businesses spring from that ideological foundation.

The Corporate Ideology Debate

Capitalism, like any other form of organized economic activity, is deeply ideological. As a system, it rests on its own set of self-justifying assumptions. Its basic tenets reflect the mindset of 17th-century British social philosopher John Locke. The sanctity of private property was central to this ideology, and it was the recognition of that sanctity that ensured the protection of an individual's rights as well as his (and only later her) fulfillment and self-respect. Competition – what Adam Smith would, nearly a century after Locke, refer to as the invisible hand – provided the mechanism for regulation. The state played a strictly limited role.[26]

Even within a capitalist system, executives face ideological choices. That choice amounts to a corporate ideology. Business organizations operating within a noncapitalist ideology – e.g., socialism – would need to develop a corporate ideology as well.[27] As George Lodge noted, Americans more readily acknowledge the ideology of socialism than the ideology of capitalism.[28] We know there is a choice within capitalism because we know there is a debate, and a long-standing debate at that, over the efficacy of the various ideological options.

During the 1990s, Al Dunlap's "stakeholders are rubbish" ideology may have seemed extreme. Nonetheless, his perspective became the dominant corporate ideology in the United States. "The idea that business strategies should be judged by the economic value they create for shareholders is well accepted in the business community," Alfred Rappaport wrote. "After all, to suggest that companies be operated in the best interests of its owners is hardly controversial."[29]

"Hardly controversial" can be taken to mean "prevailing." By 2001, the argument was being made that the shareholder primacy position was so noncontroversial, so widely accepted, that the ideological debate was essentially *over*. In "The End of History for Corporate Law" (an echo of the then popular "end of history" thesis), Henry Hansmann and Reinier Kraakman insisted that a "broad normative consensus" had emerged that "shareholders alone are the parties to whom corporate managers should be accountable."[30]

The "broad normative consensus" to which Hansmann and Kraakman referred was not universal, however. It has been contested for much of the 20th century, the debate finding its roots on the pages of the *Harvard Law Review* in the early years of the Great Depression. It was a contest played out in legalistic terms between two renowned corporate lawyers.[31] On one side stood Columbia University Law Professor Adolf Berle, and on the other, Harvard Law School Professor E. Merrick Dodd. At the time,

Berle was completing his co-authored (with Gardiner Means) *Modern Corporation and Private Property*.[32]

One of the first attempts to take full account of the evolution of the new public corporation and the role of management in leading these entities, Berle and Means noted the separation of ownership from management that had been evolving since the turn of the new century. Business was no longer *owned* and *operated* by the same person, family, or small group. Now, investors contributed, and thus risked, their own capital to a firm over which they could exercise no direct control. In large publicly held corporations, it was up to managers to make decisions on behalf of the shareholders.

In his article, Berle focused more explicitly on the primacy of shareholder interests. All powers granted to the corporation and the managers of that corporation were "at all times exercisable only for the ratable [i.e., quantifiable] benefit of shareholders."[33] The task of business leaders, then, was clear and precise: serve the financial interests of shareholders.

In a subsequent issue of the *Harvard Law Review*, Dodd joined the debate. Managers of public companies were obliged to pursue goals that went beyond making money for shareholders. Leadership was responsible for providing secure jobs for employees, quality products for consumers, and contributions to the broader society. This was a corporate ideology aligned more with United Natural Food's Steve Spinner than with Al Dunlap.

Corporations served shareholders, yes, but also employees, consumers, and the broader society. "The business corporation," Dodd argued, is "an economic institution which has a social service as well as a profit-making function."[34] For Berle, corporate managers were trustees for the interests of investors; for Dodd, it was the "broader community" which embraced employees and customers whose interests must be served by the corporation. This, presented in legal-speak, was the shareholder primacy versus stakeholder plurality ideological debate.

Berle's belief that, first and foremost, corporate leaders were obliged to pursue the interests of shareholders dominates contemporary discourse. It was Dodd's view, however, that originally won the day. Remember, these articles appeared in the context of the Great Depression and at the dawning of the New Deal. Even after the New Deal ebbed, however, stakeholder plurality prevailed. In 1940, George E. Bates, then editor of the *Harvard Business Review*, wrote a piece that surveyed the responsibilities of a public corporation's board of directors.[35] Shareholders did not receive a single mention!

As late as 1960, nearly three decades after the Berle/Dodd debate, Arch Patton, a McKinsey consultant, reflected Dodd's perspective. In

"How to Apprise Executive Performance," Patton listed a number of metrics to consider, all of which related to internal performance, including improving delivery schedules and reducing waste. Unthinkable by today's standards, measuring the impact on shareholder wealth was not mentioned.[36]

The domination of stakeholder plurality did not last. Perhaps the most significant argument in favor of shareholder primacy since Berle's piece appeared in, of all places, a Sunday *New York Times Magazine* article.

Shareholder Primacy and Agency Theory

In the years between Berle and Mead's *Modern Corporation and Private Property* and the publication of Milton Friedman's 1970 *Times'* essay, "The Social Responsibility of Business Is to Increase Its Profits," James Burnham focused attention on what he referred to as a "managerial revolution." The large public corporation had given rise to a new "dominant class," managers, with the capacity to exercise control over the dynamics of the business. In his 1941 *Managerial Revolution*, Burnham expressed no doubt, indeed warned against, the likelihood that this managerial class would exercise its control on behalf of self-serving rather than general interests.[37]

Friedman's essay echoed Burnham's insistence that managerial self-interests had to be reined in on behalf of the interests of shareholders. Friedman, the leading light of the University of Chicago's school of free-market economics, held that because shareholders "own" the corporation – a core assertion of stakeholder primacy ideology – executives needed to conduct business "in accordance with their [the shareholders] desires."[38]

As an economist, Friedman had no doubt about the nature of those shareholders desires: "to make as much money as possible while conforming to the basic rules of the society, both those embodied in law and those embodied in ethical customs."[39] Friedman proposed a principal/agent relationship between shareholders and executives: "The whole justification for permitting the corporate executive to be selected by the stockholders is that the executive is an agent serving the interests of his principal."[40] The "managerial class" that Burnham had identified nearly thirty years earlier needed to be kept focused on the interests of shareholders.

There was a factual flaw in the Friedman argument. Shareholders do not select corporate executives. They elect directors to the board and the board selects the CEO who hires other executives. Despite its flawed construct, Friedman's principal-agent position received an endorsement six years later in an influential article by economist Michael Jensen and business school dean William Meckling.[41] Appearing in the *Journal of Financial Economics*, "Theory of the Firm: Managerial Behavior, Agency Costs and Ownership Structure," served as the major statement of what became known as agency theory.

In order to connect back to Adam Smith, the authors opened with an approving quote from his 1776 *Wealth of Nations*, insisting that executives were managers:

> ... of other people's money [rather] than their own, it cannot well be expected, that they should watch over it with the same anxious vigilance with which partners in a private company frequently watch over their own. Like the stewards of a rich man, they are apt to consider attention to small matters as not for their master's honour, and very easily give themselves a dispensation from having it. Negligence and profusion, therefore, must always prevail, more or less, in the management of the affairs of such a company.[42]

Being "rational," at least in a pure economic sense of the word, executives would be motivated to enhance their own monetary advantage, even at the expense of the fiscal health of the shareholders. Not trusting leaders to subordinate their own (rational) interests to those of shareholders, Jensen and Meckling urged the construction of governance structures to monitor executives' behaviors and incentivize alignment.

The implication for corporate leaders was profound. Agency theorists rejected unchecked human discretion in decision making on the part of executives because of its inherent tendency toward self-interest. Instead, the presumed neutrality of the market would separate effective from ineffective executive actions.[43] The task of the leader, as well as the metrics by which that leader would be evaluated, became clear: make decisions that rebounded to the best interests of the shareholders, the "owners" of the corporation.

The timing of the Jensen and Meckling piece could not have been more propitious for the advancement of shareholder primacy as the soon-to-be dominant corporate ideology. Over the next decade, a "perfect storm" of forces converged to reinforce the perspective. Frank Dobbin and Dirk Zorn noted:

> It was happenstance (the baby boom) that pension investments grew by leaps and bounds and were increasingly put into the stock market, leading institutional investors to control the majority of stock in major corporations. It was happenstance that the high technology boom would replace the conventional metric of corporate success, profits, with the arms-length metric of meeting analysis's profit/loss projections.[44]

The ascendency of shareholder primacy with its implications for leadership behavior was not, however, happenstance, not a reflection of a supposedly neutral market. Rather, shareholder primacy triumphed because of the self-interested efforts of a small group of actors.

By applying a social movement framework to the emergence of shareholder primacy, Gerald Davis and Tracy Thompson noted that the ideology was imposed on rather than developed by corporations or boards of directors.[45] The key players were:

- Individual and then institutional shareholder activists, regulators who allowed for banks to own equity and required private pension funds to play a more active role in investment enhancement.[46]
- Consultants who peddled various metrics to define shareholder value.[47]
- Professors at the nation's leading business schools who adopted agency theory and taught it as received truth to the next generation of executives.[48]
- The popular press, which increasingly focused on the intricate measures of financial performance.[49]

Legal doctrine evolved as well, increasingly embracing the shareholder primacy ideology.[50]

Writing in *Economy and Society*, Robert Boyer assessed the profound impact of shareholder primacy (he referred to it as the "financialization" of business and society) on both corporations and the larger society.[51] It was an impact felt profoundly by business leaders. Under the shareholder primacy regimen, executives "are forced to review most of their management techniques" in order "to take into account the shareholder requirement for level and stability of rate of return."[52] And although shareholder primacy remains dominant, it has always been a contested ideology.

Serving the Interests of Multiple Stakeholders

In his 1932 article, Professor Dobb laid out his argument that the modern corporation was obligated to meet the needs of multiple groups. It was R. Edward Freeman who, in 1984, provided the label "stakeholder" to Dobb's interested parties. He then turned this insight into a "stakeholder theory of the firm."[53]

Freeman's idea can be stated rather simply: stakeholders were groups that could lay *legitimate* claim to the function and performance of a firm. Shareholders were included among stakeholders. But so were suppliers, customers, employees (both management and nonmanagement employees) and the host community.

The central question for Freeman was a "pure ideological" one: "For whose benefit and at whose expense should the firm be managed."[54] Stakeholder plurality offered an alternative statement of corporate ideology that could shape leader behavior and decision making:

The Chief Executive Officer (CEO) who worries only about paying dividends to stockholders, or increasing the value of their equity by earnings per share and stock price increases, is sure to be a prime candidate for unemployment through takeover. Of course, if the Price/Earnings ratio is high enough, the chances of takeover will be greatly diminished, and we see that some CEOs have emphasized the P/E ratio at the expense of making needed investments in the future.[55]

"The stakeholder concept," Freeman insisted, "provides a new way of thinking about strategic management – that is, how a corporation can and should set and implement direction."[56]

I refer to this corporate ideology as stakeholder *plurality*, using pluralism in the sense of the denial of a single, elite, and undisputed source of power and influence.[57] Instead, competing groups (interest groups, in a political sense) vie for a distribution of rewards and benefits. System stability is achieved not through imposed order or forced consensus, but through a process of piloting among those varied and at times competing interests. In this sense, leadership became an act of navigation.

In stakeholder plurality, "the interests of all stakeholders are of *intrinsic value*," wrote Thomas Donaldson and Lee Preston. "That is, each group of stakeholders merits consideration for its own sake and not merely because of its ability to further the interests of some other group, such as shareholders."[58] In a sharp contrast to stakeholder primacy, Donaldson and Preston held that under stakeholder plurality "there is no prima facie priority of one set of interests and benefits over another."[59] Rejecting the ideological position of Adolf Berle, Milton Friedman, and Alfred Rappaport, stakeholder pluralists insisted that shareholders should not be granted preferred status.

For stakeholder pluralists, the tenets of Smith's invisible hand of unfettered economic interests no longer applied. Smith assumed, argued Robin Marris and Dennis Mueller, the existence of "atomistic competition, which in turn held that the system was decentralized and that no competitor was large relative to the others," a precondition that was already under stress in 1776.[60] The ensuing Industrial Revolution changed the playing field significantly. Corporations had the heft and political clout to "internalize the benefits and externalize the costs of their actions."[61] Lower costs achieved through such time-honored devices as low labor wages and insufficient attention to health and welfare would simply be transferred to society at large. It was time, Freeman insisted, to recalibrate the ideology of corporations.

A vital distinction – and a key ideological building bloc – arose over the question of who owns the corporation. Shareholder primacy was built on the assertion that shareholders did, thus providing them with a unique claim on the attention of executive leadership. To advocates of stakeholder plurality, however, this was a legal fiction. Shareholders did *not* own the corporation. What shareholders owned were stocks; no more, no less.

Share ownership, to be sure, came with specific although limited contractual rights. Mainly, shareholders elected directors and, after passage of the Sarbanes-Oxley Act, engaged in nonbinding "say on pay" votes. "In this sense," Lynn Stout wrote, "stockholders are not different from bondholders, suppliers, and employees. All have contractual relationships with the corporate entity."[62]

If not shareholders, who then owned the corporation? To whom were corporate leaders ultimately accountable? No one owned the firm, in the stakeholder plurality ideology. "*Corporations are independent legal entities that own themselves,* just as human beings own themselves," said Stout.[63] The ultimate obligation of executives was to the corporation itself as a real entity, "an autonomous legal person."[64] It was a *social* entity at that, one created and empowered by the state and bearing reciprocal responsibilities.[65]

With shareholders removed as owners of the corporation, the fundamentals of agency theory changed dramatically. Donald Margotta insisted that Jensen and Meckling got the principal-agent relationship wrong by misidentifying the principal. Managers were agents, to be sure, but of the corporation itself, not of shareholders.[66] Steven Wallman pointed out that state laws recognize that corporations retain their own identity. Fiduciary responsibility demands that corporate directors consider the best interests of the corporation, a far different concept than the maximization of shareholder wealth.[67]

The stakeholder plurality ideology fit well with a commitment within some elements of the corporate community to sustainability and the "triple bottom line": an expression of the stakeholder plurality concept of corporate ideology that seeks an accounting of economic, environmental, and social outcomes.[68] "*Corporate citizenship,*" wrote David Cooperrider and Ronald Fry, "*is about attention to multiple, external and internal stakeholders, and relating with them in ways that foster enduring and innovative partnerships.*" For these authors, Freeman's stakeholder theory not only allowed but obliged business executives to navigate their organizations toward sustainability.[69]

Pressure on business executives to address the social impact of their companies' activities had been increasing since 1984, when an India-based subsidiary of Union Carbide experienced an environmental, social, and economic disaster. A chemical leak from its plant in Bhopal was widely considered to be the worst industrial catastrophe in history. It sparked a succession of international organizations, led by the United

Nations, to seek an appropriate balance between the economic requirement for development and growth, social needs for human dignity and
rights, and environmental needs for sustainability.[70]

Another less dramatic turning point in the rising demand for corporate environmental responsibility occurred in 1993 when Paul Hawken,
cofounder of Smith & Hawken's garden supply company, published *The
Ecology of Commerce*. "Quite simply," Hawken wrote, "our business practices are destroying life on earth." Business had been handed a "blank
check" to ignore its social responsibilities, but was also uniquely positioned to implement solutions. To forge a path forward, business leaders
needed to follow a "third way" between promoting growth and enhancing
the planet.[71]

Advocates of stakeholder plurality agreed that their ideology failed to
provide a specific algorithm that can be used to apply to "day-to-day
managerial decision-making."[72] However, neither was shareholder value
a precisely defined term, they responded.[73] It was, rather, a "rhetoric
which circulates widely and a thematic which can be variably invoked as
cause, consequence or justification."[74]

Thomas Donaldson and Thomas Dunfree suggested that the basis for
stakeholder plurality could be located not in any particular combination
of metrics but rather in the intricacies of the "implicit understanding" that
"bind industries, companies, and economic systems into moral communities." The specific terms of this contract are flexible and up for regular
reconsideration. However, the authors added, an ethical commitment to
"hypernorms" – deep moral values resting on a sense of right and wrong,
"grounded in consent," and "buttressed by the rights of individual members to voice and exit" – defines the contours of the terms.[75]

Donaldson and Dunfree asserted a universal set of principles that
define ethical behavior. In their view, ethics – at last at a meta-level – tran-
scends ideology. But the specifics by which ethical behavior is enacted
will differ depending on prevailing ideology. That is a point made by
George Lodge in the second issue of *Journal of Business Ethics*. There are
universal moral proscriptions, he agreed, but "their application, definition and institutionalization provoke disagreement and vary according to
time and place." The definition of responsible behavior "is the product
of definite social arrangements."[76] Resistance to and questioning of an
existing social order can also be ethical and will typically be embedded
in an ideology at odds with the prevailing definitions of end goals.

That's a tricky balancing act between asserting universal moral principles and recognizing the impact of ideology on the enactment of those
principles. Focus on leadership ethics became a much-addressed topic in
the 1990s and then exploded in the early 21st century, driven in part by

the highly publicized corporate scandals at companies including Enron, Arthur Andersen (those two were really the same scandal), Tyco, and WorldCom.[77]

Much of the literature on ethical leadership placed its definition of ethical behavior firmly in the stakeholder plurality camp. Truly effective ethical leaders are motivated by a concern for "others," argued Rabindra Kanungo and Manuel Mendonca in *Ethical Dimensions of Leadership*. In that view, "others" embraced a plurality of stakeholder interests.[78] But it was a bit of a reach to claim ethical concerns as the exclusive domain of stakeholder pluralists. Shareholder primacy advocates believed equally that they were embracing an ethical view of corporate responsibility. In his *New York Times* article, remember, Milton Friedman, agreed that "responsible" leaders were accountable to others. Within his ideology, others meant shareholders, not stakeholders.

What was unequivocal was that the duties and responsibilities of corporate leaders varied dramatically, depending on which corporate ideology those leaders embraced. The admonition to assume a pragmatic stance toward methodology and a consensus on facts ignored (or implicitly denied) this basic truth. All businesses operate within an ideological framework. The choices leaders make are significantly constrained by that ideology.

Looking Backward/Looking Forward

As the two leading capitalist corporate ideologies, shareholder primacy and stakeholder plurality defined the scope of discretion that impacts the decision making and action of corporate leaders. Under shareholder primacy, executives shift their focus toward cost-cutting and improved margins, stock buybacks to drive up share price, and revenue growth.[79] Corporate governance seeks to ensure that these goals are built into metrics of performance, evaluation, and compensation. CEOs are hired, evaluated, compensated, and even fired based on their capacity to deliver on shareholder value. And the impact ripples out from the corporation to society at large as the financial markets pressure governments to spend less and, more specifically, borrow less in order to prevent inflationary pressures. Simultaneously, cost cuts that work to the benefit of shareholders are increasingly passed on to government and, through taxation, the general population.

Stakeholder plurality offers a profoundly different view of the role of leaders. As officers of public corporations, leaders must always exercise their fiduciary responsibility. Under stakeholder plurality, that responsibility demands that leaders be responsive to multiple stakeholders, including but not limited to shareholders. The task of the leader, then, is to act on behalf of the corporation as a whole by keeping the relationships among stakeholders in balance and resolving conflicts when they arise. In seeking to navigate through multiple interests, corporate leaders serve only one "master": the corporation itself.

Both ideologies make assertions about what "should be" in the business organization. These assertions are, in turn, embedded in a system of overlapping structures, processes, metrics, and evaluations. For shareholder primacy, the core assertion is that the corporation is owned by the shareholder and should therefore be operated on behalf of the shareholder. For stakeholder plurality, it is that the corporation is an independent entity that has a social responsibility to a large array of stakeholders, none of which possesses a senior claim on value.

By adopting shareholder primacy, leaders seem to be accepting a single, all-important metric of effectiveness. All of their actions, including the recruitment, development, and selection of future leaders, would seem to be based entirely on an individual's capacity to deliver those results. But what happens when an individual's capacity is judged not on specific performance criteria but on other factors? How does bias shape the leadership discourse, and to what extent does the discourse shape bias?

NOTES

1 The term "sublime myth" is borrowed from Jonathan Macey, "Sublime Myths: An Essay in Honor of the Shareholder Value Myth and the Tooth Fairy," *Texas Law Review* 91 (2013), 911–24.

2 The authors distinguish a third category, "charismatic" leadership. See Katrina Bedell-Avers et al., "Charismatic, Ideological, and Pragmatic Leaders: An Examination of Leader-Leader Interactions," *Leadership Quarterly* 20 (2009), 299–315; Samuel L. Hunter et al., "First and Ten Leadership: A Historiometric Investigation of the CIP Leadership Model," *Leadership Quarterly* 22 (2011), 70–91; Michael D. Mumford and Judy R. Van Doom, "The Leadership of Pragmatism: Reconsidering Franklin in the Age of Charisma," *Leadership Quarterly* 12 (2001), 279–309; Michael D. Mumford et al., "Charismatic, Ideological, and Pragmatic Leadership: Multilevel Influences on Emergence and Performance," *Leadership Quarterly* 19 (2008), 144–60; Michael D. Mumford et al., "The Sources of Leader Violence: A Comparison of Ideological and Non-ideological Leaders," *Leadership Quarterly* 18 (2007), 217–35.

3 Mumford et al., "The Sources of Leader Violence."

4 Ideology, wrote William Mitchell, is "the structure of values and interests that informs any representation of reality." Therefore, there is "no such thing as a position outside ideology." William J.T. Mitchell, *Iconology: Image, Text, Ideology* (Chicago: University of Chicago Press, 1986), 4. On the ideology

of Booker T. Washington and his supposedly pragmatic, "go slow" position, see Pierre Denain, "An Educator's Education: Notes on the Makings of Booker T. Washington's Ideology," in Régis Durand, ed., *Myth and Ideology in American Culture* (Lilli: Centre d'Etudes et de Recherché, 1976), 152–73; Karen J. Ferguson, "Caught in 'No Man's Land': The Negro Cooperative Demonstration Service and the Ideology of Booker T. Washington, 1900–1918," *Agricultural History* 12 (Winter 1998), 33–54; and August Meier, "Negro Class Struggle and Ideology in the Age of Booker T. Washington," *Pylon* 23 (1962), 256–66.

5 Rob B. Briner et al., "Evidence-Based Management: Concept Cleanup Time?" *Academy of Management Perspectives* 23 (2009), 19–32; Mark Learmonth and Nancy Harding, "Evidence-Based Management: The Very Idea," *Public Administration* 84 (2006), 245–66; Jeffrey Pfeffer and Robert I. Sutton, "Profiting from Evidence-Based Management," *Strategy & Leadership* 34 (2006), 35–42; Denise M. Rousseau, "Is There Such a Thing as 'Evidence-Based Management'?" *Academy of Management Review* 31 (2006), 256–69.

6 Pfeffer and Sutton, "Profiting from Evidence-Based Management," 41.

7 For a critique of the epistemology behind evidence-based management, see Dennis Tourish, "'Evidence Based Management' or 'Evidence Oriented Organizing'? A Critical Realist Perspective," *Organization* 20 (March 2013), 173–92.

8 Svetozar Stojanović, "From Ideology to Pragmatism," *Society* 25 (May–June 1988), 24.

9 Macey, "Sublime Myths," 911–12. Rejection of ideology by academics was especially pronounced in the aftermath of World War II and in the midst of the Cold War. Sociologist Edward Shills denounced ideologues of both the left and the right because, he insisted, they inherently "exhibit dichotomous, 'black-white' thinking and have little patience for the compromise, bargaining, and instrumentalism characteristic of pluralistic democracies." Shills was part of an "end of ideology" school of sociology most famously articulated by Daniel Bell. See Bell, *The End of Ideology: On the Exhaustion of Political Ideas in the Fifties* (New York: Free Press, 1962); Shills, "Ideology and Civility: On the Politics of the Intellectual," *Sewanee Review* 66 (1958), 450–80. For a counterargument, see Chaim I Waxman, *The End of Ideology Debate* (New York: Funk & Wagnalls, 1969).

10 George C. Lodge, *The New American Ideology* (New York: Alfred A. Knopf, 1977), 9.

11 Frederick J. Tuner, *The Frontier in American History* (New York: H. Holt, 1920). Turner's frontier thesis was first presented as "The Significance of the Frontier in American History" at a meeting of the American Historical Association at the 1893 Chicago World's Fair. His argument was quickly and fundamentally challenged. For a review of the debate, see George R. Taylor, *The Turner Thesis: Concerning the Role of the Frontier in American History* (Lexington: Heath, 1971).

12 My discussion of the evolution of the term "ideology" comes from Michael Freeden, *Ideology: A Very Short Introduction* (Oxford: Oxford University Press, 2003); Emmet Kennedy, "Ideology from Destutt to Marx," *Journal of the*

History of Ideas 40 (July–September 1979), 353–68; Emmett Kennedy and Vincent Geoghegan, "Ideology and Utopia," *Journal of Political Ideologies* 9 (2004), 123–38; George Lichtheim, "The Concept of Ideology," *History and Theory* 4 (1965), 164–95; and Michel Wieviorka, "An Old Theme Revisited: Sociology and Ideology," *Comparative Sociology* 2 (2003), 510–21. De Tracy is quoted in Kennedy, "Ideology from Destutt to Marx," 354–5.

13 John T. Jost, "Negative Illusions: Conceptual Clarification and Psychological Evidence Concerning False Consciousness," *Political Psychology* 16 (1995), 397–424.

14 Paul Lagassé, *Columbia Encyclopedia* (New York: Columbia University Press, 2000), 1090.

15 William James, *Pragmatism and Other Writings* (New York: Penguin Books, 1907/2000), 25.

16 Ibid., 27.

17 Nietzsche quoted in George M. Frankfurter and Elton G. McGoun, "Ideology and the Theory of Financial Economics," *Journal of Economic Behavior & Organization* 39 (1999), 159.

18 Adorno, *Authoritarian Personality*.

19 Cornelis Disco, "Critical Theory as Ideology of the New Class," *Theory and Society* 8 (1979), 159–214; George M. Frankfurter and Elton G. McGoun, "Ideology and the Theory of Financial Economics," *Journal of Economic Behavior and Organization* 39 (1999), 159–77.

20 Quoted in John A. Byrne, *Chainsaw: The Notorious Career of Al Dunlap in the Era of Profit at Any Price* (New York: HarperCollins, 1999), xiv–xv.

21 Albert J. Dunlap, *Mean Business: How I Save Bad Companies and Make Good Companies Great* (New York: Simon and Schuster, 1996), ix.

22 www.unfi.com/about-us.

23 Ingalill Holmberg and Lars Stannegård, "Leadership Voices: The Ideology of 'The New Economy,'" *Leadership* 1 (2005), 357.

24 John T. Jost and Orsolya Hunyady, "Antecedents and Consequences of System-Justifying Ideologies," *Current Directions in Psychological Science* 14 (2005), 260–65.

25 Dahl, "The Concept of Power"; Lukes, *Power*; Jon K. Maner and Nicole L. Mead, "The Essential Tension between Leadership and Power: When Leaders Sacrifice Group Goals for the Sake of Self-Interest," *Journal of Personality and Social Psychology* 99 (2010), 482–97; Jojanneke Van der Toorn et al., "More than Air: Outcome Dependence, System Justification, and the Perceived Legitimacy of Authority Figures," *Journal of Experimental Social Psychology* 47 (2011), 127–38.

26 Lodge, *The New American Ideology*.

27 For a review of the literature on the varieties of capitalism, see David Coates, ed., *Varieties of Capitalism, Varieties of Approaches* (London: Palgrave, 2005); Peter A. Hall and David W. Soskice, *Varieties of Capitalism: The Institutional Foundations of Comparative Advantage* (New York: Oxford University Press, 2001); and Mira Wilkins, "Multinational Enterprises and the Varieties of Capitalism," *Business History Review* 84 (2010), 638–48.

28 Lodge, *The New American Ideology*.

29 Alfred C. Rappaport, *Creating Shareholder Value: The New Standard for Business Performance* (New York: Free Press, 1986), xiii.

30 Henry Hansmann and Reinier Kraakman, "The End of History for Corporate Law," *Georgetown Law Review* 89 (2001), 441.

31 Lynn Stout, *The Shareholder Value Myth: How Putting Shareholders First Harms Investors, Corporations, and the Public* (San Francisco: Berrett-Koehler Publishers, 2012). For a treatment of the historical context of the Berle/Dodd debate, see Richard S. Kirkendall, "A.A. Berle, Jr.: Student of the Corporation, 1917–1932," *Business History Review* 35 (Spring 1961), 43–58.

32 Adolf A. Berle and Gardiner Means, *The Modern Corporation and Private Property* (New Brunswick: Transaction Publishers, 1932/1991).

33 Adolf A. Berle, "Corporate Powers as Powers in Trust," *Harvard Law Review* 45 (May 1931), 1049.

34 E. Merrick Dodd, "For Whom Are Corporate Managers Trustees?" *Harvard Law Review* 45 (May 1932), 1157.

35 George E. Bates, "The Board of Directors," *Harvard Business Review* 19 (1940), 72–87.

36 Arch Patton, "How to Appraise Executive Performance," *Harvard Business Review* 38 (1960), 63–70.

37 James Burnham, *The Managerial Revolution* (New York: John Day, 1941). By calling attention to the newly emergent managerial elite, Burnham was, in the words of critic Alfred Kazin, "reaching American business executives, scientists, and the technocratic elite with the news that they were the leaders of the future." Economist John Kenneth Galbraith added that *The Managerial Revolution*, more so than Berle and Means' *Modern Corporation and Private Property* "changed people's minds on the nature of the modern corporation." Kazin and Galbraith are quoted in Paul Le Blanc, "From Revolutionary Intellectual to Conservative Master-Thinker: The Anti democratic Odyssey of James Burnham," *Left History* 3 (April 1995), 63.

38 The terms "stockholder" and "shareholder" can be used interchangeably, although for the past several decades, "shareholder" has been the preferred label.

39 Milton Friedman, "The Social Responsibility of Business Is to Increase Its Profits," *New York Times Magazine* 32 (September 13, 1970), 33.

40 Ibid., 122.

41 This was 1976, the same year that Friedman received the Nobel Prize in Economics. The award to Friedman did not acknowledge his free-market / antisocial responsibility position. Instead, the Royal Swedish Academy noted Friedman's "achievements in the fields of consumption analysis, monetary history and theory, and for his demonstration of the complexity of stabilization policy."

42 Quoted in Michael C. Jensen and William H. Meckling, "Theory of the Firm: Managerial Behavior, Agency Costs and Ownership Structure," *Journal of Financial Economics* 3 (1976), 305.

43 William Lazonick and Mary O'Sullivan, "Maximizing Shareholder Value: A New Ideology for Corporate Governance," *Economy and Society* 29 (2000), 13–35.

44 Frank Dobbin and Dirk Zorn, "Corporate Malfeasance and the Myth of Shareholder Value," *Political Power and Social Theory* 17 (2005), 182.
45 Gerald F. Davis and Tracy A. Thompson, "A Social Movement Perspective on Corporate Control," *Administrative Science Quarterly* 39 (1994), 141–73.
46 Julie Froud et al., "Shareholder Value and Financialization: Consultancy Promises, Management Moves," *Economy and Society* 29 (2000), 80–110.
47 Ibid.
48 Khurana, "The Curse of the Superstar CEO."
49 Andrew L. Yarrow, "The Big Postwar Story," *Journalism History* 32 (2006), 58–76.
50 Morton Horwitz makes the argument that legal doctrine evolved along with market capitalism throughout the 20th century. Horwitz, *The Transformation of American Law, 1780–1860* (Cambridge: Harvard University Press, 1976).
51 Robert Boyer, "Is a Finance Led Growth Regime a Viable Alternative to Fordism? A Preliminary Analysis," *Economy and Society* 20 (2000), 111–45.
52 Ibid., 118.
53 Freeman, *Strategic Management*.
54 E. Edward Freeman, "Stakeholder Theory of the Firm," in L.P. Hartman, ed., *Perspectives in Business Ethics* (Boston: McGraw-Hill Irwin, 2002), 174.
55 Freeman, *Strategic Management*, 9.
56 Ibid., vi.
57 This definition of plurality is from Nelson W. Polsby, *Political Innovation in America: The Politics of Policy Initiation* (New Haven: Yale University Press, 1984).
58 Thomas Donaldson and Lee E. Preston, "The Stakeholder Theory of the Corporation: Concepts, Evidence, and Implications," *Academy of Management Review* 20 (1995), 67.
59 Ibid., 68.
60 Robin Marris and Dennis C. Mueller, "The Corporation, Competition, and the Invisible Hand," *Journal of Economic Literature* 18 (March 1980), 32.
61 Freeman, "Stakeholder Theory of the Firm," 184.
62 Stout, *The Shareholder Value Myth*, 37.
63 Ibid.
64 Jean-Phillippe Robé, "Science vs. Ideology: A Comment on Lynn Stout's New Thinking on 'Shareholder Primacy,'" *Accounting, Economics, and Law* 2 (2012), 4.
65 In the 2010 Citizens United case, the U.S. Supreme Court struck down legislated restrictions on direct spending by corporations and labor unions in political campaigns. As independent entities, the court held, corporations were protected by the same free speech guarantees allowed to other persons. They were, in other words, independent legal entities.
66 Donald C. Margotta, "The Legal Meaning of Agency and Its Implications for Finance Theory," *Journal of Applied Business Research* 6 (2011), 34–39.
67 Steven M.H. Wallman, "The Proper Interpretation of Corporate Constituency Statutes and Formulation of Director Duties," *Stetson Law Review* 21 (1991), 163–96.
68 Andrew W. Savitz, *The Triple Bottom Line* (San Francisco: Wiley, 2006).

69 David Cooperrider and Ronald Fry, "Corporate Citizenship at the Core: It Is Still about Stakeholder Engagement and Relational Practices," *Journal of Corporate Citizenship* 47 (Autumn 2012), 3–7.

70 This history is traced in John Elkington, "Towards the Sustainable Corporation: Win-Win-Win Strategies for Sustainable Development," *California Management Review* 36 (Winter 1994), 90–100. Elkington is either the originator of the phrase "triple bottom line" or certainly the popularizer of the concept. See Elkington, *Cannibals with Forks: The Triple Bottom Line of 21ˢᵗ Century Business* (London: Capstone, 1997). Some scientists argue that the Triple Bottom Line is inherently delusional and nonsustainable in that it assumes that growth and ecological concerns can be reconciled. For an overview of this and other sustainability debates, see John Robinson, "Squaring the Circle? Some Thoughts on the Idea of Sustainable Development," *Ecological Economics* 48 (2004), 369–84.

71 Paul Hawken, *The Ecology of Commerce* (New York: Harper Business, 1993), 3.

72 Robert R. Phillips et al., "What Stakeholder Theory Is Not," *Business Ethics Quarterly* 13 (2003), 485.

73 Jack T. Treynor, "The Financial Objective in the Widely Held Corporation," *Financial Analysts Journal* 37 (1981), 68–71.

74 Froud et al., "Shareholder Value and Financialization," 81.

75 Thomas Donaldson and Thomas W. Dunfee, "Ties That Bind in Business Ethics: Social Contracts and Why They Matter," *Journal of Banking and Finance* 26 (2002), 1854, 1857, 1859.

76 George C. Lodge, "The Connection between Ethics and Ideology," *Journal of Business Ethics* 1 (1982), 85.

77 For examples of the important pre-Enron work, see Bernard M. Bass and Paul Steidlmeier, "Ethics, Character, and Authentic Transformational Leadership Behavior," *Leadership Quarterly* 10 (Summer 1999), 181–218; Joanne B. Ciulla, *Ethics: The Heart of Leadership* (Westport: Quorum Books, 1998); Marcus W. Dickson et al., "An Organizational Climate Regarding Ethics: The Outcome of Leader Values and the Practices that Reflect Them," *Leadership Quarterly* 12 (Summer 2001), 197–218; Harold B. Jones, Jr., "The Ethical Leader: An Ascetic Construct," *Journal of Business Ethics* 14 (1995), 867–74; Joseph C. Rost, "Leadership: A Discussion about Ethics," *Business Ethics Quarterly* 5 (1995), 129–42.

78 See, for example, Mark Bandsuch et al., "Rebuilding Stakeholder Trust in Business: An Examination of Principle-Centered Leadership and Organizational Transparency in Corporate Governance," *Business and Society Review* 113 (2008), 99–112; Refik Culpan and John Trussel, "Applying the Agency and Stakeholder Theories to the Enron Debacle: An Ethical Perspective," *Business and Society Review* 110 (2005), 59–76; Craig E. Johnson, *Meeting the Ethical Challenges of Leadership: Casting Light or Shadow* (Thousand Oaks: Sage, 2001); Rabindra Kanungo and Manuel Mendonca, *Ethical Dimensions of Leadership* (Thousand Oaks: Sage, 1996). I'll admit to being uncertain about precisely what is meant by the phrase "ethically effective leadership." The prevailing understanding is a leader who "sets the tone and builds the

culture of an organization to effectively develop and empower the people in the organization so that products, services, and mission are promoted, enhanced, and sustained while building up our civil society." In addition to seemingly promoting a rather magical view of the impact of organizational leaders, the author of this definition added parenthetically "(context and culture appropriate)." Exactly! Alex J. Pinto, "Ethics and Leadership," *International Journal of Discourse and Governance* 6 (2009), 281.

79 In May 2015 the *Wall Street Journal* noted that corporate stock buybacks had been increasing steadily over the previous decade and were on a pace to reach $1.2 trillion for the year. Dan Strumpf, "Stock Buybacks Hit New Records," *Wall Street Journal,* May 7, 2015, accessed at http://blogs.wsj.com/moneybeat/2015/05/07/stock-buybacks-hit-new-records/.

5 (White) Men Named John and the Persistence of Bias

A 2015 Upshot column in the *New York Times* ran the headline, "Fewer Women Run Big Companies than Men Named John." Among the chief executives of America's top corporations, 5.3 percent were, in fact, men named John. On the other hand, only 4.1 percent were women. There were also more CEOs named David than women. This was not a good sign.[1]

I include *white* in the chapter title and place it in parentheses for a reason. Unmentioned in the article was the race of the CEOs. That's not unusual; leadership discourse often excludes race. A review of the indices of two prominent business leadership textbooks, for instance, finds extensive listings under "gender" but *none* under "race" or "ethnicity."[2] Still, a CNN *Money* article just months earlier than the *Times'* column noted that, with the January 2015 resignation of McDonald's CEO Don Thompson, there were only five black CEOs at America's 500 biggest companies. Four men (none named "John," by the way) and one woman, Xerox's Ursula Burns, made up that group.[3]

This reality points to an underlying truth: think leader, think white male.[4]

Without minimizing the continued impact of individual prejudice, I accept Pushkala Prasad and Albert Mill's assertion that institutional "resistance can be distinguished from *individual* resistance by the structural potency of the problem."[5] Institutional resistance to women and racioethnic minorities as leaders may grow out of overt and intended acts of prejudice; but not always.[6] Gertrude Ezorsky made the argument that even if the intention of race neutral policies are to be helpful and are not the outcome of overt racism, the fact that they have a negative impact on unfairly disadvantaged racial groups makes them institutionally racist in their consequences. Individual and institutional racism exist in symbiotic kinship, enabling and reinforcing each other.[7]

The focus of this chapter, then, is on institutional resistance – what Herminia Ibarra and colleagues referred to as the "unseen barriers" – to the entry of members of particular groups, especially women and racio-ethnic minorities, into the ranks of executive leadership.[8]

In terms of leadership, that resistance manifests itself in two ways. First, popular notions of what it means to be a leader – to take charge, act decisively – slant toward gendered notions of masculinity. And sec-ond, women and racioethnic minorities are often disadvantaged in the construction of a pipeline: a career ladder that, from the outset of one's employment, offers the potential for upward mobility in the corporate hierarchy. The way in which institutional resistance becomes manifest is different for women and racioethnic minorities, and for women who are also racioethnic minorities, but remains a potent force for all outsider groups.

Labeling Outsiders

De jure barriers to equality have existed in the United States since its colonial founding. The legally supported institution of slavery, the denial of property and voting rights to women and nonwhite males, the legal segregation of races, the separate and unequal educational system, and the barring of entry into many professions all stood as external signs of institutional resistance.[9] Even after the fading of such legal barriers, vigorous resistance remained.

Whether considering women leaders, black leaders, black women lead-ers, or any other racioethnic group, we are focusing on groups that have been labeled *outsider*, individuals who have been separated from the majority of white men who hold positions of power in corporate America. Any acknowledgment of institutional resistance to the advancement of groups labeled as outsiders rests on an assumption, often unstated but vital to appreciate. Organizations are not neutral, objective, fully open configurations. Individuals are not considered solely on the basis of their potential or capacity to contribute to organizational outcomes.

An outsider designation carries symbolic weight, a weight that becomes real in its consequences. That was the point made by the sociological school of symbolic interactionism. Howard Becker titled his 1973 study of social deviance – as a sociologist, he defined deviance not in moral terms but rather as a label attached by the dominant social group to those who reside outside of that group – *Outsiders*.[10] The act of labeling works to insert distance.

A number of researchers referred to that distance as the empathy gap. "Judging the reasonableness of people's arguments and sympathiz-ing with their mental and emotional states," wrote Jeneen Interlandi in the *New York Times,* demands empathy. As *intra*group cohesion grows stronger, *inter*group gaps widen. The challenge of creating cross-group empathy, and of finding some common ground between various group identities, has proved far more daunting than many had hoped. "While social and economic factors account for some of what divides us into warring camps," noted Interlandi, "psychologists since Freud have suspected that something more fundamental is at work."[11]

A group of cognitive neuroscientists at the Massachusetts Institute of Technology set out to map the brain's empathy pathways in search of an answer, and, they hoped, a solution. "Why does understanding what someone else feels not always translate to being concerned with their welfare?" Interlandi asked. "Why is empathizing across groups so much more difficult? And what, if anything, can be done to change that calculus?"[12] Maybe the intractability of group biases and the resulting empathy gap are embedded in brain patterns. Perhaps understanding that process would help reduce intergroup conflict. These were the issues on the researchers' agenda.

That research still has miles to go. It is possible that enhanced understanding of neural activity will eventually offer important insights into individual cognition. But intragroup cohesion and intergroup differentiation serves a larger ideological purpose, one that resides not in the individual brain but in the power dynamics of society.

The words used to characterize others matter. Gender, race, and other labels, noted Cynthia Fuchs Epstein, work to preserve in-group advantage. "Dichotomous systems of thought serve the existing power structures and organization of society by reinforcing the notion of the 'we' and the 'not we,' the deserving and the undeserving."[13] To overcome that outsider status requires a shedding of the deviance label through assimilation of dominant group norms.

In many ways, the challenge of assimilation sits at the heart of leadership in business organizations. Particularly when leadership is associated with access to hierarchical power and authority, a high degree of assimilation is a baseline requirement. Prasad and Mills critically assessed business organizations as "extraordinarily monocultural entities."[14]

Although I do not find that observation to be as axiomatically problematic as did Prasad and Mills – a homogeneous culture aligned with strategy creates a level of control required of performance and *may* also offer a respectful voice to diverse ideas and approaches – the underlying impact of the observation has a profound impact on the exercise of leadership and the willingness to diversify the leadership pipeline. Research conducted by Lauren Rivera suggested that hiring and promoting based on some loosely defined measure of "cultural fit" often deteriorates into an assessment of personal similarities. A homogeneous culture may enhance organizational effectiveness, but also has the potential to become "a new form of discrimination that keeps demographic and cultural diversity down."[15]

Labels locate individuals and groups within a power and status hierarchy.[16] When we refer to a "black CEO" or a "women CEO," our language falls into the same trap. White male CEOs are simply "CEOs," thought to be "unraced" or "ungendered" and therefore universal. When the label "black" or "woman" or any other outsider group is applied *by* insiders *to* outsiders, a sense of special interest, nonneutrality, even suspicion is suggested.[17]

Gender and race are not the only two outsider labels that have constricted potential for advancement. Opportunities for upward mobility among lesbian, gay, bisexual, and transgendered employees, and institutional resistance to such mobility, have entered the discourse.[18] Women and racioethnic minorities are among the groups that face hurdles deeply rooted in history, in national culture, in usually apparent physical differences, in individual bigotry, and in institutionalized resistance.

Writing in 1973, sociologist Cynthia Fuchs Epstein described sex and race as "dominant" statuses. The civil rights movement of the early 1960s had, by then, evolved into a more militant assertion of power and call for liberation. By the late-1960s/early 1970s, women activists joined these demands. Protests at the 1968 "Miss America Pageant" – condemning the pageant as treating women as "sex objects" – brought national attention to the women's liberation movement.[19] A spate of books analyzed what was called "sexual politics"; among them, Shulamith Firestone's *The Dialectic of Sex*, Robin Morgan's *Sisterhood Is Powerful*, and Kate Millett's *Sexual Politics*, all of which appeared in 1970.[20]

Epstein joined the two movements together, referring to both sex and race as "visible and immutable" identities.[21] A focus on these dominant statuses, then, helps illuminate the nature of institutional resistance. The matter to be addressed is how institutional resistance undermines the opportunities of members of those groups. Why are there still so many white men named John sitting at the CEO desk? Let's start that inquiry by looking at the discourse on gender.

Gender-Based Institutional Resistance

For an opening, I would like to turn to a 2002 article in which consultant Sylvia Ann Hewlett sought to explode the "myth" of "having it all." That myth, in Hewlett's view, held that women could have both an effective executive career and "motherhood." However, "when it comes to career and fatherhood," Hewlett suggested, "high-achieving men don't have to deal with difficult trade-offs." Surveying an elite group of women executives, Hewlett found that "for many women, the brutal demands of ambitious careers, the asymmetries of male-female relationships, and the difficulties of bearing children late in life conspire to crowd out the possibility of having children."[22] Her focus was on biological reproduction.

There were important insights in the article, including the potency of institutional resistance at work against women who choose parenting.[23] There were also limitations. Hewlett's presumption was that men *could* have it all. They faced, in her telling, no trade-off. Given the gendered nature of home life and home work, men were seen as not needing to sacrifice or strive to achieve a home/work – often presented as a private/public sphere – balance. Men who wanted children, we were informed, had children, often waiting until later in life with younger partners. Women, conversely, began to approach menopause in their forties and thus faced a more time-constrained reproductive pressure in Hewlett's view.[24]

Hewlett was wrong. Men do make choices and trade-offs. Pressures to assimilate, to fit in, have long shaped the responses of men in the corporate setting. Men seeking upward mobility in the newly emerging post-World War II corporate order, for instance, faced their own challenge. The assimilationist pressure of that era – what was often referred to as outer-directedness or conformity – attracted an extraordinary degree of critical attention.[25]

In her study of leadership development efforts at General Electric, Karen Ward Mahar called attention to the pressure placed on up-and-coming male executives to conform to an exaggerated concept of masculinity. Executive men were praised for enjoying "hunting, fishing, good food and drink, good stories and other things men like," including "rare steaks and roast beef."[26] Regardless of whether they did enjoy these conspicuous accoutrements of postwar masculinity, they would need to be *seen* as a "man's man."[27]

Assimilation into this hyper-masculine image of corporate executives – driven in no small part by the discomfort with homosexuality that pervaded Cold War America – was the price of admission for potential male leaders at General Electric. Not all men were willing or able to fit comfortably into that culture. There was, however, a presumption that men could and should fit in.[28] Women stood outside the barriers of culture.

Men may sacrifice time at home and with their family for the demands of work, or conversely choose involvement with home and family over the requirements of career progression. Men cannot "have it all" in the sense that Hewlett intended. Still, there is no question that in this struggle for balance, men experienced a privileged position at work and an asymmetric set of assumptions at home.[29]

Even when men assumed a greater share of child care responsibility, they responded differently in the public space afforded by work. A kind of "masculine mystique" surrounded tired, overstretched fathers.[30] Unlike women who believed their advancement opportunities would be damaged if they allowed an abundance of their private sphere to spill over into the public work space, men were allowed to claim advantage. These "new men" came to be seen as "*genius warriors, tough guys* who get the job done no matter what." Men who suffered from the strains of private pressures came to be appreciated as heroes in the workplace – at least that was the finding of Marianne Cooper's study of gender culture in Silicon Valley – while women were expected to keep the private sphere private.[31]

Gender and the Leadership Pipeline

A masculine type is not necessarily a man. There is a distinction to be made between the sex of an individual and the gendered role an individual is thought to be exercising. In the context of this discussion, *sex* refers to physical distinctions between men and women. *Gender* is a socially constructed concept, a view of the nature of differences imposed by a male-dominated culture.[32]

In 1977 Erving Goffman wrote an essay on sex and gender, "The Arrangement between the Sexes." Decades earlier, Simone de Beauvoir had associated gender distinctions with the concept of the *other*. Otherness, she offered in *The Second Sex*, was a fundamental category of human thought. "Man never thinks of himself without thinking about the Other."[33] Constructing the One required labeling the Other.

Goffman echoed de Beauvoir's argument that gendered thinking reflected an oppositional paradigm. The constructs of masculinity and femininity were labels not predetermined by physical differences. "More to the point," Goffman insisted, "for these very slight biological differences – compared to all other differences – to be identified as the grounds for the kinds of social consequences felt to follow understandably from them requires a vast, integrated body of social beliefs and practices, sufficiently cohesive and all-embracing to warrant for its analysis the resurrection of unfashionable functional paradigms."[34] Gendered language adheres to a pattern that dates back centuries.

The concept of femininity as an oppositional construct to masculinity reaches back to the Middle Ages.[35] Writers, most notably Geoffrey Chaucer and John Gower, invented the term "femininity" in response to a newly emerging social and economic role being played by women.[36]

Concepts of "manhood" already existed, according to medieval literature scholar Tara Williams, and women were placed in categories relative to their relationship with men: maiden, wife, mother, and widow, with allowances made for "the sinful Eve."

The bubonic plague, which traveled westward from Asia to Europe in the early 14th century, wiped out a large portion of the male population, opening new socioeconomic possibilities for women, particularly wealthy widows. Chaucer and Gower invented a word – *femenye* in Chaucer's "Knight's Tale" – in order to label that new role. It was not a neutral term. Femininity was construed in the negative, as a force to be denied and resisted because of the threat it was seen as posing to the dominance of "manhood."[37]

Words and concepts that serve a purpose stick around, and femininity continued to attract attention and gain refinement. Carl Jung and Sigmund Freud proposed a psychoanalytic theory for the origins of gender distinctions based on attachments and desires in infancy.[38] In the 1930s, reflecting the acceptance of psychoanalysis, masculine-feminine measures found their way into personality tests; first with the Terman-Miles Attitude-Interest Analysis Tests (1936), and then the popular Minnesota Multiphasic Personality Inventory (1943).[39] All made the assumption that gender was a single dimension, either masculine or feminine, and rooted in sex-based physical distinctions.

At the same time, anthropologist Margaret Mead challenged these rigid gender lines. Her findings from "primitive societies" reported that significant gender differences were not inherently connected to sex. Rather, they were socially constructed and highly fluid notions, or temperaments.[40] Even those who accepted Mead's findings as valid, however, were able to dismiss the fundamental lesson of social constructionism by insisting they applied only to peripheral primitive societies. "Long before recorded history," wrote Garda Bowman and colleagues, "biological and economic necessity placed women as keeper of the hearth and man as the warrior-hunter in all but a few atypical cultures."[41] That gendered view was taken to be virtually if not strictly universal, driven by biological and economic necessity.

In a Different Voice, psychologist Carol Gilligan's 1982 exploration of gender differences, laid out the masculine and feminine types more fully. The masculine, Gilligan asserted, held a hierarchical and legalistic view of the world and saw responsibility as beginning with the self and then extending to others. In contrast, the feminine saw "the world as a network or web of relationships and is guided in more decision making by a desire to preserve connections." At its core, the feminine idealized attention to others, sought to maintain relationships and interdependencies, and favored personal care over rigid rules and responsibilities.[42] The gendered view of organizational leadership grew from these assumptions.

Rosabeth Moss Kanter's 1977 study of a large American corporation, focused attention on the degree to which a "masculine ethic" defined the organization. Traits associated with effective management coincided with characteristics identified as male: "a tough-minded approach to problems; analytic abilities to abstract and plan; a capacity to set aside personal, emotional considerations in the interest of task accomplishment; and a cognitive superiority in problem-solving and decision-making."[43]

Writing thirteen years later, Joan Acker pushed the argument even further, depicting business organizations as fundamentally gendered constructs. Acker had been concentrating for several decades on the gender bias of organizational research, noting, for instance, the treatment of women and men work groups in the classic Hawthorne studies.[44] She now turned her attention to gendered organizations.

To say that an organization is gendered, explained Acker, "means that advantage and disadvantage, exploitation and control, action and emotion, meaning and identity are patterned through and in terms of a distinction between male and female, masculine and feminine."[45] The processes that unfold within organizations cannot be understood without reference to gender. The underlying logic of corporations, including the very mechanisms intended to ensure gender-blind practices, reflect images of "successful, forceful masculinity."[46]

Barbara Bird and Candida Bush pushed the gendered organization thesis back even further, into the entrepreneurial founding of companies. Literature on business start-ups assumed that the "individual entrepreneur is motivated by achievement and power," is a "driven individual," is motivated solely by economic purpose, and will/should establish a "clear chain of command or hierarchy."[47] In short, the ideal entrepreneur was masculine.

In much of the discourse, the notion of a gendered organization was problematized; a construct that inherently disparaged the other; in this case, the nonmasculine. A gendered organization was a masculine organization in which the grooming of women for leadership positions was discouraged. Part of that resistance emerged from the sexism that resided in the males who served as the gatekeepers of the leadership pipeline.

Are Women Executives People?

In 1965 the *Harvard Business Review* ran the results of a survey under the (presumably ironic) title, "Are Women Executives People?" The role of the *Review* in shaping the discourse is worth paying special attention to. If there exists a quasi-official outlet for the thoughts of America's executive class, the *Review* is it.

Fourteen years after the opening of the Harvard Business School, Dean Wallace B. Donham launched the *Review* with the goal of providing business executives with the "breadth of view so urgently demanded of business administrators in this century."[48] The *Review's* ambition extended beyond providing helpful how-to articles on management techniques.

From its inception, the *Review* took a special role in presenting "the economic and social, the national and international background" that would help shape the thinking and actions of its readers.[49] As a fully owned and operated arm of Harvard University, the *Review* attracted major management theorists from the world of academics and business who mingled with economists and other intellectuals to publish in its issues. By focusing on and analyzing the great questions of the day, the *Review* editors and writers hoped to inform and guide the thoughts and actions of the country's leading business executives.[50]

Forty-one percent of male respondents in the *Review's* 1965 poll self-identified as "anti-women executives." These men argued that women were "a special kind of people with a special place – which is *not* in the ranks of management."[51] A featured quote at the outset of the article captured that attitude: "I probably should be more broad-minded – no pun intended – in exploring the possibilities of women as managers."[52] "Broad" was a dismissive gender term popular in the ring-a-ding culture of 1950s America.[53]

It is hard to imagine that such a poll conducted today would offer the same results or feature such a disparaging quote. Betty Friedan's *Feminine Mystique* had appeared before the *Review's* initial poll and helped focus attention on the role of women in a male society.[54] The legal framework certainly changed after the article.

Two decades later, a follow-up poll found some indication of improvement. "*Today, only 9% of the men and 4% of the women surveyed think that women don't want top jobs. And men, in general, are far more willing to accept women as colleagues and to see them as competent equals.*"[55]

Despite the generally positive spin applied to the 1985 survey results by the authors, not all the findings were encouraging. More than half of the respondents did not think women would ever be accepted wholly in business. Forty-seven percent of males said *they* would be "comfortable" working for a woman, but only 21 percent believed that "men" – that is, men other than themselves – "feel comfortable working for women." Fifty-nine percent of men and 83 percent of women agreed that "a woman has to be exceptional to succeed in business today," and 20 percent of men and 40 percent of women concurred that "the business community will never wholly accept women executives." That 40 percent figure from women represented a drop from 47 percent in the 1965 survey; an improvement, to be sure, but still an indicator of ongoing skepticism and a conviction that "anti-woman executive" attitudes had not disappeared entirely.

Even when organizational leaders expressed values supportive of equal opportunity and diversity, institutional resistance continued to be a factor in suppressing the grooming of women leaders. It was in the early 1970s that Virginia Schein started her stream of pioneering "think manager, think male" work. Her point was that managers of both sexes described requisite managerial characteristics in highly gendered, masculine terms. In casting a wider net beyond the United States, she found evidence of global gender bias, making it difficult for women to reach top jobs in international organizations. And her research, published shortly after the *Review's* follow-up survey results, confirmed that female attitudes had changed significantly more than their male counterparts.[56]

That deeply held and widely shared belief that managers were masculine was only one of many instances of institutionalized resistance that have been recognized in the discourse:

- A number of findings pointed to the relationship between sexually charged workplaces and the resulting hostile work environment on one hand, and a highly gendered company culture on the other. Albert Mills, for example, found a highly gendered and purposefully sexualized culture endemic throughout the airline industry. Male executives used recruitment, selection, supervision, and promotional tools, with the added reinforcement of marketing images, to shape a highly gendered workplace.[57]
- Nancy Adler uncovered a pattern of denying women the opportunities for international placement based on mistaken assumptions about women's reluctance to move overseas and the inaccurately presumed inability of women to operate effectively in some countries.[58]
- Joyce Fletcher highlighted the tendency of much of the contribution made by women in organizations – anticipating problems before they cropped up, working to keep teams functional – to get "disappeared" from performance appraisals and consideration for promotion. That disappearance occurred not because the contributions were ineffective or misaligned with the organization's strategy; they were, in fact, both effective and strategically aligned. Rather, the contributions were rendered invisible "because they are associated with the feminine, relational, or so-called softer side of organizational practice."[59]

- Joan Williams and colleagues noted that work flexibility policies designed by institutions to allow for customized hours for parents were underutilized by women employees because their use created a stigma that resulted in wage penalties, lower performance evaluations, and fewer promotions.[60]
- A major stream of the gendered discourse focused on the inflexibility of organizations in dealing with pregnancy and parenting. A hostile context created by organizations to parenting placed unreasonable and non-task-related demands on employees.[61]
- Even when women leaders were perceived as being effective, they were characterized as doing "unexpectedly" well or as being lucky rather than deserving. That backhanded kind of praise translated into a need for aspiring women leaders to prove themselves repeatedly, and *not* into rewards equal to their male counterparts.[62]
- The engineering culture so dominant in the high-technology industry was singled out by a number of authors for carrying gendered assumptions favoring males as more analytic and less emotional than females and working to the distinct disadvantage of potential women leaders in that vital sector of economic activity.[63]

When women adopted gendered assumptions themselves, the effects could also undermine their passage to leadership positions.

Her Place at the Table

A 1986 *Wall Street Journal* article by Carol Hymowitz and Timothy Schelhardt introduced readers to the concept of the glass ceiling. That image was traceable to a profile two years earlier in which magazine editor Gay Bryant suggested that women reached a certain point in their careers at which a "glass ceiling" presented a barrier, a solid roadblock to women's upward mobility.[64]

As powerful as that metaphor was, authors Alice Eagly and Linda Carli suggested it was misleading. Rather than conceptualizing roadblocks to the advancement of women in organizations as a single, invisible barrier that suddenly asserted itself near the top of the hierarchy, they preferred the image of a labyrinth through which women would be forced to navigate throughout their careers. That labyrinth "contains numerous barriers, some subtle and others quite obvious."[65]

Negotiating the labyrinth presented a complex challenge to women seeking upward mobility in an organizational hierarchy. In 2014's best-selling business book, *Lean In*, Facebook's chief operating officer Sheryl Sandberg suggested that "in addition to the external barriers created by society, women are hindered by barriers that exist within ourselves."[66]

Although Sandberg's formulation underemphasized the obstructions erected and maintained by business organizations themselves, her point that women were disadvantaged by playing the assigned feminine role was important to consider.

We, by whom Sandberg meant women who aspire to executive leadership positions, "hold back in ways both big and small, by lacking self-confidence, by not raising our hands, and by pulling back when we should be leaning in." Gendered assumptions sent "negative messages" to women: saying "it is wrong to be outspoken, aggressive, more powerful than men." Compared to men, "fewer of us aspire to senior positions." Rather than waiting for societal barriers to crumble, women should work proactively at "getting rid of these internal barriers."[67]

The blowback to Sandberg's "lean in" argument was immediate and fierce. Critics argued that she was blaming the victim for internalizing a role enforced by a male-dominated organization, offering individual solutions to institutional problems, speaking to and for a privileged class of professional women, and failing to address issues of social, political, and economic inequality.[68] Nonetheless, her underlying point – that the adaption of a feminine role disadvantages women as they negotiate a path through the labyrinth – represented a significant stream of gender discourse. Deborah Kolb, for instance, inquired into the role of gender in negotiations.

Although Kolb took negotiations as her setting, her focus was much broader than the dynamics that unfold within a well-defined negotiation structure such as a union-management or management-government context. For her, negotiations were a form of discursive formation in which participants sought to create identity.[69] Negotiations marked "the activities involved in designing jobs, doing work, avoiding work, achieving status, and establishing boundaries of authority and responsibility." The stakes ran the gamut "from a change in title and responsibility, to credit for work, support for a project, or the more routine resources for a new hire." Women entered such negotiations disadvantaged, not – in contrast to Sandberg's analysis – because of their individual characteristics, but because of the gendered nature of the workplace.[70] Practices "that appear neutral on their face" nonetheless "result in different experiences for, and treatment of women and men, and for different groups of women and men."[71] For Kolb, these patterns contributed to a "negotiated order" in which an organizational context that privileges some over others was regularly created and recreated.[72]

As women sought leadership positions in organizations, they faced a "fundamental obstacle," Kolb and colleagues noted. "A woman lacks the *presumption of credibility and competence* when she takes on a leadership role," a presumption far more likely to be granted to a man.[73] Their practical advice to women seeking to negotiate the career labyrinth on the way to top leadership positions – gather intelligence, negotiate the backing of key players, amass resources, make sure your contributions are recognized – was less interesting conceptually than their core point. "People *do* make choices. Negotiation skills *can* help structure better choices."[74] Nonetheless, women could work to improve their position within the process of negotiations that help address what Kolb refers to as second-generation biases.

When women take on parenting in a society with clear demarcations for gender roles at home, the discourse becomes even more contested.

Suggesting a "Mommy Track"

Felice Schwartz believed she was being helpful and supportive. When her article, "Management Women and the New Facts of Life," appeared in 1989, she addressed a corporate audience with the intent of helping the largely male gatekeepers see possibilities for women's career advancement.[75]

Schwartz had reason to believe she would be construed as supporting women and their journey through the corporate labyrinth. She had founded the National Scholarship Service and Fund for Negro Students shortly after World War II. Then, in 1962 she created Catalyst, a consulting firm dedicated to advancing women in business. She was still serving as Catalyst's president when the article appeared.

Schwartz never used the term, "mommy track." Nonetheless, her focus was on maternity, which she defined as "childbirth," including the "continuum that begins with an awareness of the ticking of the biological clock, proceeds to the anticipation of motherhood, includes pregnancy, childbirth, physical recuperation, psychological adjustment, and continues on to nursing, bonding, and child rearing."[76] That experience, she argued, reverberated through career interruptions, career plateauing, and turnover.

The piece opened with a statement that Schwartz admitted was "jarring," not the least because, she maintained, it was *true*. "The cost of employing women in management is greater than the cost of employing men." People were reluctant to talk about this supposed truth, but Schwartz believed that organizations and the women they employ would benefit from a thoughtful airing.[77] But just what was the evidence that women "cost more" to employ?

Schwartz cited one study conducted (by whom, it was not clear) within an unnamed company that indicated women were 2.5 times more likely than men to leave management positions. The added cost accrued from the assumption that the time and money put into the

development of these women was wasted in comparison to a like investment in men.

That was a narrow and thoroughly dubious construction of employment costs, and erected a rickety platform for the remainder of the argument. If the focus was purely on the cost of maternity leave, Schwartz
was overlooking the degree to which such leaves extracted a cost from
the women who availed themselves of the leave rather than the organization granting the leave.[78] The contribution made by well-trained women
before taking leave was not considered in Schwartz's calculation. Neither
was the cost of male turnover for reasons other than paternity; seeking a
new, higher-paying position for instance. Finally, the fact of unequal pay
for women was unacknowledged.

Schwartz added another "startling fact," one that referenced the role
of gender within organizations: "The greater cost of employing women
is not a function of inescapable gender differences. Women *are* different
from men, but what increases their cost to the corporation is princi-
pally the clash of their perceptions, attitudes, and behavior with those
of men, which is to say, with the policies and practices of male-led corporations."[79] To help organizations overcome this problem of gendered
assumptions clashing with the needs of women who were family oriented,
Schwartz had a proposal.

Although Schwartz denied seeking to "pigeonhole" women, she urged
corporate (male) executives to think of their high potential women as
falling into one of two categories. "Career-primary women" were those
who forwent parenting and were willing and able to make the same
commitments as their male counterparts. "Career-and-family women"
wanted to continue to make a contribution to the organization and find
individual fulfillment and satisfaction, but to do so in balance with the
demands of parenting.

The high-performing "career-and-family woman can be a major player
in your company," she lectured executives. "She can give you a significant business advantage as the competition for able people escalates."
And there was always the possibility that, later in her career and personal
life, she would "switch gears" and "reenter the competition for the top."[80]

The negative reaction was explosive. Betty Friedan took to the press
to voice not just opposition but outrage. Schwartz's article was "dangerous" and "retrofeminism." The "Mommy Track" was the term quickly
attached to Schwartz's concept of career-and-family women by critics. It
should really be the Mommy *Trap*, insisted Friedan. "It says to women
that if they choose to have children, they pay a permanent price. It's
another word for sex discrimination."[81]

None of these highly visible, often controversial treatments of women
and leadership in business organizations spoke about the question of race.

Were they addressing white women or all women? A number of scholars suggested that the implicit answer was white women.

"African American women are virtually excluded in the gender and leadership literature," Patricia Parker observed. Researchers had "focused on the identity and experiences of a select few – almost exclusively White, middle-class women," and then implicitly generalized in a manner that "excludes the experience of African American women, as well as other women of color and of different class statuses."[82] Just how gender and race intersected to shape leadership in organizations, then, becomes a serious topic for consideration.

Race-Based Institutional Resistance

"The problem of the 20th century is the problem of the color line," W.E.B Du Bois famously observed of the United States. Despite the occasional proclamations of a postracial society in the aftermath of Barack Obama's 2008 election, race continued to dominate American life well into the 21st century.[83] Earlier, I spent time untangling the differences between sex and gender and the impact of gender construction on women in organizations. But what about race? Is it a biologically fixed category? Or is it, like gender, a social construction, built on an impulse to define otherness?

Just What Is Race?

Perhaps the most common conception of race, certainly the dominant theory of the early 20th century, was that "humans were divided into a few distinctive racial types, each with its own fairly ingrained or even immutable characteristics." When white Europeans defined other races, Peter Wade noted in his survey of Western views of race, they arranged the categories "in a stable moral, social and intellectual hierarchy" in which they placed themselves at the top.[84]

The view of race as a biologically fixed category, however, has long been contested. Franz Boas and W.E.B. Du Bois fought against racial typologies.[85] Racial skeptics argued that race was an "intellectually bankrupt" concept that was both false and dangerous. Social constructionists insisted that race was not about biology (even if it may have been at the earliest stages of human evolution) but was a grouping created by a sociohistorical context that worked to establish, inhabit, transform, and even destroy categories.[86]

Genetic testing revived the debate over the validity of race as a biological category. Some claimed to find significant overlap between racial classifications and generic clusters. Others denounced that conclusion, insisting that the results were the outcome of ahistorical technologies whose findings were achieved through "statistical mischief."[87] Regardless of the outcome of that genetic argument, anthropologists took a stand against race as a valid biological category.

"With the vast expansion of scientific knowledge in this century," proclaimed the executive board of the American Anthropological Association in their 1998 *Statement on Race*, "it has become clear that human populations are not unambiguous, clearly demarcated, biologically distinct groups."[88] That scientific knowledge, however, cannot negate an important reality: race still stands as a way of thinking about identity and group affiliation.

A Paucity of Attention

Given the centrality of race in American life, the paucity of literature on race and leadership in corporate settings is notable. Stella Nkomo made that point on the pages of the *Academy of Management Review*. Even though it was widely accepted that race "has been a profound determinant of one's political rights, one's location in the labor market, one's access to medical care, and even one's sense of identity," the issue had largely been excluded.[89]

A 1986 survey by Taylor Cox and Nkomo found that, of the 11,804 articles published in sixteen leading management journals over the previous fifteen years, only 201 addressed issues of race or ethnicity. The thinness of the discourse is especially apparent when contrasted with the rich literature that has addressed issues of gender.

There is no consensus on why this is so. Citing Thomas Kuhn's insight that problem selection and the search for explanations occurs within a dominant paradigm, Nkomo insisted that the "study of race is an especially sensitive issue because scholars must not only be aware of how prevailing societal race relations influence their approach to the study of race but they must also understand the effects of their own racial identity and experiences on their work." Believing they were searching for universal truths, social scientists conducted their research within "the values and concerns of dominant societal groups."[90]

In a critical review of the literature on race, ethnicity, and leadership, Sonia Ospina and Erica Foldy suggested that "the inside perspective of people of color are often downplayed or ignored" because their experiences are treated as a "special case."[91] There is, researchers have largely concluded, no opportunity to form general theories.[92]

There are exceptions. A 1978 review article by Kathryn Bartol and colleagues noted that little consistent evidence had been produced to suggest that black and white leaders behaved differently. That was true regardless of the ethnic composition of the work group being led. There were some indications that systematic bias worked against black supervisors in job evaluation and assessment situations, although here the lack of "objective performance data" rendered the findings inconclusive.[93] By highlighting a small number of studies, all of which focused on the impact of race on supervisors and subordinates, that review reinforced the lack of serious consideration of race in the leadership discourse.

Three years later, Bernard Bass' *Stogdill's Handbook of Leadership* considered "Blacks and Leadership," along with "Women and Leadership" and "Leadership in Different Cultures" in a category called special conditions.[94] "A 300-year legacy of master-slave relationship is giving way by fits and jumps prompted by war, civil strife, legislation, and education," wrote Bass, "to the rise of blacks into positions of leadership in sizeable numbers."[95] The research cited in his chapter referenced how the race of individuals influenced their job evaluations by supervisors and patterns of interaction between black supervisors and black employees.[96] The research, however, was again sparse and typically set in college labs or military units rather than in business organization.

In his 1999 book with John Gabarro, *Breaking Through: The Making of Minority Executives in Corporate America*, and again in a 2001 piece, David Thomas turned his attention directly to the construction of the leadership pipeline in corporate America. Thomas' argument was fundamentally critical of corporate attempts to build a "race blind" context for executive development.

In the years preceding Thomas and Gabarro's book, legal scholars had formulated what came to be known as critical race theory, calling into question the alleged neutrality and objectivity of America's legal structure. Sure, the civil rights movement and consequent federal laws and court rulings had managed to achieve a kind of race blind posture. Equal opportunity was thought to mean access and opportunity unconstrained by factors such as race.

Critical race theorists dissented. Race-blindness actually functioned to "reproduce manifestations of group advantages and disadvantages." Laws pertaining to work-place equality, in particular, left untouched "many mechanisms able to subvert, manipulate, or obfuscate the law," resulting in an "unequal racialized balance of power."[97]

Although avoiding the rhetoric of critical race theory, Thomas and Gabarro argued that structural elements continued to support institutional resistance to minority advancement in the leadership pipeline. Individual racism surely accounted for a significant degree of resistance. "Virtually everyone writing on the career experiences of minority and women managers and professionals" – note how they tie in gender and race to their analysis – "identifies race and gender based prejudice as a major – perhaps *the* major – barrier to advancement." Thomas and

Gabarro were less focused on the "mean spirited actions of bigots," however, than on "institutionalized discrimination."[98]

The line drawn by Thomas and Gabarro separating individual bigotry from institutionalized discrimination was perhaps not as clear as the authors' suggested. A number of forces worked to the detriment of minorities to advance in the pipeline, including:

- The tendency of networks of individuals to seek each other's company – referred to as homophily – worked to build both in-group and outsider identification.[99]
- The tendency of white employees to label black subordinates as "high risk" because of negative attributions concerning attitudes toward work.[100]
- Additionally, people "habitually seem to prefer working with people who are racially similar. Thus, while superior-subordinate relationships that cross race lines may provide the interaction needed to get work done, they often fail to lead to close interpersonal bonds that form between mentor and protégé."[101]

These were ways in which individual racism gets baked into institutional processes.[102]

Jeffrey Greenhaus and colleagues identified what they labeled "treatment discrimination," which occurred "when subgroup members received fewer rewards, resources, or opportunities on the job than they legitimately deserve on the basis of job-related criteria."[103] Thomas and Gabarro added that people "systematically give higher performance ratings to members of their own racial groups." Selection committees created to first identify and then groom potential future leaders often lacked minority representation. That structural reality, combined with the high-risk attribution often ascribed to black managers "decreases even further the likelihood that minorities will be identified as having high potential."[104]

Thomas pushed these observations about institutional resistance to their logical if uncomfortable conclusion in his 2001 piece. By the time this article appeared, a kind of equal opportunity backlash had set into the cultural/legal discourse in the United States. Kicking off with the 1978 *Regents of the University of California* v. *Bakke* case, attention turned from discrimination against women and racioethnic minorities to supposed discrimination against the "innocent white male." The suggestion was that affirmative action represented discrimination *against* the majority. In this topsy-turvy paradigm, the *one* and the *other* became reversed. Citing the ideology of meritocracy and relying on the comforting delusion that racial discrimination had ceased to exist as a force, white males sought legal recourse.[105]

Thomas did not reference the increasingly conservative disposition of the U.S. court system. Nonetheless, that turn helped define the context in which he wrote. And his message was explicit. He placed it right there in his title: "race matters." To be race blind was, in essence, to be race ignorant and resistant to minority advancement. Whites and minorities "follow distinct patterns of advancement" in what are separate "tournaments" for access to top positions in organizations.[106]

In particular, future black executives found themselves parked in middle management positions for far longer periods of time than their white counterparts, who tended to achieve a "fast track" designation earlier in their careers. As a "pernicious result," many high-potential minorities "became discouraged" by what Thomas fearlessly labeled a "separate and unequal" two-tournament system.[107] Creating an environment for success, then, involved not race blindness but race consciousness to the barriers that existed within organizations.

In the cases of both gender and race, institutional resistance decisively shaped a white male leadership pipeline. But there is another question that can be asked. When women and racioethnic minority employees found themselves in leadership positions, did their behaviors in the enactment of that role mimic their white male counterparts or did it depart in some significant way? The discourse has attempted some fascinating but not entirely conclusive inquiry into just that question.

The Other Leader

In his 1981 consideration of the "special conditions" of women and black leadership, Bernard Bass noted evidence, scanty though it was at the time, that suggested women may well approach leadership differently from men. Women were less interested in dominance than were their male counterparts. When it came to race, Bass found little evidence of difference. Rather, he pointed to economic class, which he clumsily identified as a "slum subculture." Class more than race, he speculated, impacted leadership behavior.[108]

The role of economic class in shaping leadership behaviors would make a fascinating research stream, but Bass could not offer citations that dealt directly with that point. Neither, by the way, did his 1990 updated edition.[109]

In a 1980 article, Judy Rosener offered her thoughts on the "ways women lead." As more and more women were moving into positions within organizations where they were called upon to demonstrate leadership skills, it was obvious to Rosener that women "have proven that effective leaders don't come from one mold." Using the "command-and-control style generally associated with men in large, traditional organizations is not the only way to succeed." Rather than adopting "styles and habits" from men, women leaders were "drawing on the skills and attitudes developed from their shared experience as women."[110]

Rosener went even further, positing that women more than men had adopted a transformational leadership style. This article came just two years after James MacGregor Burns first proposed the transactional/transformational dichotomy, and privileged the transformational model as morally superior.[111] Her conclusion was based not on any clinical observation of leadership behaviors, but rather on surveys in which women described their own styles.

Women leaders worked more than men to convince subordinates to "transform their own self-interest into the interest of the group through concern for a broader goal." Women more than men sought to achieve that transformational goal by encouraging participation, sharing power and information, enhancing other people's self-worth, and getting "others excited about their work." And in a startling conclusion, Rosener noted that many women respondents suggested that this particular style came "naturally."[112]

The notion that women were more prone to so-called transformational behaviors than men inspired Marta Calás and Linda Smircich to compose this fictionalized but clever "help wanted" ad:

Help Wanted
Seeking transforming manager. Impatient with rituals and symbols of hierarchy. Favors strengthening networks and interrelationships, connecting with coworkers, customers, suppliers. Not afraid to draw on personal, private experience when dealing in the public realm. Not hung up by a "What's in it for me?" attitude. Focuses on the whole, not only the bottom line; shows concern for the wider needs of the community. If "managing by caring and nurturing" is your credo, you may be exactly what we need. Excellent salary and benefits, including child care and parental needs.
Contact: CORPORATE AMERICA[113]

Sound appealing? Woman friendly? There are still questions to be asked, of course. Is it true that women are more likely to be transformational than men? Is it true of all women or is this a white women stereotype? And finally, is this the best women leaders have to offer?

Since the appearance of Rosener's article, there has been some evidence in support of her contention that women lead differently from men, although those findings derived mainly from studies of women leadership in small groups. Unlike corporations or large hierarchical units, small groups tend to be loosely constructed, often made up of peers without a formally designated leader. In these cases, women seemed to prefer decentralized structures, allowing greater participation and influence than their male counterparts.[114]

That finding was contested. Other research suggested that, in leaderless groups, individuals who exhibited masculine, or at least some combination of masculine and feminine behaviors were more likely to emerge as leaders.[115] Yvonne Billing and Mats Alvesson denounced the entire debate about "feminine leadership" as "misleading and risky in terms of gender equality and social development."[116]

Perceptions matter. There are certain characteristics ascribed to leaders. In their thoughtful review of ascribed leadership characteristics, Alice Eagly and Mary Johannesen-Schmidt suggested that women leaders often make "efforts to accommodate their behavior to the sometimes conflicting demands of the female gender role."[117] The "think leader/think male" dictum applied. What Eagly and Johannesen-Schmidt described as "agentic" characteristics – assertive, controlling, confident, ambitious, dominant, forceful, daring, and competitive – were associated with males and simultaneously held to be attributes of effective leaders. "Communal" characteristics – helpful, kind, sympathetic, interpersonally sensitive, and nurturing, for instance – "are ascribed more strongly to women than men."[118]

These perceptions relating both to gender roles and ascriptions of effective leadership behaviors pressured women leaders to negotiate a tricky path. Adoption of expected leadership behaviors required an adoption of agentic traits most associated with males. There were some findings that when women leaders displayed these agentic behaviors, they were evaluated less favorably than their male counterparts.[119] They were seen as behaving in nonfeminine and thus incongruent ways.

There are numerous settings in which women leaders tend to be in the majority: in emerging markets and bottom-of-the-pyramid enterprises, even when these micro-businesses spring up in settings otherwise hostile to gender equality. The behaviors and perceptions regarding these women have not yet been evaluated.[120] What is clear, however, is that in settings where effectiveness is associated with masculinity, women leaders faced an identity negotiation that men did not automatically need to manage.

The process of identity construction is always a multilayered undertaking. Hannah Riley Bowles and Kathleen McGinn noted a "two-level game." Negotiations occur on two levels: a public level (with employers) and private level (with household members).[121] These authors were referencing gender without regard to racioethnic identity. Women who identified with a racioethnic group typically faced a challenge of even greater complexity.

Racioethnic group expectations vied, often competitively, with family and work assumptions.[122] A number of authors identified the biculturalism that shapes attitudes and behaviors, often citing the earlier work of W.E.B. Du Bois.[123] That additional boundary-spanning task, it has been suggested, shapes the leadership style of racioethnic women in ways different from white men and women.

Individuals typically hold more than one status identification.[124] Goffman insisted that identification was fluid, at least to some extent, and dependent on the social context in which the individual found herself or himself.[125] Kimberlé Crenshaw introduced the concept of intersectionality to address the challenge of multiple identities.[126] "No single identity category or social category can satisfactorily account for the meanings a person places on his/her social relations, life events and social surroundings, nor for how he or she is responded to by those surroundings," noted Eva Magnusson.[127] Because people live "multiple, layered identities," added Agnes Richardson and Cynthia Loubier, they "are members of more than one category or social group and can simultaneously experience advantages and disadvantages related to those different social groups."[128] It is at the intersection of race and gender that, it has been suggested, a unique perspective has produced a distinct style of leadership.[129]

Patricia Parker and dt ogilvie postulated a unique African American women executive, separate from a white (male or female) leader prototype. "Contemporary African American women's organizational leadership is grounded in a tradition of survival, resistance, and change that has traditionally been ignored or devalued," Parker wrote. This was a response that "began as a form of creative resistance and community building during the era of slavery," and found reinforcement during the civil rights movement and "grass roots community organizing today."[130]

Clearly intending to disrupt accepted "masculine and feminine notions of leadership" and other leadership dualisms, the authors recognized that "very little empirical research focuses on the leadership styles of African-American women."[131] Forces of both racism and sexism created a "distinct social location" which shaped social attributions. "Black women are characterized as loud, talkative, aggressive, intelligent, straightforward, and argumentative." They are often portrayed as "'Black matriarchs' represented as eminent, pathological, deviant and a threat to Black family life."[132]

Out of the singular experience of African American women came a unique leadership style, one that emphasized egalitarian relationships, self-reliance, assertiveness, creativity, and risk taking. The pressing necessity for African American women to negotiate an often contradictory identity between their workplace, community involvement, and home life demanded a skill for multicultural boundary spanning that reverberated in a positive way into their leadership style.

"Taken together," wrote Parker, "these themes challenge traditional notions of instrumental leadership as *directive* and *controlling*, and collaborative leadership as *nurturing* and *caring*." Leadership as expressed by African American women redefined control as "as interactive and personal rather than competitive and distant." Rather than enacting control in purely instrumental, even manipulative terms, leadership that resided at this axis of gender and race "becomes a means of empowerment. The leader's focus is on the other, not as a means of affirming the other person per se – although that many be a likely outcome – but as a way of assessing points of view and levels of (others' as well as their own) readiness to perform."[133]

Help Wanted

When the overt manifestation of a racioethnic or gender identity is apparent to observers, as it often – though by no means *always* – is, interaction across groups becomes more structured, more inserted in a context of "unequal power, exclusion, and discrimination."[134] The result can be institutional resistance to individual leaders on the basis of gender and race.

Institutional efforts to overcome biases have offered mixed results in terms of increasing managerial representation among white women, black women, and black men. In a far-ranging and systemic study of private sector employees covering a thirty-year period, Alexandra Kalev and colleagues concluded that efforts to target bias "through feedback (diversity evaluations) and education (diversity training) showed virtually no effect in the aggregate." Even mentoring initiatives lead to "disappointing results." Their study was not all discouraging, however. "Structures that embed accountability, authority, and expertise (affirmative action plans, diversity committees and taskforces, diversity managers and departments)," were the most effective path toward management diversity.[135]

Given that much of the discourse of feminine leadership styles appeared in the *Harvard Business Review*, it is not surprising that the literature did little to contest the prevailing ideology of corporate actions, leaving unaddressed debates over which stakeholders corporations can and should serve. In the *Review* and elsewhere, gender and race were treated as serious matters but not critical of corporate ideology.

Remember the fictional want ad proposed by Calás and Smircich? They wrote a second one, an ad that would call not for transforming, personal, and nurturing leadership – traits associated with feminine communalism – but for a more fully critical form:

Help Wanted
Seeking hysterical person. Willing to become enraged when observing worldwide exploitation, esp. when done in the name of free market economy. Ready to act in world forums to denounce such conditions. Ready to help others develop their critical voices to create a global network of well-informed peoples who won't accept being called 'less developed' or be undervalued for their own local talents and capabilities. Not afraid to call attention to the travesty of conspicuous consumption in the name of progress and demonstrate the negative long-term consequences of a 'First-World standard of living.' If you are willing to create new forms of business organizations ready to promote sane globalization for a sustainable planet.
Contact: THE WORLD[136]

That critical stance resided far outside the corporate world, however.

Looking Backward/Looking Forward

Using the dominant statuses of gender and race as a lens to leadership discourse helps us understand the startling paucity of minorities in top executive positions. Leadership is defined in highly gendered, masculine terms. The impact of typically unacknowledged and implicit racial and gender bias is felt in multiple processes: in recruitment, assessment, development, and succession processes. The leadership pipeline narrows. The result is apparent.

With the triumph of the shareholder primacy ideology, the culture of workplace diversity and work-life balance, to the extent that it was ever real and widespread, gave way to the mantra of bottom-line performance. Organizational culture became, if anything, even more masculine. Competitiveness, long working hours, and being physically present at work even when the nature of the work did not inherently demand such presence, increasingly prevailed. For women and men of all racioethnic identities, the expectations of assimilation were mediated by the ideology of shareholder primacy.

There is no evidence that this ideology created greater openness to the other in leadership positions, particularly among the dominant statuses of gender and race. Just look at the findings reported at the beginning of the chapter. It is possible that intense bottom-line focus rendered the boards that hire CEOs and the processes that produce and perpetuate the leadership pipelines all the more risk adverse. The white, male gatekeepers, perhaps, are more comfortable than ever reproducing the white male leadership model out of some deeply held suspicions about the Other versus the One.

Roesener's 1980 article on the ways women lead suggested that women were more likely than men to be transformational leaders. That argument built on a construct introduced just two years earlier by James MacGregor Burns. It may be the first instance in which Burns' political science perspective was appropriated for a business context.[137] It would soon become a torrent.

NOTES

1 Justin Wolfers, "Fewer Women Run Big Companies than Men Named John," *New York Times,* March 2, 2015, A2.
2 Northouse, *Leadership*; Yukl, *Leadership in Organizations.*
3 Taylor Cox, Jr. and Stella M. Nkomo, "Differential Appraisal Criteria Based on Race of the Ratee." *Group and Organization Studies* 11 (1986), 101–19; "Only 5 Black CEOs at 500 Biggest Companies," CNN Money, January 29, 2015, accessed at money.cnn.com/2015/01/29/news/economy/mcdonalds-ceo-diversity.
4 The persistence of bias in American society extends far beyond the world of business. A 2015 study commissioned by the University of Southern California's Annenberg's School for Communication and Journalism looked at the biases prevalent in the top-grossing U.S.-produced movies between 2007 and 2014. Women made up just over 30 percent of all speaking or named characters. In addition, 73.1 percent of all characters were white, and less than 2 percent were movies directed by women. Popular culture both reflects and reinforces biases. Reported in Manohla Dargis, "Young, White and Male? The Role Is Yours," *New York Times,* August 6, 2015, C1.
5 Pushkala Prasad and Albert J. Mills, "From Showcase to Shadow: Understanding the Dilemmas of Managing Workplace Diversity," in Pushkala Prasad et al., eds., *Managing the Organizational Melting Pot: Dilemmas of Workplace Diversity* (Thousand Oaks: Sage, 1997), 15.
6 I am taking the term "racioethnic" to "refer to biologically and/or culturally distinct groups" from Taylor Cox, Jr., "Problems with Research by Organizational Scholars on Issues of Race and Ethnicity," *Journal of Applied Behavioral Science* 40 (June 2004), 126. Cox's definition finesses the question of whether biologically distinct groups actually exist, a matter I will address later in the chapter.
7 Gertrude Ezorsky, *Racism and Justice: The Case for Affirmative Action* (Ithaca: Cornell University Press, 1991).
8 Herminia Ibarra et al., "Women Rising: The Unseen Barriers," *Harvard Business Review* 91 (September 2013), 60–67.
9 Bill Cooke has noted the absence of a consideration of slavery in depictions of the United States' growing antebellum economy. See "The Denial of

Slavery in Management Studies," *Journal of Management Studies* 40 (December 2003), 1895–918.

10 Howard S. Becker, *Outsiders: Studies in the Sociology of Deviance* (New York: Free Press, 1973).

11 Jeneen Interlandi, "The Brain's Empathy Gap: Can Mapping Neural Pathways Help Us Make Friends with our Enemies?" *New York Times*, March 19, 2015, 52.

12 Ibid., 53.

13 Cynthia Fuchs Epstein, *Deceptive Distinctions: Sex, Gender, and the Social Order* (New Haven: Yale University Press, 1988), 233.

14 Prasad and Mills, "From Showcase to Shadow," 15.

15 Lauren A. Rivera, "Guess Who Doesn't Fit In at Work," *New York Times*, May 30, 2015, accessed at www.nytimes.com/2015/05/31/opinion/sunday/guess-who-doesnt-fit-in-at-work.html?

16 Ibid.

17 Helena Liu and Christopher Baker, "White Knights: Leadership as the Heroicisation of Whiteness," *Leadership* 10 (2014), 11.

18 See, for example, Fiona Colgan et al., "Equality and Diversity in the Public Services: Moving Forward on Lesbian, Gay and Bisexual Equality?" *Human Resource Management Journal* 19 (2009), 280–301; Benjamin A. Everly and Joshua L. Schwarz, "Predictors of the Adoption of LGBT-Friendly HR Policies," *Human Resource Management* 54 (March 2015), 367–84; Michelle Fullerton, "Diversity and Inclusion: LGBT Inclusion Means Business," *Strategic HR Review* 12 (2013), 121–5; Donna M. Riley, "LGBT-Friendly Workplaces in Engineering," *Leadership & Management in Engineering* 8 (January 2008), 19–23; and Miriam Smith, "Diversity and Identity in the Non-profit Sector: Lessons from LGBT Organizing in Toronto," *Social Policy & Administration* 39 (October 2005), 463–80. For an earlier consideration of the topic, see David Shallenberger, "Professional and Openly Gay," *Journal of Management Inquiry* 3 (1994), 119–42.

19 This protest is where the popular image of bra burning came from. That image was mythical, according to historians David Farber and Beth Bailey. Protesters "filled a trash can with bras, girdles, hair curlers, and high heels." The intention, apparently, *was* to set the material on fire. But, recalled Carol Hanisch, one of the organizers of the protest, "the police department, since we were on the boardwalk, wouldn't let us do the burning." Myths can serve a purpose, and this one worked to connect – for better or worse depending on one's own ideology – the women's movement with the draft-card burning incidents that characterized at least a segment of the anti-Vietnam War movement. David Farber and Beth Bailey, *The Columbia Guide to America in the 1960s* (New York: Columbia University Press, 2001). The Hanisch quote is from Nell Greenfieldboyce, "Pageant Protest Sparked Bra Burning Myth," September 5, 2008, accessed at www.npr.org/templates/story/story.php?storyId=94240375.

20 Shulamith Firestone, *The Dialectic of Sex* (New York: William Morrow, 1970); Kate Millett, *Sexual Politics* (New York: Doubleday, 1970); Robin Morgan, ed., *Sisterhood Is Powerful: An Anthology of Writings from the Women's Liberation Movement* (New York: Random House, 1970).

21 Cynthia Fuchs Epstein, "Positive Effects of the Multiple Negative: Explain-ing the Success of Black Professional Women," *American Journal of Sociology* 78 (January 1973), 913.

22 Sylvia Ann Hewlett, "Executive Women and the Myth of Having it All," *Harvard Business Review* 80 (April 2002), 68.

23 For follow-up research on the "motherhood penalty," see Shelley J. Correll et al., "Getting a Job: Is There a Motherhood Penalty?" *American Journal of Sociology* 112 (March 2007), 1297–339.

24 Louann Brizendine, "One Reason Women Don't Make It to the C-Suite," *Harvard Business Review* 86 (June 2008), 36; Fanny M. Cheung and Diane F. Halpern, "Women at the Top: Powerful Leaders Define Success at Work + Family in a Culture of Gender," *American Psychologist* 65 (April 2010), 183–93.

25 See, for example, Solomon E. Asch, "Opinions and Social Pressure," *Scien-tific American* 193 (November 1955), 31–35; C. Wright Mills, *White Collar: The American Middle Class* (New York: Oxford University Press, 1951); David Riesman, *The Lonely Crowd: A Study of the Changing American Char-acter* (New Haven: Yale University Press, 1950).

26 "Henry V. Erben – He Gets Things Done," *GE Monogram* 25 (1948), 10–12.

27 Mahar, "'Definitely a Man's Man.'"

28 This pressure was captured in the early seasons of the television series, "*Mad Men.*" The point about homosexual anxiety and the Cold War is made in K.A. Cuordileone, "'Politics in an Age of Anxiety': Cold War Political Culture and the Crisis in American Masculinity, 1949–1960," *Journal of American History* 87 (2000), 515–45; and James Burkhart Gilbert, *Men in the Middle: Searching for Masculinity in the 1950s* (Chicago: University of Chicago Press, 2005).

29 Scott Coltrane, *Family Man: Fatherhood, Housework, and Gender Equity* (New York: Oxford University Press, 1996); Carole Pateman, *The Sexual Con-tract* (Stanford: Stanford University Press, 1988); John E. Williams and Deborah L. Best, *Measuring Sex Stereotypes: A Multination Study* (Newbury Park: Sage, 1990).

30 David Collinson and Jeff Hearn, *Men as Managers, Managers as Men: Critical Perspectives on Men, Masculinities and Management* (Newbury Park: Sage, 1996).

31 Marianne Cooper, "Being the Go-To Guy: Fatherhood, Masculinity, and the Organization of Work in Silicon Valley," *Quantitative Sociology* 23 (2000), 390.

32 Ann Oakley, *Sex, Gender, and Society* (New York: Harper & Row, 1972).

33 De Beauvoir, *Second Sex*, 69.

34 Erving Goffman, "The Arrangement between the Sexes," *Theory and Society* 4 (Autumn 1977), 302.

35 Lesley Jeffries has studied the rhetoric of "constructed opposites" in *Oppo-sition in Discourse: The Construction of Oppositional Meaning* (London: Con-tinuum, 2010).

36 Chaucer's *Canterbury Tales* appeared between 1387 and 1400. Gower, a poet and balladeer, was a contemporary and friend of Chaucer's.

37 Tara Williams, *Inventing Womanhood: Gender and Language in Later Middle English Writing* (Columbus: Ohio State University Press, 2011).

38 Two excellent histories of the psychoanalytic emergence of the masculine–feminine dichotomy can be found in Anne Constantinople, "Masculinity-Femininity: An Exception of the Famous Dictum?" *Psychological Bulletin* 89 (1973), 389–407; and Jan E. Stets and Peter J. Burke, "Femininity/Masculinity," in Edgar F. Borgatta and Rhonda J.V. Montgomery, eds., *Encyclopedia of Sociology* (New York: Macmillan, 2000), 997–1005.

39 Starke R. Hathaway and J. C. McKinley, *The Minnesota Multiphasic Personality Inventory* (New York: Psychological Corporation, 1943); and Lewis Terman and Catherine C. Miles, *Sex and Personality* (New York: McGraw-Hill, 1936).

40 Margaret Mead, *Sex and Temperament in Three Primitive Societies* (New York: Dell, 1935).

41 Garda W. Bowman et al., "Are Women Executives People?" *Harvard Business Review* 43 (July–August 1965), 15.

42 Carol Gilligan, *In a Different Voice: Psychological Theory and Women's Development* (Cambridge: Harvard University Press, 1982), 37–38. See also Carol Gilligan and Jane Attanucci, "Two Moral Orientations: Gender Differences and Similarities," *Merrill-Palmer Quarterly* 34 (1988), 223–37.

43 Kanter, *Men and Women of the Corporation*, 22.

44 "It is clear from our reexamination of the Hawthorne Studies," wrote Joan Acker and Donald Van Houten, "that the experimenters' treatment of the men in the Bank Wiring Room was very different from their treatment of the women in the Relay Assembly Test Room." Acker and Van Houten, "Differential Recruitment and Control: The Sex Structuring of Organizations," *Administrative Science Quarterly* 19 (1974), 156.

45 Joan Acker, "Hierarchies, Jobs, Bodies: A Theory of Gendered Organizations," *Gender and Society* 4 (June 1990), 146. Acker built on feminist theory of bureaucratic biases presented in Kathy E. Ferguson, *The Feminist Case against Bureaucracy* (Philadelphia: Temple University Press, 1984).

46 Acker, "Hierarchies, Jobs, Bodies," 147.

47 Barbara Bird and Candida Brush, "A Gendered Perspective on Organizational Creation," *Entrepreneurship: Theory and Practice* 26 (Spring 2002), 42.

48 George E. Bates, "Twenty Years," *Harvard Business Review* 21 (Autumn 1942), 3.

49 Ibid., 2.

50 I explore the influence of the *Harvard Business Review* more thoroughly in "Business Responsibilities in a Divided World: The Cold War Roots of the Corporate Social Responsibility Movement," *Enterprise and Society* 9 (June 2008), 314–36.

51 Bowman et al., "Are Women Executives People?" 15. The authors added, completely unself-consciously, that the view of women as a special kind of people was "a matter on which there is complete, indeed enthusiastic, agreement."

52 Ibid., 14.

53 Frank Sinatra's 1950s recording of "Lady Is a Tramp" altered the original 1937 Lorenz Hart lyric "Won't dish the dirt with the rest of the girls" to "Won't dish the dirt with the rest of the broads."

54 Friedan, The *Feminine Mystique*.

55 Charlotte Decker Sutton and Kris K. Moore, "Executive Women – 20 Years Later," *Harvard Business Review* 63 (September–October 1985), 42.

56 Virginia E. Schein, "The Relationship between Sex Role Stereotypes and Requisite Management Characteristics," *Journal of Applied Psychology* 57 (1973), 95–100; "The Relationship between Sex Role Stereotypes and Requisite Management Characteristics among Female Managers," *Journal of Applied Psychology* 60 (1975), 340–44; "Sex Role Stereotypes and Requisite Management Characteristics, Past, Present and Future," Working Paper NC 89-26 (November 1989), Western Ontario, National Centre for Management Research and Development. "A Global Look at Psychological Barriers to Women's Progress in Management," *Journal of Social Issues* 37 (2001), 675–88; Schein and Ruediger Mueller, "Sex Role Stereotyping and Requisite Managerial Characteristics: A Cross Cultural Look," *Journal of Organizational Behavior* 13 (1992), 439–47.

57 Albert J. Mills, *Sex, Strategy, and the Stratosphere: Airlines and the Gendering of Organizational Culture* (London: Palgrave, 2006). See also Jeff Hearn and F. Wendy Parkin, "Women, Men, and Leadership: A Critical Review of Assumptions, Practices, and Change in Industrialized Nations," *International Studies of Management and Organization* 16 (1986), 33–60.

58 Nancy J. Adler, "Women Do Not Want International Careers: And Other Myths about International Management," *Organizational Dynamics* 13 (1984), 66–79; Adler, "Expecting International Success: Female Managers Overseas," *Columbia Journal of World Business* 19 (1984), 79–85; Adler, "Women in Management Worldwide," *International Studies of Management and Organization* 16 (1986), 3–32.

59 Joyce K. Fletcher, *Disappearing Acts: Gender, Power, and Relational Practice at Work* (Cambridge: MIT Press, 1999), 3.

60 Joan C. Williams et al., "Cultural Schemas, Social Class, and the Flexibility Stigma," *Journal of Social Issues* 69 (2013), 209–34.

61 Emma Cahusac and Shireen Kanji, "Giving Up: How Gendered Organizational Cultures Push Mothers Out," *Gender, Work, and Organization* 21 (January 2014), 57–70; Liisa Mäkelä, "A Narrative Approach to Pregnancy-Related Discrimination and Leader-Follower Relationships," *Gender, Work, and Organization* 19 (November 2012), 677–98; Ruth Simpson, "Presenteeism, Power and Organizational Change: Long Hours as a Career Barrier and the Impact on the Working Lives of Women Managers," *British Journal of Management* 9 (1998), 37–50; Pamela Stone, *Opting Out? Why Women Really Quit Careers and Head Home* (Berkeley: University of California Press, 2007).

62 Hearn and Parkin, "Women, Men, and Leadership"; Geoffrey C. Ho et al., "Labels and Leaders: The Influence of Framing on Leadership Emergence," *Leadership Quarterly* 21 (2012), 943–52; Russell L. Kent and Sherry E. Moss, "Effects of Sex and Gender Role on Leader Emergence," *Academy of Management Journal* 37 (1994), 1335–46; Clara Kulich et al., "Where Is the

Romance for Women Leaders?," 582–601; Laurie Larwood and Marion W. Wood, *Women in Management* (Lexington: Lexington Books, 1977); Christopher Orpen, "Causal Attributions for the Success and Failure of Black and White Managers," *Journal of Occupational Behavior* 2 (April 1981), 81–87; Debbie Salas-Lopez et al., "Women Leaders: Challenges, Success, and Other Insights from the Top," *Journal of Leadership Studies* 5 (2011), 34–42; Joan C. Williams and Rachel Dempsey, *What Works for Women at Work: Four Patterns Working Women Need to Know* (New York: New York University Press, 2014).

63 Barbara Orser et al., "Perceived Career Challenges and Response Strategies of Women in the Advanced Technology Sector," *Entrepreneurship & Regional Development* 24 (January 2012), 73–93; An-Ju R. Tai and Randi L. Sims, "The Perception of the Glass Ceiling in High Technology Companies," *Journal of Leadership and Organizational Studies* 12 (2005), 16–22.

64 On the etymology of the term "glass ceiling," see Sage Reference, "Glass Ceiling," *Encyclopedia of Race, Ethnicity, and Society*, accessed at www.sage pub.com/northouse6e/study/materials/reference/reference14.1.pdf. The glass ceiling image was central to Hillary Clinton's 2012 campaign for the Democratic Presidential nomination. After losing the nomination to Barack Obama, Clinton told her followers: "Although we were not able to shatter that highest and hardest glass ceiling this time, thanks to you it has 18 million cracks in it, and the light is shining through like never before."

65 Alice H. Eagly and Linda L. Carli, *Through the Labyrinth: The Truth about How Women Become Leaders* (Boston: Harvard Business School Press, 2008), 6.

66 Sheryl Sandberg, *Lean In: Women, Work, and the Will to Lead* (New York: Alfred A. Knopf, 2014), 9.

67 Ibid.

68 See, for example, Rosa Brooks, "Recline, Don't 'Lean In' (Why I Hate Sheryl Sandberg)," *Washington Post*, February 25, 2014, accessed at www.washingtonpost.com/blogs/she-the-people/wp/2014/02/25/recline-dont-lean-in-why-i-hate-sheryl-sandberg.

69 For an analysis of discursive formulation and women leaders in organizations, see Jackie Ford, "Discourses of Leadership: Gender, Identity and Contradiction in a UK Public Sector Organization," *Leadership* 2 (February 2006), 77–90.

70 The "women don't ask" argument in negotiation literature is much closer to Sandberg's lean in formulation, although absent the trappings of corporate privilege afforded by Sandberg's position at Facebook. See Linda Babcock and Sara Laschever, *Women Don't Ask: Negotiation and the Gender Divide* (Princeton: Princeton University Press, 2003).

71 Deborah M. Kolb, "Negotiating in the Shadows of Organizations: Gender, Negotiation, and Change," *Ohio State Journal of Dispute Resolution* 28 (2013), 253, 255.

72 Deborah M. Kolb and Kathleen L. McGinn, "Beyond Gender and Negotiation to Gendered Negotiation," *Negotiation and Conflict Management Research* 2 (2009), 1–2.

73 Deborah M. Kolb et al., *Her Place at the Table: A Woman's Guide to Negotiating Five Key Challenges to Leadership Success* (San Francisco: Jossey-Bass, 2004), 3.

74 Ibid.

75 Schwartz's reflections are offered in Beverly Beyette, "A New Career Flap: What's a Mommy Track and Why Are So Many Women Upset about It?" *Los Angeles Times*, March 17, 1989, 3.

76 Felice N. Schwartz, "Management Women and the New Facts of Life," *Harvard Business Review* 67 (January–February 1989), 66.

77 Ibid., 65.

78 Evidence that maternity leave is costly to women is presented in Amelia R. Miller, "The Effects of Motherhood Timing in Career Path," *Journal of Population Economics* 24 (2011), 1071–1100.

79 Schwartz, "Management Women and the New Facts of Life," 66.

80 Ibid., 71.

81 Friedan is quoted in Beyette, "A New Career Flap."

82 Patricia S. Parker, *Race, Gender, and Leadership: Re-envisioning Organizational Leadership from the Perspectives of African American Women Executives* (Mahwah: Lawrence Erlbaum, 2005), xv.

83 For a review and debunking of the postracial myth, see Jeffrey J. Rachlinski and Gregory S. Parks, "Implicit Bias, Election '08, and the Myth of a Post-Racial America," *Cornell Law Library Scholarship@Cornell Law: A Digital Repository* (2010), accessed at http://scholarship.law.cornell.edu/cgi/viewcontent.cgi?article=1177&context=facpub.

84 Peter Wade, *Race, Nature and Culture: An Anthropological Perspective* (London: Pluto Press, 2002), 2.

85 Franz Boas, *Race, Language and Culture* (New York: Macmillan, 1940); W.E.B. Du Bois, *The Souls of Black Folks* (New York: Mead, 1909/1961).

86 In this view, "race" and "ethnicity" are virtually indistinguishable in the modern world. See Joan Ferrante and Prince Brown, Jr., *The Social Construction of Race and Ethnicity in the United States* (New York: Longman, 1998); David Theo Goldberg, *Racist Culture: Philosophy and the Politics of Meaning* (Cambridge: Blackwell, 1993); Charles W. Mills, *Blackness Visible: Essays on Philosophy and Race* (Ithaca: Cornell University Press, 1998); Michael Omi and Howard Winant, *Racial Formation in the United States: From the 1960s to the 1990s* (New York: Routledge, 1994); Tommie Shelby, "Race," in David Estlund, ed., *The Oxford Handbook of Political Philosophy* (New York: Oxford University Press, 2012), 336–53; Paul C. Taylor, *Race: A Philosophical Introduction* (Cambridge: Polity, 2004).

87 For a sense of the debate, you can read Tang et al., which found considerable overlap between genetic clusters and racial identification, higher, in fact, than between sex and sexual identification. Hua Tang et al., "Genetic Structure, Self-Identified Race/Ethnicity, and Confounding in Case-Control Association Studies," *American Journal of Human Genetics* 76 (2005), 268–75. For a highly skeptical view of the research, see Stephen Palmié, "Genomics, Divination, 'Racecraft,'" *American Ethnologist* 34 (2007), 205–22. Troy Dunster went so far as to accuse the supporters

of race and genetic overlap of finding the smallest number of individuals to sample in order to "show differences between the groups that they are trying to distinguish." See Duster, "Buried Alive: The Concept of Race in Science," in Alan H. Goodman et al., eds., *Genetic Nature / Culture: Anthropology and Science beyond the Two-Culture Divide* (Berkeley: University of California Press, 2003), 265.

88 www.americananthro.org/ConnectWithAAA/Content.aspx?ItemNumber= 2583.

89 Stella M. Nkomo, "The Emperor Has No Clothes: Rewriting Race in Organizations," *Academy of Management Review* 17 (July 1992), 488.

90 Nkomo, "The Emperor Has No Clothes," 490. Kuhn's work is *The Structure of Scientific Revolutions* (Chicago: University of Chicago Press, 1962).

91 Sonia Ospina and Erica Foldy, "A Critical Review of Race and Ethnicity in the Leadership Literature: Surfacing Context, Power and the Collective Dimensions of Leadership," *Leadership Quarterly* 20 (2009), 877.

92 A far richer body of literature has appeared examining African American school principals. For a review, see Linda C. Tillman, "African American Principals and the Legacy of *Brown*," *Review of Research in Education* 28 (2004), 101–46.

93 Kathryn M. Bartol et al., "Black versus White Leaders: A Comparative Review of the Literature," *Academy of Management Review* 3 (April 1978), 296.

94 Bernard M. Bass, *Stogdill's Handbook of Leadership: A Survey of Theory and Research* (New York: Free Press, 1981). The title of this section was altered in the 1990 third edition to "Diverse Groups," Bass, *Bass and Stogdill's Handbook* (1990).

95 Bass, *Stogdill's Handbook of Leadership* (1981), 508.

96 For example, W. Clay Hamner et al., "Race and Sex as Determinants of Ratings by Potential Employers in a Simulated Work-Sampling Task," *Journal of Applied Psychology* 59 (1974), 705–11; Walter H. Hill and William M. Fox, "Black and White Marine Squad Leaders' Perceptions of Racially Mixed Squads," *Academy of Management Journal* 16 (December 1973), 680–86; and Jerome M. Sattler, "Racial 'Experimenter Effects' in Experimentation, Testing, Interviewing, and Psychotherapy," *Psychological Bulletin* 73 (1970), 137–60.

97 Nneka Logan, "The White Leader Prototype: A Critical Analysis of Race in Public Relations," *Journal of Public Relations Research* 23 (2011), 451. For a review of critical race theory, see Kimberlé Crenshaw, *Critical Race Theory: The Key Writings That Formed the Movement* (New York: New Press, 1995).

98 David Thomas and John J. Gabarro, *Breaking Through: The Making of Minority Executives in Corporate America* (Boston: Harvard Business School Press, 1999), 26.

99 The literature of the phenomenon of homophily is reviewed in Miller McPherson et al., "Birds of a Feather: Homophily in Social Networks," *Annual Review of Sociology* 27 (2001), 415–44.

100 Jomills Henry Braddock III and James M. McPhartland, "How Minorities Continue to be Excluded from Equal Opportunities: Research on Labor

Markets and Institutional Barriers," *Journal of Social Issues* 43 (1987), 5–39.

101 Thomas and Gabarro, *Breaking Through*, 27.

102 The interaction between individual racism and institutional resistance in the United States became especially manifest in a 2014 series of fatal police shootings and their aftermath in American cities. See, for example, United States Department of Justice Civil Rights Division, *Investigation of the Ferguson Police Department* (Washington, D.C.: Department of Justice, March 4, 2015).

103 Jeffrey H Greenhaus et al., "Effects of Race on Organizational Experiences, Job Performance Evaluations, and Career Operations," *Academy of Management Journal* 33 (1990), 65.

104 Thomas and Gabarro, *Breaking Through*, 28.

105 Emilio J. Castilla and Stephen Benard, "The Paradox of Meritocracy in Organizations," *Administrative Science Quarterly* 55 (2010), 543–76; Jennifer L. Pierce, *Racing for Innocence: Whiteness, Gender, and the Backlash against Affirmative Action* (Stanford: Stanford University Press, 2012).

106 David A. Thomas, "The Truth about Mentoring Minorities: Race Matters," *Harvard Business Review* 79 (April 2001), 99–100. Edward P. Lazear and Sherwin Rosen proposed tournament theory as a way to understand the existence of wage differences in labor contracts. See Lazear and Rosen, "Rank-Order Tournaments as Optimum Labor Contracts," *Journal of Political Economy* 89 (1981), 841–64. Thomas presented his argument in more academic terms in "The Impact of Race on Managers' Experiences of Developmental Relationships (Mentoring and Sponsorship): An Intra-organizational Study," *Journal of Organizational Behavior* 11 (1990), 479–92; and "Racial Dynamics in Cross-Race Developmental Relationships," *Administrative Science Quarterly* 38 (June 1993), 169–94.

107 Thomas, "The Truth about Mentoring Minorities," 99, 101.

108 Bass, *Stogdill's Handbook of Leadership*, 510. For the 1990 edition, Bass changed the chapter title from "Blacks and Leadership" to "Leadership, Blacks, Hispanics, and Other Minorities." Bass, *Bass and Stogdill's Handbook of Leadership*.

109 Bass, *Bass and Stogdill's Handbook of Leadership*. This edition retained the "Slum Subculture" subtitle.

110 Judy B. Rosener, "Ways Women Lead," *Harvard Business Review* 68 (November–December 1980), 119.

111 Burns, *Leadership*.

112 Rosener, "Ways Women Lead," 120, 122.

113 Marta B. Calás and Linda Smircich, "Dangerous Liaisons: The 'Feminine-in-Management' Meets 'Globalization,'" *Business Horizons* (March–April 1993), 71.

114 Jennifer L. Berdahl and Cameron Anderson, "Men, Women, and Leadership Centralization over Time," *Group Dynamics: Theory, Research, and Practice* 9 (2005), 45–57.

115 Janet R. Goktepe and Craig Eric Schneier, "Role of Sex, Gender Roles, and Attraction in Predicting Emergent Leaders," *Journal of Applied Psychology* 74 (1989), 165–7; Kent and Moss, "Effects of Sex and Gender

Role on Leader Emergence"; Jill Kickul and George Neuman, "Emergent
Leadership Behaviors: The Function of Personality and Cognitive Ability in
Determining Teamwork Performance and KSAS," *Journal of Business and
Psychology* 15 (Fall 2000), 27–51.

116 Yvonne Billing and Mats Alvesson, "Questioning the Notion of Feminine
Leadership: A Critical Perspective on the Gender Labelling of Leadership,"
Gender, Work, and Organization 7 (July 2000), 144.

117 Alice H. Eagly and Mary C. Johannesen-Schmidt, "The Leadership Styles
of Women and Men," *Journal of Social Issues* 57 (2001), 785.

118 Ibid. An earlier iteration of the agentic/communal categorization appeared in
Alice H. Eagly, Wendy Wood, and Amanda B. Diekman, "Social Role The-
ory of Sex Differences and Similarities: A Current Appraisal," in Thomas
Eckes and Hanns M. Trautner, eds., *The Development of Social Psychology of
Gender* (East Sussex: Psychology Press, 2000), 123–74.

119 For example, Arthur G. Jago and Victor H. Vroom, "Sex Differences in
the Incidence and Evaluation of Participative Leader Behavior," *Journal of
Applied Psychology* 67 (1982), 776–83.

120 See, for example, Deborah Burand, "Beyond Microfinance: Creating
Opportunities for Women at the Base of the Pyramid," *International Trade
Forum* 2 (April–June, 2012), 20–21; Isabelle Guérin et al., "Women's
Empowerment: Power to Act or Power over Other Women? Lessons from
Indian Microfinance," *Oxford Development Studies* 41 (2013), 576–94.

121 Hannah Riley Bowles and Kathleen L. McGinn, "Gender in Job Negotiations: A Two-Level Game," *Negotiation Journal* 24 (October 2008),
393–410. A 2015 article by Amanda Bullough and colleagues made recommendations for entrepreneurship training among women in developing countries. See "Developing Women Leaders through Entrepreneurship Education and Training," *Academy of Management Perspectives* 29
(May 2015), 250–70.

122 DeMarcus A. Pegues and Christopher J.L. Cunningham., "Diversity in
Leadership: Where Is the Love for Racioethnic Minorities?" *Business Journal
of Hispanic Research* 4 (2010), 11–17.

123 Verónica Benet-Martínez et al., "Negotiating Biculturalism: Cultural Frame
Switching in Biculturals with Oppositional versus Compatible Cultural
Identities," *Journal of Cross-Cultural Psychology* 33 (September 200), 492–
516; Patricia S. Parker and dt ogilvie, "Gender, Culture, and Leadership:
Toward a Culturally Distinct Model of African-American Women Execu-
tives' Leadership Strategies," *Leadership Quarterly* 7 (1996), 189–214.

124 In 2015, Rachel Dolezal, the president of the NAACP's Spokane, Washington branch, was forced to resign her position when it was revealed by
her parents that she was white. Dolezal had, for years, claimed an African
American identity. And she was being truthful, she insisted. "I identify as
black."

125 Erving Goffman, *The Presentation of Self in Everyday Life* (New York:
Doubleday, 1959).

126 Kimberlé Crenshaw, "Mapping the Margins: Intersectionality, Identity Politics, and Violence against Women of Color," *Stanford Law Review* 43 (1991),
1241–99. There is considerable ongoing discussion about the meaning

and viability of the term "intersectionality." See, for example, Kathy Davis, "Intersectionality as Buzzword: A Sociology of Science Perspective on What Makes a Feminist Theory Successful," *Feminist Theory* 9 (2008), 67–85.

127 Eva Magnusson, "Women, Men and All the Other Categories: Psychologies for Theorizing Human Diversity," *Nordic Psychology* 63 (2011), 94.

128 Agnes Richardson and Cynthia Loubier, "Intersectionality and Leadership," *International Journal of Leadership Studies* 3 (2008), 143.

129 Patricia H. Collins, *Fighting Words: Black Women and the Search for Justice* (Minneapolis: University of Minnesota Press, 1998); Kathy M. Evans and Edwin L. Herr, "The Influence of Racism and Sexism in the Career Development of African-American Women," *Journal of Multicultural Counseling & Development* 19 (July 1991), 130–35.

130 Parker, *Race, Gender, and Leadership*, xiv.

131 Ibid., 59; Parker and ogilvie, "Gender, Culture, and Leadership," 196.

132 Parker and ogilvie, "Gender, Culture, and Leadership," 201.

133 Parker, *Race, Gender, and Leadership*, 69–70.

134 Patricia Hill Collins and John Solomos, "Situating Race and Ethnic Studies," in Patricia Hill Collins and John Solomos, eds., *The SAGE Handbook of Race and Ethnic Studies* (Thousand Oaks: Sage, 2010), 9.

135 Alexandra Kalev et al., "Best Practices or Best Guesses? Assessing the Efficacy of Corporate Affirmative Action and Diversity Policies," *American Sociological Review* 71 (August 2006), 611.

136 Calás and Smircich, "Dangerous Liaisons," 79.

137 It was the first I could find.

6   No Longer *Just* Managing and the Misuse of Ideal Types

"Not too long ago," noted the president of the American Management Association, a corporate training organization, "business people came to AMA to become more effective managers." No more. "Today" – this was in 1997 – "they come because they want to be more effective leaders."[1]

That distinction – that leaders are something *different from* and *superior to* managers – became orthodoxy in the business world by the late 1990s. Corporations devoted millions of dollars in an effort to inject managers with whatever it was that turned them into leaders. Business schools assured potential executive enrollees that they would learn the "noble pursuit" of organizational leadership.[2] A leadership industry blossomed, composed, noted Barbara Kellerman, "of countless leadership centers, institutes, programs, courses, seminars, workshops, experiences, trainers, books, blogs, articles, websites, webinars, videos, conferences, consultants, and coaches claiming to teach people – usually for money – how to lead."[3] Becoming a manager, even an excellent manager, was no longer sufficient. The goal now was to become a leader.

That leadership mantra often rested on an assumption: that leadership was something different from and preferred to management. Take a look at Table 6.1. It offers a list of contrasting management and leadership qualities taken from the leadership industry literature that typifies such dichotomous thinking. Now, consider the top row. Leaders emphasize "change," we are told, while managers support "stability." That change/stability contrast will come up repeatedly. But that isn't all.

Leaders explore "new roads" while managers stick to "existing paths." Leaders "set direction" while managers "plan details." Leaders are "transformational" while managers are "transactional." That's another common one.

The comparison breaks down into occasional silliness. Leaders "take the blame" while managers "blame others." Really? One distinction is a mere tautology: managers "manage work or people" and leaders "lead

Table 6.1 *Managers and Leaders Contrasted*

Area/Factors	Quality Associated with Leaders or Leadership	Quality Associated with Managers or Management
Goal	Change	Stability
Seeks	Vision and expression of values	Achievement of aims or objectives
Theoretical style	Transformational or congruent	Transactional
Conflict	Uses conflict constructively	Avoids or manages conflict
Power	Personal charisma and values	Formal authority and a hierarchical position
Blame and responsibility	Takes the blame	Blames others
Direction	Explores new roads	Travels on existing paths
Main focus	Leading people	Managing work or people
Relationship to the organization	Essential	Necessary

Note: Based on David Stanley, "Role Conflict: Leaders and Managers," *Nursing Management* 13 (September 2006), 33.

people." It's the final row of the list – "relationship to the organization" – that is the most revealing. Managers may be "necessary" to the organization, but leaders are "essential."

Aren't those two words, *necessary* and *essential*, synonyms? They are, according to *Roget's Thesaurus*. Still, the author of the matrix clearly meant to highlight some contrast. *Essential* is intended to imply something more deeply valuable than *necessary*, more fundamental to the well-being of the organization. It's important to have good managers. Leaders, however, are what separate so-so organizations from great ones.

Scholarly discourse has, for the most part, shied away from the leader versus manager dichotomy. In their 1984 *Leaders and Managers*, James Hunt and colleagues declared that the "fashion" of separating management and leadership – the word *fashion* indicating a faddish rather than a substantive use of the two terms – had been replaced by a tendency to use the terms interchangeably.[4] A 2013 comprehensive review of leadership literature by Gary Yukl observed that "most scholars seem to agree that success as a manager or administrator in modern organizations also involves leading."[5] Adding "modern" was a case of presentism. When did organizations not need leadership? But Yukl was correct in describing "most scholars" as avoiding a strict manager/leader dichotomy.

However, as the statement from the president of the AMA indicated, the management versus leadership delineation held real meaning to practitioners. That was particularly the case for those who found themselves in leadership training programs. Could leadership really be learned through rope climbing, trust falling, and white-water rafting? Participants might be initially skeptical, yet they often emerged from such programs convinced of both the validity of the distinction and the effectiveness of the engagement.[6]

One graduate told Jay Conger that "she was no longer just managing, as she had before; she was spending less time on administration and more time on leadership." *Just* managing was no longer adequate. As a consequence of a leadership training program, she insisted that she "had set up a new vision for her organization and was active in motivating staff toward its achievement."[7] And she had traveled from the management column to the leadership column over the span of a week.

It is not difficult to appreciate the appeal of leadership over management. Just look again at Table 6.1. Why settle for "formal authority and a hierarchical position" when one can stake a claim to "personal charisma and values," "passion," "vision," and "excitement"? Plus, there is that last row. Leaders are more critical to organizations than managers; essential rather than mere necessities.

"Leaders, almost by definition, are remarkable achievers and, by their example, enable others to implement and develop their concepts." This was the view of another professional leadership trainer. Managers, conversely, provided "sinister" opposition to leader-inspired innovations.[8] *Sinister*? If managers actually believed that to be true, or even if they thought their organizational higher-ups held that view, then the motivation to shed the manager label in favor of being seen to be a leader was intensified.

When not being depicted as sinister, management was seen as mundane, in contrast to the inspiring, special, even heroic characteristics of leadership. Mats Alvesson and Stefan Sveningsson pointed to a mythological distinction between what is thought to be the bureaucratic work of the manager and the "remarkable and significant" efforts that we have come to label leadership.[9] Organizational life is filled with routine acts for everyone involved. Labeling something as leadership, they suggested, gave extraordinary meaning to the mundane.

Leaders and managers represent, in Yukl's thinking, "ideal" definitions. So does transactional and transformational leadership. The formulation of ideal types can and does make a contribution to leadership discourse. Furthermore, these classifications represented a response to the same, inherent characteristic of organizations: the need for ongoing adaptation and change to an ever-dynamic environment on the one hand and the requirement for some degree of maintenance and control on the other. They are ideal types that serve an important analytic function.

One of the most common traps into which leadership scholars fall is the confusion of ideal types with real-world examples. Ideal types are not real; they do not exist in the real world. You would not know that from the literature, however, or from asking practitioners. Remember the AMA president? People do not want to be trained to be managers, they want to learn how to be leaders, as if these were two distinct realities. This is a problem worthy of further exploration.

Ideal Types as Mental Constructs and Not Concrete Reality

The creation of ideal types as an intellectual methodology is associated with the writings of German sociologist Max Weber, particularly his 1904 essay "'Objectivity' in Social Science and Social Policy." Reflecting the influence of German idealism growing from the philosophy of Immanuel Kant, Weber wrestled with the challenge of making sense out of a chaotic world, an "infinite reality" in his terms.[10] Searching for approaches that would render significant social and cultural phenomena comprehensible, he offered the notion of ideal types.[11]

Weber worked in what would today be considered a robustly cross-disciplinary manner. He identified himself as much with history and economics as he did with the newly emerging discipline of sociology, turning to ideal types as a way of opening and directing an ongoing dialogue about significant historical phenomenon. His best-known and most influential usage occurred in the 1905 *Protestant Ethic and the Spirit of Capitalism*. As a preliminary to considering ideal types in leadership discourse, it is helpful to explore Weber's use of the methodology in his seminal work.[12]

Weber wanted to understand why Protestants in comparison to Catholics were overrepresented in the merchant class that emerged in 17th- and 18th-century Europe. To help form an answer, he constructed two ideal types: the "spirit of capitalism" and "Protestants," and then analyzed the overlap between them. Weber defined the spirit of capitalism as "the pursuit of profit, and forever *renewed* profit."[13] Avarice and personal greed were nothing new to the world, Weber noted. What capitalism did was to restrain greed, or offer "at least a rational tempering, of this irrational impulse." So, that was the first ideal type.

Next came Protestantism, and more specifically, Calvinism. Weber found impulses in Protestantism that worked to comingle the religious with the secular. Following the 1517 publication of Martin Luther's *Theses*, the Reformation splintered Catholicism. Those who remained in the Roman Catholic Church retained what Weber called an "other-worldliness." Conversely, the Protestants who split from the Church in the Reformation – led by Luther and John Calvin – embraced the sanctity of "organized worldly labor."[14]

Luther, a bitter enemy of the merchant class, nonetheless advocated for a here-on-earth "calling." Calvinists generally and English Puritans in particular were far more comfortable with mercantilism than was Luther. These groups integrated the notion of a religious calling with a more secular striving for work in the here-and-now world. "The Puritan *wanted* to be a vocational man," Weber wrote, "We *must* be vocational men."[15]

Would capitalism have flourished absent the Reformation? Would Protestantism have become so forceful without the concurrent rise of the spirit of capitalism? Weber did not pretend that ideal types could offer an answer. The congruence between the two movements – Protestantism and Capitalism – was presented for us to consider, debate, and perhaps further refine. Ideal types, in other words, should be used to *start* a conversation, not to *end* it.[16]

My point in this quick review of Weber's work is to offer insight into the ideal type methodology, both what it is and what it is not. For Weber, both the "spirit of capitalism" and the "Protestant Ethic" were ideal types; they were fictions, not empirical realities. Take capitalism. Carl Diehl, in his analysis of Weber's writing, noted that capitalism, "in the sense of an economy which is oriented only by calculated capital investment and is determined only and solely by unlimited profit-seeking, has never existed anywhere."[17] Likewise, to suggest that Protestantism represented a unified, orderly movement toward worldly engagement was to defy both common sense and historical evidence. Diehl's observation, however, was not meant to be a critique of Weber and his methodology. Far from it. Weber himself acknowledged that these were mental constructs rather than empirical realities. And therein lies the central premise of ideal types.

Returning to "'Objectivity' in Social Science," Weber argued that ideal types are constructed:

by the one-sided accentuation of one or more points of view and by the synthesis of a great many diffuse, discrete, more or less present and occasionally absent concrete individual phenomena, which are arranged according to those one-sidedly emphasized viewpoints into a unified abstract construct (*Gedankenbild*). In its conceptual purity, this mental construct (*Gedankenbild*) cannot be found empirically anywhere in reality. It is a *utopia*.[18]

These ideal types were not meant to be "a description of concrete reality," noted Werner Cahnman, "or even the essential features of such a reality." Rather, as Weber himself acknowledged, they were "presuppositions" composed of "a purposefully created fiction" that was "guided by imagination."[19]

It is often far easier to appreciate what Weber did *not* mean by ideal types than what he did mean. Ideal types were *not*:

- Explanations
- Empirical phenomenon
- Models (although on this point, Weber shifted his perspective over time)
- Objective
- Statistical averages based on what actually existed

Above all, ideal types were not meant to be evaluative, normative concepts about how things *ought* to be.[20]

It was not and could never be the task of the social scientist, insisted Weber, "to provide binding norms and ideals from which directives for immediate practical activity can be derived."[21] What was left after eliminating all these characteristics was an attempt to create order out of chaos, to suggest homogeneity out of heterogeneity.[22]

This review offers insight into how and where the use of ideal types in the leadership discourse went astray. By the time the literature alighted on the transactional/transformational types, it had worked through several earlier iterations of ideal types. Construction of "general manager," "leader," and "transformational leader" types offered valuable insights into unfolding organizational processes. But to mistake these artificial constructs for empirical realities and then build training and evaluation systems based on what were intellectually constructed fictions led to a distorted appreciation for and understanding of those processes.

From "Management" to "General Management"

Although the practice of management in one form or another has been with us as long as individuals united in common effort, the study of management is relatively recent.[23] The Industrial Revolution spurred attention to the twin challenges of discipline and motivation in industrial organizations. The national expansion of industries such as railroads and telegraphy demanded consideration for the requirements of administration in a geographically dispersed organization. And the separation of ownership from management highlighted the need for managerial talent as a scarce resource.

Throughout much of the 20th century, it was quite common to see the terms "leader," "manager," and "executive" employed interchangeably in management literature.[24] There was no notion of subdividing general from functional management or leadership from management, and certainly not transformational leaders.

Table 6.2 *Transitioning from Functional to General Management*

From	To
Specialist	Generalist
Analyst	Integrator
Tactician	Strategist
Bricklayer	Architect
Problem-solver	Agenda-setter
Supporting cast	Lead role

Notes: Based on Michael D. Watkins, "Seven Transitions Good Leaders Must Make: Moving from a Functional Leader to a General Manager," *IMD: Tomorrow's Challenges* 1 (June 2012), 1–4.

Enhancing Collective Performance

Functional managers and general managers are *different,* two distinct and contrasting types. That is the prevailing view. "No matter how good a functional manager you are," INSEAD announced to potential attendees in its "Transitions to General Management" executive course, "you need a completely new perspective to succeed in general management."[25] Nothing unusual or surprising in that statement. Business schools all around the globe offer similar courses based on the notion that good functional managers do not necessarily make good general managers because the two are so different. Table 6.2 offers a map of the transition based on the writings of IMD's Michael Watkins.

Rather than focusing on analytic depth in a technical field – say, marketing, accounting, or informational technology – general managers were strategic integrators and architects with responsibility for bottom-line performance.[26] Functional managers provided the "technical expertise" necessary to provide "a significant depth of knowledge." General managers were "more adept at adapting to change," and therefore better able "to drive change through the business."[27] The similarities of the general management type on one hand and the leadership type of the other that are on display in Table 6.1 are stark. For good reason. Both are constructing ideal types around the same phenomenon.

Early Recognition of "Broad" Management Responsibilities

The need to achieve coordination in a complex organization found root in the transcontinental railway system in the United States in the mid-19th century. In contrast to small, localized businesses, railroad companies needed to augment technical know-how with skills of coordinating a far-flung, decentralized organization.[28] Writing in 1895, railroad executive George Bridge Leighton suggested that the effective modern executive needed to be a broad generalist. "He must understand the relation of the railway to the owners, to the public, and to the state," Leighton wrote. "He will have to know what to leave to subordinates and how to direct them . . . In a broad way, he must not only be a man of affairs, but lawyer, engineer, financier, economist, and accountant."[29]

By the 1850s, railroads had developed a position of "general supervisor" who was described as "an officer of general duty . . . who besides duties particular to himself is charged with the supervision and control of the whole system, subject to the President and Directors." This was, wrote business historian Alfred Chandler, a "new class" of managers.[30]

At the end of the 19th century, Francis Burton, a British naval engineer, recognized a general management responsibility. In *The Commercial Management of Engineering Works* (1899), Burton focused on what he termed a "general manager." The responsibility of the general manager, "or, as he was frequently termed in minutes and correspondence, *The manager*" was the individual "on whom, above all others, the profits of the company depend."[31] The term "general management" was interchangeable with the chief executive or managing director in Burton's view.

Engineers, including the American Frederick Taylor and the French Henri Fayol, expanded on the responsibilities of management. Starting in the 1820s, the economy of the United States had increasingly become industrialized, supplementing small, local businesses and agriculture with manufacturing and transportation. Innovations, including the electric light bulb, the automobile, and the process of mass assembly, furthered the expansion of the country's industrial base. The Bessemer process, invented by a British engineer, enabled the mass production of inexpensive steel. With ready access to both raw materials and low-cost (often immigrant) labor, U.S. steel companies grew rapidly. Carnegie and Bethlehem Steel were the major players, and a smaller company, Midvale Steel, hired a twenty-two-year-old apprentice engineer named Frederick Taylor. Like Francis Burton, Taylor thought deeply about the role of managers in the newly emerging industrial context. He focused largely on management's technical responsibilities to establish output standards to ensure that the "men" – that is, shop employees – knew what was expected of them and delivered it in the "best and cheapest way" possible.[32]

In 1914 Fayol produced what is considered the first general theory of management. Fayol's *General and Industrial Management* separated the activity of management from more specifically technical functions within the organization such as production, finance, security, and accounting. The technical functions, he noted, were not "concerned with drawing up the broad plan of operations of the business, with assembling personnel, coordinating and harmonizing effort and activity." That was the responsibility of a different group: managers.[33]

Fayol's title, published originally as *Administration Industrielle et Generale*, does suggest that general administrators were responsible for coordinating and direction-setting within the organization as something distinct from the technical aspects of business. Fayol had, after all, spent decades serving as *Directeur Général* – note the use of "general" that is this common French designation of a managing director – for Commentry-Fourchambault-Décazeville, a prominent French mining company.

Fayol's emphasis on management responsibilities was echoed by other early organizational theorists, notably Chester Barnard, Herbert Casson, Mary Parker Follett, and Sune Carlson.[34] They recognized the need for coordination and the role of top managers, or in Barnard's case, executives, in ensuring a common purpose and direction for organizational members.

The term "general manager" increasingly surfaced in early-20th-century America. References to general management could be found, for instance, in legal decisions as U.S. courts regularly considered questions of corporate liability and executive responsibility. "The implied powers of a general manager today are generally understood to be coexistent with the general scope of the business," noted a 1910 *Yale Law Review* article. The general management title was applied to the company's president, and, occasionally, other top-ranking executives who could be held responsible for the overall activities of the corporation.[35]

Those legal decisions represented an important truth about business organizations of the early 20th century. There were general managers; that is, managers with general responsibility for the profitability of the firm. There just weren't *many* general managers.

Through the first half of the 20th century, virtually all businesses were organized in a functional structure. Specialized activities – sales, finance, and manufacturing, for example – were cordoned off in their own units. Economies of scale and efficient division of labor were the intended outcome. Under this structure, a corporation typically had one general manager: the president.[36] So while some theorists examined the purpose of top management, there seemed to be no need to offer a separate consideration of general management. That changed in the 1950s.

A Revolutionary Redistribution of Responsibilities

It was in the 20th century, as the complexity of organizational structure became formalized, that general management expanded beyond the president's office. Du Pont and General Motors pioneered the multidivisional structure in the 1920s. Rather than purely functional reporting relationships, these new configurations were organized into "quasi-autonomous operating divisions (organized mainly along product, brand, or geographic lines)." Operating divisions, which were in turn subdivided into functional subunits, became "the principal basis for dividing up the task and assigning responsibility."[37]

In the multidivisional structure, managers of businesses were general managers with profit-and-loss responsibility for their divisions. The head of General Motors' Buick Division, for instance, supervised the functional managers of manufacturing and assembly. These divisional general managers oversaw and coordinated the activities of functional managers within their division. The corporate chief executive served as the general manager for the overall corporation.[38]

At first, this new structure found few takers. Corporations were reluctant to adopt a multidivisional form. It was seen as a "revolutionary" redistribution of responsibilities.[39] The political-economic dynamics of the 1950s changed that, turning the unusual into the commonplace, at least among large corporations.

In the aftermath of World War II, U.S. power and influence over world affairs generally and economic matters specifically was, if not monopolistic, at the very least dominant. This was the period labeled by Robert Sobel as the "age of giant corporations," characterized by a shift away from focused corporate strategy to what was called "circular" (now more likely to be referred to as *unrelated*) diversification.[40] In order to escape the antitrust attention of the federal government (and yes, this was during the so-called business-friendly Eisenhower administration), corporations became investment portfolios, taking on unrelated businesses in order to fuel the steady growth expected by shareholders.[41]

With the spreading adoption of the multidivisional structure, it was inevitable that general management would make its way into organizational discourse.[42] After immersing himself in General Motors, Peter Drucker surfaced with an appreciation for the role of the divisional manager with responsibility for "the long-term future of the business he runs."[43] It was in his 1954 *Practice of Management* that Drucker applied the title "manager of managers" to general managers. That title offered a valuable insight. By overseeing a functionally subdivided business unit, these divisional managers had direct responsibility for managing managers. Still Drucker did not specifically articulate a management of managers' job as one that was separable from the management of workers and of work.[44]

With the emergence of formal strategic thinking applied to business starting in the 1960s, attention focused on organizations as interconnected systems. Strategists recognized a core role for general management:

- In his 1963 article, Seymour Tilles emphasized the role of the "general manager" in adapting the organization to environmental change.[45]
- A 1969 *California Management Review* piece by H. Igor Ansoff and R.G. Brandenburg focused on "the general manager of the future." This was the level "at which managers are assigned total responsibility for effectively using the resources allocated to them in achieving the goals of the firm."[46]
- Kenneth Andrews elaborated further on this phenomenon by suggesting that the general manager must "rely for his principal support on a tier of functional managers, each more knowledgeable than himself within a particular area."[47]
- Hugo Uyterhoeven added the observation that the general manager of a division was a middle manager, accountable for performance of his unit but lacking full decision-making authority, which was held by the chief executive.[48]
- Michael Porter, with all his emphasis on economic rationality, included general management as an element of "firm infrastructure," suggesting that "infrastructure, unlike other support activities, usually supports the entire [value] chain and not individual activities."[49]

Now, there was a distinction between functional and general managers. That distinction was not front-and-center for the strategists. Porter acknowledged general management while simultaneously barely mentioning managers.[50] As an organizational behavior professor, John Kotter paid specific attention to the people performing that task.

In his 1982 *General Managers*, Kotter posited that, while functional managers oversaw specific areas of expertise and operations, the general manager was "responsible for a complex system which he cannot directly control and cannot entirely understand." General management as practiced by CEOs, group and divisional general managers, and product or market general managers required that individual managers possess the capacity to deal with "thousands of diverse issues and problems," balance short- and long-term pressures, and motivate and direct "other busy people over whom he has no formal authority."[51] Ambiguity and uncertainty, dealing with unknowns and unknowables; this is what separated general from functional managers.

It was absurd to suggest that in the real world of organizational life, functional managers never faced ambiguity and uncertainty. By confusing ideal types with reality, Kotter could suggest that not everyone, even those who were successful functional managers, would be well suited for the generalist job.

Where did this leave leadership? For some, leadership was conceptualized as a part of general management; one activity among many in
which the manager engaged. For others, it was a sphere of activity that
could and should be considered as distinct from management. And six
years after proposing the general manager as a concept different from the
functional manager, Kotter adopted that latter stance: leaders and managers *are* different. His 1988 take on leadership, however, was virtually
identical to his 1982 construct of a general manager. Before we look at
Kotter's evolution, we can trace the roots of the argument that leadership
was something exceptional back to the years of the Great Depression.

From Management to Leadership

POSDCORB. That was the acronym offered by Luther Gulick, director
of the Institute of Public Administration, in the 1930s to capture the general duties of the CEO. Because the terms administration and management had "lost all specific content," Gulick suggested that CEOs needed
to focus on a certain set of activities: planning, organizing, staffing,
directing, coordinating (which he described as "the all-important duty of
interrelating the various parts of the work"), reporting, and budgeting.[52]
Thus, the not very catchy POSDCORB.

Less than forty years later, Henry Mintzberg offered an analysis
of managerial work that attempted to supplement the generalities of
Gulick.[53] Mintzberg provided his own list of roles, subdivided into interpersonal, informational, and decisional roles. Of particular interest is one
of his interpersonal roles, a role not included in POSDCORB: the manager as "leader." The leader role, Mintzberg observed, "is clearly among
the most significant of all roles" in that it "permeates all activities."[54]

Certain activities could be characterized, said Mintzberg, as primarily about leadership: staffing (hiring, firing, evaluating, compensating),
motivating, and problem-solving. The leader – and Mintzberg explicitly
designated the formal head of the organization – is the only one "with
a very broad mandate – to put this another way, he is the only one who
can meddle at will – and his activities clearly reflect this."[55] Mintzberg
added a list of skills particular to that leadership role, including conflict
resolution and decision making under conditions of ambiguity.[56] Leadership was not something separate from management. Rather, it was a
critical component of management.

Mintzberg was emphatically not constructing an ideal type. He was
not engaging in a purposefully one-sided abstraction. Rather, he was reporting and defining empirical realities as he saw them. Leadership was
one of the roles played by managers. Two professors, Abraham Zaleznik

and John Kotter, soon redirected the discourse by engaging in ideal typing – managers and leaders – while insisting these types were empirical realities.

Leadership and Management Are Different, Aren't They?

In 1977 Zaleznik asked the stark question about managers and leaders: "Are They Different?" His answer, heavily influenced by his training in Freudian psychology, was an unequivocal "yes." To Zaleznik, these were not ideal types: they were tangible and real. And he would name names in order to make his point.

Zaleznik's 1977 article represented a definitive turning point in thinking about management and leadership. Ideas, however, rarely surface completely independent of previous discourse. Joseph Rost located the first distinction between leadership and management in the writing of sociologist Philip Selznick.[57] Rost's assessment overlooked many of the historical attempts to wrestle with the necessity of both technical expertise and general coordination. Still, it is important to acknowledge Selznick's contribution.

"Administrators" – that was how Selznick characterized managers in his 1957 *Leadership in Administration* – work to achieve organizational efficiency. Leaders, by whom Selznick meant the "statesmen" who sit atop an organization, have a different responsibility. The leader-statesman defines the mission of the organization and ensures ongoing success in an ever-changing environment.[58]

The difference in the approaches of Selznick and Zaleznik can be thought of as the distinction between a sociologist (Selznick) and a psychoanalyst (Zaleznik). Selznick looked at institutional forces; Zaleznik at personal dynamics. Managers and leaders, Zaleznik insisted, "are very different kinds of people. They differ in motivation, personal history, and in how they think and act."[59] Zaleznik insisted that his distinction was new. "The term manager and leader were used synonymously," he noted. "Both terms implied the responsibility of getting things done. The relationship was vertical" – i.e., hierarchical – "and superior and subordinate understood they were in an unequal power relationship."[60]

Zaleznik's application of Freudian psychology to corporate leadership first surfaced in his 1966 book, *Human Dimensions of Leadership*. He identified leaders as individuals desirous of building an enterprise, asserting an idea, or even leading a nation. Zaleznik here made an explicit distinction between management and leadership. He quoted Max Weber's view of bureaucratic administrators as functioning *sine ire et studio* (without anger or fondness) and focusing unemotionally on codification.

In his study of bureaucracies, Weber had indeed identified administrators as people who "carry out the order governing the organization in a rational, objective way."[61] Managers, whom Zaleznik equated with Weber's administrators, emphasized policies as a way of ensuring that everyone in the organization was treated "fairly," by which he meant "the same." That emphasis on standardization of treatment, however, worked against the possibility of recognizing outstanding individual achievement.[62] It was leaders, people "with brilliant ideas and the capacity to inspire thought and action in others," who provided the energy needed to propel an organization to greatness, not managers.[63]

Zaleznik transformed mental constructs into empirical realities. Managers and leaders were no longer purposefully created fictions. They were real: evaluative, normative prototypes about how things ought to be.

What had been incidental in his 1966 book became the centerpiece of Zaleznik's 1977 piece. Managers represented the organizational force that sought to create and reinforce order. Leaders, conversely, worked to generate "relative disorder."[64] The exemplar of the manager was Alfred P. Sloan, the executive who forged the modern General Motors, indeed the modern multibusiness corporation, out of the chaos of William Durant's initial creation.[65]

"Managers tend to view work as an enabling process," noted Zaleznik, "involving some combination of people and ideas interacting to establish strategies and make decisions."[66] Conversely, leaders – and here, Zaleznik pointed to Edwin Land, co-founder of Polaroid, and John F. Kennedy as examples – were "active instead of reactive, shaping ideas rather than responding to them." These are the folks who "develop fresh approaches to long-standing problems and open issues for new options."[67]

Even though leaders provided energy to organizations and were active and not reactive, Zaleznik also made readers aware of the potential dangers inherent in those who became leaders. "Leaders work from high risk positions," he suggested. "Indeed often are temperamentally disposed to seek out risk and danger, especially when opportunity and reward appear high." Leaders possessed hot personalities infusing their actions and reactions with strong emotions, including love and hate, in contrast to Weber's view of bureaucratic administrators as functioning with analytic detachment. Leaders were people who "may work in organizations, but they never belong to them. Their sense of who they are does not depend on memberships, work/roles, or other social indicators of identity."[68]

The next volley in the management-is-different-from-leadership argument came from John Kotter in his 1988 *The Leadership Factor*. Kotter had championed general management in his 1985 book. After Zaleznik, however, his own views veered toward the management versus leadership dichotomy. For the release of the paperback edition of *The General Manager* in 1985, Kotter referred to the book as "the first of what has become a series of works on leadership in complex organizations," even though the terms "leader" or "leadership" are absent from the index. With *The Leadership Factor*, Kotter fully embraced the management/leadership classification.

His was neither a continuation nor an endorsement of Zaleznik's work. In fact, Kotter rejected Zaleznik's hard demarcation by suggesting that management and leadership "are certainly not incompatible (indeed, more and more these days, both are needed in managerial jobs)."[69] By the time of Kotter's next book, *A Force for Change* (1990), the distinction between management and leadership was taken as a given. The ideal type had fully disappeared into a presumed empirical reality.

Kotter's research methodology asked executives to provide examples of people who were effective at management, at leadership, or at both. From that methodology, he concluded that while managers established plans, leaders produced "visions" and while managers directed activities, leaders created understanding and acceptance of desired future states. Fundamentally, managers administered the status quo while leadership mobilized people toward "*adoptive change.*"[70]

First, it was managers, then general managers, and now leaders who helped the organization move together into the future. Kotter insisted that "the two processes can work together very successfully."[71] Nonetheless, he argued, organizations have proven to be much more effective at developing managers than at producing leaders.

Zaleznik was explicit in his condemnation of managers. What he called "the managerial mystique" – the triumph of the search for order – was "only tenuously tied to reality." American industry had "lost its way, adrift in a sea of managerial mediocrity desperately needing leadership to face worldwide economic competition."[72]

Not everyone bought the premise. "Our research thus far does not demonstrate the need for this distinction," wrote Fred Fiedler and Joseph Garcia in 1987. "Leadership, as we define the term, refers to that part of organizational management that deals with the direction and supervision of subordinates rather than, for example, inventory control, fiscal management, or customer relations."[73] Still, there is no denying that the embrace of leadership as a concept distinct from and, for the most part, superior to, management became something of a fad in the discourse. As an example of such faddishness, we can look at the evolution of a popular developmental tool: the managerial grid.

In 1964 Robert Blake first published his managerial grid offering guidelines to managers seeking to support and aid people in the performance of the task. Building on the orthogonal dimensions proposed by the Ohio State and Michigan researchers, Blake emphasized high concern for both task and people. Blake's focus on managerial behavior was reinforced through a number of subsequent editions in which the grid emphasized both concern for production and concern for people. Leadership was seen as a team effort by managers working together with employees to create a "correct whole picture for organizational decision making and direction." That's where it stood until 1991 when the *managerial* grid morphed into the *leadership* grid.

"The new pursuit is visionary leadership at the top," wrote Blake and Anne McCanse, "as organizations find themselves in the midst of accelerating change, suddenly thrust upon the global scene with new financial markets, rapidly advancing technology, and a multitude of other factors that demand attention. With such a rapid fire chain of events, we may pause and reflect, 'How can my organization keep up with the competition, much less hope to get ahead?'" The grid, it should be noted, remained *exactly the same*. Now, however, it was a leadership rather than a managerial grid. Why the relabeling? "It all comes back to leadership," wrote the former advocates of a managerial grid. "Effective leadership is the key to success for the future."[74]

There was much that was voguish in this rush to leadership as a solution to organizational ills. Danny Miller and associates defined management "fads" as quick fixes that do not have a "profound effect" on performance, are embraced ritualistically, and then fade out. Fads are not without merit. Rather, they represent a typically opportunistic embrace of a particular zeitgeist, arguing typically without critical distance that a unique solution has been found for a unique situation.[75] By 1997, when executives were clamoring to become leaders rather than managers, the fad had become the new reality.

The idea of both Zaleznik and Kotter that leadership and management were different was itself a product of a particular time and place: 1970s America.

"Groping for Leadership"

The 1970s were the decade referred to by one historian as the age of "the great compression" and another as a period of "disorienting, frustrating, and frightening" challenge for Americans. The mood of the nation, noted critic Frank Rich, was "defeated, whiny, and riddled with self-doubt." As the Bicentennial celebration of the penning of the Declaration of

Independence approached, pundits wondered "whether the country even deserved to throw itself a birthday party."[76] Little surprise, then, that leadership emerged as a desirable, albeit rare, commodity; a force that would pull the country and its industry out of a pervasive malaise.

The 1970s, noted historians Beth Bailey and Burnham Farber, "was the only decade other than the 1930s wherein Americans ended up poorer than they began."[77] In fact, the "age of compression" opened with the 1973 oil embargo by the Organization of Petroleum Exporting Countries (OPEC).[78] That unprecedented action initiated a rest-of-the-decade decline in American economic fortunes. The resignation the following year of President Richard Nixon in the wake of the Watergate scandal left in place an unelected president, Gerald Ford, who had never stood for election as vice president. He was appointed in 1973 when the elected vice president, Spiro Agnew, was forced to resign due to his own scandal. Ford lacked the political platform to respond effectively to this challenge to western capitalism.[79]

Both the 1974 resignation of President Nixon and the ignoble end of the Vietnam War the following year were harbingers of what Bailey and Farber labeled the "cultural crisis" of the period.[80] The retreat from Vietnam was often depicted as America's first-ever military defeat (although one would be hard-pressed to see the Korean War as a victory). Two assassination attempts on President Ford, although inept, left a sour aftertaste. A 1979 accident at the Three Mile Island nuclear power plant seemed to undercut the desirability of turning to nuclear energy as a way of loosening the country's dependence on OPEC oil.

Above all else, it was the sagging national economy that defined the era. America's "Rust Belt" – the upper Midwestern states that hosted much of the country's industrial operations – staggered under the economic weight. "One by one," wrote historian Paul Boyer, "plagued by foreign competition, aging equipment, rising labor costs, and shifting consumer tastes, the factories that made America the world's industrial leader from the 1880s through World War II closed their gates."[81] America's global economic might was under severe challenge. Japanese companies seemed to be outperforming their American competitors. In 1980, an NBC-TV news special asked, "If Japan Can, Why Can't We?" The answer was not so clear.

Bruce Schulman located the roots of a national malaise specifically in "the unchecked, out-of-control rage of inflation."[82] Runaway inflation – in 1979 and 1980 the U.S. experienced two consecutive years of double-digit inflation for the first time since World War I – led President Jimmy Carter to institute voluntary wage and price freezes with little positive effect. A public opinion poll taken in February 1979 found only

26 percent of respondents claimed to be "highly satisfied" with "life in the nation today"; five months later, that figure plummeted to 12 percent.[83]

A lack of leadership lay behind this malaise. That, at least, was an argument being made with some frequency and prominence. *The Culture of Narcissism*, a surprise 1979 best seller by cultural historian Christopher Lasch, reflected the view that America's leaders had lost their capacity to confront the difficulties faced by society.[84] An Independence Day editorial in the *New York Post* repeated the theme: "The United States is now a victim of a loss of nerve and will, wracked by indecision and groping for a glimpse of inspirational and innovative leadership."[85]

In July 1979, President Carter delivered a nationally televised speech to address what he called the "crisis of the American spirit."[86] That "malaise speech" directly confronted the national longing for leadership:[87]

The symptoms of this crisis of the American spirit are all around us. For the first time in the history of our country, a majority of our people believe that the next five years will be worse than the past five years. Two-thirds of our people do not even vote. The productivity of American workers is actually dropping, and the willingness of Americans to save for the future has fallen below that of all other people in the Western world.

"I will do my best," the president vowed, "but I will not do it alone . . . it is time for us to join hands . . . [and] commit ourselves together to a rebirth of the American spirit."

In a comment little noted at the time, Carter suggested that the American people expected far more than competent management from public officials. Reflecting on a concern that had been voiced by a congressman – "Mr. President, you are not leading this nation, you're just managing the government" – he concluded that the public craved *leadership*. This notion that "leadership" provided the needed antidote to malaise fits perfectly with a moment in the evolving leadership discourse.

A year after Carter's malaise speech, Robert Hayes and William Abernathy wrote "Managing Our Way to Economic Decline." That title left little room for ambiguity. The authors chastised management and managers for undermining America's economic strength. "During the past several years," the authors wrote, "American business has experienced a marked deterioration of competitive vigor and a growing unease about its overall economic well-being."[88]

Hayes and Abernathy placed blame for America's declining economic performance squarely on the shoulders of managers. "What, exactly, have American managers been doing wrong," the authors asked, before providing a catalogue:

. . . guided by what they took to be the newest and best principles of management, American managers have increasingly directed their attention elsewhere. These new principles, despite their sophistication and widespread usefulness, encourage a preference for [1] analytic detachment rather than the insight that comes from 'hands on' experience and [2] short-term cost reduction rather than long-term development of technological competitiveness. It is this new managerial gospel, we feel, that has played a major role in undermining the vigor of American industry.[89]

"In our judgment," Hayes and Abernathy concluded, "the assumptions underlying these questions are prime evidence of a broad managerial failure – a failure of both vision and leadership – that over time has eroded both the inclination and the capacity of U.S. companies to innovate."[90] For Hayes and Abernathy, managers had failed as leaders.

If leadership, generally, was not up to the task, a particular variety of leadership – yet another ideal type mistaken for an objective empirical reality – emerged from the work of political scientist James MacGregor Burns. His 1978 *Leadership* introduced readers to the contrasting models of transactional and transformational leadership.

Burns' book was pivotal in the evolution of leadership discourse. Bernard Bass proclaimed it to be "seminal." Leadership discussions prior to Burns tended to focus on behaviors of individuals within groups and actions taken by those individuals to influence the behavior of others. What Burns did, noted Bass, was turn attention to "the statesmen who moved and shook the world."[91] The impact on leadership discourse among business scholars was extraordinary.

From Leadership to Transformation

Transformational leadership, defined as leadership with the capacity to "help the organization develop a vision of what it can be, to mobilize the organization to accept and work toward achieving the new vision, and to institutionalize the changes that must last over time," was soon integrated into management discourse. In their 1984 manifesto, Noel Tichy and David Ulrich extolled the capacity of transformational leadership to rescue the industrial base of the U.S. economy from the decline it had been experiencing following the OPEC embargo. "Unless the creation of this breed of leaders becomes a national agenda," Tichy and Ulrich insisted, "we are not very optimistic about the revitalization of the U.S. economy."[92]

At first, a small cadre of scholars – notably Tichy and Ulrich joined by Bernard Bass and Warren Bennis – offered articles and books on the topic.[93] That trickle turned into what Burns called "an international tidal wave of researchers and scholars" focused on transformational leadership.[94] By 1999, James Hunt noted that the study of transformational and charismatic leadership had fundamentally altered the field of leadership studies.[95]

In the three decades following the Tichy and Ulrich piece, transformational leadership grew to become the most popular approach to and source of leadership research.[96] Articles examining transformational leadership outnumbered all leadership articles using other theories – trait theory, path-goal theory, and leader-member exchange theory among them – combined.[97] In addition, transformational leadership came to dominate the pedagogy offered in leading U.S. and U.K. MBA programs, helping to set the agenda for educating future corporate executives.[98]

Central to transformational leadership discourse was the relegation of transactional leadership to a secondary, decidedly inferior status. In Burns' construct, transactional leadership was equated with political horse trading: swapping jobs for votes or subsidies for campaign contributions. All leaders, Burns admitted, did *some* of this. Still, an aura of shadiness if not outright mendacity hung over the transactional exchange. Transformational leadership provided moral elevation; transactional leadership functioned at a considerably lower level.[99]

With no apparent hesitation, that debasement of transactional leadership was endorsed by leadership scholars. The exchange process, in which rewards would be meted out in return for agreed-upon performance, could bring about "changes of degree," but not the type of fundamental realignment that was apparently called for.[100]

Transactional leadership, Bernard Bass insisted, could be "a prescription for mediocrity," especially "if the leader relies heavily on passive management-by-exception, intervening with his or her group only when procedures and standards for accomplishing tasks are not being met." To complete this equation of transactional leadership with bad management, Bass insisted that "such a manager espouses the popular adage, 'If it ain't broke, don't fix it.' He or she stands in the back of the caboose of a moving freight train and says, 'Now I know where we are going.'"[101]

Transformational leadership, conversely, was more moral, more uplifting for both leaders and followers. It was the only style suited to the turbulent, challenging environment in which business executives lived. Transformational leaders, wrote Bass and Paul Steidlmeier in a 20th-century reflection of Thomas Carlyle, were aware of "what is right, good, important, and beautiful" and are able to "elevate followers to go beyond their self-interests for the good of their group, organization, or society."[102]

Did the success of a corporate enterprise truly depend on the elevation of employees to some higher order? Did effort on behalf of organizational success rely on the relegation of self-interests to organizational goals on the part of followers? Did "authentic transformational leaders," in fact, ever set aside their own self-interests on behalf of "what is right, good, important, and beautiful"? And were contingency rewards based on the expectation of contracted performance necessarily the enemy of high performance? To the original transformational leadership advocates – and "advocates" they were – the answers to these questions were self-evident: yes, yes, yes, and yes.

In order to convince themselves and others that this ideal type – the transformational leader – was an empirical reality, the early advocates engaged in a fiction, one that posited a decidedly transactional leader, and a bit of a bully at that, as the exemplar of transformation.

The Iacocca Phenomenon

Positioning Lee Iacocca, president of Chrysler from 1978 to 1992, as a transformational leader prototype was a founding assertion in the early discourse. The 1984 Tichy and Ulrich article referred to Iacocca as "one of the most dramatic examples of transformational management and organizational revitalization in the early 1980s." Iacocca had "provided the leadership to transform the company from the brink of bankruptcy to profitability."[103] Their claim for transformation rested on assertion rather than evidence. "As a result of Iacocca's leadership," they insisted, "by 1984 Chrysler had earned record profits, had obtained high levels of employee morale, and had helped employees generate a sense of meaning in their work." Iacocca had altered the culture of the corporation to a "lean and hungry team looking for victory."

A turnaround argument for Chrysler appeared valid at the time of the article. Placing that result on the shoulders of the CEO was, at the very least, a shortcut for explaining the multiple forces at play both inside Chrysler and in the larger external environment. Furthermore, the authors provided no evidence for their claim that Iacocca had transformed the culture, lifted employee morale, and generated a "sense of meaning" for those employees. Tichy and Ulrich, in fact, made no attempt to suggest that their conclusions were based on data collected either by them or others.

That lack of substantiation did not prevent them from insisting that Iacocca's transformational leadership presented a salve for American industry: "Lee Iacocca's high visibility and notoriety may be the important missing element in management today," argued Tichy and Ulrich. "There seems to be a paucity of transformational leader role models at all levels of the organization."[104] The drab leaders of other industrial giants – sluggish, colorless, and noncharismatic – became foils for the exciting and apparently effective style of Iacocca.

Neither did the lack of evidence stop others from repeating the claim of Chrysler's transformation under Iacocca. In their 1985 *Leaders: Strategies for Change*, Warren Bennis and Burt Nanus simply imported Tichy and Ulrich's claim: "Almost exclusively because of Iacocca's leadership, by 1983 Chrysler made a profit, boosted employee morale, and helped employees generate a sense of meaning in their work." *Almost exclusively.*

To demonstrate Iacocca's right to the mantle of transformational leadership, Bennis and Nanus repeated Tichy and Ulrich's insistence that Iacocca had overseen a culture change at Chrysler. "Over a period of a year or two, the internal culture was transformed to that of a lean and hungry team looking for victory – and competent enough to achieve it."[105] The authors were even more emphatic than were Tichy and Ulrich. "Our concept of power and leadership, then, is molded on the Iacocca phenomenon." Once again, no claim of research was offered or supporting evidence presented. Unlike Tichy and Ulrich, however, Bennis and Nanus could include one citation: Tichy and Ulrich. They were not advancing scholarship; they were bolstering the Iacocca myth.

The Myth

Lee Iacocca's launch as a nationally recognized figure can be traced to his first (of three) appearances on the cover of *Time Magazine* in April 1964.[106] At the time, Iacocca headed the Ford Division, which accounted for 80 percent of that corporation's total sales. Iacocca and his staff were credited with "launching most of the major themes that dominate the U.S. auto industry today: the return to car racing, the intensified appeal to the youth market, and the trend to the low-priced sports car [the Mustang]."[107] For Iacocca, ascendency to mythical "folk hero" status was just beginning.

In November 1978, Iacocca became president of Chrysler. The company that had once been the number two automaker in the U.S. – with a 25 percent market share in 1940 – had fallen to the brink of bankruptcy. In 1978, Chrysler lost over $200 million, then over $1 billion the following year. The poor reputation of Chrysler products (Chrysler, Dodge, and Plymouth were its brands) in terms of both styling and quality eroded the company's market share. When Iacocca arrived at Chrysler, the company had 80,000 unsold vehicles worth nearly one-quarter of a billion dollars sitting in dealer lots, and owed $4 billion.[108]

Like the rest of the automotive industry – indeed, like American basic industry generally – Chrysler increasingly found itself on the losing end of competition with Japanese companies, especially Toyota and Nissan (then marketed in the U.S. under the brand name "Datsun"). Japanese auto manufacturers, which had produced a total of 32,000 vehicles in 1950, now manufactured over eleven million cars, allowing Japan to surpass the U.S. as the largest auto-producing nation.

At the core of the Japanese challenge was the increasing productivity of Japanese factories compared with their U.S. counterparts. In particular, Toyota's revolutionary production system, which included quality circles, voluntary improvement programs, and new just-in-time inventory control systems that reduced waste and idle time, allowed Japanese makers to improve quality and lower costs simultaneously. Automobiles were not alone in falling behind Japanese competition – the U.S. steel, appliances, and electronics industries were also deeply challenged – but there was something emblematic about the role of automobiles in U.S. culture.

Iacocca commenced turnaround efforts at Chrysler with cost cutting, starting with his own salary. He accepted only $1 of his contracted $360,000, seeing this as a symbolic gesture of shared sacrifice. In a move considered radical by much of the business community and highly controversial within the labor movement, Iacocca convinced United Auto Workers' president Douglas Fraser to accept a seat on the Chrysler board. That gesture allowed Chrysler to win wage concessions from the union three years ahead of those granted to GM and Ford, accounting for a three-year $1 billion labor cost advantage over its domestic competitors.[109]

When financial restructuring, which removed $400 million in debt and added $300 million in loans, proved insufficient to fuel recovery, Iacocca, Fraser, and Detroit Mayor Coleman Young traveled to Washington, D.C. They won approval of a $1.5 billion federal loan guarantee, signed by President Carter in the waning days of his administration. That guarantee further aided Chrysler by allowing the corporation to roll forward its recent losses and pay no taxes through 1985.

Product innovations at Chrysler helped as well. The erosion of Chrysler's market share had been severe throughout the 1970s. Volkswagen had gained a foothold in the U.S. market, but it was mainly Japanese brands that ate away at Chrysler and the other U.S.-based automakers. Under Iacocca, Chrysler responded by reducing the number of platforms and emphasizing front-wheel-drive cars with smaller four-cylinder engines. Drastic cost-cutting accompanied by the offshoring of assembly to Canada allowed Chrysler to slash its breakeven point on domestically produced autos, thus keeping prices low while generating a profit.

And the most significant new car development of the 1980s emerged from Iacocca's Chrysler: the minivan. Built on Chrysler's K-platform, the

Dodge Caravan and twin Plymouth Voyager combined a station wagon and a van. Ford and GM had small vans at the time, but both were built on truck platforms, resulting in limited appeal to suburban consumers. The minivan concept had been developed at Ford during the Iacocca years by product design master Hal Sperlich. Ford did not pursue the idea and fired Sperlich in the mid-1970s. Sperlich joined Chrysler where he was soon reunited with his old boss. Iacocca gave Sperlich the go-ahead and the minivan helped revitalize the car market.

By the early 1980s, the U.S. auto industry as a whole was experiencing a recovery. The end of 1970s "stagflation" – the combination of slow growth and inflation – and a dramatic decline in interest rates, released pent-up demand for *all* cars.[110] Eventually, the United Auto Workers made wage concessions to Ford and GM. Political pressure led to a "voluntary" limit on the number of Japanese imports, affording U.S. automakers a temporary cushion (temporary because, by the mid-1980s, Japanese makers began manufacturing their cars in the United States to circumvent import limitations) against foreign competition.

However, while the entire industry recovered, Chrysler outpaced its domestic competitors, achieving larger percentage increases in U.S. sales than either GM or Ford. In 1982 Chrysler posted its first profitable quarter in five years. Overall, 1982 ended in a $68 million loss. But 1983 was a different story. With profits of nearly $1 billion, Chrysler repaid its government debt seven years early; a "miracle," observed the *Saturday Evening Post*.[111]

The identification of Iacocca as an essentially *American* hero – "the American underdog winning the battle of preserving the American dream" – was carefully and consciously cultivated by Iacocca himself.[112] Chrysler's ad campaign frequently used the word "American." The K-car was roomy enough to hold not six *passengers* but "six Americans." The ads typically employed a red, white, and blue color scheme for their back-drop.[113] With the launch of various K-car models, Iacocca proclaimed, "This is the beginning of the reindustrialization of the American auto-mobile industry."[114]

Even beyond the automobile industry, Iacocca offered himself and Chrysler as a tonic for America's loss of confidence. Iacocca opened a 1984 TV ad, for instance, by saying, "A lot of people think America can't cut the mustard any more, that quality counts for nothing and hard work for even less. And commitment? That went out with the hula hoop." To combat that pessimism, Iacocca offered hope, promising – from Chrysler at least – "quality, hard work, and commitment, the stuff America was made of."[115]

By 1984, the U.S. economy was far healthier than it had been when Iacocca assumed control of Chrysler. Although some heavy industries, including steel, continued to shed jobs, the American economy overall was expanding. Unemployment had fallen to just over 7 percent, inflation had dropped to under 4 percent, and corporate earnings were healthy. It was in that environment that Iacocca's self-titled memoir appeared.

Released in 1984, at the peak of Chrysler's recovery, it took exactly three weeks for *Iacocca* to reach number one on the *New York Times'* best-seller list. In 1984 *Iacocca* was the best-selling nonfiction book of the entire year. In 1985, the same. "It is," said a buyer for book chain B. Dalton, "one of the biggest books of our lifetime."[116] Iacocca was now, unquestionably, a CEO superstar.[117] But had he actually transformed anything? Despite the claims made by his admirers, the answer was a simple and unequivocal no.

Iacocca was certainly part of the team that saw Chrysler pull back from the brink of economic catastrophe. But in order to depict him as a transformational leader, Tichy and Ulrich claimed that he had overseen a major overhaul of Chrysler's culture. What was the evidence? The authors provide none. There were data available, however.

Improved quality, which can be used as an outcome proxy for transformed internal processes and which sat at the crux of the Japanese alternative approach to manufacturing, did not happen at Chrysler under Iacocca. His promise, made in television ads, that Chrysler quality would rival imports and "beat the Japanese at their own game," was demonstrably unmet. An examination of the overall quality of Chrysler models between 1982 and 1991 as reported by *Consumer Reports* and publicly available at the time shows consistent ratings of "much worse than average" quality performance for the Plymouth minivan, the Chrysler La Baron ("If you can find a better car, buy it"), and consistent "average" performance by the Dodge minivan. In contrast, the Honda Accord was annually rated as "much better than average."[118]

Likewise, the product innovation that Chrysler undertook in Iacocca's early years – reliance on smaller, gas-efficient cars, front-wheel drive, and the minivan – ended by mid-decade. In 1985 Iacocca began using the cash generated from auto sales to diversify the corporate portfolio: bidding unsuccessfully for Hughes Aerospace and purchasing Gulfstream Aerospace. Corporate diversification is a legitimate strategy to pursue; but in this case, Iacocca was following General Motors (the corporation that outbid Chrysler for Hughes) rather than innovating. Iacocca brought nothing new to the management of Chrysler or the auto industry generally.

What came next for Iacocca and Chrysler proved both disheartening and diminishing. The myth did not hold up well. Iacocca found himself in frequent and increasingly bitter conflict with the Chrysler board, raising questions, at the very least, about the alignment of his goals with those of the company. Chrysler fell further behind both the Japanese and domestic competitors. As a result, the company faced another financial crisis in 1991. Failure to name a successor on Iacocca's part led the board to force Iacocca to retire.[119] In 1995, a bitter Iacocca joined forces with Chrysler stockholder Kirk Kerkorian to launch a hostile, and ultimately unsuccessful, takeover bid.[120]

And what was the evidence that Iacocca's executive behavior conformed to the transformational leader prototype presented by Bass, Bennis, Tichy, and the other promoters of the concept? To examine that question, we can turn to Iacocca's own description of his management approach, both in his days at Ford and at Chrysler. This is material that was readily available to but ignored by the authors as they were constructing the fiction of Iacocca as the transformational leader prototype.

In the 1964 *Time Magazine* cover story – he was head of the Ford Division at the time – Iacocca admitted to secretly tape-recording dealership sales people and threatening them with losing their jobs if their performance was deemed unsatisfactory. Demanding superior performance is well within the realm of executive responsibility. But secret tape-recording suggests at the very least questionable ethics at the expense of moral uplift. It is his rationale for that action that is particularly informative: "It worked, because all of a sudden a guy [an auto salesman] is face to face with the reality of his mortgage payments."[121] There is nothing especially transformational, paradigm-bending, or "good, important, and beautiful" in either the behavior or the rationale that Iacocca offered.

There was much in his autobiography to rebut the conclusion that Iacocca's style was transformational. Of particular interest was his description of negotiations with the United Auto Workers to convince them to accept wage cuts: "I had to lay it on the line. I talked tough to them. 'Hey, boys,' I said, 'I've got a shotgun at your head. I've got thousands of jobs available at seventeen bucks an hour. I've got none at twenty. So you'd better come to your senses.'" At a second meeting, he recalled saying, "You've got until morning to make a decision. If you don't help me out, I'm going to blow your brains out. I'll declare bankruptcy in the morning and you'll all be out of work."[122] These words describe an approach that is wholly and dramatically at odds with the transformational model.

In short, it is possible to make a strong case for Iacocca as a turnaround leader in his initial years. He made key decisions and participated in a remarkable recovery for a nearly bankrupt industrial giant. He was, during this period, an effective CEO and perhaps, even, a "hero." It is far less possible to accept uncritically the argument that he oversaw the transformation of Chrysler or that his behavioral style fits a transformational prototype. And the fact that Chrysler quickly fell behind its competitors as the decade continued and faced a second near-bankruptcy crisis in 1991 undermines the claim of substantive transformation.

Iacocca was a fiction disguised as a real type. Not all the discourse of the period, however, accepted the underlying premise of the transformational construct quite so readily.

An Alternative View

A number of leadership scholars had, in the 1970s, focused on the exchange – unfortunately labeled the "vertical dyad linkage" – between leaders and followers. Reciprocity, in the view of the discourse that shed its awkward label and adopted Leader-Member Exchange (LMX), could lead to interdependencies between leader and follower. That resulting interdependency could range from a reciprocal partnership to a pure overseer role in which only contractual behavior was exchanged and influence was entirely downward.[123]

A more sweeping defense of transactional leadership had appeared several years prior to Burns' book. In his 1973 *Rebel Leadership*, sociologist James Downton focused on the leadership of mass movements.[124] His attention was not on business organizations. (Neither, remember, was Burns' focus on business.) Rather, Downton sought to analyze the leader-follower dynamic in various "rebellious" situations, ranging from the Russian Revolution to the Black Muslim movement in the United States. Downtown saw his work in juxtaposition with a popular book by Eric Hoffer published in 1951, *The True Believer*.[125]

As were so many others of his generation, Hoffer was moved to consider the twin totalitarian mass movements of Nazism and Communism, which he equated. All fanatical mass movements, he suggested, regardless of their particular ideological positions, were the same in one key regard. They were fueled by a misguided urge on the part of followers to achieve some degree of self-esteem.[126]

Downton was not convinced of the universality of Hoffer's conclusion. Rather than considering Hitler and Stalin, two obvious targets for condemnation, Downton wondered whether people in rebellious political movements might be acting as rational human decision makers rather than irrational fanatics. To help arrive at an answer, Downton looked at the exchange that lay at the heart of all leader-follower engagements. He concluded that transactional leadership contained the capacity to mobilize and energize followers to a rational commitment to a leader and to the purpose of that leader's calling.

Downton's book preceded Burns' *Leadership* by five years, so he was not explicitly rebutting that work. There is no denying, however, that he positioned the transactional leader-follower exchange, potentially at least, in a far more positive light.

That exchange-benefit relationship sat at the core of transactional leadership. Leadership was, by its nature, transactional, insisted Downton. But his take on transactions had nothing to do with "horse trading." Rather, transactions, with the inherent reciprocity of benefits and obligations, recognized the autonomy of all parties. That was true, at least, for what Downton called "positive transactions" in which individuals consciously weighed alternative modes of behavior and made an informed, consensual choice. Once a positive leader-follower bond was forged, groups were situated to make the kinds of adaptations and changes required of a dynamic external environment.

And what of charisma, that force which was claimed by transformational leadership as its exclusive domain? Not so, insisted Downton. Remember, he was engaging these concepts several years before the introduction of transformational leadership. Still, he placed charisma squarely inside the transactional construct. Charisma was basically a psychological exchange. In recognizing the "*manifestly* transcendental authority" of a leader, the follower offers both deference and affection.[127] It may have been an irrational exchange, but the terms were explicit and understandable. The follower moves closer to an ideal and becomes socialized into a larger group. Even the notion of radical change can be seen as an element of transactional leadership as the follower willingly adopts the leader's new model of behavior.

Transactional leadership possessed, in Downton's analysis, the potential to transform. His conceptualization obliterated what would become the abiding and widely accepted dichotomization that Burns and others had inserted between transactional leadership and transformational outcomes. That doesn't suggest, however, that the discourse was creating an artificial tension within organizations between the need for stability and the requirement for dynamic responsiveness. That tension was real.

Recognizing the Tension

General managers, leaders, and transformational leaders are all ideal types. Furthermore, they are the *same* ideal types under different labels. Look at this list of characteristics:

- Capacity to operate effectively under conditions of ambiguity and uncertainty
- Requirement to achieve coordinated activity on behalf of the organization
- Need to set the overall scope and direction of the business
- Engagement in ongoing adaptation and change

These are characteristics of an ideal type, but *which* ideal type? General manager? Leader? Transformational leader? The answer, clearly, is "yes, all three." They were interchangeable labels. Between his 1982 and 1988 books, Kotter's general managers became leaders. Likewise, Bernard Bass appropriated Zaleznik's "managers" and relabeled them "transactional leaders."[128]

The reason leadership discourse continuously returns to these types is the need to wrestle with a fundamental fact of all organizations: maintenance and adaptation have always existed as a core tension.

By the late 1950s, multibusiness corporations had become the dominant source of economic activity in the American economy. Organizational sociologist Amitai Etzioni turned his attention to how these behemoths functioned, focusing particular attention on how leadership unfolded. In a 1959 *Administrative Science Quarterly* piece, he drew attention to the necessity of an "authority structure" for the achievement of organizational goals. It was in this piece that he drew a distinction between two types of authority.

Managers – that's the label Etzioni applied – have "(line) authority because they direct the major goal activity."[129] These are the folks in organizations who issue orders and take responsibility for actions. Experts, who he labeled "staff," have authority as well, this based on "intensive knowledge in a limited area." In a foreshadowing of Zaleznik's argument about fundamental distinctions between the psychology of managers and leaders, Etzioni suggested that line management called for different personality types from staff experts. "Managers are more committed or loyal to their specific organizations than are experts" who direct their loyalties primarily "toward their professional reference and membership groups."[130]

The notion that organizations need to maintain some degree of order while simultaneously responding to a dynamic external environment reached perhaps its fullest recognition in James Thompson's 1967 impressive statement of administrative theory, *Organizations in Action*. Only "sheltered" organizations, by which Thompson meant businesses with either "unlimited resources" or a "monopolistic position" could afford to take an "office-holding view" of administration.[131] Otherwise, the formal authority required to maintain unified direction needed to be supplemented.

Thompson referred to the requirement to manage the tension between unity of direction and responsiveness to external dynamism as "co-alignment." It was precisely the maintenance of co-alignment that provided the central challenge of administration. The task of administration was not just to maintain direction but also to decide "how and how fast to change the design, structure, or technology of the organization."[132]

Both change and stasis were critical in organizational life; a business cannot survive without either.

Toward the end of this concise, insightful work, Thompson made a point of noting a "personality variable" that might tend to bias administrators toward certainty and away from the embrace of the challenge of change.[133] His reference was to intolerance-to-ambiguity, a concept arising out of the work of Egan Frankel-Brunswick in the late 1940s.

Individuals with a high intolerance for ambiguity, Frankel-Brunswick argued, experienced ambiguous situations – situations involving novelty, complexity, insolubility, unpredictability, and uncertainty – as a source of either discomfort or stress.[134] That discomfort or stress, referred to in psychological literature as anxiety, led individuals to reject or avoid ambiguous situations. When facing a decision in the face of ambiguity, these high-intolerance-for-ambiguity individuals tended to delay, waiting for more data to add greater predictability. And perhaps most troubling of all for organizations, individuals with high intolerance for ambiguity found decision making under conditions of stress to be especially difficult, often putting off decisions to mitigate the discomfort.[135]

Thompson's insight into a fundamental tension between ambiguity and certainty, between change and stability, avoided any clear-cut creation of ideal types. But the ideal types reviewed here certainly fit into this schema. The general management task is to administer the tension in such a way as to create co-alignment. Leaders might be those individuals more comfortable with ambiguity and managers more comfortable with predictability. But remember, these are ideal types, not real things. And this is precisely where so much of the discourse has gone sour.

Nowhere can we see the consequence of ideas more starkly than with the emergence of transformational leadership and its claimed superiority to the mundane task of "just managing." There was a time – that is, the period before the effusive praise and unrealistic hopes pinned on transformational leaders – when the ideal CEO was valued for strategic thinking, industry knowledge, and organizational commitment. The infusion of charisma into the presumed requirements of a CEO and the expectation that salvation could be attained by hiring a transformational leader, bespoke a deep misunderstanding of how and why organizations perform the way they do.

Time and again, management scholars engaged in a process of relabeling: from managers to general managers to transformational leaders. Each represented an ideal type, the *same* ideal type. Weber had suggested the ideal type methodology as a way of shaping discourse, and these various types have done that. However, many of these writers using these ideal types ignored Weber's admonishment not to confuse them with empirical realities. When leaders were presented in contrast to managers, when transformational leaders were presented as superior to transactional leaders, that confusion became misleading, even disingenuous.

Transactions between leaders and followers, for instance, offer the opportunity to expand the field of reciprocity while recognizing the agency of all parties to the transaction. Yet the transformational advocates denounced the potential value of the leader-follower transaction in favor of some abstract notion of transformation.

Looking Backward/Looking Forward

Each dichotomy – general management versus functional management, leadership versus management, and transactional versus transformational – represented a conceptual response to a particular historical context. General management became important in response to the diversification of corporations in the 1950s and 1960s. Leadership emerged from the economic turmoil and disillusionment that characterized the 1970s, while transformational leadership appealed to the hunger for renewal.

This is not to suggest that the rhetoric of general management and leadership were *just* faddish reactions to events of the day. There was some element of faddishness, certainly, as there is in much of management discourse. But each represented an ideal type that can, if used appropriately, provide useful insight. However, when used inappropriately, as has often been the case throughout the literature, ideal types distort understanding and misdirect energies.

A decade after the appearance of transformational leadership, yet another ideal type – global leadership – appeared and soon assumed a central position in the discourse. Global leadership was offered as more than an extension of domestic leadership; rather, it was positioned as a way to address the unique challenges of a globally connected, intensively dynamic world. And like all other ideal types, it was a fiction; a useful fiction for opening a discussion (as all well-constructed ideal types are), but not a fully realized and distinct empirical type.

NOTES

1 David Fagiano, "Managers vs. Leaders: A Corporate Fable," *Management Review* 86 (1997), 5.
2 That quote from Stanford University is found in Tourish, *Dark Side*, 103.
3 Barbara Kellerman, *The End of Leadership* (New York: Harper Business, 2012), xiii. For another critical examination of the emergent leadership industry, see Jeffrey Pfeffer, *Leadership BS: Fixing Workplaces and Careers One Truth at a Time* (New York: HarperCollins, 2015).

4 James G. Hunt et al., eds., *Leaders and Managers: International Perspectives on Managerial Behavior and Leadership* (New York: Pergamon Press, 1984), 5.

5 Yukl, *Leadership in Organizations*, 7.

6 Jay A. Conger, *Learning to Lead: The Art of Transforming Managers into Leaders* (San Francisco: Jossey-Bass, 1992).

7 Ibid., 5.

8 Peter Baskett, "Leaders Not Managers," *Resuscitation* 50 (2001), 3.

9 Mats Alvesson and Stefan Sveningsson, "Managers Doing Leadership: The Extra-ordinization of the Mundane," *Human Relations* 56 (2003), 1438.

10 On Weber's intellectual roots, see Fritz Ringer, *Max Weber: An Intellectual Biography* (Chicago: University of Chicago Press, 2004). The quote is from Max Weber, *The Methodology of the Social Sciences* (New York: Free Press, 1949), 72.

11 The concept was already in play among German economic historians, so Weber considered ideal types to be a well-established methodology to aid interpretation. Tore Lindbekk, "The Weberian Ideal-Type: Development and Continuities," *Acta Sociologica* 35 (1992), 285–97.

12 Historian Les Standiford said of this work that it "remains for many the most influential and provocative in Western social thought," and the New York Public Library listed *The Protestant Ethic* among its "books of the century." Standiford, *Meet You in Hell: Andrew Carnegie, Henry Clay Frick, and the Bitter Partnership That Transformed America* (New York: Crown, 2005), 23; and www.nypl.org/voices/print-publications/books-of-the-century.

13 Max Weber, *The Protestant Ethic and the Spirit of Capitalism* (New York: Norton, 1905/2009), 5.

14 Ibid., 41.

15 Ibid., 65.

16 David Lindenfeld calls attention to another analytical devise, the psychological archetypes offered by Carl Jung as a way of categorizing individual subconsciousness. "Jungian Archetypes and the Discourse of History," *Rethinking History: The Journal of Theory and Practice* 13 (2009), 217–34.

17 Carl Diehl, "The Life and Work of Max Weber," *Quarterly Journal of Economics* 38 (1923), 97.

18 Weber, *The Methodology of the Social Sciences*, 90.

19 Werner J. Cahnman, "Ideal Type Theory: Max Weber's Concept and Some of Its Derivations," *Sociological Quarterly* 6 (1963), 269. Weber's quote on presuppositions is from *The Methodology of the Social Sciences*, 92. Weber quoted on fiction in Jon Hendricks and C. Breckinridge Peters, "The Ideal Type and Sociological Theory," *Acta Sociologica* 16 (1973), 32.

20 For a thoughtful and appreciative critique of Weber's own use of ideal types, see Donald McIntosh, "The Objective Bases of Max Weber's Ideal Types," *History and Theory* 16 (October 1977), 265–79.

21 Weber, *The Methodology of the Social Sciences*, 52.

22 Hendricks and Peters, "The Ideal Type and Sociological Theory."

23 Daniel A. Wren and Arthur G. Bedeian, *The Evolution of Management Thought*, 6th edition (San Francisco: Wiley, 2009).

24 The equation of leaders with top executives was made in D.S. Bridgeman, "Success in College and Business," *Personnel Journal* 9 (1930), 1–19; Glen U. Cleeton and Charles W. Mason, *Executive Ability: Its Discovery and Development* (Yellow Springs: Antioch Press, 1934); Gowin, *Selection and Training*; Johnson O'Connor, *Psychometrics* (Cambridge: Harvard University Press, 1934); Daniel Starch, *How to Develop Your Executive Ability* (New York: Harper, 1943); and F.W. Taussig and C.S. Joslyn, *American Business Leaders* (New York: Macmillan, 1932).

25 View at www.youtube.com/watch?v=zt78FGz-OEc.

26 Ibid., 2–3.

27 The quotes are from Tia Benjamin's post, "A Functional Specialist vs. a Management Generalist" at smallbusiness.chron.com/functional-specialist-vs-.management-generalist.

28 Alfred D. Chandler, Jr., *The Visible Hand: The Managerial Revolution in American Business* (Cambridge: Belknap Press, 1977).

29 Leighton quoted in Jeffery L. Cruikshank, *A Delicate Experiment: The Harvard Business School, 1908–1945* (Boston: Harvard Business School Press, 1987), 7–8.

30 Chandler, *The Visible Hand*, 101, 123.

31 Francis G. Burton, *The Commercial Management of Engineering Works* (Manchester: Scientific Publishing, 1899), 44.

32 Taylor, *Shop Management*, 21.

33 Fayol, *General and Industrial Management*, 5.

34 Barnard, *The Functions of the Executive*; Sune Carlson, *Executive Behavior: A Study of the Work* (Stockholm: Strömberg, 1951); Mary Parker Follett, "The Process of Control," in Luther Gulick and L. Urwick, eds., *Papers on the Science of Administration* (New York: Institute of Public Administration, 1937), 159–70.

35 See, for example, "Corporations: Implied Authority of General Manager," *Michigan Law Review* 11 (1913), 403–4; "Corporations: Independent Actions of General Manager," *Michigan Law Review* 14 (1916), 506; and "Corporations: Powers of the President and General Manager," *Columbia Law Review* 23 (1923), 784–5. The quote is from "Corporations, General Manager, Implied Authority," *Yale Law Review* 19 (March 1910), 383.

36 Oliver E. Williamson, *Markets and Hierarchies: Analysis and Antitrust Implications* (New York: Free Press, 1975). This is what Williamson labeled the Unitary or U-form corporation.

37 Ibid., 136. This is what Williamson identified as the M-form corporation.

38 As organizations grew in complexity, additional layers of general management were added. The strategic business unit, for example, inserted a mediating layer of general management between the business and the corporate general managers.

39 Alvin Brown, *Organization: A Formulation of Principles* (New York: Hibbert, 1945), 208.

40 Robert Sobel, *The Age of Giant Corporations: A Microeconomic History of American Business, 1914–1994* (Westport: Greenwood Press, 1993).

41 The federal government acted under the auspices of the Celler–Kefauver Act, passed under the previous Democratic administration with the intent of controlling corporate mergers. For a thorough analysis, see Neil Fligstein, *The Transformation of Corporate Control* (Cambridge: Harvard University Press, 1990).

42 The spread of the multidivisional form to European corporations in the 1960s and 1970s is chronicled in Andrea Colli et al., eds., *Mapping European Corporations: Strategy, Structure, Ownership and Performance* (London: Routledge, 2012); and Richard Whittington and Michael Meyer, *The European Corporation: Strategy, Structure and Social Science* (Oxford: Oxford University Press, 2000).

43 Peter F. Drucker, *Concept of the Corporation* (New York: John Day, 1946), 51. Sloan's terminology is from Sloan, *My Years with General Motors*.

44 Peter F. Drucker, *The Practice of Management* (New York: Harper, 1954), 12.

45 Tilles, "The Manager's Job."

46 H. Igor Ansoff and R.G. Brandenburg, "The General Manager of the Future," *California Management Review* 11 (Spring 1969), 61.

47 Kenneth R. Andrews, *The Concept of Corporate Strategy* (Homewood: Dow Jones-Irwin, 1971), 1.

48 Hugo E.R. Uyterhoeven, "General Managers in the Middle," *Harvard Business Review* 50 (March–April 1972), 75–85.

49 Porter, *Competitive Advantage*, 43.

50 In conducting a review of research published in the first decade of the *Strategic Management Journal*, Dan Schendel, the founding president of the Strategic Management Society, noted very little attention to leadership. Schendel, "On Strategic Leadership," *Strategic Management Journal* 10 (1989), 1–3.

51 John P. Kotter, *The General Managers* (New York: Free Press, 1982), 10–11.

52 Luther Gulick, "Notes on the Theory of Organization," in *Papers on the Science of Administration*, 13.

53 Mintzberg cited Fayol as one of the originators of this "classic school" of composite functions. Fair enough. Fayol had his own list: planning, organize, command, coordination, and control. Still, I would argue that Mintzberg undervalues the totality of Fayol's contribution, including the separation of managerial activities from technical activities.

54 Mintzberg, *Nature of Managerial Work*, 61.

55 Ibid., 62.

56 Mintzberg suggested that leadership skills were "so closely related to innate personality" that "it may be difficult to effect really significant behavioral change in the classroom." Mintzberg, *The Nature of Managerial Work*, 190.

57 Joseph C. Rost, *Leadership for the Twenty-First Century* (New York: Praeger, 1991).

58 Philip Selznick, *Leadership in Administration: A Sociological Interpretation* (New York: Harper & Row, 1957).

59 Abraham Zaleznik, "Managers and Leaders: Are They Different?" *Harvard Business Review* 55 (1977), 70.

60 Abraham Zaleznik, *The Managerial Mystique: Restoring Leadership in Business* (New York: Harper & Row, 1989), 12.

61 Max Weber, *Economy and Society: An Outline of Interpretive Sociology*, Vols. 1–2 (Berkeley: University of California Press, 1978), 49.

62 Abraham Zaleznik, *Human Dimensions of Leadership* (New York: Harper & Row, 1966), 71.

63 Ibid., 3.

64 Zaleznik, "Managers and Leaders," 68.

65 Not everyone agrees that Sloan was a prototypical manager. Bernard Bass labeled Sloan a charismatic leader and Warren Bennis associated Sloan with Thomas Edison, John D. Rockefeller, and other "great leaders." When ideal types are equated with empirical realities, such confusion is inevitable. See Bernard M. Bass, *Leadership and Performance beyond Expectations* (New York: Free Press, 1985), and Warren Bennis, *Why Leaders Can't Lead: The Unconscious Conspiracy Continues* (San Francisco: Jossey-Bass, 1989), 63.

66 Zaleznik, "Managers and Leaders," 71.

67 Ibid., 71–72.

68 Ibid., 74.

69 Kotter, *The Leadership Factor*, 26.

70 John A. Kotter, *A Force for Change: How Leadership Differs from Management* (New York: Free Press, 1990), 5.

71 Ibid., ix.

72 Zaleznik, *The Managerial Mystique*, 2, 11.

73 Fred E. Fiedler and Joseph E. Garcia, *New Approaches to Effective Leadership: Cognitive Resources and Organizational Performance* (New York: Wiley, 1987), 3.

74 Blake, *The Managerial Grid*, 57. Subsequent iterations of the *managerial* grid appeared in Robert R. Blake and Jane S. Mouton, *Building a Dynamic Corporation through Grid Organization Development* (Reading: Addison-Wesley, 1969); and Robert R. Blake et al., *Change by Design* (Reading: Addison-Wesley, 1990); and Robert R. Blake and Anne A. McCanse, *Leadership Dilemmas – Grid Solutions* (Houston: Gulf Publishing, 1991).

75 Danny Miller et al., "How to Detect a Management Fad – and Distinguish It from a Classic," *Business Horizons* 47 (August 2004), 7–16. See also David Collins, *Management Fads and Buzzwords: Critical-Practical Perspectives* (London: Routledge, 2000).

76 Frank Rich, "A Distant Mirror," *New York Times Sunday Book Review* (August 3, 2014), 16.

77 Beth Bailey and David Farber, *America in the 70s* (Lawrence: University of Kansas Press, 2004), xi.

78 A number of observers argued that the decade of decline actually commenced in 1971 when President Nixon announced that the United States would no longer convert dollars to gold at a fixed value, thus completely abandoning the gold standard. See, for example, Nye, "Soft Power," 154.

79 Judith Stein, *Pivotal Decade: How the United States Traded Factories for Finance in the Seventies* (New Haven: Yale University Press, 2010).

80 Bailey and Farber, *America in the 70s*. Direct U.S. military involvement in Vietnam ceased in 1973 with the Paris Peace Accords. In 1975 the South Vietnamese government formally collapsed as North Vietnamese troops captured

Saigon. The iconic image of American helicopters evacuating the Embassy marked the final withdrawal.

81 Paul E. Boyer, *Promises to Keep: The United States since World War II* (Boston: Houghton Mifflin, 1999), 379.

82 Bruce J. Schulman, *The Seventies: The Great Shift in American Culture, Society, and Politics* (New York: Free Press, 2001), 131.

83 George H. Gallup, *The Gallup Poll: Public Opinion, 1979* (Wilmington: Scholarly Resources Inc., 1980).

84 Christopher Lasch, *The Culture of Narcissism: American Life in an Age of Diminishing Expectations* (New York: Norton, 1979). Lasch, a harsh critic of capitalism, believed that Carter and most readers had misinterpreted the book's thesis, which was aimed at capitalism as an alienating ideology that left citizens little alternative but to turn inward. See Andrew Hartman, "Christopher Lash: Critic of Liberalism, Historian of Its Discontents," *Rethinking History: The Journal of Theory and Practice* 13 (2009), 499–519. Lasch attempted to make his point more clearly in his follow-up book, *The Minimal Self: Psychic Survival in Troubled Times* (New York: Norton, 1984). Sales were not nearly as robust.

85 *New York Post*, July 2, 1979, 25.

86 The text to the speech is reprinted in Kevin *Mattson, What the Heck Are You Up To, Mr. President? Jimmy Carter, America's "Malaise," and the Speech That Should Have Changed the Country* (New York: Bloomsbury, 2009), 207–17.

87 Although Carter never used the term "malaise," the dictionary meaning of the word – a general sense of depression or unease – is well suited for both the text and tone of the address. The speech can be viewed at youtube.com/watch?v=1IlRVy7oZ58.

88 Robert H. Hayes and William J. Abernathy, "Managing Our Way to Economic Decline," *Harvard Business Review* 58 (July–August 1980), 67.

89 Ibid., 68.

90 Ibid., 69.

91 Bass, "A Seminal Shift."

92 Noel M. Tichy and David O. Ulrich, "SMR Forum: The Leadership Challenge – A Call for the Transformational Leader," *Sloan Management Review* 26 (Fall 1984), 59.

93 Although not nearly so prominent, I was an early adopter of the transformational leadership paradigm. See Bert A. Spector, "Transformational Leadership: The New Challenge for U.S. Unions," *Human Resource Management* 26 (1987), 3–16.

94 Burns is quoted in Bernard M. Bass and Ronald E. Riggio, *Transformational Leadership* (New Jersey: Psychology Press, 2005).

95 James G. Hunt, "Transformational / Charismatic Leadership's Transformation of the Field: An Historical Essay," *Leadership Quarterly* 19 (1999), 129–45.

96 John Antonakis, "Transformational and Charismatic Leadership," in David Day and John Antonakis, eds., *The Nature of Leadership* (Thousand Oaks: Sage, 2012), 256–88; Northouse, *Leadership*.

97 Kevin B. Lowe and William L. Gardner, "Ten Years of the *Leadership Quarterly*: Contributions and Challenges for the Future," *Leadership Quarterly* 11 (2001), 459–514; Judge and Piccolo, "Transformational and Transactional Leadership"; Bass and Riggio, *Transformational Leadership*.

98 Kellerman, *The End of Leadership* ; Tourish, *Dark Side*.

99 Burns would subsequently own up to over-dichotomizing the notions of transformation and transaction in leadership. "I tried to present the conceptual frameworks of transforming leadership and transactional leadership as a contrast as though there is no connection between them. I know that this is wrong. There is a stronger connection between transforming and transactional leadership than I led readers to believe." Burns, "Forward," in Richard A. Couto, ed., *Reflections on Leadership* (Lanham, MD: University Press of America, 2007), viii.

100 Bass, *Leadership and Performance*, 5.

101 Bernard M. Bass, "From Transactional to Transformational Leadership: Learning to Share the Vision," *Organizational Dynamics* 18 (1990), 21.

102 Bernard M. Bass and Paul Steidlmeier, "Ethics, Character, and Authentic Transformational Leadership Behavior," *Leadership Quarterly* 10 (Summer 1999), 191.

103 Tichy and Ulrich, "SMR Forum," 59.

104 Ibid., 60.

105 Warren Bennis and Burt Nanus, *Leaders: Strategies for Taking Charge* (New York: Harper Business, 1985), 17, 145.

106 Henry Ford also appeared on *Time's* cover three times; Alfred Sloan twice. In terms of modern corporate executives, Bill Gates appeared four times and Steve Jobs five, including once being named "Man of the Year."

107 "Ford's Young One," *Time*, April 17, 1964.

108 Dimitry Anastakis estimates that Chrysler's debt accounted for nearly 10 percent of all U.S. corporate debt. Anastakis, "The Last Automotive Entrepreneur? Lee Iacocca saves Chrysler, 1978–1986," Business History Conference (2007), accessed at www.thebhc.org/sites/default/files/anastakis_0.pdf.

109 Michael Moritz and Barrett Seaman, *Going for Broke: Lee Iacocca's Battle to Save Chrysler* (New York: Doubleday, 1984).

110 By late 1981 the prime interest rate had dropped to 15.75 percent, a high figure by later standards but a major relief from the 21.5 percent rate of the previous year.

111 John Stuller, "Lee Iacocca and an America That's Back on Its Feet," *Saturday Evening Post* (October 1984), 46.

112 Judie M. Thorpe, "Lee Iacocca and the Generation of Myth in the Spokesman Advertising Campaign for Chrysler from 1980–1984," *Journal of American Culture* 11 (1998), 44.

113 Iacocca, *Iacocca*, 265.

114 Quoted in Moritz and Seaman, *Going for Broke*, 323.

115 The commercial can be viewed at www.yourememberthat.com/media/9309/1984_Lee_Iacocca_Chrysler_commercial.

116 Quoted in *New York Times*, July 17, 1985.

117 Rakesh Khurana suggested that Lee Iacocca was the first modern so-called charismatic CEO. Considering that the subtitle of Khurana's book included the phrase: "the irrational quest for charismatic CEOs," this was not meant to be a compliment. *Searching for a Corporate Savior: The Irrational Quest for Charismatic CEOs* (Princeton: Princeton University Press, 2002).

118 *Consumer Reports*, 1989 (Yonkers: Consumer Union, 1990); *Consumer Reports 1994* (Yonkers: Consumer Union, 1995). *Consumer Reports* used as its categories "much worse than average," "worse than average," "average," "better than average," and "much better than average."

119 Doron B. Levin, *Behind the Wheel at Chrysler: The Iacocca Legacy* (New York: Harcourt Brace, 1995).

120 Iacocca's fragile relationship with employers came to light in 1986. While still chairman of Chrysler, Iacocca was appointed to head the Statue of Liberty-Ellis Island Foundation, a federal advisory commission established by the U.S. Department of Interior. Iacocca was fired from that position by the secretary of interior. At first, the reason given was "conflict of interest" between Iacocca's advisory role and his active role in raising private funds for restoration. When the dispute became public, the secretary also suggested that Iacocca needed to be removed because he did not seem open to discourse and debate from other commission members. "This borders on being un-American," Iacocca retorted. There was also speculation that the Reagan White House was not inclined to provide a platform to the executive who was being mentioned as a possible presidential candidate for the Democrats in 1988. Robert Pear, "Iacocca and Secretary of Interior Clash Over Statue Panel Ouster," *New York Times*, February 1, 1986, A1.

121 "Ford's Young One," *Time*, April 17, 1964, 94. It is useful to remember that because dealerships in the United States are independent businesses, not owned by the auto companies, the sales people who Iacocca was secretly taping were not employed by Chrysler. Thus, he had no legal standing to fire them, although he undoubtedly possessed the power and influence to see to it that they were fired.

122 Iacocca, *Iacocca*, 245.

123 Fred Dansereau et al., "A Vertical Dyad Linkage Approach to Leadership in Formal Organizations," *Organizational Behavior and Human Performance* 13 (1975), 46–78; George Graen and William Schiemann, "Leader-Member Agreement: A Vertical Dyad Linkage Approach," *Journal of Applied Psychology* 63 (1978), 206–12.

124 James V. Downton, Jr., *Rebel Leadership: Commitment and Charisma in the Revolutionary Process* (New York: Free Press, 1973).

125 James V. Downton, Jr., personal correspondence with author, August 1, 2014.

126 Eric Hoffer, *The True Believer: Thoughts on the Nature of Mass Movements* (New York: Harper, 1951).

127 Downton, *Rebel Leadership*, 77.

128 Bass, *Leadership and Performance beyond Expectations*, 13.

129 Amitai Etzioni, "Authority Structure and Organizational Effectiveness," *Administrative Science Quarterly* 4 (1959), 45.

130 Ibid., 46.
131 Thompson, *Organizations in Action*, 152.
132 Ibid., 148.
133 Ibid., 153.
134 Egan Frankel-Brunswick, "Intolerance of Ambiguity as an Emotional and Perceptual Personality Variable," *Journal of Personality* 18 (1948), 108–43.
135 Stanley Burder, "Intolerance of Ambiguity and Need for Closure," *Psychological Reports* 43 (1978), 638; Sebastien Grenier et al., "Uncertainty and Intolerance of Ambiguity: Similarities and Differences," *Personality and Individual Differences* 39 (2005), 593–600; Christian Luhmann et al., "Intolerance of Uncertainty and Decisions about Delayed, Probabilistic Rewards," *Behavior Therapy* 42 (2011), 378–86; Charles D. Smock, "The Influence of Psychological Stress on the 'Intolerance of Ambiguity,'" *Journal of Abnormal Psychology* 50 (1955), 177–82.

7 Globalization and the Challenge of Complexity

Corporations live in a state of dynamic complexity.[1] They are by their nature complex mechanisms, composed of many moving parts: divisions, subsidiaries, functional units, and employees at all levels, not to mention multiple stakeholders: government regulators, labor unions, public interest groups, and so on. These components all interact with each other, sometimes in predictable but more often in unexpected, even surprising ways.

As organizations expand into new product and service lines, new markets, and new geographies; and as they adopt new processes, reconfigure supply chains, create new partnerships, and embrace new business models, complexity increases exponentially. Simultaneously, the environment in which these multiple components operate and interact – technology, competition, labor markets, laws and regulations, cultures, currencies, national and regional political and economic forces, not to mention natural emergencies – is in constant flux.

Given the understanding that all organizations exist in a state of constant tension between unity of direction and responsiveness to external dynamism and the belief that leaders need to navigate businesses through that tension, it seems apparent that the leadership challenge has never been as salient as it is today. Now, more than ever, we need not just leaders but *global* leaders capable of meeting the unique challenges of extreme volatility, uncertainty, complexity, and ambiguity.

Right?

Well, not so fast.

Take the unfathomably popular acronym VUCA: volatility, uncertainty, complexity, and ambiguity. It is used to express the supposedly unique environment facing leaders. The VUCA world has rendered leadership "more difficult than ever."[2]

Military leaders coined the term in the early 1990s to describe the destabilized world conditions precipitated by the fall of Communism and the end of the Cold War.[3] The US-USSR confrontation had provided

192

at least the clarity of a single enemy. Now, without that focus, the world of military leadership had become far more . . . well, VUCA.

But are we to believe that military commanders in Normandy in 1945, in Korea in 1950, in Berlin in 1961, or, for that matter, in the Vietnam "fog of war" *ever* experienced their conditions as stable, certain, simple, and clear? Of course not. This is simply a spurious attribution imposed on the past by presentists. Nonetheless, those who favored the formulation were convinced that they now lived in a *uniquely* VUCA world.

Organizational life has always been and will continue to be complex. Management theorists, it turns out, have long recognized a tension inherent in the management of organizations between the ever-present need to maintain some degree of control and stability while at the same time creating a capacity to respond to complexity and dynamism. As far back as the early 20th century, Henri Fayol pointed to the need to both administer a stable organization and to anticipate (*prévoyance*) the future.[4] Chester Barnard articulated the requirement for executives to respond to a "fluctuating environment of physical, biological, and social materials, elements, and forces." It was the task of the executive to engage in the complex process of readjustment of the internal dynamics of the business to the constantly changing external environment.[5]

It is easy to conclude from reading contemporary literature that, starting in the 1990s, globalization provided a new source of ever-escalating complexity. Global leaders – just the latest in a long line of ideal types – faced challenges unknown to their predecessors. "Globalization," wrote Rosabeth Moss Kanter in 1995, "is surely one of the most powerful and pervasive influences on nations, businesses, workplaces, communities, and lives at the end of the twentieth century."[6] The world had become "flat." Competitors everywhere were capable of competing anywhere.[7] And then there was the unique technology of the Internet with its apparently boundless capacity to forge globally connected webs. Even "local" businesses found themselves at the end of complex, globally dispersed supply chains, often in direct competition with foreign-based companies.

Surely, globalization can be traced back further than that, for example to the 1960s when the United Nations began calling attention to and advocating for a "new international order." By enhancing the movement of goods, knowledge, capital, and people across national borders, international trade could help promote "prosperity for all."[8] That was the mission of the United Nations Conference on Trade and Development (UNCTAD).

Starting in 1995, UNCTAD published an annual index of transnationality, defined as "the extent to which a firm's activities were located abroad."[9] The World Trade Organization (WTO), an outgrowth of the

1947 General Agreement on Tariffs and Trade, set out to promote international trade through the reduction of government-constructed barriers, placing particular pressure on tariffs that had been put into place originally as a protection for both new and threatened domestic industries.

There were critics who argued that the foreign direct investments that UNCTAD promoted and the tariff reductions called for by WTO bolstered the position of wealthy nations vis-à-vis poorer ones. Free trade, in this view, was seen as a detriment to the evolution of new business in emerging economies that needed protection in order to take root. Rather than promoting "prosperity for all," the reality of globalization was a widening gap between wealthy nations and poor, and a growing chasm between socioeconomic groups within individual countries.[10] That critique, however, did nothing to detract from the sense that globalization was a relatively new phenomenon with a unique set of challenges.[11]

We can accept globalization as a source of complexity and a challenge to leaders without buying into the suggestion that this is a *new* phenomenon or that global leaders are a distinct empirical reality. The scope of the term "global" has certainly expanded. Still, global trade has been a regular feature of economic activity starting in the premodern world.

The Internet is hardly the first technology to expand and connect the world simultaneously. Historians avoid the tranquility fallacy by analyzing the 15th century when advances in shipbuilding and navigation provided a prominent boost to global trade. Brazilian sugar, English wool, and – horribly – African people became part of an expanding commercial network. Trading companies created novel organizing techniques to deal with the complexities and ambiguities of their own global environment. Shipbuilding operations, centered in Amsterdam and Antwerp, served an emerging multinational market. An ongoing stream of technological innovation – the Guttenberg printing press, steam engines, transcontinental cables, telegraph/telephone/television, and air flight – added to the volatility and complexity of the world.[12] From this perspective, the Internet can be seen as a continuous evolution of rather than a discontinuous break in the march toward global interconnectedness.

There is evidence that the pace of internationalization steadily increased, at least for a time. An index of global connectedness compiled annually by Pankaj Ghemawat and Steven Altman found steady growth in both foreign trade and foreign direct investment from the 1980s through the onset of the Great Recession.[13] Nonetheless, Ghemawat argued, the world is not nearly so "flat" as advocates of the concept suggest: "The levels of internationalization associated with cross-border migration, telephone calls, management research and education, private charitable giving, patenting, stock investment, and trade, as a fraction of gross domestic product (GDP), all stand much closer to 10 percent than 100 percent."[14]

Globalization is real. It is just not the uniquely singular defining characteristic of our times in contrast to earlier times. Merchants in any decade could say, justifiably, that they lived in an era of unprecedented globalization. What is relatively recent is the proposal of the global leader as an ideal type, something distinct in the world of leadership. The sectioning off of "global" from other types of leadership focused attention on what was believed to be the special, unique circumstances facing global corporations.

Locating the Global in Leadership

Marketing professor Theodore Levitt is credited with introducing the expression *globalization* to business. "The globalization of markets is at hand," he proclaimed in 1983.[15] Based on new technologies, particularly television, Levitt predicted a homogenization of global markets. We were living in "the republic of technology," he noted (remember, this was 1983). And, he insisted, "the earth is flat."[16] Given the commercial purpose inherent in the conduct of business, "the global company will shape the vectors of technology and globalization" by pushing those vectors "toward their own convergence," a convergence that would create a unified global market.[17]

The term global leadership began showing up in management literature in the 1990s.[18] Christopher Bartlett and Sumantra Ghoshal addressed the challenge of managing in a global organization in their 1989 book on "transnationals," and elaborated further three years later with an article asking, "What is a global manager?"[19]

Nancy Adler made a claim for global leadership as a unique construct. Unlike "its domestic counterpart," she maintained, global leadership theory "is concerned with the interaction of people and ideas among cultures, rather than either with the efficacy of particular leadership styles within the leader's home country or with the comparison of leadership approaches among leaders from various countries – each of whose domain is limited to issues and people within their own cultural environment."[20] This is an important and valuable insight. It is not, however, a new theory of leadership. Rather, it suggests a contingency approach in which leadership style needs to be responsive to organizational context.

One of the defining features of that global context is the fact that global companies operate across multiple national borders. Complexity is an outcome of that reality. In his critique of traditional contingency theory, Keith Grint noted the fallacy of maintaining that leaders reacted to a scientifically objective, verifiable, and uncontested understanding of their environment.[21] In fact, interpreting the environment and communicating that interpretation is a fundamental leadership task.

For organizations moving across country borders, the newly expanding environment is best understood not as an independent variable determining leadership behavior, but as an outcome of how leaders see that environment. Starting in 1980, especially with the work of Dutch social psychologist Geert Hofstede, an understanding of that global environment began to focus on the diversity represented by separate "national cultures."

Leadership and National Culture

National culture was a formulation intended to capture a collective set of values. In this view, it stood as a kind of shared character that shaped the thought processes and behaviors of individual members. National culture was an important, certainly influential construct. Corporate leaders have relied on Hofstede's findings of national culture diversity to design systems and adopt styles. Academics were attracted to the quantifiable nature of the categorization.[22] Despite the many questions that have been raised over time concerning the validity of his methodology, the appropriateness of his categories, and the rigor of his conclusions, Hofstede's work added useful complexity to how executives viewed the world.[23]

It is possible to recall a time in the not-so-distant past when executives scanned their global environment – looking at the nations in which the activities in their business models were undertaken – and saw a largely homogeneous world. Consider a 1971 article entitled "Understand Your Overseas Work Force." The authors concluded that, despite "stereotyped assumptions," there existed "considerable similarity in the work goals of employees around the world." National cultural differences "are not nearly so great as some might think."[24] In devising strategies and policies, corporate leaders needed to recognize those similarities. And remember, Theodore Levitt's important 1983 "earth is flat" article envisioned globalization as an increasingly homogeneous world. Hofstede offered a useful anecdote to such Anglo-centric thinking.

Differences across Cultures

Hofstede had been wrestling for years with notions of motivation and how to help managers "predict" – that was his word – employee behaviors. As head of IBM's personnel research department, he initiated a massive employee attitude study. The IBM survey asked employees at all levels and countries to rank-order the importance of various work goals, from a sense of personal accomplishment and growth, to an opportunity for autonomy, a sense of job security, good pay and benefits, and a successful company. What Hofstede concluded in his early analysis was that different groups of employees – clerical workers, unskilled laborers, and managers – tended to cluster together in their self-described work motivations. National culture was acknowledged as another factor that could influence answers, but it was seen as "relatively minor"; certainly "smaller than the occupational differences described here."[25] To bolster his argument, Hofstede cited the above-mentioned 1971 "Overseas Work Force" article.

Very quickly, however, Hofstede's analysis bent toward national culture as the factor with the greatest explanatory power over employee attitudes. In a 1975 piece, for instance, he focused on employees in his native Netherlands, noting a "significant difference between the work-goal importance scores of Dutchmen and other Europeans." Here was evidence, he insisted, "of the Dutch national character."[26] When the full results came out in 1980, in an *Organizational Dynamics* article and the influential *Culture's Consequences*, the notion of national cultural differences and their impact on employee behavior became firmly embedded in the discourse.[27]

The specific dimensions by which Hofstede distinguished national cultures – power distance, uncertainty avoidance, individualism-collectivism, masculinity-femininity, and, in later iterations, time orientation – are well known.[28] Of particular interest here is the connection he drew between national cultural differences and leadership. Leadership needed to be culturally sensitive, he insisted. After all, "subordinateship" (his term for followership) differed across cultures. "Leaders cannot choose their styles at will," he reasoned, because "what is feasible depends to a large extent on the cultural conditioning of a leader's subordinates."[29]

Hofstede's study was not specifically focused on leadership theories. The implication of Hofstede's work was to beware of assuming that *any* theory of leadership could be applied universally. That warning – that there was no such thing as a globally applicable leadership theory – was countered in a study conducted by Robert House and his colleagues at the Global Leadership and Organizational Behavior Effectiveness (GLOBE) project.

The GLOBE study explicitly delved into the relationship between national culture and leadership.[30] The goal was to determine how leadership effectiveness was viewed in various cultures. They did not study leadership practice, leadership effectiveness, or even organizational effectiveness. They focused instead on *views* of leadership effectiveness. The theoretical grounding for their inquiry was implicit leadership theory, which extrapolated prototypes from the "preferred leader attributes or behaviors" of followers.[31]

Rather than looking at individual nations as Hofstede did, the GLOBE researchers created what they called cultural clusters ("Nordic Europe," for instance, which included Denmark, Sweden, and Finland, and "Confucian Asia," which included China, Singapore, and Japan) to inform their analysis. There were, not surprisingly, significant differences in how leadership was viewed across clusters. Nordic Europeans expected their leaders to be long-term oriented, with an emphasis on orderliness, modesty, cooperation, and power sharing. Confucian Asian cultures, on the other hand, expected their leaders to make independent decisions. The GLOBE prototypes consisted of an undifferentiated stew of traits (orderly and modest, for example), cognitive styles (long-term oriented), and, perhaps, behaviors (independent decision making).

The finding of cultural differences in leadership style was to be expected. It conformed, after all, to Hofstede's earlier argument. What surprised many observers, although apparently not the researchers themselves (they admittedly "expected" it from the outset), was that there seemed to be some universals as well.[32]

Across all clusters, some leadership attributes were found to be desirable: trustworthy, dynamic, motivator, were among the vague and subjective attributes. Likewise, there were attributes found to be universally negative: dictatorial, ruthless, and egocentric, among them. Now, the GLOBE researchers made a major conceptual leap by converting these desirable (and undesirable) characteristics into a particular theory of leadership – a decidedly western, even U.S.-based, one at that – as *the* globally applicable theory of leadership.

Building on their finding of universally desirable and undesirable attributes, the researchers went to "charismatic / value-based leaders" as the universally applicable model. Why? Because they associated that style with a set of rosy end values "such as dignity, peace, order, beauty, and freedom," and not necessarily "linked to other values." By adopting some of the excess of the transformational leadership literature – transformational leaders seek "beauty and freedom" – and then imposing a single construct on a cluster of attributes, values, and behaviors the researchers reflected their own assumptions.

If we focus on the specifics of the GLOBE findings and avoid their sweeping theoretical conclusion, we can see evidence that how leaders think *is* vital; a key element of their capacity to be effective. That approach gained considerable traction in the body of discourse that argued for something called a *global mindset*. To understand the notion of a global mindset, we have to first unpack the concept and look at a mindset absent the global modifier.

A Global Mindset

Mindset is typically conceptualized as a cognitive orientation, one that shapes how an individual selects, processes, and formulates responses to stimuli from the external environment.[33] Ryan Hamilton and colleagues added that mindsets are more than specific responses to particular situations. Rather, they are "sticky." Once formulated, they create a readiness "to respond in a particular way" to a wide variety of situations.[34]

Nobody can process the impossible breadth and depth of information available in the world, Hamilton and colleagues reasoned, so people turn to cognitive filters. To help guide that process, people develop assumptions and rule-of-thumb heuristics to help guide them. The variety and complexity of the data they allow in for consideration varies widely. A mindset is a cognitive orientation, a set of heuristics constructed by individuals to help navigate a complex environment. So, what happens when we add the adjective "global"?

Consideration of global mindsets started with Howard Perlmutter's classic 1969 article in the *Columbia Journal of World Business*. His concern was with "primary attitudes" – he did not use the term mind-set – among "international executives."[35] There was nothing especially complex in Perlmutter's findings. He identified three clusters of such primary attitudes: ethnocentric, polycentric, and geocentric. But his was far from a simplistic argument. Perlmutter's point was that dominant executive attitudes (he admitted there was "some degree" of each attitude in every organization) shaped the nature of the interaction between corporate headquarters and international subsidiary units, impacting many elements of organizational design.

Take authority and decision making. Ethnocentrism, which was home-country oriented, led to high decision-making authority placed in the hands of corporate headquarters relative to subsidiaries. Polycentrism, which was host-country oriented, led to decentralization of decision making by placing authority in the hands of subsidiaries relative to corporate headquarters. Finally, geocentricity, which was world-oriented, led to collaborative headquarters-subsidiary decision making.

Note that Perlmutter treats the multinational corporation not as a single type but as one of three prototypes. It is the prevailing primary attitudes of executives that help shape the strategy and structure called upon by these organizations as they evolve toward multinational operations.

As the evolution toward multinational operations proceeded over the next several decades that followed Perlmutter's article, a thesis emerged from a number of writers that geocentrism would provide superior results. For Christopher Bartlett and Sumantra Ghoshal, geocentrism could best be produced through organizational design, specifically a matrix structure in which responsibilities and relationships around product, market, and functional operations intersected.

The requirement for "transnational" leaders – that was their term – was to recognize that "assets and resources are widely dispersed but mutually supportive" across the global organization; "the roles and responsibilities of organizational units are differentiated but interdependent," and "knowledge and initiatives are linked through a worldwide learning capability that assures the efficient development and diffusion of innovations."[36]

Matrixed leadership was neither especially new nor uniquely global. In the previous decade, books by Jay Galbraith and Stanley Davis and Paul Lawrence had heralded the usefulness of matrix structures for complex domestic organizations operating in complex environments. Bartlett and Ghoshal applied the term "transnational" to their matrixed "solution."[37]

Placing emphasis on strategic capabilities rather than structure, Yves Doz, José Santos, and Peter Williamson introduced their own term: metanational. Some global businesses, even those that Bartlett and Ghoshal classified as transnational, owed their global competitiveness to advantages built up within their home country. Metanationals represented a different set, companies that learned *from* the world. They lacked a full complement of domestically grown advantages. From their earliest days, these companies were forced to look beyond their home base for innovation and integration capacities. For companies such as Finland's Nokia and Switzerland's ABB, leaders needed to recognize and develop "a global canvas dotted with pockets of technology, market intelligence, and capabilities." It is in the ability to first sense and then mobilize this knowledge that creates the capacity "to innovate more effectively than their rivals."[38]

Both sets of authors realized the degree to which the implementation of an effective approach would challenge the thinking of executives. Corporate leaders, said Doz and colleagues, were typically more comfortable developing products in the home country and then exporting them to new markets, a clear example of the ethnocentric mindset prevailing. For Bartlett and Ghoshal, the requirement was to create a "matrix in the minds" of executives.[39]

Matrix structures represented complex interactions while introducing ambiguity and uncertainty. A matrix of the mind suggested that willingness to live and ability to thrive within that type of environment would be a prerequisite for global leaders. The Bartlett and Ghoshal response tightly coupled a mindset with a structure. For Doz, Santos, and Williamson, the required mindset grew out of a particular set of circumstances: companies that were "born in the wrong place" and had to look at the world in toto for competitive advantage.[40]

When training consultant Stephen Rhinesmith introduced the term global mindset to the discourse in a 1992 article, he set off the word global in quotation marks, indicating some uncertainty about just what that modifier meant.[41] He proposed that a global mindset allowed the individual to "scan the world from a broad perspective, always looking for unexpected trends and opportunities to achieve our personal, professional, or organizational objectives."[42]

Rhinesmith emphasized characteristics including openness, a willingness to balance contradictory forces, a belief in processes rather than structure, and a willingness to "flow with change."[43] When these characteristics, the "being" side of management, were matched by key competencies, the "doing" side, the global mindset would help organizations "take a major step" toward "becoming more globally competitive – and toward enabling our global managers to be more fulfilled and effective."[44] In truth, there was little in Rhinesmith's formulation that was specifically global. One could easily drop the global adjective altogether and make an argument that openness, a willingness to balance contradictory forces, and so on could be seen as useful characteristics for any and all leaders.

Unquestionably, the pairing of the global mindset concept with increasing internationalization in the business world struck a responsive chord. "Strategic leaders must have a global mindset," Michael Hitt and colleagues insisted.[45] *Must* have. Corporate trainer Stephen Cohen agreed: "Effective global leadership requires a global mindset."[46] But Rhinesmith's description offered little specificity on which to build.

Paula Caligiuri's stream of work attempted to add detail to the definition of what she termed "cultural agility." She focused on the capacity of expatriates – not specifically leaders but managers generally – to work successfully in nonnative cultures.[47] Cultural agility demanded that individuals "read" – that is, sense, interpret, and formulate actions – their cultural milieu. Culturally agile managers demonstrate openness, flexibility, and low ethnocentrism.[48] Caligiuri intended the concept as an examination of an individual's capacity to cope with environmental changes due to entry into new (i.e., unfamiliar) cultural situations. Coping allowed individuals to experience unfamiliarity with lower levels of depression, stress, worry, and exhaustion than people with less cultural flexibility.[49]

What all of these writers agreed upon was the notion that globalization implied complexity. Levy and colleagues, for instance, defined a global mindset as "*a highly complex cognitive structure characterized by an openness to and articulation of multiple cultural and strategic realities on both global and local levels, and the cognitive ability to mediate and integrate across the multiplicity.*"[50] The particular challenge of leading in a complex environment may be the defining element in the rather vague notion of global leadership. In fact, rather than discussing global leadership, why not focus on complexity leadership?[51]

The Cognitive Challenge for Leaders

"Globalization," Henry Lane and colleagues suggested, "is a manifestation of complexity." That complexity arises from "conditions of multiplicity, interdependence, and ambiguity, all of which are related." In addition, those conditions are in a state of constant flux. For global leaders, then, "predicting the future is impossible, and trying to control global organizational outcomes may be dysfunctional."[52]

Multiplicity – of competitors, customers, value chains, governments, and stakeholders – is one, but only one of the conditions of complexity. Each of those elements is interconnected to each other. All of this is characterized by ambiguity, by confusion around cause-and-effect relationships, and by the likelihood of multiple interpretations of the continually changing state of the global environment.

Are executives up to the cognitive challenge posed by complexity? When faced with a situation of complexity – complex organizations in complex environments – leaders deal with problems for which there were no definitive, objective solutions, what Horst Rittel and Melvin Webber called "wicked problems."[53] Imagine railroad executives in the mid-19th century and corporate executives overseeing newly emergent multidivisional structures a hundred years later. All faced wicked problems. Globalization did not create complexity; it added an additional element.

When Levy and colleagues defined global mindset, they recognized its foundation in the mental processes of individuals who possessed "*a highly complex cognitive structure.*"[54] They were not alone in exploring the benefits of cognitive complexity as an aspect of global leadership.[55] But a matter often left underexplored by management writers was what, precisely, *is* cognitive complexity? For that, we need to turn to cognitive and brain scientists.

Cognitive scientist Stellan Ohlsson offered the idea of "deep learning."[56] The difficulty of mental navigation in a complex environment is that past experience is an inadequate, misleading, and perhaps even foolhardy clue to the future. The future is not a mirror image of the past. It is something that is different; not only that, but different in a fundamentally unpredictable way. For that reason, extrapolating from the past is an ill-suited methodology for navigating from the present into the future. If the future cannot be predicted, leaders must nonetheless chart a course that expands the possibility of effective action.

This is a tense, even paradoxical requirement. Cognitively complex individuals embrace conflict, encourage open discourse, expect diversity of cognition, reject either/or choices, welcome paradoxes, tolerate failures, and plan for contingencies.[57] The question is: will leaders see these tensions as opportunities to exploit or problems to ameliorate, as positives or negatives.

Cognitive complexity is an individual trait. An individual with cognitive complexity has the ability to both differentiate – to perceive multiple dimensions in an array of external stimuli – and to integrate those multiple dimensions.[58] This is not the same, and in fact, has no apparent relationship to, what we think of as traditional measures of intelligence.[59] High intelligence (at least as measured by our most popular intelligence tests) and high cognitive complexity are simply not the same.

Individuals with low cognitive complexity, wrote Lars Larson and Kendrith Rowland, "are characterized as having categorical black-white perceptions as well as relatively few but rigid rules of integration." High cognitive complexity individuals, on the other hand, "are characterized as perceiving more differences in their environment and [are] better able to assimilate contradictory cues."[60]

How and why individuals acquire this trait is a matter that continues to generate debate.[61] There is some recent research to suggest the existence of a biologically based capacity for cognitive complexity.[62] Paula Caligiuri and colleagues discussed the usefulness of global assignments in impacting openness and flexibility.[63] The two streams together suggest that both selection and development – selecting leaders who have already demonstrated cognitive complexity and providing them with global assignments to develop that capacity further – offer the most promising route to evolving global leadership.

As vital as cognitive complexity is, however, it is not the whole story. In his 1936 *Esquire* article titled "The Crack-up," F. Scott Fitzgerald famously observed that "the test of a first-rate intelligence is the ability to hold two opposed ideas in the mind at the same time, and still retain the ability to function."[64] A "first-rate intelligence" implies a capacity to integrate thinking and doing.

Individuals with behavioral complexity have access to a range of roles that they are able to play.[65] Let's put behavioral complexity into a specifically leadership context. Robert Quinn articulated a wide variety of roles that a leader can play, including a politically astute broker, a task-oriented director, a performance monitor, as well as a facilitator of opinions and consensus.[66] Those roles may, at times, suggest contradictory pressures: the desire to reach consensus and the need to achieve performance objectives, for instance. A leader with behavioral complexity will be able to assume multiple roles effectively and to understand and interpret the environment in a way that guides that selection process.[67]

It is possible, perhaps even likely, that as both the internal and external environments become increasingly complex, no individual will be able to match that complexity with his or her cognitive abilities. That challenge may well require a leadership *team*.

From Individual to Team Complexity

In their 1992 "What Is a Global Manager?" article, Bartlett and Ghoshal asserted that the skills needed to be an effective global leader did not reside in an individual but rather in a combination of perspectives and competencies from business managers, country managers, and functional managers.[68] The hope that a "first-rate intelligence" can emerge from a team presumed that teams can develop a level of cognitive complexity that surpasses the collective capacities of its individual members.

Top management teams, wrote Amy Edmundson and colleagues, are meant to provide a mechanism "to cope with the turbulence and complexity in the external environment that has complicated the task of executive leadership." Teamwork among CEOs and their direct reports potentially allows corporate leaders "to engage in an inclusive, participative process through which diverse members grapple with difficult issues to make decisions and build commitment to implementing them."[69] Donald Hambrick, with his attention to upper echelon theory, emphasized that "leadership of a complex organization is a shared activity, and the collective cognitions, capabilities, and interactions of the entire [top management team] enter into strategic behaviors."[70]

Teams are differentiated from collections of individuals in that team members share both purpose and responsibility for achieving an outcome.[71] Types of teams differ considerably based on the interdependence of their task. One typology, offered by Scott Page, distinguished between disjunctive and conjunctive tasks.[72] Disjunctive tasks require only one person to be effective for the team to succeed. These are not really teams at all but rather collections of specialists and advisors with a common goal: help the top person succeed. They are not designed nor particularly intended to engage in the kind of dialectical thinking that will view issues from multiple perspectives and arrive at the most economical and reasonable reconciliation of required collective action for outcomes.

In contrast, teams created to address conjunctive tasks require rich, reciprocal interdependence in which the inputs and outputs of each member occur in a dynamic, consequential manner.[73] For such teams, group processes are intended to facilitate the full engagement of members in wrestling with difficult issues, making decisions, and engaging in actions necessary to implement those decisions.[74]

The actual nature of a task, however, is less significant than the interpretation and understanding of the nature of that task held by team members. Is a top executive team focused on assuring that the CEO succeeds, on the assumption that a clear, single leadership voice will optimize effective decision making? Or do top executives view their task as addressing complexity in which only interdependent action will lead to effectiveness? If the belief of top team members, including and especially the hierarchically powerful CEO, is that the task is disjunctive, then the top team is not likely to seek collective cognition.[75]

The potential for teams to address conjunctive tasks is based on some notion of collective cognition. However, the leap from individual to collective cognition is not an obvious one. Cognitive complexity is, after all, an individual attribute. Can a leadership *team* develop a collective, group-level cognitive process? And if so, under what conditions? Do teams cognate at all, or do they simply accumulate the outputs of separate individual cognitions?

There is considerable debate on that point within the behavioral and brain sciences. In his faddishly titled but rigorously argued *Supersizing the Mind*, Andy Clark insisted on the possibility of a synergistic effect that is larger than the individuals who make up that system.[76] Teams of individuals can develop a shared cognition, one capable of complexity beyond any and all team members. That shared cognition, then, is different from the accumulated knowledge that a team can also arrive at. What makes his position so compelling, and so controversial, is that he goes far beyond the notion of collective knowledge.

Pooling individual knowledge can lead to positive team outcomes. Teams often benefit from the fact that members collectively know more than any individual team members. They do so by amassing their knowledge base. Anyone who has conducted a team problem-solving exercise has seen this phenomenon in action. Teams can accumulate knowledge when individual members first share their own knowledge and then acknowledge the contribution of other members.

Not all teams, however, are willing and able to develop and exploit accumulated knowledge. Members of poorly performing teams may fail to share what they know with each other. The contribution of individual members may be dismissed as untrustworthy. Team members may be inhibited by any number of external and internal factors (gender, age, race, hierarchy, expertise, and personality among them) from contributing their own knowledge to the pool. Under optimum conditions, however, the collective whole knows more than any one individual due to the distribution and sharing of each one's knowledge.[77]

Accumulated knowledge can be helpful to a leadership team. It was not, however, what Andy Clark had in mind when he addressed collective cognitive capacity. For Clark (and he is certainly not alone in his contention), individual team members can go further. They can actually incorporate each other's cognitive capacity into their own internal processes resulting in higher-order cognition for both the individual members and for the collective.

This is a compelling and appealing thesis. Top leadership teams can, in theory, engage collectively in the kind of complex thinking required of a complex organization operating in a complex environment.[78] We are still left to wonder, is collective cognition a likely outcome of a top leadership team deliberating strategy and tactics within a dynamically complex context? In order to consider that question, we need to appreciate the special characteristics and dynamics of a top team as compared to other teams in an organization.[79]

The top leadership team is composed of CEOs and their direct reports. These will most likely be divisional profit-center heads (either product or market-based divisions or some combination) and functional cost-center heads (say, the chief financial, legal, marketing, and information technology officers). A number of writers have implicitly accepted Andy Clark's hypothesis that a top leadership team is, in theory, capable of operating in a way in which individual members combine their personal cognition to achieve the goal of shared cognitive complexity.[80]

However, Yves Doz and Mikko Kosonen recognized the extreme difficulty, even unlikelihood, that cognitive complexity would emerge from a top team.[81] Top leadership teams aren't really teams at all. Don't count on them exerting truly shared leadership.

For most companies, Doz and Kossemen insisted, the "CEO continues to set strategic targets and holds the heads of the main business units or functions accountable for achieving them." Department heads operate like "semi-autonomous feudal barons, using considerable discretion to achieve their goals." This is true even when executives are given a stake in total company performance through stock options. Top team meetings "become highly ritualized, and little time is allotted for free-flowing exchange"[82] This is not teamwork in any real sense and not likely to produce team leadership. At best, these teams may provide valuable and diverse advice to the CEO who will then make key decisions.[83]

The CEO is an institutional feature of all top leadership teams. Powerful CEOs can centralize decision making, constraining open discussion. And the chances are good that one or more of the team members has designs on that top position, setting up a win/lose career competition that mitigates collective processes.[84] And then there is the question of diversity. Unless these teams are diverse, there is little likelihood of expanded cognitive complexity by virtue of team interaction.

It is the element of diversity among members that allows teams the opportunity to match external environmental complexity with internal cognitive complexity. Top leadership teams that enhance membership diversity and encourage members to challenge one another's thinking have the opportunity to develop a more complete understanding of their choices, create a richer range of options, and arrive at higher-quality decisions.[85] Challenges arise from different approaches to seeing a problem, to understanding the environment, and to envisioning a response.

As the organization expands beyond national borders, leadership may flow from the diversity of the countries of origin for top team (and board) members. Often, differences in the country-of-origin of members are taken as a useful proxy for cultural diversity. The assumption that passport diversity equates with cognitive diversity, however, is dubious.

Particularly when the experiences, values, motivations, and biases of team members overlap, they are more likely to find consensus but far less likely to engage in the open debate, advocacy and inquiry, and problem-solving process that are required of complexity. If team members, regardless of their passport homes, share a way of thinking, a common approach to problems, a single paradigm for addressing the organization and its environment, then collective cognitive capacity is unlikely to be enhanced.

To acknowledge the obvious, executives do not find themselves on top teams randomly. They have all arrived through the same chute, traveling a path through the corporation (or hired from the outside by the corporation). Constructing a leadership pipeline typically involves not a search for diversity of thinking, but rather a desire for commonality.

The notion of "fit" works toward homogeneity rather than heterogeneity. The emphasis on corporation culture has the impact of favoring some ways of thinking over others. A common corporate culture may have a positive impact on corporate performance. Leaders at companies including General Electric, Southwest Air, Nordstrom's, and In-N-Out Burgers certainty believe that to be the case. Still, human resource policies relating to selection, promotion, and development intended to reinforce individual "fit" and cultural homogeneity do little to promote cognitive diversity.

And then there is the construction of the top leadership team that needs to be considered. This is not just any cross-functional team, not any passport-diverse team. This is a tightly structured, profoundly hierarchical team. There is, for the most part, one CEO. That individual may have a highly commanding style, demanding tight control over the team.[86] Membership on the team is the result of promotion up the ranks, or of an acquisition that landed the CEO of the target company in the acquiring corporation's C-suite. Removing an individual from the team because of a failure to contribute cognitive diversity is no simple matter, even assuming such diversity was both desired and identifiable. "Finally," noted Kathleen Eisenhardt and colleagues, some top leadership teams "may avoid conflict simply because of fear that endless debate will lead to slow decision making and divert attention from critical issues."[87]

Collective cognitive complexity is an ideal, a theoretical possibility suggested by cognitive science. It is difficult to escape the conclusion, however, that top teams really function as advisory groups to a powerful individual. It can be a team capable of generating collective cognitive complexity, but the institutional conditions make that unlikely. That is not to say that a top leadership team cannot contribute. Certainly, it could be better able to process input than any individual, undoubtedly an asset in the huge complicated world of multinational companies.

Looking Backward/Looking Forward

Leadership theorists have long understood the complex nature of organizations. That complexity, both internal and external, has steadily increased throughout the 19th and 20th centuries, and continues to do so. To the degree that we understand complexity as a core component of leadership, we can look at the capacity of leaders, both as individuals and as members of teams, to manage complexity. For that reason, cognitive complexity has become a key focal point of the discourse.

The complexity of mindset and behavior that resides within an organization's leadership is intended to match the complexity of the environment in which those leaders seek to be effective. That's the reason many organizations look to leadership teams as a mechanism for enhancing cognitive capacity. The way leadership teams are constructed, however, often undermines the capacity that organizations seek to create by echoing hierarchy and reinforcing compliance rather than allowing for messy, inventive thinking. That limitation will be problematic particularly as complexity continues to grow.

In her review of the global leadership literature, Joyce Osland noted a tendency to create a definition of global leadership simply by extrapolating from "traditional domestic leadership definitions."[88] It's hard to conclude that scholars have moved beyond the assertion that global leadership is different from domestic leadership because global organizations and their contexts are more complex. Managing complex organizations in complex environments is a challenge for *all* leaders. Some purely domestic organizations may be highly complex, while some global organizations might be relatively less so. Rather than considering global leaders as an ideal type, we can think of leadership generally as residing in the challenge to navigate a course for complex organizations through complex environments.

NOTES

1 This is a term employed by Peter Senge, *The Fifth Discipline: The Art and Practice of the Learning Organization* (New York: Doubleday, 1990).

2 Mike Doheny et al., "Agile Operations for Volatile Times," *McKinsey Quarterly* 3 (2012), 126.

3 George W. Casey, Jr., "Leading in a 'VUCA' World," *Fortune*, April 7, 2014, 75–76.

4 Wren and Bedeian, *The Evolution of Management Thought*, 221.

5 Barnard, *The Functions of the Executive*, 6.

6 Rosabeth Moss Kanter, *World Class: Thriving Locally in the Global Economy* (New York: Simon and Schuster, 1995), 11.

7 Thomas L. Friedman, *The World Is Flat: A Brief History of the Twenty-First Century* (New York: Farrar, Straus, and Giroux, 2006). Friedman did not maintain that globalization was a new phenomenon. Rather, he recognized various eras of globalization.

8 http://unctad.org/en/Pages/About%20UNCTAD/A-Brief-History-of-UNCTAD.aspx.

9 United Nations Conference on Trade and Development, *The Universe of the Largest Transnational Corporations* (New York: United Nations, 2007), 1. UNCTAD's index of transnationally relies on such quantitative measures as the ratio of foreign sales to total sales, the ratio of foreign assets to total assets, and the ratio of foreign employees to total employees. In search of a more complete measure of a firm's internationalization, Daniel Sullivan created an index compiled of various measures of performance, structure, and attitudes. He does not measure attitudes directly – a virtual impossibility anyway – but rather uses the number of years top managers have been on nondomestic assignments and the dispersion of firm operations. Daniel Sullivan, "Measuring the Degree of Internationalization of the Firm," *Journal of International Business Studies* 25 (1994), 325–42.

10 For a critique of globalization and its effects, see Dani Rodrik, *The Globalization Paradox: Democracy and the Future of the World Economy* (New York: Norton, 2011).

11 The contemporary debate over tariffs echoes earlier concerns over the potential impact of foreign trade on domestic industries. There was a time when

the United States was more of a developing than a developed economy, and protective tariffs served the interests of early merchants. Throughout much of the 19th century, manufacturers supported protective tariffs as a way of buffering new industries. Populists and progressives, conversely, advocated lowering tariffs as a way of benefiting consumers. Tariffs were also, until the advent of a federal income tax in 1913, the major source of revenue for the federal government. See Judith Goldstein, *Ideas, Interests, and American Trade Policy* (Ithaca: Cornell University Press, 1993), and Edward S. Kaplan and Thomas W. Ryley, *Prelude to Trade Wars: American Tariff Policy, 1890–1922* (Westport: Greenwood Press, 1994).

12 For a general history of trade, see William J. Bernstein, *A Splendid Exchange: How Trade Shaped the World* (New York: Atlantic Monthly Press, 2008). For a history of Brazilian sugar trade, see Daniel Strum, *The Sugar Trade: Brazil, Portugal and the Netherlands, 1595–1630* (Stanford: Stanford University Press, 2013). On the Atlantic slave trade, see William A. Pettigrew, *Freedom's Debt: The Royal African Company and the Politics of the Atlantic Slave Trade, 1672–1752* (Chapel Hill: University of North Carolina Press, 2013). For a novelistic treatment of the extraordinary complexity of 17th-century Dutch global trade, see Jessie Burton, *The Miniaturist: A Novel* (New York: Ecco, 2014).

13 Pankaj Ghemawat and Steven A. Altman, *DHL Global Connectedness Index 2014: Analyzing Global Flows and Their Power to Increase Prosperity,* accessed at www.dhl.com/en/about_us/logistics_insights/studies_research/global_connect edness_index/global_connectedness_index.html#.VOeer3zF-Sr.

14 Pankaj Ghemawat, "Why the World Isn't Flat," *Foreign Policy* 159 (March–April 2007), 58.

15 Theodore Levitt, "The Globalization of Markets," *Harvard Business Review* 61 (May–June 1983), 92. The claim that this represented the first application of the term to business is from Levitt's *New York Times* obituary. Barnaby J. Feder, "Theodore Levitt, 81, Who Coined the Term 'Globalization', Is Dead," *New York Times*, July 6, 2006, accessed at www.nytimes.com/2006/07/06/business/06levitt.html?_r=0.

16 Levitt's previous use of this rather striking metaphor was not acknowledged in Friedman's *The World Is Flat*. As a work by a journalist, however, the book contained few citations.

17 Levitt, "The Globalization of Markets," 102. His use of the expression is from page 100.

18 The term "global leadership" appeared in a different context much earlier. American presidents, for example, particularly in the wake of World War II, were often characterized as practicing global leadership. See, for example, Louis W. Koenig, "Truman's Global Leadership," *Current History* 39 (October 1960), 225–9. Truman, Koenig argued, "was the first President to give the presidency an enduring 'peacetime' global orientation" (228). Even in that context, the term recognized the complexity, ambiguity, and extremely high stakes associated with global leadership.

19 Christopher A. Bartlett and Sumantra Ghoshal, *Managing across Borders: The Transnational Solution* (Boston: Harvard Business School Press, 1989); "What

Is a Global Manager?" *Harvard Business Review* 20 (September–October 1992), 124–32.

20 Nancy J. Adler, "Global Leadership: Women Leaders," in Mark E. Mendenhall, et al., eds., *Developing Global Business Leaders: Policies, Processes, and Innovations* (Westport: Quorum Books, 2001), 77.

21 Grint, "Problems, Problems, Problems."

22 M.L. Jones, "Hofstede – Culturally Questionable?" *University of Wollongong Research Online* (2007), accessed at http://ro.uow.edu.au/cgi/viewcontent.cgi?article=1389&context=commpapers.

23 Criticisms of the research methodology, not to mention his use of data from within a single company with its own distinctive culture, abound. To be sure, a body of research has argued in favor of Hofstede's findings as valid. See, for example, Brendan McSweeney, "Hofstede's Model of National Cultural Differences and Their Consequences: A Triumph of Faith – A Failure of Analysis," *Human Relations* 55 (2002), 89–118; Peter B. Smith, "Culture's Consequences: Something Old and Something New," *Human Relations* 55 (2002), 119–35; and Mikael Søndergaard, "Hofstede's Consequences: A Study of Reviews, Citations, and Replications," *Organization Studies* 15 (1994), 447–56.

24 David Sirota and J. Michael Greenwood, "Understand Your Overseas Work Force," *Harvard Business Review* 49 (January–February 1971), 53.

25 Geert Hofstede, "The Colors of Collars," *Columbia Journal of World Business* 7 (September–October 1972), 79.

26 Geert Hofstede, "The Importance of Being Dutch: National and Occupational Differences in Work-Goal Importance," *International Studies of Management & Organization* 5 (Winter 1975/1976), 25.

27 Geert Hofstede, *Culture's Consequences: International Differences in Work-Related Values* (Newbury Park: Sage, 1980).

28 Geert Hofstede, *Culture and Organizations: Software of the Mind* (New York: McGraw-Hill, 1991); Hofstede, "The Universal and the Specific in 21st Century Global Management," *Organizational Dynamics* 28 (1999), 34–43.

29 Hofstede, *Culture's Consequences*, 57.

30 Robert J. House et al., *Culture, Leadership, and Organizations: The GLOBE Study of 62 Societies* (Thousand Oaks: Sage, 2004).

31 Ibid., 56. For their definition of implicit leadership theory, the authors cite Robert G. Lord and Karen J. Maher, *Leadership and Information Processing: Linking Perceptions and Performance* (Boston: Unwin Hyman, 1991).

32 House et al., *Culture, Leadership, and Organizations*, 673.

33 Peter Gollwitzer, "Action Phases and Mind-Sets," in E. Tony Higgins and Richard M. Sorrentino, eds., *Handbook of Motivation and Cognition* (New York: Guilford Press, 1990), 63; Rachel Clapp-Smith and Gretchen Vogelgesang Lester, "Defining the 'Mindset' in Global Mindset: Modeling the Dualities of Global Leadership," in Joyce Osland et al., eds., *Advances in Global Leadership*, Vol. 8 (UK: Emerald, 2014), 209.

34 Ryan Hamilton et al., "Being of Two Mindsets: Switching Mindsets Exhausts Self-Regulatory Resources," *Organizational Behavior and Human Decision Processes* 115 (2011), 14.

35 Howard V. Perlmutter, "The Tortuous Evolution of the Multinational Corporation," *Columbia Journal of World Business* 4 (January–February 1969), 11.

36 Bartlett and Ghoshal, *Managing across Borders*, 182.

37 Jay Galbraith, *Developing Complex Organizations* (Reading: Addison-Wesley, 1973); Stanley Davis and Paul R. Lawrence, *Matrix* (Reading: Addison-Wesley, 1977).

38 Yves Doz et al., *From Global to Metanational: How Companies Win in the Knowledge Economy* (Boston: Harvard Business School Press, 2001), 1, 5

39 Bartlett and Ghoshal, *Managing across Borders*, 227.

40 The metanational thesis received further elaboration in a 2007 piece by José Santos from which the "born in the wrong place" quote comes. "Strategy Lessons from Left Field," *Harvard Business Review* 85 (April 2007), 20.

41 This is the first use I could find of the term in Business Source Complete.

42 Stephen H. Rhinesmith, "Global Mindsets for Global Managers," *Training & Development* 46 (October 1992), 63.

43 Ibid., 64.

44 Ibid., 68.

45 Michael A. Hitt et al., "Strategic Leadership for the 21st Century," *Business Horizons* 53 (September–October 2010), 441.

46 Stephen L. Cohen, "Effective Global Leadership Requires a Global Mind-Set," *Industrial and Commercial Training* 42 (2010), 3–10.

47 Paula Caligiuri, *Cultural Agility: Building a Pipeline of Successful Global Professionals* (San Francisco: Jossey-Bass, 2013).

48 Paula Caligiuri and Victoria Di Santo, "Global Competence: What Is It, and Can It Be Developed through Global Assignments?" *Human Resource Planning* 24 (2001), 27–35.

49 Cecilia Cheng et al., "Unpacking Cultural Differences in Interpersonal Flexibility: Role of Culture-Related Personality and Situational Factors," *Journal of Cross-Cultural Psychology* 42 (2011), 426. Anthropologists find little explanatory power in the notion of the flexibility of a culture in explaining individual perceptions, and indeed, empirical research has failed to find any significant differences between the rates of individual flexibility within a wide array of cultures and countries. For a summary of the anthropological view, see Edwin A. Cook, "Cultural Flexibility: Myth and Reality," *Antropos* 3 (1966), 831–8. Cheng et al. summarize the research on individual flexibility across counties in "Unpacking Cultural Differences in Interpersonal Flexibility."

50 Orly Levy et al., "What We Talk About When We Talk About 'Global Mind-Set': Managerial Cognition in Multinational Corporations," *Journal of International Business Studies* 38 (2007), 244.

51 A newly emerging literature explores complexity leadership theory. See, for example, Benyamin B. Lichtenstein et al., "Complexity Leadership Theory: An Interactive Perspective on Leading in Complex Adaptive Systems," *Complexity and Organization* 8 (2006), 2–12; and Mary Uhl-Bien and Russ Marion, "Complexity Leadership in Bureaucratic Forms of Organizing: A Meso Model," *Leadership Quarterly* 20 (2009), 631–50.

52 Henry W. Lane et al., "Globalization: Hercules Meets Buddha," in Henry W. Lane et al., eds., *The Blackwell Handbook of Global Management: A Guide to Managing Complexity* (Malden: Blackwell Publishing, 2004), 4.

53 Horst W.J. Rittel and Melvin M. Webber, "Dilemmas in a General Theory of Planning," *Policy Sciences* 4 (1973), 155–9. John C. Camillus applied Rittel and Webber to the process of strategy formulation in "Strategy as a Wicked Problem," *Harvard Business Review* 86 (May 2008), 99–106.

54 Levy et al., "What We Talk About When We Talk About 'Global Mindset,'" 244.

55 See, for example, Lisa Dragoni and Kristie McAlpine, "Leading the Business: The Criticality of Global Leaders' Cognitive Complexity in Setting Strategic Directions," *Industrial and Organizational Psychology* 5 (2012), 237–40; and Jonathon R.B. Halbesleben et al., "Awareness of Temporal Complexity in Leadership of Creativity and Innovation: A Competency-Based Model," *Leadership Quarterly* 14 (2003), 433–54.

56 Stellan Ohlsson, *Deep Learning: How the Mind Overrides Experience* (Cambridge: Cambridge University Press, 2011).

57 For a fascinating article on the paradoxes inherent in organizational leadership, see Wendy K. Smith and Marianne W. Lewis, "Toward a Theory of Paradox: A Dynamic Equilibrium Model of Organizing," *Academy of Management Review* 36 (2011), 381–403.

58 Deborah M. Kolb and Jean Bartunek, *Hidden Conflict in Organizations: Uncovering Behind-the-Scenes Disputes* (Newbury Park: Sage, 1992), 274.

59 Robert Hooijberg et al., "Leadership Complexity and Development of the Leaderplex Model," *Journal of Management* 23 (1997), 378.

60 Lars L. Larson and Kendrith M. Rowland, "Leadership Style and Cognitive Complexity," *Academy of Management Journal* 17 (1974), 38.

61 One stream of the debate asks the question: does cognitive complexity reflect, shape, or interact reciprocally with personality traits. To pursue this stream, see Mark C. Bowler et al., "Further Evidence of the Impact of Cognitive Complexity on the Five-Factor Model," *Social Behavior and Personality* 40 (2012), 1083–98.

62 Jan-Emmanuel De Neve et al., "Born to Lead? A Twin Design and Genetic Association Study of Leadership Role Occupancy," *Leadership Quarterly* 24 (2013), 46.

63 Paula Caligiuri, "Developing Global Leaders," *Human Resource Management Review* 16 (2006), 219–28; Caligiuri and Di Santo, "Global Competence"; Paula Caligiuri and Ibraiz Tarique, "Dynamic Cross-Cultural Competencies and Global Leadership Effectiveness," *Journal of World Business* 47 (2012), 612–22; Elaine Farndale et al., "Balancing Individual and Organizational Goals in Global Talent Management: A Mutual-Benefits Perspective," *Journal of World Business* 49 (2014), 204–14.

64 "One should, for example," Fitzgerald added, "be able to see that things are hopeless and yet be determined to make them otherwise." F. Scott Fitzgerald, "The Crack-Up," in Edmund Wilson, ed., *The Crack-Up* (New York: New Directions, 1945), 69.

65 Hooijberg et al., "Leadership Complexity."

66 Robert E. Quinn, *Beyond Rational Management: Mastering the Paradoxes and Competing Demands of High Performance* (San Francisco: Jossey-Bass, 1988).

67 Daniel R. Denison et al., "Paradox and Performance: Toward a Theory of Behavioral Complexity in Managerial Leadership," *Organization Science* 6 (September–October 1995), 524–40.

68 Bartlett and Ghoshal, "What Is a Global Manager?"

69 Amy Edmundson et al., "A Dynamic Model of Top Management Team Effectiveness: Managing Unstructured Task Streams," *Leadership Quarterly* 14 (2003), 298.

70 Donald C. Hambrick, "Upper Echelons Theory: An Update," *Academy of Management Review* 32 (April 2007), 334.

71 Spector, *Implementing Organizational Change*, 93–94.

72 Scott E. Page, *The Difference: How the Power of Diversity Creates Better Groups, Firms, Schools, and Society* (Princeton: Princeton University Press, 2007). Page reaches a conclusion with which I strongly dissent but which I want to acknowledge. "Diversity works best on disjunctive tasks," he argued, "because multiple approaches can be tried simultaneously, and one good idea means success for everyone" (xv). I would suggest, rather, that if and when diversity can add to cognitive complexity, it can enhance the capacity of the entire team to respond in multiple ways to the challenges of dynamic complexity.

73 I am borrowing here from the classic definition of reciprocal interdependence offered by Thompson, *Organizations in Action*.

74 Amy C. Edmundson et al., "A Dynamic Model of Top Management Team Effectiveness," 298.

75 Donald Hambrick, and Phyllis A. Mason, "Upper Echelons: The Organization as a Reflection of Its Top Managers," *Academy of Management Review* 9 (1984), 193–206. See also Hambrick, "Putting Top Managers Back in the Strategy Picture."

76 Andy Clark, *Supersizing the Mind: Embodiment, Action, and Cognitive Extension* (Oxford: Oxford University Press, 2008).

77 This definition of collective knowledge is from Alice Lan, "Tacit Knowledge, Organizational Learning and Societal Institutions: An Integrated Framework," *Organizational Studies* 21 (2000), 491.

78 There are, as is to be expected, critiques of these conclusions. See, for example, Fred Adams and Ken Aizawa, *The Bounds of Cognition* (Oxford: Blackwell Publishing, 2008). Even these authors accept the theoretical possibility of collective cognition. Their main criticism of Clark is that he has not demonstrated that the phenomenon he has found is anything more than accumulative and shared knowledge.

79 Mark Healey and colleagues have offered a typology of shared cognition in teams. See "When Teams Agree While Disagreeing: Reflexion and Reflection in Shared Cognition," *Academy of Management Review* 40 (July 2015), 399–422. They distinguish between automatic, intuitive mental models that team members may hold on the one hand and reasoned, deliberated models on the other.

80 Kathleen M. Eisenhardt et al., "How Top Management Teams Can Have a Good Fight," *Harvard Business Review* 75 (July–August 1997), 77–85.

81 Yves L. Doz and Mikko Kosenen, "The New Deal at the Top," *Harvard Business Review* 85 (June 2007), 98–104.

82 Ibid., 98, 100, 101.

83 That dour view is echoed by Edmundson et al., "A Dynamic Model of Top Management Team Effectiveness"; Kathleen M. Eisenhardt et al., "Conflict and Strategic Choice: How Top Management Teams Disagree," *California Management Review* 39 (Winter 1997), 42–62; Donald C. Hambrick, "Top Management Groups: A Conceptual Integration and Reconsideration of the Team Label," in Staw and Cummings, eds., *Research in Organizational Behavior* (Greenwich: JAI Press, 1983), 171–214; Hambrick, "Fragmentation and Other Problems CEOs Have with Their Top Management Teams," *California Management Review* 37 (April 1995), 110–27; Jon R. Katzenbach, *Teams at the Top* (Boston: Harvard Business School Press, 1998).

84 Paula Jarzabkowski and Rosalind H. Searle, "Harnessing Diversity and Collective Action in the Top Management Team," *Long Range Planning* 37 (2004), 399–419.

85 Eisenhardt et al., "How Top Management Teams Can Have a Good Fight."

86 One of the techniques associated with highly innovative teams, rotating leadership, is functionally impossible on a top management team. See Jason P. Davis and Kathleen M. Eisenhardt, "Rotating Leadership and Collaborative Innovation: Recombination Processes in Symbiotic Relationships," *Administrative Science Quarterly* 56 (2011), 159–201.

87 Eisenhardt et al., "Conflict and Strategic Choice," 44.

88 Joyce Osland, "An Overview of Global Leadership Literature," in Mark E. Mendenhall et al., eds., *Global Leadership: Research, Practice, and Development* (New York: Routledge, 2013), 40.

Epilogue: Key Moments in Leadership Discourse and a Plausible Chronological Narrative

My goal in *Discourse on Leadership* has been to present a narrative of the unfolding conversation, with particular focus on how leadership was understood and articulated within a business context. I hold no conceit that this is the only possible narrative, and certainly not the *true* narrative in any positivist sense. Rather, what I have offered is, I hope, a plausible story, one built on descriptions of actual artifacts, as well as on representation. I have represented the artifacts of my study – books, articles, and other writings – as being interrelated to each other, as well as with the historical context in which they were first offered.

The act of historical representation afforded me the opportunity to bring to light themes, interactions, and meaning interwoven throughout the discourse. In doing so, I did not present my findings in strict chronological order. And yet, there is a timeline, a sequence in which one event manifestly occurred before or after another. Freud wrote about Moses as a leader after Carlyle's lectures and before Burns' opus. For this epilogue, I will revisit the events that provided raw data for the preceding narrative, and now do so in chronological order.

This is not meant to be a simple sequence, however, not *just* a timeline. I am presenting this timeline in order to support an "order of meaning" intended to treat individual events as part of "an integrated whole."[1] It is the provision of a plot structure that renders chronological events into what White calls a "comprehensible story."[2] And it is a conversation that starts in Victorian England.

A Timeline

1840 Thomas Carlyle delivered his "Great Man" lectures in a period of crisis and upheaval: the aftermath of the French Revolution and the Napoleonic wars and in the midst of the Industrial Revolution. Victorian England searched for alternative sources of strength, direction, wisdom, and uplift. Carlyle had an answer.

"For, as I take it," he explained in the first of his six public presentations, "Universal History, the history of what man has accomplished in this world, is at bottom the History of the Great Men who have worked here."[3] Although dismissed or ignored by most current scholars, the theory has demonstrated impressive staying power. Writers who venerated transformational leaders and their capacity to save failing companies often fell in line behind a kind of great man hypothesis. And 174 years after Carlyle's lecture, even in the face of well-publicized executive misdeeds, CEO pay continued to spiral upward. The belief that it was the "Great Man" who sat at *the* vital center of corporate performance was alive and well.

1864   In April of this year, Abraham Lincoln awaited a vote in the U.S. Senate on the Thirteenth Amendment aimed at ending slavery. In a contemplative mood, Lincoln wrote a humble letter to a colleague. "I claim not to have controlled events," he observed, "but confess plainly that events have controlled me." Perhaps he was being overly humble. Still, it is a useful statement of the constant interplay that unfolds between an individual leader, even one who could arguably be labeled a "great man," and the context that helps shape events and determine outcomes.

1873   Lincoln was far from alone in questioning the capacity of any individual to control events. The most fully articulated counter-argument to Carlyle's Great Man appeared in Herbert Spencer's 1873 *Study of Sociology*. Spencer was influenced by newly emergent theories of evolution, most specifically the work of French biologist Jean-Baptiste Lamarck. Spencer's thoughts were also shaped by the ongoing work of French philosopher Auguste Comte who published a series of books between 1830 and 1842 under the title *The Course in Positive Philosophy*. Spencer became a founding voice in the field of sociology and a leading critic of Carlyle's Great Man Theory. He considered not just individuals but also the larger social forces that shaped both individual actions and the manner in which people responded to individuals. "Even if we were to grant the absurd supposition that the genesis of the great man does not depend on the antecedents furnished by the society he is born in," Spencer wrote, "there would still be the quite sufficient facts that he is powerless in the absence of the material and mental accumulations which his society inherits from the past, and that he is powerless in the absence of the co-existing population, character, intelligence, and social arrangements."[4] Which was more significant: the individual?

The context? Some combination of the two? This ongoing dialectic would continue to be played out over the span of the leadership discourse.

1893   Frederick Jackson Turner's address to the American Historical Association helped establish the myth that it was the interaction between American settlers and the frontier that forced the shedding of ideological trappings by demanding that settlers respond pragmatically to their challenging environment. This nonideological picture of Americans, their values, and institutions has been pervasive, impacting how leaders and organizations are viewed and studied.

1895   In the United States, railroads were among the earliest industries to face the need for the management of a national as opposed to a local organization. The Union Pacific and Central Pacific railroad lines joined in Promontory, Utah, in 1869 to create the first intercontinental track. As a consequence, railroad companies became both organizationally complex and geographically dispersed. George Bridge Leighton suggested that the effective modern executive needed to be a broad generalist. That individual "must understand the relation of the railway to the owners, to the public, and to the state. He will have to know what to leave to subordinates and how to direct them . . . In a broad way, he must not only be a man of affairs, but lawyer, engineer, financier, economist, and accountant."[5] In this reflective article, Leighton offered an early insight into the systemic nature of organizations and the complex requirements of executive leadership that would become central to the general management and leadership constructs as elaborated a century later.

1899   The Industrial Revolution in England relied on the shipping of raw materials and finished products. A British naval engineer, Francis Burton, offered an early view of general management in *The Commercial Management of Engineering Works*. Based on increasing complexity and expanding reach, the need for a responsible individual "on whom, above all others, the profits of the company depend" became manifest.[6] Burton placed overall responsibility in the hands of a single office holder sitting atop the organization's hierarchy. Accordingly, he understood the term general management to be interchangeable with chief executive or managing director. It was not until organizations grew to become multibusiness conglomerates that the general management role spread beyond the chief executive office, with Alfred Sloan's General Motors leading the way in the 1920s.

1904 Prussian-born, German-educated Max Weber used the essay "'Objectivity' in Social Science and Social Policy" to introduce his notion of ideal types. It was only after World War II, when English translations of his work became available, that Weber's theories begin to impact thought in the United States. Weber saw ideal types as a way of synthesizing "a great diffuse, discrete, more or less present and occasionally absent concrete individual phenomena" and arranging these phenomena one-sidedly in order to create a "unified abstract construction." Ideal types, he insisted, were mental constructs that "cannot be found empirically anywhere in reality."[7] In instances including transformational and global leadership, leadership discourse regularly confused ideal types with empirical realities.

1907 Philosopher William James delivered a lecture addressing the "pragmatic method." A deeply U.S.-based construct, pragmatism focused on the practical consequences of decisions, and was said to exist free of dogmas and doctrines. James' notion of pragmatism ironically echoed the original definition of ideology first offered by French theorist Antoine Destutt de Tracy as a science of ideas that "supposes nothing doubtful or unknown" and is concerned only with the "practical consequences" of knowledge.[8] By 1867, just over seven decades after de Tracy's coinage, the term was adopted by Friedrich Engels and Karl Marx to denote an expression of bourgeois class interests; a false consciousness. Thereafter, the conception of ideology attracted a wide array of negative adjectives: dogmatic, deceptive, manipulative, rigid, and doctrinaire among them. Nonetheless, in the 1970s in *The New American Ideology*, George Lodge would declare the argument that American society generally and American business in particular is purely pragmatic and not ideological to be "nonsense."

1911 Starting in the 1820s, the economy of the United States increasingly became industrialized, supplementing small, local businesses and agriculture with manufacturing and transportation. Innovations including the electric light bulb, the automobile, and the process of mass assembly furthered the expansion of the country's industrial base. The Bessemer process enabled the mass production of inexpensive steel. With ready access to both raw materials and low-paid (often immigrant) labor, U.S. steel companies grew rapidly. Carnegie and Bethlehem Steel were the major players, while a smaller company, Midvale Steel, hired a twenty-two-year-old apprentice engineer named Frederick

Taylor. Like Francis Burton, Taylor thought deeply about the role of managers in the newly emerging industrial context. In *The Principles of Scientific Management*, Taylor described the duties of management to include the scientific analysis of each organizational task and the placement of the right man within each job. Managers would also be expected to "heartily cooperate with the men" so as to ensure that "all the work is done" in the most-efficient way possible.[9]

1914   Francis Burton in England and Frederick Taylor in the United States focused on the roles of managers in new industrial firms. In France, yet another engineer, Henri Fayol, offered a set of more general principles for managers to follow. Fayol spent decades serving as *Directeur Général* for a prominent French mining company he had helped start in 1860. Many of the fourteen proscriptions contained in *General and Industrial Management* – division of labor, use of authority, centralization of decision-making among them – came with a suggestion not to go too far. He concluded his list by urging that everyone in a firm engage in the pursuit of common interests. The fields of transformational leadership and organizational culture, both of which blossomed in the 1980s, would likewise hold out hope that competing interests within the organization could be subsumed by a common purpose, one defined by management.

1916   It was in 1908 that French psychologist Alfred Binet along with colleague Théodore Simon first published a pioneering intelligence test. Now, eight years later, William Stern and Lewis Terman developed a measure of intelligence known as intelligence quotient (IQ). These tests would become a part of the U.S. military's "manpower" planning once the country entered the war the following year, with particular attention on intelligence as a trait thought to be predictive of leadership effectiveness.

1918   With the United States now engaged in World War I, the country's military sought a disciplined approach to leadership identification and development. The analysis was heavily influenced by the field of industrial psychology, newly emergent from the 1913 publication of Hugo Munsterberg's *Psychology and Industrial Efficiency*. One of the earliest articulations of trait theory, Enoch Gowin's *Selection and Training of the Business Executive*, argued that, in order to identify the right people to serve as executives, businesses should look for those who possess the right characteristics. There is a hint of Carlyle's Great Man here, although absent his emphasis on godly intervention and human subservience. Gowin offered a list of characteristics that included integrity, initiative, perseverance, health, aggressiveness, organizing abilities, and judgment. Typical of trait theorists, Gowin engaged in a fragmented, nonsystemic attempt to identify the universals of effective leadership.

1921 Benjamin Seebohm Rowntree emerged from his World War I service to the British government convinced that management's attention to human factors and industrial democracy would lead to higher efficiencies of operation.[10] His *The Human Factor in Business* reflected a critique of Frederick Taylor and anticipated the human relations movement that came to be associated with Eton Mayo and Fritz Roethlisberger. The call was for leaders, typically first-line supervisors, to pay attention to social interactions, always with the goal of increasing operational efficiencies.

1931 With the Great Depression in its earliest stage and Herbert Hoover still in the White House, lawyer Adolf Berle articulated a corporate ideology that placed the interests of shareholders at the center of a corporation's concerns. The large public corporation was a relatively new phenomenon, and Berle pondered the implications of separating ownership (in his view, this meant shareholders) from management. By defining a shareholder-centric purpose for the public firm, Berle was delineating the arena for executive action and suggesting the appropriate metrics of evaluation. Berle's "Corporate Powers as Powers in Trust" insisted that all powers granted to the corporation and the managers of that corporation were "at all times exercisable only for the ratable benefit of shareholders."[11] That was a powerful "only." Corporate executives who failed to keep shareholder interest in the forefront of their thoughts and actions were not meeting their responsibilities.

1932 A year after Berle's essay, the debate was joined by E. Merrick Dodd's "For Whom Are Corporate Managers Trustees?" The nature of the modern public corporation demanded the pursuit of interests beyond "only" making money for shareholders. Public companies were required to consider their responsibilities to provide secure jobs for employees, quality products for consumers, all while contributing to the broader society. This was a contrasting view of the role of corporations in society and placed significantly different demands on the role played by corporate executives. Throughout the New Deal and well into the post-World War II years, it was Dodd's definition of corporate ideology and the consequent responsibilities of executives rather than Berle's that dominated. Later advocates of sustainability and the "triple bottom line" – an accounting of economic, environmental, and social outcomes – built on Dodd's expression of corporate ideology. The debate over corporate ideology would continue to unfold with its competing notions of how corporate leaders should define success and how their performance should be measured.

1935   In *Sex and Temperament in Three Primitive Societies*, anthropologist Margaret Mead challenged rigid gender lines. She found that significant gender differences were not inherently connected to sex. Rather, they were socially constructed and highly fluid notions. Even those who accepted Mead's findings were able to dismiss the fundamental lesson of social constructionism. Biological and economic necessity "placed women as keeper of the hearth and man as the warrior-hunter in all but a few atypical cultures."[12] That gendered view significantly shaped the attitudes of male executives.

1936   America's great novelist, F. Scott Fitzgerald, wrote that "the test of a first-rate intelligence is the ability to hold two opposing ideas in the mind at the same time, and still retain the ability to function."[13] The statement earned its place here because of the succinct description it provided concerning the challenge of leading complex organizations in complex environments. This was Fitzgerald's insight that married behavioral complexity ("the ability to function") with complex cognition.

1937   Sigmund Freud had an explanation for the enduring influence of Carlyle's Great Man Theory. The need for a great man was primal, even universal. In *Moses and Monotheism*, he argued that the great man was "the father that lives in each of us from his childhood days." That father figure combined "the decisiveness of thought, strength of will, self-reliance, and independence" that all humans seek. Unlike Carlyle, however, Freud did not view this drive for a father figure with unalloyed celebration. In his conviction that he was "doing the right thing," the great man's actions "may pass into ruthlessness." Therefore, "one cannot help but being afraid of him."[14] Both Italian Fascists and German Nazis celebrated Carlyle as a founding theorist of their authoritarian views. Freud had good reason to be far less celebratory. The year prior to *Moses and Monotheism*'s 1937 release, he left Vienna for London.

Luther Gulick, an expert in public administration, was about as far removed from Carlyle and Freud as you could get. Much closer in spirit to Frederick Taylor and Henri Fayol, Gulick's "Notes on a Theory of Organization" introduced POSDCORB, an acronym intended to draw attention to the main duties of a CEO: planning, organizing, staffing, directing, coordinating (which he described as "the all-important duty of interrelating the various parts of the work"), reporting, and budgeting.[15] Defining leadership through listing roles and activities would continue to appeal to writers on the subject.

In the same volume that Gulick's POSDCORB chapter appeared, Mary Parker Follett offered "The Process of Control." Paying less attention to the techniques of management than to its underlying philosophy, she developed a notion of managerial control that expanded its scope beyond hierarchical authority. Control in organizations, Follett argued, was co-created by those who managed and those who were managed. She paid attention to work environment and group dynamics, thus breaking from Taylor's insistence on highly segmented and specialized tasks. The followership literature of the 1980s and 1990s would echo Follett's call for co-created organizational purpose.

1938 Management historian Morgen Witzel proclaimed Chester Barnard's *The Functions of the Executive* to be "one of the most profound books on management ever written – as well as one of the most difficult to read."[16] A former New Jersey Bell president, Barnard rejected Scientific Management and urged executives to pay attention to effectiveness as well as efficiency. Like Mary Parker Follett, Barnard emphasized intangibles. Trust, empathy, and intuition would all be needed for executives to be successful.

1941 In *The Managerial Revolution*, James Burnham voiced an awareness of and warning against the rise of a managerial class in large public corporations. With his general pessimism regarding human nature, Burnham warned that this newly emergent class would seek to enhance its own self-interests at the expense of the larger goals of the business. That view would be echoed in the 1970s by advocates of agency theory. Alfred Chandler made the same point about the rise of "managerial capitalism" in his 1977 *The Visible Hand*. For Chandler, however, the evolution of a managerial class was a far more positive development.

1943 With the United States in the Second World War, the military worked to understand the dynamics of effective leadership. As had been the case in the previous world war, the conceptual underpinning of that analysis was supplied primarily by psychologists. And again, the emphasis was on individuals, the traditional domain of the field of psychology. Who were these people who aspired to become officers? Were some individuals more likely to be effective than others? In 1943 Leon Pennington and Romeyn Hough wrote a textbook, *The Psychology of Military Leadership*, suggesting a number of traits – decisiveness, force and aggressiveness, tact, energy, and humanity, even appearance, among them – that could be used to guide the development of capable officers. That search for a combination of traits that could predict effectiveness in leadership constituted what Walter Palmer in 1974 labeled a near-obsessive search among psychologists for "the Holy Grail": a definitive cluster of leadership traits.[17] It was a search that never found a satisfactory answer but continued to attract attention.

1947   This was the year that Max Weber's *Wirtschaft und Gesellschaft*, published posthumously in German in 1922, first appeared in English translation. Weber interjected the notion of charismatic authority into the broad social science discourse. "Both rational and traditional authority are specifically forms of everyday routine control of action," argued Weber, "while the charismatic type is the direct antithesis of this."[18] Echoing Carlyle's conception of the great man, Weber held that the source of charisma was a gift received from God. Individuals who held such authority would be "obeyed" by virtue of the "personal trust in his revelation, his heroism, or his exemplary qualities."[19] Charisma explicitly entered the business leadership discourse, absent the notion of divine intervention, in the 1970s.

1948   The lure of trait theory was persistent, but some scholars resisted. In "Personal Factors Associated with Leadership," Ralph Stogdill conducted an extensive review of the literature and concluded that "a person does not become a leader by the possession of some combination of traits."[20] Stogdill's research focus remained on individuals, but with attention to behaviors rather than skills.

1949   It was University of Chicago-trained sociologist Samuel Stouffer who convinced the U.S. Army to allow him to survey troops at or near the front line during World War II to determine their attitudes toward officers. Stouffer's results, published in 1949, suggested that troops preferred officers who treated them with respect and did not take special favors for themselves; hardly a surprising outcome. What was missing from the study was any attempt to relate how the feelings of the troops concerning their officers impacted how fighting units actually performed in battle. Is liking your supervisor or feeling respected and well treated a requirement for effective combat performance? That question was unasked, let alone answered. Still, *The American Soldier* made for fascinating reading, not the least for the story about how the study came to be in the first place.

1950   Theodor Adorno's *Authoritarian Personality* suggested that a particular constellation of personality traits could shape a "potentially fascistic individual."[21] For a time, the U.S. military used his F-Scale test as a way to weed out officer candidates. But criticism of Adorno's methodology as well as ideological unease with his suggestion that fascism could occur in the United States led to dwindling influence. This was 1950, the year that Senator Joseph McCarthy began his anticommunist campaign in the United States. An ideologically ripe term like "fascism" invited trouble.

1954   With the emergence of postwar prosperity and economic growth – GNP increased from $221 billion in 1945 to $284 billion in 1950 – the large, diversified corporation became the dominant player in American economic life. This was the "age of giant corporations," and in 1953 the CEO of General Motors insisted that "for years I thought what was good for the country was good for General Motors and vice versa." At the same time, Peter Drucker emerged as the principal chronicler of and first guru to those corporations. His *Concept of the Corporation* appeared in 1946, reflecting on a two-year study of the multidivisional operations of General Motors. In 1954, with *The Practice of Management*, Drucker applied the lessons he had taken away from his General Motors experience, and noted the rise of a new cadre of general managers. This wasn't quite a theory of general management, which would only appear in the 1980s. But it did offer an important insight into the internal dynamics of corporations. As firms continued to expand – in the 1950s, that expansion was into both multiple countries and multiple industries – there would be an increased need for coordination and general management.

1955   Robert Katz's "Skills of an Effective Administrator" added to the argument being advanced by Stogdill that far too much emphasis had been placed on traits. In searching for the "ideal executive," Katz urged asking not "what good executives *are* (their innate traits and characteristics)," but rather "what they *do* (the kinds of skills which they exhibit in carrying out their jobs effectively)."[22] But there is a key conceptual misstep here, one that too often appears in the leadership discourse. Katz equated "do" (behaviors) with "skills" (competencies). *Behaviors* and *skills* are not interchangeable concepts. Just what do scholars mean when they claim to be focusing on behaviors? In leadership literature, that is rarely clear.

1957   Philip Selznick's *Leadership in Administration* focused on leadership, one of the earliest management books to do so. The leaders or "statesmen" who headed organizations had a particular responsibility: to define the mission of the organization and ensure ongoing success is an ever-changing environment. These responsibilities, associated with the role of top leadership, would be critical to virtually all of the leadership discourse of the 1980s and beyond.

Systems thinking started to receive serious academic attention in World War II England when a group of mathematicians and social scientists coalesced around a field they labeled cybernetics: a science of systems. In his 1957 *Cybernetics and Management*, Stafford Beer, a founding member of the cybernetics school, noted that the business organization was an example of an "extremely complex" system in which "no precisely detailed prediction can be given."[23] The challenge of managing dynamic complexity would come to define a core task of organizational leaders.

Since World War I, social scientists, particularly psychologists, played a role in aiding the U.S. military. In Cold War America, that research took on a renewed sense of urgency. Funding from the Department of Defense and private industry fueled an unprecedented growth in the broad field of social science. A group of Ohio State researchers under the direction of Carroll Shartle set out to analyze individual leader behavior. The underlying assumption that effective leaders always behaved in a certain way regardless of setting or situation was illusionary. Despite claims to rigorous scientific research, the methodology employed by the Ohio State researchers to reach their conclusions was dubious. Their results, published in Ralph Stogdill and Alvin Coons' 1957 *Leader Behavior: Its Description and Measurement*, determined that the "ideal leader" was someone who was "high" (that is, strong) on two orthogonally related dimensions: "initiating structure" and "consideration." The Ohio State findings were repeated, in only slightly varied forms, by other researchers and in Robert Blake's popular 1964 "Managerial Grid." In all these cases, the authors constructed insightful ideal types – effective leaders were individuals who focused simultaneously on people and task – but ignored Weber's insistence that ideal types were abstract constructs that "cannot be found empirically anywhere in reality."[24]

1958 Trait theories remained popular, as did the counterargument. Michael Mescon wrote in the *Journal of the Academy of Management* that "there is no recognizable stereotyped cluster of traits or qualities which universally distinguished the leader from the non-leader."[25] That hardly settled the issue.

1959 Consideration of power as a concept is often missing from leadership discourse. In an important early exception, John French and Richard Snyder published an essay, "Leadership and Interpersonal Power," in which they insisted that leaders needed interpersonal power in order to be effective. At the same time, they noted, the exercise of power within an organization amounted to leadership. Thus did the two concepts – leadership and power – become isomorphic. That conclusion was echoed in Rosabeth Moss Kanter's 1977 *Men and Women of the Corporation*. Organizational bureaucracies, she argued, had a tendency to render their participants powerless. By dispersing power, these giant bureaucracies undermined the capacity of anyone inside to amass sufficient resources to get something done. Individuals who were capable of rising above the erosion of power inherent in a bureaucracy attracted followers and thus became leaders.

1960 In "How to Apprise Executive Performance," McKinsey consultant Arch Patton told corporations to focus on such metrics as delivery schedules and waste. These were all internal performance measures. After the triumph of the shareholder primacy ideology in the 1970s, it would be unthinkable not to include, even favor, measuring the impact of executive actions on shareholder wealth.

The alliance between the social sciences and what President Eisenhower labeled the "military-industrial complex" attracted remarkably little critical assessment within the academic community.[26] Sociologist C. Wright Mills offered an ongoing call for a critical sociology during the 1950s with *The Power Elite* (1956) and *The Sociological Imagination* (1959). That critical posture only entered the mainstream of social science discourse with the widespread criticism of the Vietnam War later in the 1960s. There was an important exception, however. In 1960 historian Loren Baritz surveyed the state of social science research in *The Servants of Power*, critiquing the degree to which that research was called upon not to advance social justice but to "attack age-old problems of costs and worker loyalty with new weapons designed to fit the needs and problems of the twentieth century."[27] A decade later, Alvin Gouldner continued this critical assessment of the social sciences in the United States with *The Coming Crisis of Western Sociology*. Gouldner noted the rejection of fundamental theory in favor of the pursuit of "continuity, codification, convergence, and cumulation."[28] That tacit alliance between research and industry continued to shape organizational and management research until the challenge of the critical management/critical leadership movement that took root largely outside of the United States starting in the early 21st century.

1961   This was the year that Yale psychologist Stanley Milgram published the startling results of his obedience study. With no recourse to physical force, lab technicians convinced subjects to administer what they took to be potentially lethal punishment to people hidden from their sight but near enough to hear their protests. Like many social scientists who lived through World War II, Milgram was haunted by the ability of Hitler to achieve obedience from the German people. Could that happen in the United States? Milgram's study was ethically and methodologically flawed, but the conclusion was shocking nonetheless. Yes, it could happen. Remember Freud's admonition that "one cannot help but being afraid" of leaders who were father figures? Milgram seemed to be confirming that caution: leaders can get people to act immorally, even with a modicum of authority.

1962   Historian August Meier's "Negro Class Struggle and Ideology in the Age of Booker T. Washington" may seem to be only peripherally related to leadership discourse. But it represents an important rebuke to a number of leadership scholars who adopted a position that favored "pragmatic" over ideological leadership. Washington was labeled as a pragmatic leader in contrast to the ideology of W.E.B. Du Bois. As Meier and other historians of race relations noted, Washington was deeply ideological. That shouldn't be a surprise. Leadership is always an ideological assertion of legitimacy and authority, even when the leaders insist they are being purely pragmatic.

1963   The notion of strategy and strategic leadership had not yet been articulated when Seymour Tilles wrote "The Manager's Job: A Systems Approach." Attention to strategic thinking in political philosophy can be traced back to Chinese (Han Fei),

Greek (Hesiod), and Islamic (Al-Farabi) thinkers. The writings of Machiavelli, especially *The Prince* (1513), counseled state leaders to take advantage of strategic opportunities when they arose. Systems thinking – appreciating and analyzing how various elements of an organism interacted with each other and with their host environment – had made scientific headway during and immediately after World War II. Additionally, Bruce Henderson pioneered a systems approach to corporate portfolio planning that eventually became codified in his famous cash-cow/dog/star/question-mark matrix. Tilles, a colleague of Henderson, made a vital leap from the concept of systems thinking to the minds and actions of general managers. It was time for executives to move beyond the clichéd definitions of how they did their jobs. Forget about lists of separate, independent, and disjointed activities. The job of a general manager was to define the company as a system: "How do things as a company all fit together?"[29] Those responsible for the organization needed to both think and act strategically.

1964   Do you want an example of strategic leadership, even before the term was coined? You couldn't do any better than reading Alfred Sloan's surprise best seller, *My Years with General Motors*. Do not expect insightful revelations about any of the "darker side" of his GM stewardship. He was a powerful thinker and leader who devised strategies for competing in multiple automobile segments and designed a corporation intended to serve that purpose. Before getting too impressed with his legacy, recall how GM slid into near oblivion in the years following his departure. Under his direct leadership, however, GM outpaced Ford to become the largest and most profitable industrial concern in the world.

1965   This was the year that gender became manifest in the leadership discourse. Issues of inclusiveness and discrimination increasingly entered public debate. Gender-based analysis began appearing with Simone de Beauvoir's *Second Sex* (1949) and Betty Friedan's manifesto, *The Feminine Mystique* (1963). The U.S. Supreme Court's *Brown v. Board of Education* (1954) ruling overturned the 1896 decision in *Plessy* v. *Ferguson* that allowed states to construct "separate but equal" public facilities. Although a landmark ruling, the integration of American society awaited a social activism movement, highlighted by the Montgomery Bus Boycott (1955–1956), the Greensboro, North Carolina sit-ins (1960) and the mass movement led by Martin Luther King and galvanized by his 1963 "I Have a Dream" speech. The *Harvard Business Review* is to be congratulated for looking at the attitudes of male corporate leaders toward the possibility of women executives. Well, maybe not congratulated, exactly, depending on whether you read their title – "Are Women Executives People?" – as intended irony or dated sexism. The survey of executives found that 41 percent of male respondents identified themselves as "anti-women executives." A follow-up poll published by the *Review* in 1985 found that more than half of the respondents did not think women would *ever* be accepted wholly in business. Fifty-nine percent of men and 83 percent of women agreed that "a woman has to be exceptional to succeed in business today," and 20 percent of men and 40 percent of women concurred that "the business community will never wholly accept women executives."[30] With the 1965 piece, the matter was on the table, where it would stay. Race, however, remained far less visible as a topic.

1967   Much like Philip Selznick's 1957 *Leadership in Administration*, James Thompson intended his *Organizations in Action* to offer a general theory of organizations. Thompson noted an inherent organizational tension between control and autonomy, stasis and change, unity of direction and responsiveness to external dynamism. The ideal administrator, his term for what John Kotter would later label general manager, needed to achieve "co-alignment" between these contrary forces. It was precisely the maintenance of co-alignment that provided the central challenge of administration.

Much of the leadership research conducted in the United States involved a search for some elusive universal formula: a particular set of traits, roles, or behaviors that would result in enhanced effectiveness for individual leaders. Fred Fiedler was among those who suggested the futility of such a search. In *A Theory of Leadership Effectiveness*, he maintained that the behaviors needed to produce effectiveness were situational rather than absolute. Effectiveness derived from the degree of congruence between how leaders enacted their roles and the situation in which they found themselves. A rich stream of situational leadership theory flowed from the work of Paul Hersey and Kenneth Blanchard, Robert House, Warren Schmidt and Robert Tannenbaum, and Victor Vroom and Phillip Yetton, among others. The research, however, mainly placed its bet on the goal of identifying effective individual leaders who could adapt to shifting environmental dynamics.

1969   In the decades following World War II, American executives increasingly looked overseas for new markets. That search was fueled in part by an economic concern that the production capacity built up during the war would overwhelm domestic demand. Cold War ideology also positioned the expansion of international trade as an antidote to the appeal of Communism in the "underdeveloped world." The Bretton Woods Agreement of 1944 sought to create a global economic system based on free trade, convertible currencies, and fixed exchange rates through the International Monetary Fund (IMF) and the International Bank for Reconstruction and Development (the World Bank). The U.S. dollar replaced gold as the anchor of the international monetary system, and the Marshall Plan built demand for U.S. goods and expertise in war-torn Europe. Howard Perlmutter's 1969 *Columbia Journal of World Business* article responded to this rising internationalization by focusing attention on "international executives," top managers of companies that found themselves competing in more than one country. His concern was with the "primary attitudes" that shaped decision making on the part of these international executives. How, exactly, did these individuals think about the world and how to best position their own organizations to compete successfully? He identified three clusters of such primary attitudes: ethnocentric, polycentric, and geocentric. That typology would be echoed in several key studies of globalization in the following decades, notably Christopher Bartlett and Sumantra Ghoshal's 1989 *Managing across Borders* and Yves Doz, José Santos and Peter Williamson's 2001 *From Global to Metanational,* as well as the concept of a global mindset, which emphasized how leaders *think.*

1970   Remember the debate from the 1930s between Adolf Berle and E. Merrick Dodd concerning the purpose of the public corporation? Dodd's position that corporate leaders were accountable not just to shareholders but to the broader society began to lose dominance with Milton Friedman's "The Social Responsibility of Business Is to Increase its Profits." The article laid out the fundamentals of what would become the shareholder primacy ideology and agency theory. The goal of shareholders was "to make as much money as possible while conforming to the basic rules of the society."[31] Friedman argued that shareholders "selected" corporate executives – not true, but compelling– who would then act as their agents.

1971   Global business increasingly entered the leadership discourse. In "Understand Your Overseas Work Force," David Sirota and

Michael Greenwood urged executives to avoid "stereotyped assumptions" when it came to understanding their non-U.S. workforce. People everywhere were more alike, more homogeneous, than executives might think. This was nine years before Geert Hofstede published his work on cultural differences, so the statement that national cultural differences "are not nearly so great as some might think" may have seemed comforting, and not startling.[32]

1973   In a 1973 article, sociologist Cynthia Fuchs Epstein described sex and race as "dominant" statuses. The civil rights movement of the early 1960s had, by then, evolved into a more militant assertion of power and a call for liberation. By the late-1960s/early 1970s, women activists joined these demands. Protests at the 1968 Miss America Pageant – which was condemned as treating women as "sex objects" – brought national attention to the women's liberation movement. A spate of books analyzed "sexual politics," among them, Shulamith Firestone's *The Dialectic of Sex*, Robin Morgan's *Sisterhood Is Powerful*, and Kate Millett's *Sexual Politics*, all of which appeared in 1970. Epstein joined the two movements, referring to both sex and race as "visible and immutable" identities.[33] Race and gender status impacted the construction of leadership pipelines in organizations, severely restricting the diversity of top corporate executives.

From Henri Fayol through Luther Gulick, scholars had worked to identify key executive roles. What distinguished Henry Mintzberg's *The Nature of Managerial Work* was, in part, his observational methodology. In terms of leadership discourse, one of his conclusions stood out. He identified a vital management role missing from Gulick's POSDCORB: the manager as "leader." The leader role, Mintzberg observed, "is clearly among the most significant of all roles" in that it "permeates all activities."[34] It wouldn't be long before scholars were drawing a hard line of demarcation between leaders and managers. For Mintzberg, however, managers could and should be leaders.

His book is rarely read these days and long out of print. That's a shame. Sociologist James Downton's 1973 *Rebel Leadership* offered a spirited defense for what he termed "transactional leadership." In the coming years, that construct would be likened to horse-trading (by James MacGregor Burns) and dismissed as a prescription for mediocrity (by Bernard Bass). Not at all, Downton insisted. Transactional leadership contained the capacity to mobilize and energize followers behind a rational, informed commitment to a leader and to the purpose of that leader's calling. That exchange-benefit relationship sat at the core of transactional leadership, honoring the independence and agency of all parties.

1974   Ralph Stogdill's first edition of *Handbook of Leadership: A Survey of Theory and Research* appeared.[35] With over 6,000 citations to previous literature, the book helped establish the serious and robust nature of leadership as a field of inquiry.

1976   Milton Friedman's 1970 take on agency theory – shareholders were the principal "owners" of the corporation and executives operated as their agents – received elaboration from Michael Jensen and William Mackling's "Theory of the Firm." A number of social forces – the rise of shareholder activists and regulations requiring private pension funds to play a more active role in managing their members' investments – led to expanded focus on the rate of return for shareholder investments. Jensen and Meckling worried that, left to their own devices, executives would be motivated to enhance their individual monetary advantage at the expense of the fiscal health of the shareholders. Jensen and Meckling urged the construction of governance structures to monitor executives' behaviors, reduce agency costs (that is, the costs of an incongruence between shareholder and executive economic interests), and incentivize alignment. Over the next decade, shareholder activists and institutional investors would apply pressure to institutionalize agency theory and shareholder primacy, while finance professors at the nation's leading business schools taught the ideology to the next generation of executives as if it were received truth.

1977   I've already mentioned Kanter's *Men and Women of the Corporation* in regards to the interdependence of power and leadership in bureaucratic organizations. This 1977 study of a large American corporation is best known and most influential for its conclusion that the organization was defined by a "masculine ethic." Later research, for example, Joan Acker's "Hierarchies, Jobs, Bodies" in 1990, would elaborate on the notion of a gendered organization. The underlying logic of gendered organizations, Acker said, reflected images of "successful, forceful masculinity."[36] As a result, leadership pipelines included fewer women than men, the CEO office was filled largely by men, and the very concept of leadership was construed in highly gendered terms. How we speak about things both reflects and reinforces how we think about them, and how we act.

Labeling theory, which flowed from the sociological school of symbolic interactionism, attached implication to the choice of words used to characterize others. In "The Arrangement between the Sexes," Erving Goffman focused specifically on gendered language, and the degree to which a language bias "establishes 'he' before 'she,' 'man' before 'woman, 'his' before 'hers,' in phrases which couple the two, allows 'man' to stand for humankind and employs 'his' as a proper relative pronoun for semi-definite terms such as 'individual,' male designations clearly being the 'unmarked' form."[37] It was Virginia Schein who did pioneering work during this decade concerning the degree to which requisite managerial characteristics were articulated in highly gendered, masculine terms. Her "think manager, think male" research found evidence of global gender bias, making it difficult for women to reach top jobs in organizations.

In 1977 the leadership discourse was primed for an eruption. America was deeply ensnared in a combination inflation-recession. Two years earlier, the Vietnam War had ignobly collapsed into what was widely perceived to be the first-ever American military defeat. Both a president (Nixon) and a vice president (Agnew) had resigned in disgrace. The interim president (Ford) had been twice targeted by would-be assassins. Despite tall ships and flag-waving parades, the 1976 Bicentennial celebration did little to lift the country out of its national malaise. Perhaps what was needed was leadership, "inspirational and innovative leadership."[38] Not so fast, wrote Jeffrey Pfeffer in "The Ambiguity of Leadership." We like to believe that individuals can triumph over "a complex set of interactions."[39] It was a comforting illusion and seemed to make solutions relatively easy. Get better leaders. But causes were far more complex and solutions far more difficult to achieve. Pfeiffer's insight was largely ignored by early transformational leadership writers. In the thrall of Lee Iacocca's short-term turnaround at Chrysler, for example, Noel Tichy and David Ulrich wrote, "As a result of Iacocca's leadership, by 1984 Chrysler had earned record profits, had obtained high levels of employee morale, and had helped employees generate a sense of meaning in their work."[40] This was far closer to Carlyle's conception of a *great man* than to Pfeiffer's suggestion that multiple and complex elements determined organizational performance.

In 1973, Henry Mintzberg had insisted that leadership was one of the primary roles of managers. In his 1977 "Managers and Leaders: Are They Different?," Abraham Zaleznik came to a radically different conclusion. Managers and leaders were different, not just in how they enacted their roles within organizations but in their personality and psychological makeup. Managers represented the organizational force that sought to create and reinforce order. Conversely, leaders were "active instead of reactive, shaping ideas rather than responding to them." These are the folks who "develop fresh approaches to long-standing problems and open issues for new options."[41] In subsequent work, Zaleznik condemned the "managerial mystique" that had caused American industry to lose "its way, adrift in a sea of managerial mediocrity desperately needing leadership to face worldwide economic competition."[42]

Weber's concept of charisma as a source of authority had been introduced in the 1947 translation of *Wirtschaft und Gesellschaft*. Now Robert House stripped the concept of its godly grace and brought it into the business world. No longer a gift from God, charisma now stood for the personal abilities of an individual leader to command loyalty and devotion and to inspire followers to achieve extraordinary results. In short order, transformational leadership writers laid claim to the concept, labeling charisma "the most important component in the larger concept of transformational leadership."[43]

1978 It was James MacGregor Burns' *Leadership*, more than any other single work, that shaped contemporary leadership discourse. Burns focused on leadership writ large, with its attention to statesmen, movement leaders, and presidents. With the assassination of two admired leaders – John Kennedy (1963) and Martin Luther King (1968) – fresh in his mind, and the contrasting example of Hitler still a source of profound unease, Burns set out to construct a moral vision of leadership. His contrast between transactional and transforming leadership quickly became a core concept and accepted truth. Following Burns, scholars celebrated the potential of transforming leadership over the exchange model that had been favored in Downton's earlier *Rebel Leadership*. Transformational leadership, wrote Burns, "is more potent" in that "it seeks to satisfy higher needs, and engages the full person of the follower." As a result, transformational leadership and *not* transactional leadership "converts followers into leaders and may convert leaders into moral agents."[44] Burns' conceptualization let lose "an international tidal wave of researchers and scholars" focused on transformational leadership.[45]

Articles examining transformational leadership outnumbered all leadership articles using other theories – trait theory, path-goal theory, and leader-member exchange theory among them – combined.

1979 Andrew Pettigrew probably did not realize he was standing at the precipice of a flood of attention to organizational culture when he published "On Studying Organizational Cultures." His focus was on the scholarly examination of organizations. He issued an explicit call for the integration of sociological and anthropological insights. After all, he wrote, "it is all too easy to forget the less rational and instrumental, the more expressive social tissue around us that gives those tasks meaning." Mary Parker Follett's 1937 emphasis on underlying managerial philosophy and work environment was now conceptualized as culture, what Pettigrew defined as "the system of such publically and collectively accepted meanings operating for a given group at a given time."[46] The unexpected success of Japanese competition in the United States – most notably in the auto industry – fueled widespread interest in culture and its apparent claim on organizational excellence. A torrent of best-selling books followed, examining both Japanese and American companies for evidence of high performance cultures. Edgar Schein's 1985 *Organizational Culture and Leadership* placed corporate leaders at the center of organizational culture. They were the ones responsible for the creation and maintenance of that culture.

Marxist historian Christopher Lasch delivered one of the most unlikely best sellers ever with *The Culture of Narcissism*. He reflected the view that America's leaders had lost their capacity to confront the difficulties faced by society. Lasch's insight helped explain why transformational leadership became so appealing as an antidote to prevailing disillusionment and malaise.

Business leaders have long engaged in what can be recognized as strategic decision making. Starting with H. Igor Ansoff's *Strategic Management*, the field of strategy gained not just academic legitimacy but also key analytic frameworks. The following year, Michael Porter published *Competitive Strategy*, and five years later, *Competitive Advantage*. Porter paid little attention to the role of executives in formulating and implementing strategy. Ansoff, however, focused on strategic leaders and the actions they could take to ensure "the future growth and profitability potential of the firm."[47]

1980   In "Managing Our Way to Economic Decline," Robert Hayes and William Abernathy chastised American managers for undermining the country's economic health. All the latest analytic, planning, and controlling techniques learned by managers to improve performance had worked instead to undermine "the vigor of American industry." This was "a failure of both vision and leadership."[48] Their conclusion both reflected and reinforced the separation of leadership from management that had been offered by Zaleznik three years earlier, and supported the search for transformative leadership that characterized much of the discourse in the upcoming decade.

Was it possible that women leaders were more likely than their male counterparts to adopt a transformational leadership style? Absolutely, according to Judy Rosener's 1980 "Ways Women Lead." Gender had appeared on the pages of the *Harvard Business Review* with their 1965 survey and in Kanter's 1977 *Men and Women of the Corporation*. Now, Rosener placed gender and leadership squarely in her sights and insisted that, rather than adopting "styles and habits" from men, women leaders were "drawing on the skills and attitudes developed from their shared experience as women."[49] Rosener's findings attracted both support and disagreement.

One of the defining features of a global business context is the fact that companies often operate across multiple national borders. The meaning of engagement in a global context and the implications for business leaders and their organizations is not obvious. For some, a global environment evoked the image of a highly homogeneous world in which individuals were pretty much the same world over. The nature of an organization's environment is, in fact, not a scientifically objective, indisputable truth. Rather, it is open to interpretation. The act of interpreting that environment is a fundamental leadership task. In his 1980 book, *Culture's Consequences*, Geert Hofstede provided leaders with a clear, quantifiable (if methodologically dubious) framework. Organizational leaders needed to be culturally sensitive to significant national cultural differences. Employees differed across cultures. "Leaders cannot choose their styles at will," he reasoned, because "what is feasible depends to a large extent on the cultural conditioning of a leader's subordinates."[50]

1982   With the Black Power and Women's Liberation movements of the 1960s and 1970s, the concept of power began assuming a liberating rather than oppressive aspect. In his 1982 essay "The Subject and Power," French philosopher/historian Michel Foucault called attention to the humanizing potential implicit in the exercise of power. The mixture of power and knowledge, he argued, could act as a countervailing force in "opposition against secrecy, deformation, and mystifying representations imposed on people."[51] Empowerment soon entered the management discourse, with Warner Burke insisting that "empowering others" was the central responsibility of leaders. Although empowerment advocates claimed to be calling for the reallocation of authority, there was little doubt that upper management retained final decision-making authority.

As far back as the late 19th century, writers had noted a need for generalists to manage complex business organizations. John Kotter's 1982 *General Managers* offered the most fully elaborated view of the general manager's role yet. Kotter posited that, while functional managers oversaw specific areas of expertise and operations, a general manager was "responsible for a complex system which he cannot directly control and cannot entirely understand."[52] And not everyone, even those who were successful functional managers, would be well suited for the generalist job.

1984   It is perfectly understandable why Chrysler CEO Lee Iacocca became something of a folk hero in America. His story seemed to offer a counternarrative to America's steep industrial decline of the 1970s. But how did he gain the uncritical adoration of leadership scholars? His 1984 memoir, *Iacocca*, put on full, unapologetic display Iacocca's macho, bullying management style. "You've got until morning to make a decision," he quoted himself as telling UAW leaders. "If you don't help me out, I'm going to blow your brains out. I'll declare bankruptcy in the morning and you'll all be out of work"[53] This was the same year that Noel Tichy and David Ulrich extolled the capacity of transformational leadership to rescue the industrial base of the U.S. economy from decline, citing Iacocca as Exhibit A. In reality, Iacocca failed to transform leadership, Chrysler, or America's industrial base.

It was a magazine editor, Gay Bryant, who introduced the "glass ceiling" metaphor to indicate a barrier, a solid roadblock, that kept women from rising into leadership roles in organizations. That image would become central in articulating the institutional resistance that faced women seeking upward mobility in corporations. In a 2008 book, Alice Eagly and Linda Carli suggested that rather than seeing roadblocks to the advancement of women in organizations in terms of a single, invisible ceiling that suddenly asserted itself near the top of the hierarchy, a more accurate image would be of a labyrinth which "contains numerous barriers, some subtle and others quite obvious."[54]

1985   Even as transformational leadership was beginning to dominate the discourse, James Meindl and colleagues countered with a series of articles on what he called the "romance of leadership." In a 1985 co-authored *Administrative Science Quarterly* piece, Meindl referred to leadership as a "socially constructed reality." Organizations and the public both obsess over and celebrate leadership. Echoing Pfeiffer's 1977 "The Ambiguity of Leadership," the authors positioned leadership as a simple, even simplistic way for people to understand complex interactions. How and why do organizations succeed or fail? The leadership construct offered a single answer: because of the individual in charge. "In our view, the social construction of organization process has elevated the concept of leadership to a lofty status and level of significance. Such realities emphasize leadership, and the concept has thereby gained a brilliance that exceeds the limits of normal scientific inquiry."[55] Freud helped explain why we look for strong individual leaders. Meindl helped analyze how such a search distorted our understanding of organizations and their performance.

1988   It was Robert E. Kelley's "In Praise of Followers" that positioned following to a process distinct from leading. He added *-ship* to the end of the word in order to emphasize the point that, just as there can be effective leadership, there can be effective and thus ineffective followership. Enthusiasm, intelligence, and self-reliant participation and assertiveness; these were the qualities that allowed followers and their organizations to succeed even in the absence of strong leadership.

John Kotter did not position his 1988 *The Leadership Factor* as a significant break from his previous study of general managers. Nonetheless, this book fully embraced and popularized the management/leadership dichotomy that Abraham Zaleznik had articulated in 1977. Kotter rejected Zaleznik's hard demarcation by suggesting that management and leadership "are certainly not incompatible (indeed, more and more these days, both are needed in managerial jobs)."[56] In his follow-up study, the 1990 *A Force for Change*, that distinction between management and leadership was taken as a given. The ideal type had fully disappeared into a presumed empirical reality.

1989   Felice Schwartz intended "Management Women and the New Facts of Life" to be helpful and supportive to women executives while offering sound advice to the male gatekeepers of organizational careers. And she never used the phrase "Mommy Track." Rather, she urged corporate leaders to think of their high potential women as falling into one of two categories: career-primary women and career-and-family women. Outrage greeted her suggestion. Betty Friedan denounced the argument as "dangerous" and "retrofeminsm." The Mommy Track really should be called the Mommy *Trap*, insisted Friedan: "It says to women that if they choose to have children, they pay a permanent price. It's another word for sex discrimination."[57]

1990   The journal *Leadership Quarterly* launched with an oddly defensive opening editorial by Bernard Bass. "Despite comments to the contrary by those who have not had the opportunity to examine much of what has been accomplished in the past half century," Bass insisted, "we do know quite a lot about who attempts to lead in a designated situation, who emerges as a leader, and what are the consequences."[58] The journal became the main outlet for positivist, traditional leadership analysis.

In a *Foreign Policy* essay, political scientist Joseph Nye distinguished two types of power. Traditional or "hard" power depended on coercion, typically manifest through military might; while "soft" or "co-optive" power occurred when "one country gets other countries to *want* what it wants." Soft power was available to a country when "its culture and ideology are attractive." Followers will consequently channel or limit their activities in ways the dominant state prefers.[59] Although writing exclusively about international relations, Nye's conceptualization provided a basis for appreciating the power of organizational culture in granting legitimacy to leaders and softening resistance among followers.

1991   Robert Blake and Anne McCanse's *Leadership Dilemmas – Grid Solutions* seemed at first glance to be just the latest iteration of Blake's managerial grid, originally published in 1964. But there was an important difference: what had been a *managerial* grid now morphed into a *leadership* grid. "Not too long ago," noted the president of the management training group, the American Management Association in 1997, "business people came to the AMA to become more effective managers." Not anymore. "They come because they want to be more effective leaders."[60] There was, in truth, much that was faddish in the rush to leadership as a solution to organizational ills.

1992   Global leadership began appearing as a new ideal type during the 1990s. Christopher Bartlett and Sumantra Ghoshal addressed the challenge of managing in a global organization in their 1989 book on "transnationals," and elaborated further three years later with their 1992 "What Is a Global Manager?" Nancy Adler was to define global leadership as "concerned with the interaction of people and ideas among cultures, rather than either with the efficacy of particular leadership styles within the leader's home country or with the comparison of leadership approaches among leaders from various countries."[61] This definition suggested not a new theory of leadership pertaining to global organizations but an application of contingency theory to the complexity created by operating in multiple markets and across multiple cultures.

    Stephen Rhinesmith introduced the term "global mindset" to the discourse in a 1992 *Training & Development* article. A global mindset allowed an individual to "scan the world from a broad perspective, always looking for unexpected trends and opportunities to achieve our personal, professional, or organizational objectives."[62] By 2010, Michael Hitt and colleagues were insisting that strategic leaders *must* have a global mindset in order to be effective. Paula Caligiuri offered the term "cultural agility" in 2013 to focus on an individual's capacity to cope with environmental change due to entry into a new, unfamiliar cultural situation.

1993   Pressure on corporate leaders to take into account the impact of their actions on host communities and the environment had been building since 1984 when an India-based subsidiary of Union Carbide experienced an environmental, social, and economic disaster. That chemical leak sparked a succession of international organizations, led by the United Nations, to seek an appropriate balance between the economic requirement for development and growth, social needs for human dignity and rights, and environmental needs for sustainability. In his 1993 *The Ecology of Commerce*, Paul Hawken wrote, "Quite simply, our business practices are destroying life on earth." Business had been handed a "blank check" to ignore its social responsibilities, but was also uniquely positioned to implement solutions. To forge a path forward, business leaders needed to frame a "third way" between promoting growth and enhancing the planet.[63] Attention to sustainability and the triple bottom line fit into the stakeholder plurality ideology of requiring business leaders to find a path forward that reconciled multiple, often competing interests.

1996   By the mid-1990s, gender had entered the mainstream of leadership discourse. Race attracted far less attention. A 1986 survey found that, of the articles published in sixteen leading management journals in the previous fifteen years, less than 2 percent addressed issues of race or ethnicity. Furthermore, literature on gender tended to remain silent on matters of race, implicitly assuming that the experience of all women was the same. Not so, insisted Patricia Parker and dt ogilvie in their 1996 "Gender, Culture, and Leadership." The authors postulated a unique African American women executive, distinct from a white (male or female) leader prototype.

1997   Ira Chaleff continued the discourse on followership with *The Courageous Follower*. Followers bore a responsibility, a moral obligation, to be "shapers" rather than "implementers." Courageous followers were the opposite of those subjects who obeyed the directives of Stanley Milgram's lab technicians. Rather, they demonstrated the courage to assume responsibility for themselves and their organization and to challenge leaders when leader actions violate their own sense of what was right and effective. In yet another echo of the work of Mary Parker Follett, Chaleff insisted that leaders and followers were co-contributors to the operations and outcomes of their organization.

1999   Writing in the *Journal of Economic Behavior & Organization*, George Frankfurter and Elton McGoun insisted that all management rested on ideological assumptions. The argument had been made previously, notably by Reinhard Bendix, Barbara Czarniawska-Joerges, Howell John Harris, and Richard Weiss.[64] Coming at the apex of the shareholder primacy era and just before claims for the superiority of nonideological, pragmatic leadership, Frankfurter and McGoun's article, "Ideology and the Theory of Financial Economics," called attention to the deep and pervasive ideology of contemporary business. Leaders guide organizations that are "imbued with certain beliefs and cast in certain language that make it out to be what its believers want it to be and not the way things in any sense 'are.'"[65]

2000   There is a dark side to leadership, one either denied or ignored by many participants in the conversation. Barbara Kellerman broke from the tacit alliance of scholars, James MacGregor Burns foremost among them, who insisted on labeling evil tyrants including Hitler as power wielders rather than leaders. In "Hitler's Ghost: A Manifesto," Kellerman insisted that leadership scholars needed to confront "the dark side of who we are and what we do." Power and leadership were inseparable concepts. To learn leadership without confronting the reality of power and the potential for bad outcomes was "to whistle in the dark."[66]

2001   By the time David Thomas' article, "The Truth about Mentoring Minorities: Race Matters," appeared, a kind of equal opportunity backlash had set into the cultural/legal discourse in the United States. Kicking off with the 1978 *Regents of the University of California* v. *Bakke* case, attention turned from discrimination against women and racioethnic minorities to supposed discrimination against the "innocent white male." The suggestion was that affirmative action represented discrimination *against* the majority. In this topsy-turvy paradigm, the *one* and the *other* became reversed. Citing the ideology of meritocracy and relying on the delusion that discrimination had ceased to exist as a force, white males sought legal recourse. Thomas would have none of it. To be race blind (that is, to decline to take race into account when making decisions or designing process under the claim that such "equal" treatment was fair), he insisted, was, in essence, to be race ignorant and resistant to minority advancement. Whites and minorities "follow distinct patterns of advancement" in what are separate "tournaments" for access to top positions in organizations.[67]

2002   Sylvia Ann Hewlett sought to explode the "myth" of having it all. That myth held that women could have both an effective executive career and motherhood. They couldn't, Hewlett insisted. "When it comes to career and fatherhood," she suggested, "high-achieving men don't have to deal with difficult trade-offs." Surveying an elite group of women executives, Hewlett found that "for many women, the brutal demands of ambitious careers, the asymmetries of male-female relationships, and the difficulties of bearing children late in life conspire to crowd out the possibility of having children."[68] There were important insights in the article, including the institutional resistance at work against women who choose maternity. But the "myth of having it all," which Hewlett ascribed to women alone, applied to both sexes. Still, there is no question that in this struggle for balance, men maintained a privileged position at work and an asymmetric set of assumptions at home.

The Harvard Business Review has always been in the forefront of publishing articles extolling the virtue of CEOs as individual leaders on whose shoulders rest the fate of corporations, the country, even – at least in rhetoric that was prominent during the Cold War – the "Free World." Nonetheless, Rakesh Khurana's 2002 "The Curse of the Superstar CEO" appeared on its pages in September to offer a well-articulated dissent. There were understandable reasons for skepticism. The previous year, Enron had collapsed in an accounting scandal that implicated its top leaders, individuals who had previously been treated as superstars by the business press. In 2002, as Congress moved to criminalize at least some of the worse behaviors on display with the Sarbanes-Oxley Act, Khurana wrote, "I have concluded that the widespread, quasi-religious belief in the powers of charismatic leaders is problematic for a number of reasons," he wrote. "First, faith exaggerates the impact CEOs have on companies. Second, the idea that CEOs must have charisma leads companies to overlook many promising candidates and to consider others who are unsuited for the job. Finally, charismatic leaders can unstabilize organizations in dangerous ways." Reflecting the romance of leadership stream offered by James Meindl and colleagues, Khurana acknowledged that major "events are easier to understand when we can attribute them to the actions of prominent individuals rather than having to consider the interplay of social, economic, and other interpersonal forces that shape and constrain even the most heroic individual efforts. With the mythology of the frontier and the veneration of rugged individualism, Americans were especially vulnerable to the distortions and wishful thinking that supported the "curse."[69]

In addition to the list of leadership traits thought to contribute to effectiveness, Daniel Goleman and colleagues added "emotional intelligence." In their 2002 *Primal Leadership*, Goleman suggested that social awareness, self-management, and empathy were key to leadership performance.[70] Did any mix of personality traits of any individual figure significantly into organizational performance? That matter remained unsettled.

2004   Hofstede's pathbreaking exposition of cultural differences focused only tangentially on leadership. The study undertaken by Robert House and colleagues, published in 2004 as *Culture, Leadership, and Organizations: The GLOBE Study of 62 Societies*, placed leaders at the center of their attention. Like Hofstede, they found cultural differences relating to expectations placed on leaders. At the same time, they located what they held to be a set of universally desirable and undesirable attributes. The GLOBE researchers turned these characteristics into a particular theory of leadership – a decidedly western, even U.S.-based one at that – as *the* globally applicable theory of leadership: "charismatic / value-based leaders" stood as the universally applicable model.

"Enough leadership." That was how Henry Mintzberg titled his rather frustrated opinion piece. It was time, past time, to move beyond the "cult of leadership." He recalled reading a piece in *Fortune* extolling Lou Gerstner's turnaround at IBM. "All by himself?" Articles from the late 1970s and early 1980s had called on business to move beyond the domination of management. Mintzberg now held that the pendulum had swung too far in search of individual corporate saviors. It was time, he insisted, to abandon "the dysfunctional separation of leadership from management." He ended by quoting from Bertolt Brecht's play, *Life of Galileo*. "Unhappy the land that has no heroes," one character proclaims. Another rebuts, "No. Unhappy the land that needs heroes."[71]

Globalization was not a phenomenon unique to the late 20th century. It is, however, a manifestation of organizational and environmental complexity with which leaders have always needed to contend. That was the point made by Henry Lane and colleagues in their 2004 article, "Globalization: Hercules Meets Buddha." Complexity arises from "conditions of multiplicity, interdependence, and ambiguity, all of which are related." In addition, those conditions are in a state of constant flux. For global leaders, then, "predicting the future is impossible, and trying to rigidly control global organizational outcomes may be dysfunctional."[72] To be an effective leader in a complex environment would require both cognitive and behavioral complexity. That was true for both global and domestic leaders.

2005   As if to confirm that Carlyle's Great Man Theory and the more contemporary manifestation of trait theory was alive and well, Anthony Mayo and Nitin Nohria wrote that leaders *are* different from the rest of us. They possess "an almost uncanny ability to understand the context they live in."[73] It was left unstated whether this "uncanny ability" was a gift from God, an innate trait, or some learned capacity.

If *Leadership Quarterly* represented mainstream academic research, the founding of *Leadership* offered voice to a more critical stream of inquiry. The notion of critical management studies, with its attention to ideology, power distribution, conflicting interests within organizational settings, and contested understanding of performance, took root largely outside of the

United States.[74] *Leadership* founding editors David Collinson and Keith Grint extended critical thinking into leadership studies with their intention to address and overcome "the superficial ideas of management and academic consultants" whose work had undermined "the intellectual integrity of leadership as a legitimate and important field of study."[75]

2007   In the original "Romance of Leadership" article, Meindl and colleagues insisted that leadership was a social construction rather than an empirical reality. Sociologists Peter Berger and Thomas Luckmann had introduced the concept of the social construction of knowledge in their classic 1966 *Social Construction of Reality*. A social construction was a mental image, not a tangible object. As distinct from Weber's ideal types, social construction built on the acceptance of the image within a social group as a representation of reality. Gail Fairhurst's 2007 *Discursive Leadership* noted that leadership was a social construct rather than a physical object that existed independently of people's understanding. "Leadership" need not have existed, nor is the way it is currently understood determined by the nature of things; it is not inevitable.[76]

In a foreword to a 2007 book on leadership, James MacGregor Burns owned up to overdichotomizing the notions of transaction and transformation. "I tried to present the conceptual frameworks of transforming leadership and transactional leadership as a construct as though there is no connection between them," he admitted. "I know that this is wrong." He fell into the trap of confusing ideal with real types. "There is a stronger connection between transforming and transactional leadership than I led readers to believe."[77]

2008   Followership is another social construction, one intended to draw attention to the interactive and interdependent role of leaders and followers in producing outcomes. For Joseph Rost, however, the concept was an "outmoded" holdover, a dated and dangerous remnant of a bygone industrial era. Within that industrial paradigm, followers could never "participate in the leadership decision-making process authentically." Decision making remains "the leader's prerogative."[78]

Birgit Carroll and colleagues argued against the very idea of a competency model of leadership effectiveness. In their 2008 "Leadership as Practice: Challenging the Competency Paradigm," the authors said it was time to stop thinking of leaders as "acting and performing in isolation from others and context." The idea that individuals could achieve outstanding performance for their organizations "by adopting the same generic prescribed behaviors rather than being cognizant and compensatory where one is stronger and weaker" was nonsense.[79] And all promoted individual causation over a more thorough appreciation of complex organizational dynamics.

The United States elected Barack Obama, the first African American president in 2008. Despite proclamations of a post-racial society in the election's aftermath, the presence of African Americans in executive suites continued to be low, a reflection of the persistence of bias in the construction and maintenance of the leadership pipeline in American corporations.

2010   In *Supersizing the Mind*, philosopher Andy Clark insisted that teams of individuals could develop a shared cognition, one capable of complexity beyond any and all team members. What made his argument so compelling was that shared cognition went far beyond the notion of collective knowledge. Clark did not address business teams, but there was promise for top executive teams to engage collectively in the kind of shared leadership built on cognitive complexity. However, a number of scholars noted the unlikelihood that CEOs and their direct reports would truly operate as a fully functional team. In their 2007 "New Deal at the Top," for example, Yves Doz and Mikko Kosonen noted the tendency of top management team meetings to "become highly ritualized," with the CEO setting direction and allotting little time "for free-flowing exchange."[80]

2011   Evolutionary psychologists Mark van Vugt and Anjana Anuja wrote in *Naturally Selected* that human beings are natural-born followers: "Individuals who possessed the cognitive ability for followership thrived better than those lacking it."[81] Previous studies of human attachment by John Bowlby argued that infants come into the world biologically preprogrammed to form attachments to authority figures. The appeal of strong, individual authority figures is undeniable.

2012   Barbara Kellerman offered a critical assessment of the industry that had emerged first in the United States as a result of the faddishness of leadership. That industry, she wrote in *The End of Leadership*, was composed of a conglomeration "of countless leadership centers, institutes, programs, courses, seminars, workshops, experiences, trainers, books, blogs, articles, websites, webinars, videos, conferences, consultants, and coaches claiming to teach people – usually for money – how to lead."[82] The leadership industry trafficked in a fiction: that ideal types were real and could be recreated through training programs.

The same year that Kellerman offered her critical appraisal of the leadership industry, consultant Olivia Fox Cabane wrote a book that treated charisma as a kind of parlor trick. *The Charisma Myth* "exposed" the myth that charisma was something exceptional. Cabane held that she could teach executives charm, persuasion, and a firm handshake, thus endowing them with personal magnetism.

In *The Shareholder Value Myth*, legal scholar Lynn Stout suggested that the shareholder primacy ideology first articulated by Adolf Berle and reinforced by Milton Friedman, Michael Jensen and William Mackling, and much of the popular press and business media in the late 20th century amounted to "just that – an ideology, not a legal requirement or a practical necessity of modern business life."[83] Corporate leaders faced an ideological choice then; to work solely on behalf of shareholders or to define their purpose more broadly by the needs of multiple stakeholders.

In 2012 transformational and charismatic leadership, the constructs that had dominated the discourse since the 1980s, received some scathing critical assessments from non-U.S. scholars. Dennis Tourish's *The Dark Side of Transformational Leadership* urged a halt to the "preoccupation with leaders who hold followers in thrall by dint of their rabble-rousing oratorical gifts; who offer an appealing simplicity of purpose in the face of life's complexities; who compel a transformation in follower attitudes . . . [and who] promise to right all wrongs, only to add fresh layers of hurt to an already besmirched human condition."[84] He was especially disturbed by the degree to which transformational leadership advocates excused macho bullying in the name of transformation.

As if Tourish's work was not critical enough, Daan van Knippenberg and Sim Sitkin published an extensive review piece in the *Academy of Management Annals* arguing that the science behind charismatic-transformational research was seriously flawed, enough so that the entire concept needed to be scrapped. It was time for the leadership field "to stop escalating our commitment" to transformational leadership, "and move on to more productive endeavors." That move, the authors concluded, "could be truly transformational!"[85]

2014 By the time Sheryl Sandberg's best seller, *Lean In*, appeared, there were a number of prominent women sitting atop American corporations: Ursula Burns of Xerox, Virginia Rometty of IBM, Indra Nooyi of PepsiCo, and Meg Whitman of Hewlett-Packard among them. Sandberg herself was serving as Facebook's chief operating officer. Still, the number of women executives remained disproportionately low. Sandberg suggested that "in addition to the external barriers created by society, women are hindered by barriers that exist within ourselves." Gendered assumptions sent "negative messages" to women: saying "it is wrong to be outspoken, aggressive, more powerful than men." Compared to men, "fewer of us aspire to senior positions." Rather than waiting for institutional barriers to crumble, women should work proactively at "getting rid of these internal barriers."[86] Although Sandberg's formulation underplayed the obstructions erected and maintained by business organizations themselves, her basic point that the adaption of a feminine role disadvantages women as they negotiate a path through the labyrinth represented a significant stream of gender discourse. Deborah Kolb's work on the role of gender in negotiations, for example, never lost sight of the institutional resistance that imposed barriers on women. Nonetheless, Kolb insisted that women could work to improve their position within the process of negotiation for organizational advancement and in actualizing leadership roles.

The world financial crisis starting in 2008 raised profound questions about the quality of corporate leadership. And yet, shareholders in the United States continued to venerate these executives, rewarding them with ever-escalating compensation packages. Writing in a 2014 *Washington Post* blog, Nancy Koehn suggested that the continuing upward spiral of CEO pay even in the midst of well-publicized executive misdeeds could be attributed directly to an ongoing belief in the "Great Man" theory articulated by Thomas Carlyle in 1840.

Looking Backward/Looking Forward

I intended this chronological reordering of key contributions to the leadership discourse to be more than a recap. It offers additional insight into the nature of the unfolding discussion over the decades. One of my goals was to demonstrate that academics are not isolated from the prevailing swings of public mood and national culture. Rather, theory building is profoundly impacted by the social milieu in which those theories are advanced.

In the United States, the buildup that accompanied participation in two major 20th-century wars encouraged a search for specific traits and characteristics that could help first identify and then train military leaders. The merger of social sciences into the military-industrial complex of the Cold War poured funding into behavioral research, while an understandable revulsion of Hitler's capacity to command obedience led to deep suspicion of the exercise of power.

The evolution of leadership discourse demonstrates the significant role played by historical context in shaping that discourse. The 1970s emerged as the formative decade of that discourse. The centrality of James MacGregor Burns' *Leadership*, with its attention to leaders as statesmen, is widely acknowledged. It's far-ranging impact demonstrates that especially innovative work can encourage others to follow its lead.

Looking beyond Burns' book, consider what else the decade brought forth:

- Henry Mintzberg's examination through observation of the role of managers which, in his view, included leadership;
- Cynthia Fuchs Epstein's analysis of the interactive effects of sex and race on black women professionals;
- James Downton's defense of transactional leadership;
- The first appearance of Ralph Stogdill's massive survey;
- The articulation of agency theory by Michael Jensen and William Mackling;
- Rosabeth Moss Kanter's examination of both power and gender (and the interrelationship between the two);
- Abraham Zaleznik's bifurcation of leadership and management roles;
- Jeffrey Pfeffer's doubts about the impact of leadership;
- Robert House's insertion of Max Weber's charismatic authority into the discourse;
- Andrew Pettigrew's consideration of organizational culture;
- H. Igor's Ansoff's opening of the concept of strategic leadership;
- Michel Foucault's analysis of power as a potentially humanizing and empowering force.

I have contextualized this intense focus in terms of the crisis in spirit and loss of faith in leaders and institutions that characterized America's malaise. Even so, it is an impressive roster of contributions, one that shaped the ensuing discourse for decades.

It is also possible to observe a degree of coherence and focus that permeates what may seem to be a disjointed, even chaotic field. Let's start with the recognition that the discourse on leadership often traffics in assumptions of individual causation. Particularly as it plays out in the world of business, the consequence is a search for just the "right" leader; a CEO with the traits, skills, and/or personality that can turn around an ailing company and ensure future success. This perspective is hardly unique to business organizations. Companies exist within the context of a larger society and a broader culture. Leadership discourse did not create this desire for heroic individuals. It often reinforces it, however.

The appeal of any narrative that relies on individual causation is obvious. Human agency is more or less upheld (unless and until leaders exert sufficient power to demand compliance and dominate followers). The popular press and management writers are able to construct tales emphasizing the rise and occasional fall of powerful, compelling, and prominent individuals. These individuals then pen memoirs to pass on their leadership secrets to others. Success is attributed to their unique sets of skills, failure to the shortcomings of others. More serious scholars offer theories to explain organizational success and failure in terms of individual traits and behaviors. As a consequence, various approaches to trait theory – finding some particular mix of characteristics that supports individual leadership effectiveness – are inherent to the discourse.

A recurring theme throughout the discourse has been the confusion of ideal with real types. Ideal types serve a useful discursive purpose: to *start* a conversation. Too often, however, leadership scholars used ideal types – managers versus leaders, transactional versus transformational leaders, domestic versus global leaders among them – to *end* a conversation. The discourse should not abandon ideal types as a methodology for inquiry; it's a valuable tool. What is needed is the recognition of the distinction between idealized concepts and empirical realities.

Complexity has also provided an ongoing focal point for inquiry. Once we place ourselves in the eyes of the beholder and abandon the habit of viewing the past as embellished reminiscence, we can see that leaders have always faced complexity. Organizational theory has long recognized and addressed the role of leaders in navigating complexity.

Complexity creates a need for coordination, for integrating the multiple pieces of the organization with each other and with the dynamics of the external environment. Appreciation of the need for coordinated effort, and the requirement for an organizational force to help achieve that coordination – variously labeled "management," "general management," and "leadership" – is vital to the discourse.

For organizations to survive, organizational members must exercise some degree of coherence and control. Simultaneously, they must recognize the dynamic complexity of their internal constitution and external environment. Managing these dynamics is the task of many people at multiple levels of the organization. Some scholars have called for a separation of these two roles: managers deal with coherence and control while leaders address dynamic complexity and responsiveness. That separation relies entirely on the confusion of ideal with real types.

The discourse has always paid close attention to the behaviors of non-leaders as well as leaders. To be sure, attitudes have varied considerably. As the conversation unfolded within a military setting, a premium was placed on obedience, a willingness of followers to obey the orders of combat leaders without hesitation. In the decades following World War II, an understandable reaction to Hitler accentuated the alienating, toxic possibilities of obedience.

A more nuanced view of followership emerged in later decades, emphasizing the independent agency of nonleaders to act critically, thoughtfully, and constructively. It may be futile to hope that business organizations will completely abandon the notion of follower resistance as a negative force to be overcome. The possibilities of learning from resistance, of treating it as a discomforting but valuable source of insight, can and should be more fully emphasized and explored.

The ideological underpinnings of business leadership are typically either ignored or denied. It is necessary, then, to look beyond the parameters of the leadership discourse to find an examination of the construct and the impact of ideology on leader actions. The lack of attention to or denial of ideology saps the discourse of considerable robustness. A more fully considered analysis of leadership would recognize that all economic systems rest on ideological assumptions and that all business leaders make ideological choices.

There are many complex forces at play in explaining the alarming dearth of women and racioethnic minorities in positions of executive leadership positions. Many, but not all, of those forces reside outside of the organization itself. An important factor contributing to the persistence of bias is the construction of leadership itself, which typically rests on gendered assumptions about masculine and feminine roles. It is the idea of leadership as a strong, forceful, take-charge approach that expects women either to adopt a role that challenges assumptions about femininity or upend the construct itself. Compounding the persistence of bias in organizational life is the impact of individual prejudices against women and racioethnic minorities, as well as institutional barriers that constrict the leadership pipeline.

It may be too soon to declare an end to the transformational and charismatic leadership cycle that took root in the wake of the 1970s and has dominated the discourse in the ensuing decades. There seems to be no obvious letup in the intense research focus emanating from U.S. universities. Yet, countervailing positions taken by a number of scholars in 2013 suggest a more critical posture.

I would stake a claim for greater emphasis on transactional leadership as a way of recognizing participant agency and situational analysis as an approach to contextualizing the role executive leaders play. Although these approaches may lack the notion of grand (and grandiose) idealization of individual heroes, they will allow a more fully satisfying exploration of the topic of leadership.

I started this review of the discourse with a Scottish philosopher. I'd like now to go full circle and end with another, Walter Bryce Gallie. It was more than a century after Thomas Carlyle's lectures, in March 1956, when a small group of philosophers gathered in London under the auspices of the Aristotelian Society. Gallie delivered a paper in which he discussed what he called "essentially contested concepts."

"There are disputes which, although not resolvable by argument of any kind, are nevertheless sustained by perfectly respectable arguments and evidence," Gallie observed. These disputes amounted to "essentially contested concepts." These concepts must be "internally complex," he added, "which in turn allows discourse to focus on multiple elements in endless sequence and combination."[87]

Leadership is just such an essentially contested concept.

NOTES

1 I am quoting here from Hayden White, *The Content of the Form: Narrative Discourse and Historical Representation* (Baltimore: John Hopkins University Press, 1987), 9.
2 Hayden White, "The Historical Text as Literary Artifact," in Roger H. Canary and Henry Kozicki, eds., *The Writing of History: Literary Form and Historical Understanding* (Madison: University of Wisconsin Press, 1978), 53.
3 Carlyle, *On Heroes*, 21.
4 Spencer, *The Study of Sociology*, 31.
5 Leighton quoted in Cruikshank, *A Delicate Experiment*, 7–8.
6 Burton, *The Commercial Management of Engineering Works*, 44.
7 Weber, *The Methodology of the Social Sciences*, 90.
8 De Tracy is quoted in Kennedy, "Ideology from Destutt to Marx," 354–5.
9 Taylor, *The Principles of Scientific Management*, 20.
10 Benjamin Seebohm Rowntree, *The Human Factor in Business: Experiments in Industrial Democracy* (London: Longmans, Green, 1921). Witzel notes that despite being a "bitter commercial rival" of Rowntree's, Edward Cadbury also expressed a "strong social conscience and desire to serve society" combined with a "hard-headed" approach to commerce. *A History of Management Thought*, 118.

11 Berle, "Corporate Powers as Powers in Trust," 1049.

12 Bowman et al., "Are Women Executives People?," 15.

13 Fitzgerald, "The Crack-Up," 69.

14 Freud, *Moses and Monotheism*, 170.

15 Gulick, "Notes on the Theory of Organization," 13.

16 Witzel, *A History of Management Thought*, 151.

17 Palmer, "Management Effectiveness," 283.

18 Weber, *The Theory of Social and Economic Organizations*, 361.

19 Weber, "Three Pure Types of Authority," 216.

20 Stogdill, "Personal Factors Associated with Leadership," 35–71.

21 Adorno, *Authoritarian Personality*, 1.

22 Katz, "Skills of an Effective Administrator," 33–34.

23 Beer, *Cybernetics and Management*, 12.

24 Weber, *The Methodology of the Social Sciences*, 90.

25 Mescon, "The Dynamics of Industrial Leadership," 14.

26 The term "military-industrial complex" is typically credited to Eisenhower's reference in his farewell address delivered in January 1961, although it echoed earlier constructs, for instance C. Wright Mills' characterization of the new elites in *The Power Elites* (New York: Oxford University Press, 1956).

27 Baritz, *Servants of Power*, 198.

28 Gouldner, *Coming Crisis of Western Sociology*, 17.

29 Tilles, "The Manager's Job," 73.

30 Bowman et al., "Are Women Executives People?"; Sutton and Moore, "Executive Women – 20 Years Later."

31 Friedman, "The Social Responsibility of Business," 33.

32 Sirota and Greenwood, "Understand Your Overseas Work Force," 53.

33 Epstein, "Positive Effects of the Multiple Negative," 913.

34 Mintzberg, *Nature of Managerial Work*, 61.

35 Ralph M. Stogdill, *Handbook of Leadership: A Survey of Theory and Research* (New York: Free Press, 1974).

36 Acker, "Hierarchies, Jobs, Bodies," 147.

37 Goffman, "The Arrangement between the Sexes," 302.

38 *New York Post*, July 2, 1979, 25.

39 Pfeffer, "The Ambiguity of Leadership," 109.

40 Tichy and Ulrich, "SMR Forum," 59.

41 Zaleznik, "Managers and Leaders," 71–72.

42 Zaleznik, *The Managerial Mystique*, 2, 11.

43 Bass, "Leadership: Good, Better, Best," 34.

44 Burns, *Leadership*, 4.

45 Burns is quoted in Bass and Riggio, *Transformational Leadership*.

46 Pettigrew, "On Studying Organizational Cultures," 574.

47 Ansoff, "Conceptual Underpinnings of Systematic Strategic Management," 2.

48 Hayes and Abernathy, "Managing Our Way to Economic Decline," 67, 91.

49 Rosener, "Ways Women Lead," 119.

50 Hofstede, *Culture's Consequences*, 57.

51 Foucault, "The Subject and Power," 781.

52 Kotter, *The General Managers*, 10–11.

53 Iacocca, *Iacocca*, 245.
54 Eagly and Carli, *Through the Labyrinth*, 6.
55 Meindl et al., "The Romance of Leadership," 78.
56 Kotter, *The Leadership Factor*, 26.
57 Friedan is quoted in Beyette, "A New Career Flap."
58 Bernard M. Bass, "Toward a Meeting of Minds," *Leadership Quarterly* 1 (1990), unpaginated.
59 Ibid., Nye, "Soft Power," 166–7.
60 Fagiano, "Managers vs. Leaders," 5.
61 Adler, "Global Leadership," 77.
62 Rhinesmith, "Global Mindsets for Global Managers," 63.
63 Hawken, *The Ecology of Commerce*, 3.
64 Reinhard Bendix, *Managerial Ideologies in the Course of Industrialization* (New Brunswick: Transaction Publishers, 1956/2001); Barbara Czarniawska-Joerges, *Ideological Control in Nonideological Organizations* (New York: Praeger, 1988); Richard M. Weiss, *Managerial Ideology and the Social Control of Deviance* (New York: Praeger, 1986); Richard M. Weiss and Lynn E. Miller, "The Concept of Ideology in Organizational Analysis: The Sociology of Knowledge or the Social Psychology of Beliefs?" *Academy of Management Review* 12 (1987), 104–16.
65 Frankfurter and McGoun, "Ideology and the Theory of Financial Economics," 161.
66 Kellerman, "Hitler's Ghost," 68.
67 Thomas, "The Truth about Mentoring Minorities," 99, 101.
68 Hewlett, "Executive Women and the Myth of Having It All," 68.
69 Khurana, "The Curse of the Superstar CEO," 3.
70 Goleman et al., *Primal Leadership*.
71 Henry Mintzberg, "Enough Leadership," *Harvard Business Review* 82 (November 2004), 22.
72 Lane et al., "Globalization: Hercules Meets Buddha," 4.
73 Mayo and Nohria, "Zeitgeist Leadership," 45.
74 For key founding texts in critical management theory, see Valérie Fournier and Chris Grey, "At a Critical Moment: Conditions and Prospects for Critical Management Studies," *Human Relations* 53 (2000), 7–32; Christopher Grey and Hugh Willmott, eds., *Critical Management Studies: A Reader* (Oxford: Oxford University Press, 2005).
75 David Collinson and Keith Grint, "Editorial: The Leadership Agenda," *Leadership* 1 (February 2005), 5.
76 Gail Fairhurst, *Discursive Leadership: In Conversation with Leadership Psychology* (London: Sage, 2007).
77 Burns, "Foreword," viii.
78 Rost, "Followership: An Outmoded Concept," 55.
79 Carroll et al., "Leadership as Practice," 365.
80 Doz and Kosonen, "The New Deal at the Top," 101.
81 Van Vugt and Ahuja, *Naturally Selected*, 22.
82 Kellerman, *The End of Leadership*, xiii.
83 Stout, *The Shareholder Value Myth*, 3.
84 Tourish, *Dark Side*, 13.

85 Daan Van Knippenberg and Sim B. Sitkin, "A Critical Assessment of Charismatic-Transformational Leadership Research: Back to the Drawing Board?" *Academy of Management Annals* 7 (2013), 50.

86 Ibid.

87 Walter Bryce Gallie, "Essentially Contested Concepts," *Proceedings of the Aristotelian Society* 56 (1956), 169, 171.

References

I did not set out to compile an all-encompassing bibliography of the leadership literature. That would be a practical impossibility anyway. Neither can I claim that I used and cited all of the "best" or most "worthwhile" works. To make that kind of judgment would be both arrogant and foolhardy. This bibliography is not intended to match the completeness of citations offered by the various excellent leadership textbooks, certainly not the thousands of references that have appeared in the multiple editions of *Stogdill's Handbook of Leadership*.

I do realize that the list of references below is quite enormous. This *is* a history of the discourse on leadership. The books and articles produced over the years that addressed the topic, either indirectly (for example, Margaret Mead's 1935 *Sex and Temperament in Three Primitive Societies*) or head on (for example, Bernard Bass's 1990 "From Transactional to Transformational Leadership: Learning to Share the Vision"), make up my database.

Additionally, I have taken seriously the challenge of tracing the movement of ideas from person to person and across years, decades, and centuries. The list below reflects what I took to be the nature of my task in writing *Discourse on Leadership: A Critical Appraisal*.

Achilles, Paul S. and Edith Mulhall Achilles. "Estimates of the Military Value of Certain Character Qualities." *Journal of Applied Psychology* 1 (December 1917): 305–16.

Acker, Joan. "Hierarchies, Jobs, Bodies: A Theory of Gendered Organizations." *Gender and Society* 4 (June 1990): 139–58.

Acker, Joan and Donald Van Houten. "Differential Recruitment and Control: The Sex Structuring of Organizations." *Administrative Science Quarterly* 19 (1974): 152–63.

Adams, Fred and Ken Aizawa. *The Bounds of Cognition*. Oxford: Blackwell Publishing, 2008.

Adler, Nancy J. "Expecting International Success: Female Managers Overseas." *Columbia Journal of World Business* 19 (1984): 79–85.

Adler, Nancy J. "Women Do Not Want International Careers: And Other Myths about International Management." *Organizational Dynamics* 13 (1984): 66–79.

Adler, Nancy J. "Women in Management Worldwide." *International Studies of Management and Organization* 16 (1986): 3–32.

Adler, Nancy J. "Global Leadership; Women Leaders." In *Developing Global Business Leaders: Policies, Processes, and Innovation*, edited by Mark E. Mendenhall, Torsten N. Kuhlmann, and Günter Stahl, 73–97. Westport: Quorum Books, 2001.

Adorno, Theodor W. *The Authoritarian Personality*. New York: Harper & Row, 1950.

Ageton, Arthur A. *Naval Leadership and the American Bluejacket*. New York: McGraw-Hill, 1944.

Agho, Augustine O. "Perspectives of Senior-Level Executives on Effective Followership and Leadership." *Journal of Leadership & Organizational Studies* 16 (November 2009): 159–66.

Allaire, Yvan and Mihaela E. Firsirotu. "Theories of Organizational Culture." *Organization Studies* 5 (1984): 193–226.

"All in a Day's Work: A Roundtable with Raymond Gilmartin, Frances Hesselbein, Frederick Smith, Lionel Tiger, Cynthia Tragge-Lakra, and Abraham Zaleznik." *Harvard Business Review* 79 (December 2001): 55–66.

Allport, Gordon W. and Henry S. Odbert. "Trait Names: A Psycho-Lexical Study." *Psychological Monograph* 47 (1936): 1–171.

Alvesson, Mats and Stefan Sveningsson. "Managers Doing Leadership: The Extra-ordinization of the Mundane." *Human Relations* 56 (2003): 1435–59.

Anastakis, Dimitry. "The Last Automotive Entrepreneur? Lee Iacocca Saves Chrysler, 1978–1986." Business History Conference (2007). Accessed at www.thebhc.org/sites/default/files/anastakis_0.pdf.

Andrews, Kenneth R. *The Concept of Corporate Strategy*. Homewood, IL: Dow Jones-Irwin, 1971.

Ankersmit, Frank R. *Historical Representation*. Stanford: Stanford University Press, 2001.

Anshen, Melvin. "The Manager and the Black Box." *Harvard Business Review* 37 (1959): 85–92.

Ansoff, H. Igor. *Strategic Management*. New York: Wiley, 1979.

Ansoff, H. Igor. "Conceptual Underpinnings of Systematic Strategic Management." *European Journal of Operational Research* 19 (1985): 2–19.

Ansoff, H. Igor and R.G. Brandenburg. "The General Manager of the Future." *California Management Review* 11 (Spring 1969): 61–72.

Antonakis, John. "Transformational and Charismatic Leadership." In *The Nature of Leadership*, edited by David Day and John Antonakis, 256–88. Thousand Oaks, CA: Sage.

Ansbacher, H.L. "German Military Psychology." *Psychology Bulletin* 38 (1941): 370–92.

Appelbaum, Jerome. "Father and Son: Freud Revisits his Oedipus Complex in *Moses and Monotheism*." *American Journal of Psychoanalysis* 72 (2012): 166–84.

Arendt, Hannah. *Eichmann in Jerusalem: Report on the Banality of Evil*. New York: Viking, 1963.

Argyris, Chris and Donald A. Schön. *Organizational Learning: A Theory of Action Perspective*. Reading, MA: Addison-Wesley, 1978.

Asch, Solomon E. "Opinions and Social Pressure." *Scientific American* 193 (November 1955): 31–35.

Ashby, W. Ross. *An Introduction to Cybernetics*. New York: Wiley, 1956.

Atkinson, Rick. *The Guns at Last Light: The War in Western Europe, 1944–1945*. New York: Henry Holt, 2013.

Babcock, Linda and Sara Laschever. *Women Don't Ask: Negotiation and the Gender Divide*. Princeton: Princeton University Press, 2003.

Bachrach, Peter and Morton S. Baratz. "Two Faces of Power." *American Political Science Review* 56 (December 1962): 947–52.

Bailey, Beth and David Farber. *America in the 70s*. Lawrence: University of Kansas Press, 2004.

Bandsuch, Mark, Larry Pate, and Jeff Thies. "Rebuilding Stakeholder Trust in Business: An Examination of Principle-Centered Leadership and Organizational Transparency in Corporate Governance." *Business and Society Review* 113 (2008): 99–112.

Baritz, Loren. *The Servants of Power: A History of the Use of Social Science in American Industry*. Middletown: Wesleyan University Press, 1960.

Barnard, Chester I. *The Functions of the Executive*. Cambridge: Harvard University Press, 1938.

Bartlett, Christopher A. and Sumantra Ghoshal. *Managing across Borders: The Transactional Solution*. Boston: Harvard Business School Press, 1989.

Bartlett, Christopher A. and Sumantra Ghoshal. "What Is a Global Manager?" *Harvard Business Review* 20 (1992): 124–32.

Bartlett, Christopher A. and Sumantra Ghoshal. "Changing the Role of Top Management: Beyond Strategy to Purpose." *Harvard Business Review* 72 (1994): 79–88.

Baskett, Peter. "Leaders Not Managers." *Resuscitation* 50 (2011): 3–5.

Bartol, Kathryn, Charles L. Evans, and Melvin T. Stith. "Black versus White Leaders: A Comparative Review of the Literature." *Academy of Management Review* 3 (April 1978): 293–304.

Bass, Bernard M. *Stogdill's Handbook of Leadership: A Survey of Theory and Research*. New York: Free Press, 1981.

Bass, Bernard M. *Leadership and Performance beyond Expectations*. New York: Free Press, 1985.

Bass, Bernard M. "Leadership: Good, Better, Best." *Organizational Dynamics* 13 (Winter 1985): 26–40.

Bass, Bernard M. *Bass and Stogdill's Handbook of Leadership: Theory, Research, and Managerial Implications*. New York: Free Press, 1990.

Bass, Bernard M. "From Transactional to Transformational Leadership: Learning to Share the Vision." *Organizational Dynamics* 18 (1990): 19–31.

Bass, Bernard M. "Toward a Meeting of Minds." *Leadership Quarterly* 1 (1990): unpaginated.

Bass, Bernard M. "A Seminal Shift: The Impact of James Burns' *Leadership*." *Leadership Quarterly* 4 (1993): 375–7.

Bass, Bernard M. and Bruce J. Avolio. "Transformational Leadership and Organizational Culture." *International Journal of Public Administration* 17 (March 1994): 541–55.

Bass, Bernard M. and Paul Steidlmeier. "Ethics, Character, and Authentic Trans-formational Leadership Behavior." *Leadership Quarterly* 10 (Summer 1999): 181–218.

Bass, Bernard M. and Ronald E. Riggio. *Transformational Leadership*, 2nd edition. New Jersey: Psychology Press, 2005.

Bates, George E. "The Board of Directors." *Harvard Business Review* 19 (1940): 72–87.

Bates, George E. "Twenty Years." *Harvard Business Review* 21 (Autumn 1942): 1–4.

Bauman, Zygmunt. *Modernity and the Holocaust*. Ithaca: Cornell University Press, 2000.

Becker, Howard S. *Outsiders: Studies in the Sociology of Deviance*. New York: Free Press, 1973.

Becker, Howard S. "Culture: A Sociological View." *Yale Review* 71 (1982): 513–27.

Bedell-Avers, Katrina, Samuel T. Hunter, Amanda D. Angie, Dawn L. Eubanks, and Michael D. Munford. "Charismatic, Ideological, and Pragmatic Lea-ders: An Examination of Leader-Leader Interactions." *Leadership Quarterly* 20 (2009): 299–315.

Beer, Michael and Bert Spector. "Organizational Diagnosis: Its Role in Organiza-tional Learning." *Journal of Counseling and Development* 71 (1993): 642–50.

Beer, Stafford. *Cybernetics and Management*. London: English University Press, 1959.

Bell, Daniel. *The End of Ideology: On the Exhaustion of Political Ideas in the Fifties*. New York: Free Press, 1962.

Bell, David V.J. *Power, Influence, and Authority: An Essay in Political Linguistics*. New York: Oxford University Press, 1975.

Bendix, Reinhard. *Managerial Ideologies in the Course of Industrialization*. New Jersey: Transaction Publishers, 1956/2001.

Benet-Martínez, Verónica, Janxin Leu, Fiona Lee, and Michael W. Morris. "Negotiating Biculturalism: Cultural Frame Switching in Biculturals with Oppositional versus Compatible Cultural Identities." *Journal of Cross-Cultural Psychology* 33 (September 2002): 492–516.

Benjamin, Tia. "A Functional Specialist vs. a Management Generalist." Accessed at http://smallbusiness.chron.com/functional-specialist-vs-management-generalist-36000.html.

Bennis, Warren G. *Why Leaders Can't Lead: The Unconscious Conspiracy Continues*. San Francisco: Jossey-Bass, 1989.

Bennis, Warren G. and Burt Nanus. *Leaders: Strategies for Taking Charge*. New York: Harper Business, 1985.

Berdahl, Jennifer L. and Cameron Anderson. "Men, Women, and Leadership Centralization over Time." *Group Dynamics: Theory, Research, and Practice* 9 (2005): 45–57.

Berle, Adolf A. "Corporate Powers as Powers in Trust." *Harvard Law Review* 45 (1932): 1049–474.

Berle, Adolf A. and Gardiner Means. *The Modern Corporation and Private Property*. New Brunswick: Transaction Publishers, 1932/1991.

Bernstein, Richard J. *Freud and the Legacy of Moses.* Cambridge: Cambridge University Press, 1998.

Bernstein, William J. *A Splendid Exchange: How Trade Shaped the World.* New York: Atlantic Monthly Press, 2008.

Beyette, Beverly. "A New Career Flap: What's a Mommy Track and Why Are So Many Women Upset about It?" *Los Angeles Times,* March 17, 1989. 3.

Biddle, Bruce J. and Edwin J. Thomas. "The Nature and History of Role Theory." In *Role Theory: Concepts and Research,* edited by Bruce J. Biddle and Edwin Thomas, 3–19. New York: Wiley, 1966.

Bierstedt, Robert. "An Analysis of Social Power." *American Sociological Review* 15 (December 1950): 730–38.

Bigelow, John. "Presentism and Properties." *Philosophical Perspectives* 10 (1996): 35–52.

Billing, Yvonne Due and Mats Alvesson. "Questioning the Notion of Feminine Leadership: A Critical Perspective on the Gender Labeling of Leadership." *Gender, Work, and Organization* 7 (July 2000): 144–57.

Bird, Barbara and Candida Brush. "A Gendered Perspective on Organizational Creation." *Entrepreneurship: Theory and Practice* 26 (Spring 2002): 41–65.

Blake, Robert R. *The Managerial Grid: Key Orientations for Achieving Production through People.* Houston: Gulf Publishing, 1964.

Blake, Robert R. and Anne A. McCanse. *Leadership Dilemmas – Grid Solutions.* Houston: Gulf Publishing, 1991.

Blake, Robert R. and Jane S. Mouton. *Building a Dynamic Corporation through Grid Organization Development.* Reading: Addison-Wesley, 1969.

Blake, Robert R., Jane S. Mouton, and Anne A. McCanse. *Change by Design.* Reading: Addison-Wesley, 1990.

Blass, Thomas. *The Man Who Shocked the World: The Life and Legacy of Stanley Milgram.* New York: Basic Books, 2004.

Bligh, Michelle C., Jeffrey C. Kohles, and Rajnandini Pillai. "Romancing Leadership: Past, Present, and Future." *Leadership Quarterly* 22 (2011): 1058–77.

Blom, Philipp. *The Vertigo Years: Change and Culture in the West, 1900–1914.* New York: Basic Books, 2008.

Blom, Philipp. *Fracture: Life and Culture in the West, 1918–1938.* New York: Basic Books, 2015.

Boas, Franz. *Race, Language and Culture.* New York: Macmillan, 1940.

Bolden, Richard and Jonathan Gosling. "Leadership Competencies: Time to Change the Tune?" *Leadership* 2 (2006): 147–63.

Booth, Charles and Michael Rowlinson. "Management and Organizational History: Prospects." *Management and Organizational History* 1 (2006): 5–30.

Bossche, Chris R.V. *Carlyle and the Search for Authority.* Columbus: Ohio State University Press, 1991.

Bowers, David G. and Stanley E. Seashore. "Predicting Organizational Effectiveness with a Four-Factor Theory of Leadership." *Administrative Science Quarterly* 11 (1966): 238–63.

Bowlby, John. *Attachment and Loss.* New York: Basic Books, 1969.

Bowler, Mark C., Jennifer L. Bowler, and John G. Cope. "Further Evidence of the Impact of Cognitive Complexity on the Five-Factor Model." *Social Behavior and Personality* 40 (2012): 1083–98.

Bowles, Hannah Riley and Kathleen L. McGinn. "Gender in Job Negotiations: A Two-Level Game." *Negotiation Journal* 24 (October 2008): 393–410.

Bowman, Garda W., N. Beatrice Worthy, and Stephen Greyser. "Are Women Executives People?" *Harvard Business Review* 43 (July–August 1965): 14–33.

Boyatzis, Richard E. *The Competent Manager: A Model for Effective Performance.* New York: Wiley, 1982.

Boyer, Paul E. *Promises to Keep: The United States since World War II.* Boston: Houghton Mifflin, 1999.

Boyer, Robert. "Is a Finance Led Growth Regime a Viable Alternative to Fordism? A Preliminary Analysis." *Economy and Society* 20 (2000): 111–45.

Braddock, Jomills Henry, III, and James M. McPhartland. "How Minorities Continue to Be Excluded from Equal Opportunities: Research on Labor Markets and Institutional Barriers." *Journal of Social Issues* 43 (1987): 5–39.

Branson, Richard. *Losing My Virginity: How I Survived, Had Fun, and Made a Fortune Doing Business My Way.* New York: Crown, 2011.

Braun, Susanne, Claudia Peus, Silke Weisweiler, and Dieter Frey. "Transformational Leadership, Job Satisfaction, and Team Performance: A Multilevel Mediation Model of Trust." *Leadership Quarterly* 24 (2013): 270–83.

Bray, Douglas W. and Donald L. Grant. "The Assessment Center in the Management of Potential for Business Management." *Psychological Monographs* 80 (1966): 1–27.

Bridgeman, D.S. "Success in College and Business." *Personnel Journal* 9 (1930): 1–19.

Briner, Rob B., David Denyer, and Denise M. Rousseau. "Evidence-Based Management: Concept Cleanup Time?" *Academy of Management Perspectives* 23 (2009): 19–32.

Brizendine, Louann. "One Reason Women Don't Make It to the C-Suite." *Harvard Business Review* 86 (June 2008): 36.

Brooks, Rosa. "Recline, Don't 'Lean In' (Why I Hate Sheryl Sandberg)." *Washington Post*, February 25, 2014. Accessed at www.washingtonpost.com/blogs/she-the-people/wp/2014/02/25/recline-dont-lean-in-why-i-hate-sheryl-sandberg.

Brown, Alvin. *Organization: A Formulation of Principles.* New York: Hibbert, 1945.

Bryman, Alan, David Collinson, Keith Grint, Brad Jackson, and Mary Uhl-Bien, eds. *The SAGE Handbook of Leadership.* Los Angeles: Sage, 2011.

Buhle, Mari Jo. *Feminism and Its Discontents: A Century of Struggle with Psychoanalysis.* Cambridge: Harvard University Press, 1998.

Bullough, Amanda, Mary Sully De Luque, Dina Abdelzaher, and Wynona Heim. "Developing Women Leaders through Entrepreneurship Education and Training." *Academy of Management Perspectives* 29 (May 2015): 250–70.

Burand, Deborah. "Beyond Microfinance: Creating Opportunities for Women at the Base of the Pyramid." *International Trade Forum* 2 (April–June, 2012): 20–21.

Burder, Stanley. "Intolerance of Ambiguity and Need for Closure." *Psychological Reports* 43 (1978): 638.

Burke, W. Warner. "Leadership as Empowering Others." In *Executive Power: How Executives Influence People and Organizations*, edited by Suresh Srivastva, 51–77. San Francisco: Jossey-Bass, 1986.

Burnham, James. *The Managerial Revolution*. New York: John Day, 1941.

Burns, James MacGregor. *Leadership*. New York: Harper, 1978.

Burns, James MacGregor. *Transforming Leadership: A New Pursuit of Happiness*. New York: Atlantic Monthly Press, 2003.

Burton, Francis G. *The Commercial Management of Engineering Works*. Manchester: Scientific Publishing, 1899.

Burton, Jessie. *The Miniaturist: A Novel*. New York: Ecco, 2014.

Bush, H. K. "What Historians Think about Spielberg's *Lincoln*." *Cineaste* 38 (Spring 2013): 13–19.

Butler, Jay G. "On Power and Authority: An Exchange on Concepts." *American Sociological Review* 25 (October 1960): 731–2.

Byrne, John A. *Chainsaw: The Notorious Career of Al Dunlap in the Era of Profit at Any Price*. New York: HarperCollins, 1999.

Cabane, Olivia Fox. *The Charisma Myth: How Anyone Can Master the Art and Science of Personal Magnetism*. New York: Portfolio, 2012.

Cahnman, Werner J. "Ideal Type Theory: Max Weber's Concept and Some of Its Derivations. *Sociological Quarterly* 6 (1963): 268–80.

Cahusac, Emma and Shireen Kanji. "Giving Up: How Gendered Organizational Cultures Push Mothers Out." *Gender, Work, and Organization* 21 (January 2014): 57–70.

Calás, Marta B. and Linda Smircich. "Dangerous Liaisons: The 'Feminine-in-Management' Meets 'Globalization.'" *Business Horizons* 36 (March–April 1993): 71–80.

Caligiuri, Paula. "Developing Global Leaders." *Human Resource Management Review* 16 (2006): 219–28.

Caligiuri, Paula. *Cultural Agility: Building a Pipeline of Successful Global Professionals*. San Francisco: Jossey-Bass, 2013.

Caligiuri, Paula and Victoria Di Santo. "Global Competence: What Is It, and Can It Be Developed through Global Assignments?" *Human Resource Planning* 24 (2001): 27–35.

Caligiuri, Paula and Ibraiz Tarique. "Dynamic Cross-Cultural Competencies and Global Leadership Effectiveness." *Journal of World Business* 47 (2012): 612–22.

Camillus, John C. "Strategy as a Wicked Problem." *Harvard Business Review* 86 (May 2008): 99–106.

Cannella, Albert A., Jr. "Upper Echelons: Donald Hambrick on Executives and Strategy." *Academy of Management Executive* 15 (2001): 36–42.

Carlson, Sune. *Executive Behavior: A Study of the Work*. Stockholm: Strömberg, 1951.

Carlyle, Thomas. *On Heroes, Hero-Worship, and the Heroic in History.* New Haven: Yale University Press, 1841/2013.

Carmichael, Stokely and Charles V. Hamilton. *Black Power: The Politics of Liberation in America.* New York: Vintage, 1967.

Carroll, Brigid, Lester Levy, and David Richmond. "Leadership as Practice: Challenging the Competency Paradigm." *Leadership* 4 (2008): 363–79.

Carsten, Melissa K. and Mary Uhl-Bien. "Ethical Followership: An Examination of Followership Beliefs and Crimes of Obedience." *Journal of Leadership and Organizational Studies* 20 (2013): 49–61.

Carsten, Melissa K., Mary Uhl-Bien, Bradley J. West, Jaime L. Patera, and Rob McGregor. "Exploring Social Constructions of Followership: A Qualitative Study." *Leadership Quarterly* 21 (2010): 543–62.

Cartwright, Dorwin, ed. *Studies in Social Power.* Ann Arbor: Institute for Social Research, 1959.

Cartwright, Dorwin and Alvin F. Zander. *Group Dynamics Research and Theory.* Evanston: Row, Peterson, 1960.

Casey, Jr., George W. "Leading in a 'VUCA' World." *Fortune* 7 (April 2014): 75–76.

Castilla, Emilio J. and Stephen Bernard. "The Paradox of Meritocracy in Organizations." *Administrative Science Quarterly* 55 (2010): 543–76.

Chaleff, Ira. *The Courageous Follower: Standing Up To and For Our Leaders.* San Francisco: Berrett-Koehler Publishers, 1997.

Chandler, Alfred D., Jr. *The Visible Hand: The Managerial Revolution in American Business.* Cambridge: Belknap Press, 1977.

Chatman, Jennifer A. and Sandra Eunyoung Cha. "Leading by Leveraging Culture." *California Management Review* 45 (Summer 2003): 20–34.

Cheng, Cecilia, Feixue Wang, and Debra L. Golden. "Unpacking Cultural Differences in Interpersonal Flexibility: Role of Culture-Related Personality and Situational Factors." *Journal of Cross-Cultural Psychology* 42 (2011): 425–44.

Cheung, Fanny M. and Diane F. Halpern. "Women at the Top: Powerful Leaders Define Success at Work + Family in a Culture of Gender." *American Psychologist* 65 (April 2010): 183–93.

Chisholm, Roderick. "Referring to Things That No Longer Exist." *Philosophical Perspectives* 4 (1990): 545–56.

Ciulla, Joanne B. *Ethics: The Heart of Leadership.* Westport: Quorum Books, 1998.

Clanchy, Michael. *From Memory to Written Record: England, 1066–1307.* Oxford: Blackwell, 1993.

Clapp-Smith, Rachel and Gretchen Vogelgesang Lester. "Defining the 'Mindset' in Global Mindset: Modeling the Dualities of Global Leadership." In *Advances in Global Leadership,* edited by Joyce Osland, Ming Li, and Ying Wang, 205–28. London: Emerald, 2014.

Clark, Burton R. "The Organizational Saga in Higher Education." *Administrative Science Quarterly* 17 (June 1972): 178–84.

Clark, Andy. *Supersizing the Mind: Embodiment, Action, and Cognitive Extension.* Oxford: Oxford University Press, 2008.

Cleeton, Glen U. and Charles W. Mason. *Executive Ability: Its Discovery and Development.* Yellow Spring: Antioch Press, 1934.

Clegg, Stewart. "Organization and Control." *Administrative Science Quarterly* 26 (December 1981): 545–62.

Clegg, Stewart. "Theories of Power." *Theory, Culture & Society* 17 (2000): 139–47.

Coates, David, ed. *Varieties of Capitalism, Varieties of Approaches.* London: Palgrave, 2005.

Cohen, Stephen L. "Effective Global Leadership Requires a Global Mindset." *Industrial and Commercial Training* 42 (2010): 3–10.

Colgan, Fiona, Tessa Wright, Chris Creegan, and Aidan McKearney. "Equality and Diversity in the Public Services: Moving Forward on Lesbian, Gay and Bisexual Equality?" *Human Resource Management Journal* 19 (2009): 280–301.

Colli, Andrea, Abe De Jong, and Martin Jes Iversen, eds. *Mapping European Corporations: Strategy, Structure, Ownership and Performance.* London: Routledge, 2012.

Collins, David. *Management Fads and Buzzwords: Critical-Practical Perspectives.* London: Routledge, 2000.

Collins, Patricia H. *Fighting Words: Black Women and the Search for Justice.* Minneapolis: University of Minnesota Press, 1998.

Collins, Patricia Hill and John Solomos. "Situating Race and Ethnic Studies." In *The SAGE Handbook of Race and Ethnic Studies,* edited by Patricia Hill Collins and John Solomos, 3–23. Thousand Oaks: Sage, 2010.

Collinson, David L. "Rethinking Followership: A Post-Structuralist Analysis of Follower Identity." *Leadership Quarterly* 17 (2006): 179–89.

Collinson, David L. and Jeff Hearn. *Men as Managers, Managers as Men: Critical Perspectives on Men, Masculinities and Managements.* Thousand Oaks: Sage, 1996.

Collinson, David L. and Stephen Ackroyd. "Resistance, Misbehavior, and Dissent." In *Oxford Handbook of Work and Organization,* edited by Stephen Ackroyd, Rosemary Batt, Paul Thompson, and Pamela S. Tolbert, 305–26. Oxford: Oxford University Press, 2005.

Collinson, David L. and Keith Grint. "Editorial: The Leadership Agenda." *Leadership* 1 (February 2005): 5–9.

Coltrane, Scott. *Family Man: Fatherhood, Housework, and Gender Equity.* New York: Oxford University Press, 1996.

Conger, Jay A. "Leadership: The Art of Empowering Others." *Academy of Management Executive* 3 (1989): 17–24.

Conger, Jay A. *Learning to Lead: The Art of Transforming Managers into Leaders.* San Francisco: Jossey-Bass, 1992.

Constantinople, Anne. "Masculinity-Femininity: An Exception of the Famous Dictum?" *Psychological Bulletin* 89 (1973): 389–407.

Consumer Reports 1989. Yonkers: Consumer Union, 1990.

Consumer Reports 1994. Yonkers: Consumer Union, 1995.

Cook, Edwin A. "Cultural Flexibility: Myth and Reality." *Anthropos* 3 (1966): 831–8.

Cooke, Bill. "The Denial of Slavery in Management Studies." *Journal of Management Studies* 40 (December 2003): 1895–918.

Cooper, Marianne. "Being the Go-To Guy: Fatherhood, Masculinity, and the Organization of Work in Silicon Valley." *Quantitative Sociology* 23 (2000): 397–402.

Cooperrider, David and Ronald Fry. "Corporate Citizenship at the Core: It Is Still about Stakeholder Engagement and Relational Practices." *Journal of Corporate Citizenship* 47 (Autumn 2012): 3–7.

"Corporations, General Manager, Implied Authority." *Yale Law Review* 19 (March 1910): 383.

"Corporations: Independent Actions of General Manager." *Michigan Law Review* 14 (1916): 506.

"Corporations: Implied Authority of General Manager." *Michigan Law Review* 11 (1913): 403–4.

"Corporations: Powers of the President and General Manager." *Columbia Law Review* 23 (1923): 784–5.

Correll, Shelley J., Stephen Bernard, and In Pail. "Getting a Job: Is There a Motherhood Penalty?" *American Journal of Sociology* 112 (March 2007): 1297–339.

Couto, Richard A., ed. *Reflections on Leadership*. Lanham, MD: University Press of America, 2007.

Cox, Taylor, Jr. "Problems with Research by Organizational Scholars on Issues of Race and Ethnicity." *Journal of Applied Behavioral Science* 40 (June 2004): 124–45.

Cox, Taylor, Jr., and Stella M. Nkomo. "Differential Appraisal Criteria Based on Race of the Ratee." *Group and Organization Studies* 11 (1986): 101–19.

Crenshaw, Kimberlé. "Mapping the Margins: Intersectionality, Identity Politics, and Violence against Women of Color." *Stanford Law Review* 43 (1991): 1241–99.

Crenshaw, Kimberlé. *Critical Race Theory: The Key Writings That Formed the Movement*. New York: New Press, 1995.

Crossman, Brian and Joanna Crossman. "Conceptualizing Followership: A Review of the Literature." *Leadership* 7 (2011): 481–97.

Cruikshank, Jeffrey L. *A Delicate Experiment: The Harvard Business School, 1908–1945*. Boston: Harvard Business School Press, 1987.

Culpan, Refik and John Trussel. "Applying the Agency and Stakeholder Theories to the Enron Debacle: An Ethical Perspective." *Business and Society Review* 110 (2005): 59–76.

Cuordileone, K.A. "'Politics in an Age of Anxiety': Cold War Political Culture and the Crisis in American Masculinity, 1949–1960." *Journal of American History* 87 (2000): 515–45.

Czarniawska-Joerges, Barbara. *Ideological Control in Nonideological Organizations*. New York: Praeger, 1988.

Dahl, Robert A. "The Concept of Power." *Behavioral Science* 2 (1957): 201–15.

Dale, Ernest. "Contributions to Administration by Alfred P. Sloan, Jr., and GM." *Administrative Science Quarterly* 10 (September 1967): 32–62.

Dansereau, Fred, George Graen, and William J. Haga. "A Vertical Dyad Linkage Approach to Leadership in Formal Organizations." *Organizational Behavior and Human Performance* 13 (1975): 46–78.

Danto, Arthur C. *Analytical Philosophy of History*. Cambridge: Cambridge University Press, 1965.

Dargis, Manohla. "Young, White and Male? The Role Is Yours." *New York Times*, August 6, 2015, C1.

Davis, Gerald F. and Tracy A. Thompson. "A Social Movement Perspective on Corporate Control." *Administrative Science Quarterly* 39 (1994): 141–73.

Davis, Jason P. and Kathleen M. Eisenhardt. "Rotating Leadership and Collaborative Innovation: Recombination Processes in Symbiotic Relationships." *Administrative Science Quarterly* 56 (2011): 159–201.

Davis, Kathy. "Intersectionality as Buzzword: A Sociology of Science Perspective on What Makes a Feminist Theory Successful." *Feminist Theory* 9 (2008): 67–85.

Davis, Stanley and Paul R. Lawrence. *Matrix*. Reading: Addison-Wesley, 1977.

Dawson, Doyne. "The Origins of War: Biological and Anthropological Theories." *History and Theory* 35 (February 1996): 1–28.

Day, David V., John W. Fleenor, Leanne E. Atwater, Rachael E. Strum, and Rob A. McKee. "Advances in Leader and Leadership Development: A Review of 25 Years of Research and Theory." *Leadership Quarterly* 25 (2014): 63–82.

Deal, Terrence A. and Allan A. Kennedy. *Corporate Cultures: The Rites and Rituals of Corporate Life*. Reading: Addison-Wesley, 1982.

De Beauvoir, Simone. *The Second Sex*. New York: Knopf, 1952.

Denain, Pierre. "An Educator's Education: Notes on the Makings of Booker T. Washington's Ideology." In *Myth and Ideology in American Culture*, edited by Régis Durand, 152–73. Lilli: Centre d'Etudes et de Recherché, 1976.

De Neve, Jan-Emmanuel, Slava Mikhaylov, Christopher T. Dawes, Nicholas A. Christakis, and James H. Fowler. "Born to Lead? A Twin Design and Genetic Association Study of Leadership Role Occupancy." *Leadership Quarterly* 24 (2013): 45–60.

Denis, Jean-Louis, Ann Langley, and Viviane Sergi. "Leadership in the Plural." *Academy of Management Annals* 6 (June 2012): 211–83.

Denison, Daniel R., Robert Hooijberg, and Robert E. Quinn. "Paradox and Performance: Toward a Theory of Behavioral Complexity in Managerial Leadership." *Organization Science* 6 (September–October 1995): 524–40.

Department of the Army. *Army Leadership: Competent, Confident, Agile (Field Manual 22-100)*. Washington, D.C.: Department of the Army, 2006.

De Vos, Jan. "From Milgram to Zimbardo: The Double Birth of Postwar Psychology/Psychologization." *History of the Human Sciences* 23 (2010): 156–75.

Dickson, Marcus W., Brent D. Smith, Michael W. Grojean, and Mark Ehrhart. "An Organizational Climate Regarding Ethics: The Outcome of Leader Values and the Practices That Reflect Them." *Leadership Quarterly* 12 (Summer 2001): 197–218.

Diehl, Carl. "The Life and Work of Max Weber." *Quarterly Journal of Economics* 38 (1923): 67–107.

Digman, John M. "Personality Structure: Emergence of the Five-Factor Model." *Annual Review of Psychology* 41 (1990): 417–40.

Disco, Cornelis. "Critical Theory as Ideology of the New Class." *Theory and Society* 8 (1979): 159–214.

Dobbin, Frank and Dirk Zorn. "Corporate Malfeasance and the Myth of Shareholder Value." *Political Power and Social Theory* 17 (2005): 179–98.

Dodd, E. Merrick. "For Whom Are Corporate Managers Trustees?" *Harvard Law Review* 45 (1932): 1145–63.

Doheny, Mike, Venu Nagali, and Florian Weig. "Agile Operations for Volatile Times." *McKinsey Quarterly* 3 (2012): 126–31.

Donaldson, Thomas and Thomas W. Dunfee. "Ties That Bind in Business Ethics: Social Contracts and Why They Matter." *Journal of Banking and Finance* 26 (2002): 1853–65.

Donaldson, Thomas and Lee E. Preston. "The Stakeholder Theory of the Corporation: Concepts, Evidence, and Implications." *Academy of Management Review* 20 (1995): 65–91.

Downton, James V., Jr. *Rebel Leadership: Commitment and Charisma in the Revolutionary Process*. New York: Free Press, 1973.

Doz, Yves L. and Mikko Kosonen. "The New Deal at the Top." *Harvard Business Review* 85 (June 2007): 98–104.

Doz, Yves L., José Santos, and Peter Williamson. *From Global to Metanational: How Companies Win in the Knowledge Economy*. Boston: Harvard Business School Press, 2001.

Dragoni, Lisa and Kristie McAlpine. "Leading the Business: The Criticality of Global Leaders' Cognitive Complexity in Setting Strategic Directions." *Industrial and Organizational Psychology* 5 (2012): 237–40.

Dray, William H. *Philosophy of History*. Englewood Cliffs: Prentice-Hall, 1964.

Drucker, Peter F. *Concept of the Corporation*. New York: John Day, 1946.

Drucker, Peter F. *The Practice of Management*. New York: Harper, 1954.

Du Bois, W.E.B. *The Souls of Black Folks*. New York: Mead, 1909/1961.

Dunlap, Albert J. and Bob Andelman. *Mean Business: How I Save Bad Companies and Make Good Companies Great*. New York: Simon and Schuster, 1996.

Durepos, Gabrielle and Albert J. Mills. "Actor-Network Theory, ANTi-History and Critical Organizational Historiography." *Organization* 19 (2011): 1–19.

Duster, Troy. "Buried Alive: The Concept of Race in Science." In *Genetic Nature / Culture: Anthropology and Science beyond the Two-Culture Divide*, edited by Alan H. Goodman, Deborah Heath, and M. Susan Lindee, 258–77. Berkeley: University of California Press, 2003.

Eagly, Alice H. and Linda L. Carli. *Through the Labyrinth: The Truth about How Women Become Leaders*. Boston: Harvard Business School Press, 2008.

Eagly, Alice H., and Mary C. Johannesen-Schmidt. "The Leadership Styles of Women and Men." *Journal of Social Issues* 57 (2001): 781–97.

Eagly, Alice H., Wendy Wood, and Amanda B. Diekman. "Social Role Theory of Sex Differences and Similarities: A Current Appraisal." In *The Development of Social Psychology of Gender*, edited by Thomas Eckes and Hanns M. Trautner, 123–74. East Sussex: Psychology Press, 2000.

Eccles, Tony. "The Deceptive Allure of Empowerment." *Long Range Planning* 26 (1993): 13–21.

Edmundson, Amy C., Michael A. Roberto, and Michael D. Watkins. "A Dynamic Model of Top Management Team Effectiveness: Managing Unstructured Task Streams." *Leadership Quarterly* 14 (2003): 297–325.

Edmundson, Mark. "Defender of the Faith?" *New York Times Sunday Magazine*, September 9, 2007. Accessed at www.nytimes.com/2007/09/09/magazine/09wwln-lede-t.html?pagewanted=all&_r=0.

Eidelson, Roy and Jean Maria Arrigo. "How the American Psychological Association Lost Its Way." *Los Angeles Times*, July 30, 2015: 31.

Eisenhardt, Kathleen M., Jean L. Kahwajy, and L.J. Bourgeois III. "Conflict and Strategic Choice: How Top Management Teams Disagree." *California Management Review* 39 (Winter 1997): 42–62.

Eisenhardt, Kathleen M., Jean L. Kahwajy, and L.J. Bourgeois III. "How Top Management Teams Can Have a Good Fight." *Harvard Business Review* 75 (July–August 1997): 77–85.

Elkington, John. "Towards the Sustainable Corporation: Win-Win-Win Strategies for Sustainable Development." *California Management Review* 36 (Winter 1994): 90–100.

Elkington, John. *Cannibals with Forks: The Triple Bottom Line of 21st Century Business*. London: Capstone, 1997.

Emirbayer, Mustafa and Ann Mische. "What Is Agency?" *American Journal of Sociology* 103 (January 1998): 962–1023.

Epstein, Cynthia Fuchs. "Positive Effects of the Multiple Negative: Explaining the Success of Black Professional Women." *American Journal of Sociology* 78 (January 1973): 912–35.

Epstein, Cynthia Fuchs. *Deceptive Distinctions: Sex, Gender, and the Social Order*. New Haven: Yale University Press, 1988.

Etzioni, Amitai. "Authority Structure and Organizational Effectiveness." *Administrative Science Quarterly* 4 (1959): 43–67.

Evans, Kathy M. and Edwin L. Herr. "The Influence of Racism and Sexism in the Career Development of African-American Women." *Journal of Multicultural Counseling & Development* 19 (July 1991): 130–35.

Evans, Richard J. *In Defense of History*. New York: Norton, 1999.

Everly, Benjamin A. and Joshua L. Schwarz. "Predictors of the Adoption of LGBT-Friendly HR Policies." *Human Resource Management* 54 (March 2015): 367–84.

Ewick, Patricia and Susan Silbey. "Subversive Stories and Hegemonic Tales: Toward a Sociology of Narrative." *Law & Society Review* 29 (1995): 197–226.

Ezorsky, Gertrude. *Racism and Justice: The Case for Affirmative Action*. Ithaca: Cornell University Press, 1991.

Fagiano, David. "Managers vs. Leaders: A Corporate Fable." *Management Review* 86 (1997): 5.

Fairhurst, Gail. *Discursive Leadership: In Conversation with Leadership Psychology*. London: Sage, 2007.

Farago, Ladislas. *German Psychological Warfare*. New York: G.P. Putnam's Sons, 1942.

Farber, David. *Sloan Rules: Alfred P. Sloan and the Triumph of General Motors.* Chicago: University of Chicago Press, 2002.

Farber, David and Beth Bailey. *The Columbia Guide to America in the 1960s.* New York: Columbia University Press, 2001.

Farndale, Elaine, Pai Avinash, Paul Sparrow, and Hugh Scullion. "Balancing Individual and Organizational Goals in Global Talent Management: A Mutual-Benefits Perspective." *Journal of World Business* 49 (2014): 204–14.

Faulkner, Richard S. *The School of Hard Knocks: Combat Leadership in the American Expeditionary Forces.* College Station: Texas A&M University Press, 2012.

Fayol, Henri. *General and Industrial Management.* London: Pitman, 1914/1949.

Feder, Barnaby J. "Theodore Levitt, 81, Who Coined the Term 'Globalization,' Is Dead," *New York Times,* July 6, 2006. Accessed at www.nytimes.com/2006/07/06/business/06levitt.html?_r=0.

Ferrante, Joan and Prince Brown, Jr. *The Social Construction of Race and Ethnicity in the United States.* New York: Longman, 1998.

Ferguson, Karen J. "Caught in 'No Man's Land': The Negro Cooperative Demonstration Service and the Ideology of Booker T. Washington, 1900–1918." *Agricultural History* 12 (Winter 1998): 33–54.

Ferguson, Kathy E. *The Feminist Case against Bureaucracy.* Philadelphia: Temple University Press, 1984.

Fiedler, Fred E. *A Theory of Leadership Effectiveness.* New York: McGraw-Hill, 1967.

Fiedler, Fred E. and Joseph E. Garcia. *New Approaches to Effective Leadership: Cognitive Resources and Organizational Performance.* New York: Wiley, 1987.

Fiorina, Carly. *Tough Choices: A Memoir.* New York: Portfolio, 2006.

Firestone, Shulamith. *The Dialectic of Sex.* New York: William Morrow, 1970.

Fitzgerald, F. Scott. "The Crack-Up." In *The Crack-Up,* edited by Edmund Wilson, 69–74. New York: New Directions, 1945.

Fleishman, Edwin A. "The Description of Supervisory Behavior." *Journal of Applied Psychology* 37 (February 1953): 1–6.

Fleishman, Edwin A., Michael D. Mumford, Stephen J. Zaccaro, Kerry-Yarkin Levin, Arthur L. Korotkin, and Michael B. Hein. "Taxonomic Effects in the Description of Leader Behavior: A Synthesis and Functional Interpretation." *Leadership Quarterly* 2 (1991): 245–87.

Fleming, Peter and André Spicer. *Contesting the Corporation: Struggle, Power and Resistance in Organizations.* Cambridge: Cambridge University Press, 2007.

Fleming, Robin. "Writing Biography at the Edge of History." *American Historical Review* 114 (June 2009): 606–14.

Fletcher, Joyce K. *Disappearing Acts: Gender, Power, and Relational Practice at Work.* Cambridge: MIT Press, 1999.

Fligstein, Neil. *The Transformation of Corporate Control.* Cambridge: Harvard University Press, 1990.

Follett, Mary Parker. "The Process of Control." In *Papers on the Science of Administration,* edited by Luther Gulick and L. Urwick, 159–70. New York: Institute of Public Administration, 1937.

Ford, Jackie. "Discourses of Leadership: Gender, Identity and Contradiction in a UK Public Sector Organization." *Leadership* 2 (February 2006): 77–90.

"Ford's Young One." *Time Magazine*, April 17, 1964: 92–102.

Foucault, Michel. *The Archaeology of Knowledge.* New York: Pantheon, 1972.

Foucault, Michel. *Discipline and Punish: The Birth of the Prison.* New York: Vintage, 1979.

Foucault, Michel. "The Subject and Power." *Critical History* 8 (Summer 1982): 777–95.

Fournier, Valérie and Chris Grey. "At a Critical Moment: Conditions and Prospects for Critical Management Studies." *Human Relations* 53 (2000): 7–32.

Fox, Suzy and Paul E. Spector. "A Model of Work Frustration-Aggression." *Journal of Organizational Behavior* 20 (1999): 915–31.

Frankel-Brunswick, Egan. "Intolerance of Ambiguity as an Emotional and Perceptual Personality Variable." *Journal of Personality* 18 (1948): 108–43.

Frankfurter, George M. and Elton G. McGoun. "Ideology and the Theory of Financial Economics." *Journal of Economic Behavior and Organization* 39 (1999): 159–77.

Freeden, Michael. *Ideology: A Very Short Introduction.* Oxford: Oxford University Press, 2003.

Freeman, E. Edward. *Strategic Management: A Stakeholder Approach.* Boston: Pitman, 1984.

Freeman, E. Edward. "Stakeholder Theory of the Firm." In *Perspectives in Business Ethics*, edited by L.P. Hartman, 171–81. Boston: McGraw-Hill Irwin, 2002.

French, John R.P., Jr., and Richard Snyder. "Leadership and Interpersonal Power." In *Studies in Social Power*, edited by Dorwin Cartright, 118–49. Ann Arbor: Institute for Social Research, 1959.

Freud, Sigmund. *Group Psychology and the Analysis of the Ego.* New York: Liveright Publishing, 1921/1967.

Freud, Sigmund. *Moses and Monotheism.* New York: Vantage, 1939/1967.

Friedan, Betty. *The Feminine Mystique.* New York: Norton, 1963.

Friedman, Milton. "The Social Responsibility of Business Is to Increase Its Profits." *New York Times Magazine* 32 (September 13, 1970): 32–33, 122–4.

Friedman, Thomas L. *The World Is Flat: A Brief History of the Twenty-First Century.* New York: Farrar, Straus and Giroux, 2006.

Frieze, Deborah and Margaret Wheatley. "It's Time for the Heroes to Go Home." *Leader to Leader* 62 (2011): 27–32.

Froud, Julie, Colin Haslam, Sukhdev Johal, and Karel Williams. "Shareholder Value and Financialization: Consultancy Promises, Management Moves." *Economy and Society* 29 (2000): 80–110.

Fuller, Mark B. "Business as War." *Fast Company*, 1994. Accessed at fastcompany.com/55076/business-war.

Fullerton, Michelle. "Diversity and Inclusion: LGBT Inclusion Means Business." *Strategic HR Review* 12 (2013): 121–5.

Galbraith, Jay. *Developing Complex Organizations.* Reading: Addison-Wesley, 1973.

Gallie, Walter Bryce. "Essentially Contested Concepts." *Proceedings of the Aristotelian Society* 56 (1956): 167–98.

Gallup, George H. *The Gallup Poll: Public Opinion, 1979.* Wilmington: Scholarly Resources Inc., 1980.

Gandz, Jeffrey. "The Employee Empowerment Era." *Business Quarterly* 55 (Autumn 1990): 74–80.

Gandz, Jeffrey and Frederick G. Bird. "The Ethics of Empowerment." *Journal of Business Ethics* 15 (1996): 383–92.

Geoghegan, Vincent. "Ideology and Utopia." *Journal of Political Ideologies* 9 (June 2004): 123–38.

Ghemawat, Pankaj. "Why the World Isn't Flat." *Foreign Policy* 159 (March–April 2007): 54–60.

Ghemawat, Pankaj and Steven A. Altman. *DHL Global Connectedness Index 2014: Analyzing Global Flows and Their Power to Increase Prosperity*, 2014. Accessed at www.dhl.com/en/about_us/logistics_insights/studies_research/global_ connectedness_index/global_connectedness_index.html#.VOeer3zF-Sr.

Gibb, Cecil A. "The Principles and Traits of Leadership." *Journal of Abnormal and Social Psychology* 42 (1947): 267–84.

Gilbert, James Burkhart. *Men in the Middle: Searching for Masculinity in the 1950s.* Chicago: University of Chicago Press, 2005.

Gilligan, Carol. *In a Different Voice: Psychological Theory and Women's Development.* Cambridge: Harvard University Press, 1982.

Gilligan, Carol and Jane Attanucci. "Two Moral Orientations: Gender Differences and Similarities." *Merrill-Palmer Quarterly* 34 (1988): 223–37.

Goffee, Robert and Gareth Jones. "Followership: It's Personal, Too." *Harvard Business Review* 79 (December 2001): 148.

Goffman, Erving. *The Presentation of Self in Everyday Life.* New York: Doubleday, 1959.

Goffman, Erving. *Frame Analysis: An Essay on the Organization of Experience.* Cambridge: Harvard University Press, 1974.

Goffman, Erving. "The Arrangement between the Sexes." *Theory and Society* 4 (Autumn 1977): 301–31.

Goktepe, Janet R. and Craig Eric Schneier. "Role of Sex, Gender Roles, and Attraction in Predicting Emergent Leaders." *Journal of Applied Psychology* 74 (1989): 165–7.

Goldberg, David Theo. *Racist Culture: Philosophy and the Politics of Meaning.* Cambridge: Blackwell, 1993.

Goldhagen, Daniel Johan. *Hitler's Willing Executioners: Ordinary Germans and the Holocaust.* New York: Knopf, 1996.

Goldstein, Judith. *Ideas, Interests, and American Trade Policy.* Ithaca: Cornell University Press, 1993.

Goleman, Daniel, Richard E. Boyatzis, and Annie McKee. *Primal Leadership: Realizing the Power of Emotional Intelligence.* Boston: Harvard Business School Press, 2002.

Gollwitzer, Peter. "Action Phases and Mind-Sets." In *Handbook of Motivation and Cognition*, edited by E. Tory Higgins and Richard M. Sorrentino, 53–92. New York: Guilford Press, 1990.

Goode, William J. *The Celebration of Heroes: Prestige as a Social Control System.* Berkeley: University of California Press, 1978.

Goodwin, Doris Kearns. *A Team of Rivals: The Political Genius of Abraham Lincoln.* New York: Simon & Schuster, 2005.

Goodwin, Doris Kearns. "Leadership Lessons from Abraham Lincoln." *Harvard Business Review* 87 (April 2009): 44–48.

Gouldner, Alvin W. *The Coming Crisis of Western Sociology.* New York: Basic Books, 1970.

Gowin, Enoch B. *Selection and Training of the Business Executive.* New York: Macmillan, 1918.

Graen, George and William Schiemann. "Leader-Member Agreement: A Vertical Dyad Linkage Approach." *Journal of Applied Psychology* 63 (1978): 206–12.

Grant, Adam M. "Leading with Meaning: Beneficiary Contact, Prosocial Impact, and the Performance Effects of Transformational Leadership." *Academy of Management Journal* 55 (2012): 458–76.

Gray, Judy H. and Iain L. Densten. "How Leaders Woo Followers in the Romance of Leadership." *Applied Psychology: An International Review* 56 (2007): 558–81.

Greenfieldboyce, Nell. "Pageant Protest Sparked Bra Burning Myth." *National Public Radio*, September 5, 2008. Accessed at www.npr.org/templates/story/story.php?storyId=94240375.

Greenhaus, Jeffrey H., Saroj Parasuraman, and Wayne M. Wormley. "Effects of Race on Organizational Experiences, Job Performance Revaluations, and Career Operations." *Academy of Management Journal* 33 (1990): 64–86.

Grenier, Sebastien, Anne-Marie Barrette, and Robert Ladouceur. "Uncertainty and Intolerance of Ambiguity: Similarities and Differences." *Personality and Individual Differences* 39 (2005): 593–600.

Grey, Christopher and Hugh Willmott, eds. *Critical Management Studies: A Reader.* Oxford: Oxford University Press, 2005.

Grint, Keith. *The Arts of Leadership.* Oxford: Oxford University Press, 2000.

Grint, Keith. "Problems, Problems, Problems: The Social Construction of 'Leadership.'" *Human Relations* 58 (2005): 1467–94.

Grint, Keith. "The Sacred in Leadership: Separation, Sacrifice and Silence." *Organization Studies* 31 (2010): 89–107.

Guérin, Isabelle, Santhosh Kumar, and Isabelle Agier. "Women's Empowerment: Power to Act or Power over Other Women? Lessons from Indian Microfinance." *Oxford Development Studies* 41 (2013): 576–94.

Gulick, Luther H. and Lyndall F. Urwick, eds. *Papers on the Science of Administration.* New York: Columbia University, 1937.

Guthey, Eric, Timothy Clark, and Brad Jackson. *Demystifying Business Celebrity.* London: Routledge, 2010.

Halbesleben, Jonathon R.B., Milorad M. Novicevic, Michael G. Harvey, and M. Ronald Buckley. "Awareness of Temporal Complexity in Leadership of Creativity and Innovation: A Competency-Based Model." *Leadership Quarterly* 14 (2003): 433–54.

Hall, Peter A. and David W. Soskice. *Varieties of Capitalism: The Institutional Foundations of Comparative Advantage.* New York: Oxford University Press, 2001.

Hambrick, Donald C. "Putting Top Managers Back in the Strategy Picture." *Strategic Management Journal* 10 (1989): 5–15.

Hambrick, Donald C. "Fragmentation and Other Problems CEOs Have with Their Top Management Teams." *California Management Review* 37 (April 1995): 110–27.

Hambrick, Donald C. "Upper Echelons Theory: An Update." *Academy of Management Review* 32 (April 2007): 334–43.

Hambrick, Donald C. and Phyllis A. Mason. "Upper Echelons: The Organization as a Reflection of Its Top Managers." *Academy of Management Review* 9 (1984): 193–206.

Hambrick, Donald C. and Sydney Finkelstein. "Managerial Discretion: A Bridge between Polar Views of Organizations." In *Research in Organizational Behavior 9*, edited by Larry L. Cummings and Barry M. Staw, 359–406. Greenwich: JAI Press, 1987.

Hamilton, Ryan, Kathleen D. Vohs, Anne-Laure Sellier, and Tom Meyvis. "Being of Two Mindsets: Switching Mindsets Exhausts Self-Regulatory Resources." *Organizational Behavior and Human Decision Processes* 115 (2011): 13–24.

Hammer, W. Clay, Jay S. Kim, Lloyd Baird, and William J. Bigoness. "Race and Sex as Determinants of Ratings by Potential Employers in a Simulated Work-Sampling Task." *Journal of Applied Psychology* 59 (1974): 705–11.

Haney, David Paul. *The Americanization of Social Science: Intellectuals and Public Responsibility in the Postwar United States.* Philadelphia: Temple University Press, 2008.

Hannah, David R. and Christopher D. Zatzick. "An Examination of Leader Portrayals in the U.S. Business Press following the Landmark Scandals of the Early 21st Century." *Journal of Business Ethics* 79 (2008): 361–77.

Hansmann, Henry and Reinier Kraakman. "The End of History for Corporate Law." *Georgetown Law Review* 89 (2001): 439–68.

Hardesty, D.J. and W.S. Jones. "Characteristics of Judged High Potential Management Personnel – The Operations of an Industrial Assessment Center." *Personnel Psychology* 21 (1968): 85–98.

Hardy, Cynthia and Sharon Leiba-O'Sullivan. "The Power behind Empowerment: Implications for Research and Practice." *Human Relations* 51 (1998): 451–82.

Hartman, Andrew. "Christopher Lash: Critic of Liberalism, Historian of Its Discontents." *Rethinking History: The Journal of Theory and Practice* 13 (2009).

Haslam, S. Alexander, Stephen D. Reicher, and Michael J. Platow. *The New Psychology of Leadership: Identity, Influence and Power.* New York: Psychology Press, 2011.

Hathaway, Starke R. and J.C. McKinley. *The Minnesota Multiphasic Personality Inventory.* New York: Psychological Corporation, 1943.

Hawken, Paul. *The Ecology of Commerce.* New York: Harper Business, 1993.

Hawley, Amos H. "Community Power and Urban Renewal Success." *American Journal of Sociology* 68 (January 1963): 422–31.

Hayes, Robert H. and William J. Abernathy. "Managing Our Way to Economic Decline." *Harvard Business Review* 58 (July–August 1980): 67–77.

Healey, Mark P., Timo Vuori, and Gerald R. Hodgkinson. "When Teams Agree While Disagreeing: Reflexion and Reflection in Shared Cognition." *Academy of Management Review* 40 (July 2015): 399–422.

Hearn Jeff and F. Wendy Parkin, "Women, Men, and Leadership: A Critical Review of Assumptions, Practices, and Change in Industrialized Nations." *International Studies of Management and Organization* 16 (1986): 33–60.

Heifetz, Ronald A. *Leadership without Easy Answers*. Cambridge: Belknap Press, 1994.

Hemphill John K. and Alvin E. Coons. "Development of the Leader Behavior Description Questionnaire." In *Leader Behavior: Its Description and Measurement*, edited by Ralph M. Stogdill and Alvin E. Coons, 6–38. Columbus: Ohio State University Bureau of Business Research, 1957.

Henderson, Bruce D. *Henderson on Corporate Strategy*. Cambridge: Abt Books, 1979.

Hendricks, Jon and C. Breckinridge Peters. "The Ideal Type and Sociological Theory." *Acta Sociologica* 16 (1970): 31–40.

"Henry V. Erben – He Gets Things Done." *GE Monogram* 25 (1948): 10–12.

Herman, Ellen. *The Romance of American Psychology: Political Culture in the Age of Experts*. Berkeley: University of California Press, 1995.

Hersey, Paul and Kenneth Blanchard. "Life-Cycle Theory of Leadership." *Training and Development Journal* 23 (1969): 26–34.

Hewlett, Sylvia Ann. "Executive Women and the Myth of Having It All." *Harvard Business Review* 80 (April 2002): 66–73.

Hexter, J.H. "The Rhetoric of History." *History and Theory* 6 (1967): 3–13.

Higham, John. "American Intellectual History: A Critical Appraisal." *American Quarterly* 13 (1961): 219–33.

Hill, Walter H. and William M. Fox. "Black and White Marine Squad Leaders' Perceptions of Racially Mixed Squads." *Academy of Management Journal* 16 (December 1973): 680–86.

Hirschman, Albert O. *Exit, Voice, and Loyalty: Responses to Decline in Firms, Organizations, and States*. Cambridge: Harvard University Press, 1970.

Hitt, Michael A., Katalin Takacs Haynes, and Roy Serpa. "Strategic Leadership for the 21st Century." *Business Horizons* 53 (September – October 2010): 437–44.

Ho, Geoffrey, Margaret Shih, and Daniel J. Walters. "Labels and Leaders: The Influence of Framing on Leadership Emergence." *Leadership Quarterly* 21 (2012): 943–52.

Hoffer, Eric. *The True Believer: Thoughts on the Nature of Mass Movements*. New York: Harper, 1951.

Hofstede, Geert. "The Colors of Collars." *Columbia Journal of World Business* 7 (September–October 1972): 72–81.

Hofstede, Geert. "The Importance of Being Dutch: National and Occupational Differences in Work-Goal Importance." *International Studies of Management & Organization* 5 (Winter, 1975/1976): 5–28.

Hofstede, Geert. *Culture's Consequences: International Differences in Work-Related Values*. Newbury Park: Sage, 1980.

Hofstede, Geert. *Culture and Organizations: Software of the Mind*. New York: McGraw-Hill, 1991.

Hofstede, Geert. "The Universal and the Specific in 21st Century Global Management." *Organizational Dynamics* 28 (1999): 34–43.

Hollander, Edwin P. "Authoritarianism and Leadership Choice in a Military Setting." *Journal of Abnormal and Social Psychology* 49, no. 3 (1954): 365–70.

Holmberg, Ingalill and Lars Stannegård. "Leadership Voices: The Ideology of 'The New Economy.'" *Leadership* 1 (2005): 353–74.

Hooijberg, Robert, James G. Hunt, and George E. Dodge. "Leadership Complexity and Development of the Leaderplex Model." *Journal of Management* 23 (1997): 375–408.

Hoption, Colette B., Amy Christie, and Julian Barling. "Submitting to the Follower Label: Followership, Positive Affect and Extra-role Behaviors." *Journal of Psychology* 220 (2012): 221–30.

Horwitz, Morton. *The Transformation of American Law, 1780–1860*. Cambridge: Harvard University Press, 1976.

House, Robert J. "A Path Goal Theory of Leader Effectiveness." *Administrative Science Quarterly* 16 (September 1971): 321–39.

House, Robert J. "A 1976 Theory of Charismatic Leadership." In *Leadership: The Cutting Edge*, edited by James G. Hunt and Lars Larson, 189–207. Carbondale: University of Southern Illinois Press, 1977.

House, Robert J., Paul J. Hanges, Mansour Javidan, Peter W. Dorfman, and Vipin Gupta. *Culture, Leadership, and Organizations: The GLOBE Study of 62 Societies*. Thousand Oaks: Sage, 2004.

Hunt, James G. "Transformational / Charismatic Leadership's Transformation of the Field: An Historical Essay." *Leadership Quarterly* 19 (1999): 129–45.

Hunt, James G., Dian-Marie Hosking, Chester A. Schriesheim, and Rosemary Stewart, eds. *Leaders and Managers: International Perspectives on Managerial Behavior and Leadership*. New York: Pergamon Press, 1984.

Hunter, Samuel T., Liliya Cushenbery, Christian Thoroughgood, Johanna E. Johnson, and Gina Scott Ligon. "First and Ten Leadership: A Historiometric Investigation of the CIP Leadership Model." *Leadership Quarterly* 22 (2011): 70–91.

Iacocca, Lee and William Novak. *Iacocca: An Autobiography*. New York: Bantam Books, 1984.

Ibarra, Herminia, Robin Ely, and Deborah Kolb. "Women Rising: The Unseen Barriers." *Harvard Business Review* 91 (September 2013): 60–67.

Interlandi, Jeneen. "The Brain's Empathy Gap: Can Mapping Neural Pathways Help Us Make Friends with our Enemies?" *New York Times*, March 19 (2015): 50–55, 63.

Jago, Arthur G. and Victor H. Vroom. "Sex Differences in the Incidence and Evaluation of Participative Leader Behavior." *Journal of Applied Psychology* 67 (1982): 776–83.

James, William. *Pragmatism and Other Writings*. New York: Penguin Books, 1907/2000.

Janis, Irving L. *Victims of Groupthink: A Psychological Study of Foreign Policy Decisions and Fiascos*. Boston: Houghton Mifflin, 1972.

Jarzabkowski, Paula and Rosalind H. Searle. "Harnessing Diversity and Collective Action in the Top Management Team." *Long Range Planning* 37 (2004): 399–419.

Jaques, Elliott. *The Changing Culture of a Factory: A Study of Authority and Participation in an Industrial Setting*. London: Tavistock Publications, 1951.

Jeffries, Lesley. *Opposition in Discourse: The Construction of Oppositional Meaning*. London: Continuum, 2010.

Jenkins, Keith. "'Nobody Does It Better' Radical History and Hayden White." *Rethinking History* 12 (March 2008): 59–74.

Jenkins, Keith. *At the Limits of History: Essays on Theory and Practice*. London: Routledge, 2009.

Jenkins, Keith and Alun Munslow. "Introduction." In *The Nature of History Reader*, edited by Keith Jenkins and Alun Munslow, 1–18. London: Routledge, 2004.

Jensen, Michael C. and William H. Meckling. "Theory of the Firm: Managerial Behavior, Agency Costs and Ownership Structure." *Journal of Financial Economics* 3 (1976): 305–60.

Johnson, Craig E. *Meeting the Ethical Challenges of Leadership: Casting Light or Shadow*. Thousand Oaks: Sage, 2001.

Jones, Harold B. "The Ethical Leader: An Ascetic Construct." *Journal of Business Ethics* 14 (1995): 867–74.

Jones, M.L. "Hofstede – Culturally Questionable?" *University of Wollongong Research Online* (2007). Accessed at ro.uow.edu.au/cgi/viewcontent.cgi?article=1389&context=commpapers.

Jost, John T. "Negative Illusions: Conceptual Clarification and Psychological Evidence concerning False Consciousness." *Political Psychology* 16 (1995): 397–424.

Jost, John T. and Orsolya Hunyady. "Antecedents and Consequences of System-Justifying Ideologies." *Current Directions in Psychological Science* 14 (2005): 260–65.

Judge, Timothy A. and Ronald F. Piccolo. "Transformational and Transactional Leadership: A Meta-analytic Test of Their Relative Validity." *Journal of Applied Psychology* 89 (2004): 755–68.

Kalev, Alexandra Kalev, Frank Dobbin, and Erin Kelly. "Best Practices or Best Guesses? Assessing the Efficacy of Corporate Affirmative Action and Diversity Policies." *American Sociological Review* 71 (August 2006): 589–617.

Kanigel, Robert. *The One Best Way: Frederick Winslow Taylor and the Enigma of Efficiency*. New York: Viking, 1997.

Kanter, Rosabeth Moss. *Men and Women of the Corporation*. New York: Basic Books, 1977.

Kanter, Rosabeth Moss. *World Class: Thriving Locally in the Global Economy*. New York: Simon and Schuster, 1995.

Kanungo, Rabindra and Manuel Mendonca. *Ethical Dimensions of Leadership*. Thousand Oaks: Sage, 1996.

Kaplan, Edward S. and Thomas W. Ryley. *Prelude to Trade Wars: American Tariff Policy, 1890–1922*. Westport: Greenwood Press, 1994.

Katz, Robert L. "Skills of an Effective Administrator." *Harvard Business Review* 33 (January–February 1955): 33–42.

Katzenbach, Jon R. *Teams at the Top*. Boston: Harvard Business School Press, 1998.

Keegan, John. *A History of Warfare*. New York: Knopf, 1993.

Kellerman, Barbara. "Hitler's Ghost: A Manifesto." In *Cutting Edge Leadership 2000*, edited by Barbara Kellerman and Larraine R. Matusak, 65–68. College Park, MD: Center for the Advanced Study of Leadership, 2000.

Kellerman, Barbara. *Bad Leadership: What It Is, How It Happens, Why It Matters*. Boston: Harvard Business School Press, 2004.

Kellerman, Barbara. *Followership: How Followers are Creating Change and Changing Leaders*. Boston: Harvard University Press, 2008.

Kellerman, Barbara. *The End of Leadership*. New York: HarperCollins, 2012.

Kelley, Robert E. "In Praise of Followers." *Harvard Business Review* 66 (November 1988): 142–9.

Kelley, Robert E. "Rethinking Followership." In *The Art of Followership: How Great Followers Create Great Leaders and Organizations*, edited by Ronald E. Riggio, Ira Chaleff and Jean Lipman-Blumen, 5–16. San Francisco: Jossey-Bass, 2008.

Kennedy, Emmet. "'Ideology' from Destutt to Marx." *Journal of the History of Ideas* 40 (July–September 1979): 353–68.

Kennedy, Emmet and Vincent Geoghegan. "Ideology and Utopia." *Journal of Political Ideologies* 9 (2004): 123–38.

Kent, Russell L. and Sherry E. Moss. "Effects of Sex and Gender Role on Leader Emergence." *Academy of Management Journal* 37 (1994): 1335–46.

Kets de Vries, Manfred F.R. "The Spirit of Despotism: Understanding the Tyrant Within." *Human Relations* 59 (2006): 195–220.

Khurana, Rakesh. "The Curse of the Superstar CEO." *Harvard Business Review* 80 (September 2002): 2–8.

Khurana, Rakesh. *Searching for a Corporate Savior: The Irrational Quest for Charismatic CEOs*. Princeton: Princeton University Press, 2002.

Kickul, Jill and George Neuman. "Emergent Leadership Behaviors: The Function of Personality and Cognitive Ability in Determining Teamwork Performance and KSAS." *Journal of Business and Psychology* 15 (Fall 2000): 27–51.

Kiechel, Walter, III. *The Lords of Strategy: The Secret Intellectual History of the New Corporate World*. Boston: Harvard Business Press, 2010.

Kirkendall, Richard S. "A.A. Berle, Jr.: Student of the Corporation, 1917–1932." *Business History Review* 35 (Spring 1961): 43–58.

Kirkendall, Richard S., ed. *The Organization of American Historians and the Writing and Teaching of American History*. New York: Oxford University Press, 2011.

Kirkpatrick, Shelley A. and Edwin A. Locke. "Leadership: Do Traits Matter?" *Academy of Management Executive* 5 (1991): 48–60.

Knights, David and Majella O'Leary. "Leadership, Ethics and Responsibility to the Other." *Journal of Business Ethics* 67 (2006): 125–37.

Koehn, Nancy F. "Great Men, Great Pay? Why CEO Compensation Is Sky High," June 12, 2014. Accessed at www.washingtonpost.com/opinions/great-men-great-pay-why-ceo-compensation-is-sky-high/2014/06/12/6e49d796-d227-11e3-9e25-188ebe1fa93b_story.html.

Koenig, Louis W. "Truman's Global Leadership." *Current History* 39 (October 1960): 225–9.

Kolb, Deborah M. "Negotiating in the Shadows of Organizations: Gender, Negotiation, and Change." *Ohio State Journal of Dispute Resolution* 28 (2013): 241–62.

Kolb, Deborah M. and Jean Bartunek. *Hidden Conflict in Organizations: Uncovering Behind-the-Scenes Disputes.* Newbury Park: Sage, 1992.

Kolb, Deborah M. and Kathleen L. McGinn. "Beyond Gender and Negotiation to Gendered Negotiation." *Negotiation and Conflict Management Research* 2 (2009): 1–17.

Kolb, Deborah M., Judith Williams, and Carol Frohlinger. *Her Place at the Table: A Woman's Guide to Negotiating Five Key Challenges to Leadership Success.* San Francisco: Jossey-Bass, 2004.

Koppes, Laura L. *Historical Perspectives in Industrial and Organizational Psychology.* Mahwah: Lawrence Erlbaum Associates, 2007.

Kotter, John P. *The General Managers.* New York: Free Press, 1982.

Kotter, John P. *Power and Influence: Beyond Formal Authority.* New York: Free Press, 1985.

Kotter, John P. *The Leadership Factor.* New York: Free Press, 1988.

Kotter, John P. *A Force for Change: How Leadership Differs from Management.* New York: Free Press, 1990.

Kovjanic, Snjezana, Sebastian C. Schuh, Klaus Jonas, Niels Van Quaquebeke, Rolf Dick. "How Do Transformational Leaders Foster Positive Employee Outcomes? A Self-Determination-Based Analysis of Employees' Needs as Mediating Link." *Journal of Organizational Behavior* 33 (2012): 1031–52.

Krzyzewski, Mike and Donald T. Phillips. *Leading with the Heart: Coach K's Successful Strategies for Basketball, Business, and Life.* New York: Warner Books, 2000.

Kuhn, Thomas. *The Structure of Scientific Revolutions.* Chicago: University of Chicago Press, 1962.

Kuklick, Bruce. "Myth and Symbol in American Studies." *American Quarterly* 24 (October 1972): 435–50.

Kulich, Clara, Michelle K. Ryan, and S. Alexander Haslam. "Where Is the Romance for Women Leaders? The Effects of Gender on Leadership Attributions and Performance-Based Pay." *Applied Psychology: An International Review* 56 (2007): 582–601.

Kunda, Gideon. *Engineering Culture: Control and Commitment in a High-Tech Corporation.* Philadelphia: Temple University Press, 1992.

Kurke, Lance B. and Howard E. Aldrich. "Mintzberg Was Right! A Replication and Extension of the Nature of Managerial Work." *Management Science* 29 (August 1983): 975–84.

Lagassé, Paul, ed. *Columbia Encyclopedia*, 6th edition. New York: Columbia University Press, 2000.

Lan, Alice. "Tacit Knowledge, Organizational Learning and Societal Institutions: An Integrated Framework." *Organizational Studies* 21 (2000): 487–513.

Lane, Henry W., Martha L. Maznevski, and Mark E. Mendenhall. "Globalization: Hercules Meets Buddha." In *The Blackwell Handbook of Global Management: A Guide to Managing Complexity*, edited by Henry W. Lane, Martha L. Maznevski, Jeanne McNett, and Mark E. Mendenhall, 1–25. Malden: Blackwell Publishing, 2004.

Larson, Lars L. and Kendrith M. Rowland. "Leadership Style and Cognitive Complexity." *Academy of Management Journal* 17 (1974): 37–45.

Larwood, Laurie and Marion W. Wood. *Women in Management*. Lexington: Lexington Books, 1977.

Lasch, Christopher. *The Culture of Narcissism: American Life in an Age of Diminishing Expectations*. New York: Norton, 1979.

Lasch, Christopher. *The Minimal Self: Psychic Survival in Troubled Times*. New York: Norton, 1984.

Lazear, Edward P. and Sherwin Rosen. "Rank-Order Tournaments as Optimum Labor Contracts." *Journal of Political Economy* 89 (1981): 841–64.

Lazonick, William and Mary O'Sullivan. "Maximizing Shareholder Value: A New Ideology for Corporate Governance." *Economy and Society* 29 (2000): 13–35.

Learmonth, Mark and Nancy Harding. "Evidence-Based Management: The Very Idea." *Public Administration* 84 (2006): 245–66.

Le Blanc, Paul. "From Revolutionary Intellectual to Conservative Master-Thinker: The Anti-democratic Odyssey of James Burnham." *Left History* 3 (April 1995): 49–81.

Lemon, M.C. *The Discipline of History and the History of Thought*. London: Routledge, 1995.

Levin, Doron B. *Behind the Wheel at Chrysler: The Iacocca Legacy*. New York: Harcourt Brace, 1995.

Levitt, Theodore. "The Globalization of Markets." *Harvard Business Review* 61 (May–June 1983): 92–102.

Levy, Orly, Schon Beechler, Sully Taylor, and Nakiye A. Boyacigiller. "What We Talk About When We Talk About 'Global Mindset': Managerial Cognition in Multinational Corporations." *Journal of International Business Studies* 38 (2007): 231–58.

Lichtenstein, Benyamin B., Mary Uhl-Bien, Russ Marion, Anson Seers, James D. Orton, and Craig Schreiber. "Complexity Leadership Theory: An Interactive Perspective on Leading in Complex Adaptive Systems." *Complexity and Organization* 8 (2006): 2–12.

Lichtheim, George. "The Concept of Ideology." *History and Theory* 4 (1965): 164–95.

Likert, Rensis. *New Patterns of Management*. New York: McGraw-Hill, 1961.

Lincoln, Abraham. Letter to Albert G. Hodges (April 4, 1864). Accessed at www.abrahamlincolnonline.org/lincoln/speeches/hodges.htm.

Lindbekk, Tore. "The Weberian Ideal-type: Development and Continuities." *Acta Sociologica* 35 (1992): 285–97.

Lindenfeld, David. "Jungian Archetypes and the Discourse of History." *Rethinking History: The Journal of Theory and Practice* 13 (2009): 217–34.

Lipman-Blumen, Jean. *The Allure of Toxic Leaders: Why We Follow Destructive Bosses and Corrupt Politicians – And How We Can Survive Them.* New York: Oxford University Press, 2005.

Liu, Helena and Christopher Baker. "White Knights: Leadership as the Heroicisation of Whiteness." *Leadership* 10 (2014): 1–29.

Lodge, George C. *The New American Ideology.* New York: Alfred A. Knopf, 1977.

Lodge, George C. "The Connection between Ethics and Ideology." *Journal of Business Ethics* 1 (1982): 85–98.

Logan, Nneka. "The White Leader Prototype: A Critical Analysis of Race in Public Relations." *Journal of Public Relations Research* 23 (2011): 442–57.

Lord, Robert G. and Karen J. Maher. *Leadership and Information Processing: Linking Perceptions and Performance.* Boston: Unwin Hyman, 1991.

Lovejoy, Arthur O. *The Great Chain of Being: Study of the History of an Idea.* Cambridge: Harvard University Press, 1936.

Lowe, Kevin B. and William L. Gardner. "Ten Years of the *Leadership Quarterly*: Contributions and Challenges for the Future." *Leadership Quarterly* 11 (2001): 459–514.

Luhmann, Christian C., Kanako Ishida, and Greg Hajcak. "Intolerance of Uncertainty and Decisions Delayed, Probabilistic Rewards." *Behavior Therapy* 42 (2011): 378–86.

Lukes, Steven. *Power: A Radical View.* London: Palgrave Macmillan, 1974.

Macey, Jonathan. "Sublime Myths: An Essay in Honor of the Shareholder Value Myth and the Tooth Fairy." *Texas Law Review* 91 (2013): 911–24.

Macfie, Alexander Lyon. "A Possible (Common-Sense) Defense of (My) History: A Response to Keith Jenkins." *Rethinking History* 13 (September 2009): 345–55.

Maciag, Drew. "When Ideas Had Consequences – Or, Whatever Happened to Intellectual History?" *Reviews in American History* 39 (2011): 741–51.

Magnusson, Eva. "Women, Men and All the Other Categories: Psychologies for Theorizing Human Diversity." *Nordic Psychology* 63 (2011): 88–114.

Mahar, Karen Ward "'Definitely a Man's Man': Executive Culture at General Electric, 1945–1960." Paper presented at the annual meeting for Business History Conference, Columbus, Ohio, March 21–23, 2013.

Mäkelä, Liisa. "A Narrative Approach to Pregnancy-Related Discrimination and Leader-Follower Relationships." *Gender, Work, and Organization* 19 (November 2012): 677–98.

Malcolm, Norman. *Problems of Mind: Descartes to Wittgenstein.* New York: Harper, 1971.

Maller, J.B. "Studies in Character and Personality in German Psychological Literature." *Psychological Bulletin* 30 (1933): 209–32.

Maloş, Raul. "The Most Important Leadership Theories." *Annals of Economic Studies* 1 (January 2012): 413–20.

Maner, Jon K. and Nicole L. Mead. "The Essential Tension between Leadership and Power: When Leaders Sacrifice Group Goals for the Sake of Self-Interest." *Journal of Personality and Social Psychology* 99 (2010): 482–97.

Margotta, Donald G. "The Legal Meaning of Agency and Its Implications for Finance Theory." *Journal of Applied Business Research* 6 (2011): 34–39.

Marris, Robin and Dennis C. Mueller. "The Corporation, Competition, and the Invisible Hand." *Journal of Economic Literature* 18 (March 1980): 32–63.

Marrou, Henri-Irénée. *The Meaning of History.* Baltimore: Helicon, 1966.

Martin, John Levi. "The Authoritarian Personality, 50 Years Later: What Questions Are There for Political Psychology?" *Political Psychology* 22 (2001): 1–26.

Martin, Raymond. "Causes, Conditions, and Causal Importance." *History and Theory* 21 (February 1982): 53–74.

Marwick, Arthur. *The Nature of History.* London: Macmillan, 1970.

Marwick, Arthur. "Two Approaches to Historical Study: The Metaphysical (Including 'Postmodernism') and the Historical." *Journal of Contemporary History* 30 (January 1995): 5–35.

Mattson, Kevin. *What the Heck Are You Up To, Mr. President? Jimmy Carter, America's "Malaise," and the Speech That Should Have Changed the Country.* New York: Bloomsbury, 2009.

Maxwell, John C. *The 21 Irrefutable Laws of Leadership: Follow Them and People Will Follow You.* Nashville: Thomas Nelson, 1998.

Mayo, Anthony J. and Nitin Nohria. "Zeitgeist Leadership." *Harvard Business Review* 83 (October 2005): 45, 60.

McArthur, Dan. "Good Ethics Can Sometimes Mean Better Science: Research Ethics and the Milgram Experiments." *Science and Engineering Ethics* 15 (2009): 69–79.

McClelland, David C. *Power: The Inner Experience.* New York: Irvington Publishers, 1975.

McCraw, Thomas K. "Introduction: The Intellectual Odyssey of Alfred D. Chandler." In *The Essential Alfred Chandler: Essays toward a Historical Theory of Big Business*, edited by Thomas K. McCraw, 1–21. Boston: Harvard Business School Press, 1988.

McCullagh, C. Behan. "What Do Historians Argue About?" *History and Theory* 43 (February 2004): 18–28.

McDonald, John. *A Ghost's Memoir: The Making of Alfred P. Sloan's My Years with General Motors.* Boston: MIT Press, 2003.

McIntosh, Donald. "The Objective Bases of Max Weber's Ideal Types." *History and Theory* 16 (October 1977): 265–79.

McKinnon, Neil and John Bigelow. "Presentism, and Speaking of the Dead." *Philosophical Studies* 160 (2012): 253–63.

"McKinsey-Academy Book Awards." *Academy of Management Journal* 8 (June 1965): 150–59.

McLaren, Patricia Genoe, Albert J. Mills, and Terrance G. Weatherbee, eds. *The Routledge Companion to Management and Organizational History.* London: Routledge, 2015.

McPherson, Blair. "No More Heroes." *Human Resource Management International Digest* 16 (2008): 6–9.

McPherson, Miller, Lynn Smith-Lovin, and James M. Cook. "Birds of a Feather: Homophily in Social Networks." *Annual Review of Sociology* 27 (2001): 415–44.

McSweeney, Brendan. "Hofstede's Model of National Cultural Differences and Their Consequences: A Triumph of Faith – A Failure of Analysis." *Human Relations* 55 (2002): 89–118.

Mead, Leonard C. "A Program of Human Engineering." *Personnel Psychology* 1 (1948): 303–7.

Mead, Margaret. *Sex and Temperament in Three Primitive Societies*. New York: Dell, 1935.

Meek, V. Lynn. "Organizational Culture: Origins and Weaknesses." *Organization Studies* 9 (1988): 453–73.

Megill, Allan. "Five Questions on Intellectual History." *Rethinking History: The Journal of Theory and Practice* 15 (2011): 489–510.

Meier, August. "Negro Class Struggle and Ideology in the Age of Booker T. Washington." *Phylon* 23 (1962): 256–66.

Meindl, James R. and Sanford B. Ehrlich. "The Romance of Leadership and the Evaluation of Organizational Performance." *Academy of Management Journal* 30 (1987): 91–109.

Meindl, James R., Sanford B. Ehrlich, and Janet M. Dukerich. "The Romance of Leadership." *Administrative Science Quarterly* 30 (March 1985): 78–102.

Mendenhall, Mark H., Joyce S. Osland, Allan Bird, Gary R. Oddou, Martha L. Maznevski, Michael J. Stevens, and Günter K. Stahl. *Global Leadership: Research, Practice, and Development*. New York: Routledge, 2013.

Mescon, Michael H. "The Dynamics of Industrial Leadership." *Journal of the Academy of Management* 1 (1958): 13–21.

Milgram, Stanley. "Behavioral Study of Obedience." *Journal of Abnormal and Social Psychology* 67 (1963): 371–78.

Miller, Amelia R. "The Effects of Motherhood Timing in Career Path." *Journal of Population Economics* 24 (2011): 1071–100.

Miller, Danny, Jon Hartwick, and Isabelle Le Breton-Miller. "How to Detect a Management Fad – and Distinguish It from a Classic." *Business Horizons* 47 (August 2004): 7–16.

Millett, Kate. *Sexual Politics*. New York: Doubleday, 1970.

Mills, Albert J. "Organization, Gender, and Culture." In *Gendering Organizational Analysis*, edited by Albert J. Mills and Peta Tancreed, 93–111. London: Sage, 1992.

Mills, Albert J. *Sex, Strategy, and the Stratosphere: Airlines and the Gendering of Organizational Culture*. London: Palgrave, 2006.

Mills, Charles W. *Blackness Visible: Essays on Philosophy and Race*. Ithaca: Cornell University Press, 1998.

Mills, C. Wright. *White Collar: The American Middle Class*. New York: Oxford University Press, 1951.

Mills, C. Wright. *The Power Elite*. New York: Oxford University Press, 1956.

Mink, Louis O. "History and Fiction as Modes of Comprehension." *New Literary History* 1 (Spring 1970): 541–56.

Mintzberg, Henry. "Structured Observation as a Method to Study Managerial Work." *Journal of Management Studies* 7 (February 1970): 87–104.

Mintzberg, Henry. "Managerial Work: Analysis from Observation." *Management Science* 18 (1971): 97–110.

Mintzberg, Henry. *The Nature of Managerial Work*. Englewood Cliffs: Prentice-Hall, 1973.

Mintzberg, Henry. "The Strategy Concept II: Another Look at Why Organizations Need Strategies." *California Management Review* 30 (Fall 1987): 25–32.

Mintzberg, Henry. "The Fall and Rise of Strategic Planning." *Harvard Business Review* 72 (January–February 1994): 107–14.

Mintzberg, Henry. "Enough Leadership." *Harvard Business Review* 82 (November 2004): 22.

Mintzberg, Henry and James A. Waters. "Of Strategies, Deliberate and Emergent." *Strategic Management Journal* 6 (1985): 257–72.

Mitchell, William J.T. *Iconology: Image, Text, Ideology*. Chicago: University of Chicago Press, 1986.

Mohr, Lawrence. *The Causes of Human Behavior: Implications for Theory and Method in the Social Sciences*. Ann Arbor: University of Michigan Press, 1996.

Morgan, Gareth. *Images of Organization*. Beverly Hills: Sage, 1986.

Morgan, Robin, ed. *Sisterhood Is Powerful: An Anthology of Writings from the Women's Liberation Movement*. New York: Random House, 1970.

Moritz, Michael and Barrett Seaman. *Going for Broke: Lee Iacocca's Battle to Save Chrysler*. New York: Doubleday, 1984.

Mumford, Michael D. and Judy R. Van Doom. "The Leadership of Pragmatism: Reconsidering Franklin in the Age of Charisma." *Leadership Quarterly* 12 (2001): 279–309.

Mumford, Michael D., Allison L. Antes, Jay J. Caughron, and Tamera L. Friedrich. "Charismatic, Ideological, and Pragmatic Leadership: Multilevel Influences on Emergence and Performance." *Leadership Quarterly* 19 (2008): 144–60.

Mumford, Michael D., Jazmine Espejo, Samuel T. Hunter, Katrina E. Bedell-Avers, Dawn L. Eubanks, and Shane Connelly. "The Sources of Leader Violence: A Comparison of Ideological and Non-ideological Leaders." *Leadership Quarterly* 18 (2007): 217–35.

Munslow, Alun. *The Routledge Companion to Historical Studies*. London: Routledge, 2000.

Munslow, Alun. "Where Does History Come From?" *History Today* 52 (March 2002): 18–20.

Munslow, Alun. *Deconstructing History*. London: Routledge, 2006.

Munslow, Alun. "Why Should Historians Write about the Nature of History (Rather than Just Do It)?" *Rethinking History* 11 (December 2007): 613–25.

Munslow, Alun. "Managing the Past." In *The Routledge Companion to Management and Organizational History*, edited by Patricia Genoe McLaren et al., 131. London: Routledge, 2015.

Munsterberg, Hugo. *Psychology and Industrial Efficiency.* Boston: Houghton-Mifflin, 1913.

Musto, Marcello. "Revisiting Marx's Concept of Alienation." *Socialism and Democracy* 24 (November 2010): 79–101.

Napoli, Donald S. *Architects of Adjustment: The History of the Psychological Profession in the United States.* Port Washington, NY: Kennikat Press, 1981.

Neustadt, Richard E. *Presidential Power: The Politics of Leadership.* New York: Wiley, 1960.

Nice, David C. "The Warrior Model of Leadership: Classic Perspectives and Contemporary Relevance." *Leadership Quarterly* 9 (1998): 321–33.

Nkomo, Stella M. "The Emperor Has No Clothes: Rewriting Race in Organizations." *Academy of Management Review* 17 (July 1992).

Nord, Walter R. and Suzy Fox. "The Individual in Organizational Studies: The Great Disappearing Act?" In *Studying Organization: Theory and Method,* edited by Stewart Clegg and Cynthia Hardy, 142–68. Thousand Oaks: Sage, 1999.

Northouse, Peter G. *Leadership: Theory and Practice.* Thousand Oaks, CA: Sage, 2013.

Nye, Joseph S., Jr. "Soft Power." *Foreign Policy* 80 (Autumn 1990): 153–71.

Nye, Joseph S., Jr. *Soft Power: The Means to Success in World Polices.* New York: Public Affairs, 2004.

Oakley, Ann. *Sex, Gender, and Society.* New York: Harper & Row, 1972.

O'Connor, Johnson. *Psychometrics.* Cambridge: Harvard University Press, 1934.

Ohlsson, Stellan. *Deep Learning: How the Mind Overrides Experience.* Cambridge: Cambridge University Press, 2011.

Olick, Jeffrey K. *The Politics of Regret: On Collective Memory and Historical Responsibility.* New York: Routledge, 2007.

Omi, Michael and Howard Winant. *Racial Formation in the United States: From the 1960s to the 1990s.* New York: Routledge, 1994.

"Only 5 Black CEOs at 500 Biggest Companies." CNN Money, January 29, 2015. Accessed at money.cnn.com/2015/01/29/news/economy/mcdonalds-ceo-diversity.

Orillia, Francesco. "Dynamic Events and Presentism." *Philosophical Studies* 160 (2012): 407–14.

Orpen, Christopher. "Causal Attributions for the Success and Failure of Black and White Managers." *Journal of Occupational Behavior* 2 (April 1981): 81–87.

Orser, Barbara, Allan Riding, and Joanne Stanley. "Perceived Career Challenges and Response Strategies of Women in the Advanced Technology Sector." *Entrepreneurship & Regional Development* 24 (January 2012): 73–93.

Osland, Joyce S., Ming Li, and Ying Wang, eds. *Advances in Global Leadership,* Vol. 8. London: Emerald, 2014.

Ospina, Sonia and Erica Foldy. "A Critical Review of Race and Ethnicity in the Leadership Literature: Surfacing Context, Power and the Collective Dimensions of Leadership." *Leadership Quarterly* 20 (2009): 876–96.

O'Toole, James. "Lordstown: Three Years Later." *Business and Society Review* 13 (Spring 1975): 64–71.

Ouchi, William. *Theory Z: How American Business Can Meet the Japanese Challenge.* Reading: Addison-Wesley, 1981.

Padilla, Art, Robert Hogan, and Robert B. Kaiser. "The Toxic Triangle: Destructive Leaders, Susceptible Followers and Conducive Environments." *Leadership Quarterly* 18 (2007): 176–94.

Page, Scott E. *The Difference: How the Power of Diversity Creates Better Groups, Firms, Schools, and Society.* Princeton: Princeton University Press, 2007.

Palmer, Walter J. "Management Effectiveness as a Function of Personality Traits of the Manager." *Personnel Psychology* 27 (1974): 283–95.

Palmié, Stephen. "Genomics, Divination, 'Racecraft.'" *American Ethnologist* 34 (2007): 205–22.

Parker, Patricia S. *Race, Gender, and Leadership: Re-envisioning Organizational Leadership from the Perspectives of African American Women Executives.* Mahwah: Lawrence Erlbaum, 2005.

Parker, Patricia S. and dt ogilvie. "Gender, Culture, and Leadership: Toward a Culturally Distinct Model of African-American Women Executives' Leadership Strategies." *Leadership Quarterly* 7 (1996): 189–214.

Parsons, Talcott and Edward Shils. *Toward a General Theory of Action.* Cambridge: Harvard University Press, 1951/1962.

Pascale, Richard Tanner and Anthony G. Athos. *The Art of Japanese Management: Applications for American Executives.* New York: Simon & Schuster, 1981.

Pateman, Carole. *The Sexual Contract.* Stanford: Stanford University Press, 1988.

Patton, Arch. "How to Appraise Executive Performance." *Harvard Business Review* 38 (1960): 63–70.

Pear, Robert. "Iacocca and Secretary of Interior Clash Over Statue Panel Ouster." *New York Times*, February 1, 1986: A1.

Pegues, DeMarcus A. and Christopher J.L. Cunningham. "Diversity in Leadership: Where *Is* the Love for Racioethnic Minorities?" *Business Journal of Hispanic Research* 4 (2010): 11–17.

Pelletier, Kathie L. "Leader Toxicity: An Empirical Investigation of Toxic Behavior and Rhetoric." *Leadership* 6 (2010): 373–89.

Pennington, Leon A. and H.W. Case. "A Course in Military Psychology." *Psychological Bulletin* 39(6) (1942): 377–80.

Pennington, Leon A. and Romeyn B. Hough, Jr. *The Psychology of Military Leadership.* New York: Prentice-Hall, 1943.

Perlmutter, Howard V. "The Tortuous Evolution of the Multinational Corporation." *Columbia Journal of World Business* 4 (January–February 1969): 9–18.

Peters, Thomas J. and Robert H. Waterman. *In Search of Excellence: Lessons from America's Best-Run Companies.* New York: Harper & Row, 1982.

Pettigrew, Andrew M. "On Studying Organizational Cultures." *Administrative Science Quarterly* 24 (December 1979): 570–81.

Pettigrew, William A. *Freedom's Debt: The Royal African Company and the Politics of the Atlantic Slave Trade, 1672–1752.* Chapel Hill: University of North Carolina Press, 2013.

Pfeffer, Jeffrey. "The Ambiguity of Leadership." *Academy of Management Review* 2 (January 1977): 104–12.

Pfeffer, Jeffrey. *Power in Organizations*. Marshfield: Pitman, 1981.

Pfeffer, Jeffrey. *Managing with Power: Politics and Influence in Organizations.* Boston: Harvard Business School Press, 1992.

Pfeffer, Jeffrey. *Leadership BS: Fixing Workplaces and Careers One Truth at a Time.* New York: HarperCollins, 2015.

Pfeffer, Jeffrey and Robert I. Sutton. "Profiting from Evidence-Based Management." *Strategy & Leadership* 34 (2006): 35–42.

Phillips, Robert, R. Edward Freeman, and Andrew C. Wicks, "What Stakeholder Theory Is Not." *Business Ethics Quarterly* 13 (2003): 479–502.

Piderit, Sandy Kristin. "Rethinking Resistance and Recognizing Ambivalence: A Multidimensional View of Attitudes toward an Organizational Change." *Academy of Management Review* 25 (2000) 783–94.

Pierce, Jennifer L. *Racing for Innocence: Whiteness, Gender, and the Backlash against Affirmative Action.* Stanford: Stanford University Press, 2012.

Pinto, Alex J. "Ethics and Leadership." *International Journal of Discourse and Governance* 6 (2009): 277–83.

Polsby, Nelson W. *Political Innovation in America: The Politics of Policy Initiation.* New Haven: Yale University Press, 1984.

Popper, Micha. "Toward a Theory of Followership." *Review of General Psychology* 15 (2011): 29–36.

Porter, Michael E. *Competitive Strategy: Techniques for Analyzing Industries and Competitors.* New York: Free Press, 1980.

Porter, Michael E. *Competitive Advantage: Creating and Sustaining Superior Advantage.* New York: Free Press, 1985.

Porter, Michael E. "From Competitive Advantage to Corporate Strategy." *Harvard Business Review* 65 (May–June 1987): 43–50.

Porter, Theodore M. "Introduction: Positioning Social Science in Cold War America." In *Cold War Social Science: Knowledge Production, Liberal Democracy, and Human Nature*, edited by Mark Solovey and Hamilton Cravens, ix–xv. New York: Palgrave, 2012.

Potterfield, Thomas A. *The Business of Employee Empowerment: Democracy and Ideology in the Workplace.* Westport: Quorum Books, 1999.

Powel, Colin. *It Worked for Me: In Life and Leadership.* New York: Harper, 2012.

Prasad, Pushkala and Albert J. Mills. "From Showcase to Shadow: Understanding the Dilemmas of Managing Workplace Diversity." In *Managing the Organizational Melting Pot: Dilemmas of Workplace Diversity*, edited by Pushkala Prasad, Albert J. Mills, Michael Elmes and Anshuman Prasad, 3–27. Thousand Oaks: Sage, 1997.

Putnam, Linda L., David Grant, Grant Michelson, and Leanne Cutcher. "Discourse and Resistance: Targets, Practices, and Consequences." *Management Communication Quarterly* 19 (August 2005): 5–18.

Quinn, Robert E. *Beyond Rational Management: Mastering the Paradoxes and Competing Demands of High Performance.* San Francisco: Jossey-Bass, 1988.

Rachlinski, Jeffrey J. and Gregory S. Parks. "Implicit Bias, Election '08, and the Myth of a PostRacial America." *Cornell Law Library Scholarship@Cornell Law: A Digital Repository* (2010). Accessed at http://scholarship.law.cornell.edu/cgi/viewcontent.cgi?article=1177&context=facpub.

Raelin, Joseph A. *Leaderful Organizations: How to Bring Out Leadership in Everyone*. San Francisco: Berrett-Koehler, 2003.

Ranson, Stewart, Bob Hinings, and Royston Greenwood. "The Structuring of Organizational Structures." *Administrative Science Quarterly* 25 (March 1980): 1–17.

Rappaport, Alfred C. *Creating Shareholder Value: The New Standard for Business Performance*. New York: Free Press, 1986.

Repp, Charles. "What's Wrong with Didacticism?" *British Journal of Aesthetics* 52 (2012): 271–86.

Rhinesmith, Stephen H. "Global Mindsets for Global Managers." *Training & Development* 46 (October 1992): 63–68.

Rich, Frank. "A Distant Mirror." *New York Times Sunday Book Review* (August 3, 2014): 16.

Richards, Graham. *Putting Psychology in Its Place: Critical Historical Perspectives*, 3rd edition. London: Routledge, 2000.

Richardson, Agnes and Cynthia Loubier. "Intersectionality and Leadership." *International Journal of Leadership Studies* 3 (2008): 142–61.

Riesman, David. *The Lonely Crowd: A Study of the Changing American Character*. New Haven: Yale University Press, 1950.

Riley, Donna M. "LGBT-Friendly Workplaces in Engineering." *Leadership & Management in Engineering* 8 (January 2008): 19–23.

Ringer, Fritz. *Max Weber: An Intellectual Biography*. Chicago: University of Chicago Press, 2004.

Rittel, Horst W.J. and Melvin M. Webber. "Dilemmas in a General Theory of Planning." *Policy Sciences* 4 (1973): 155–9.

Rivera, Lauren A. "Guess Who Doesn't Fit In at Work." *New York Times*. May 30, 2015. Accessed at www.nytimes.com/2015/05/31/opinion/sunday/guess-who-doesnt-fit-in-at-work.html?

Robé, Jean-Phillippe. "Science vs. Ideology: A Comment on Lynn Stout's New Thinking on 'Shareholder Primacy.'" *Accounting, Economics, and Law* 2 (2012): 1–11.

Roberts, Wess. *The Leadership Secrets of Attila the Hun*. New York: Grand Central Publishing, 1989.

Robinson, John. "Squaring the Circle? Some Thoughts on the Idea of Sustainable Development." *Ecological Economics* 48 (2004): 369–84.

Robinson, Sandra L. and Rebecca J. Bennett. "A Typology of Deviant Workplace Behaviors: A Multidimensional Scaling Study." *Academy of Management Journal* 38 (April 1995): 555–72.

Rodrik, Dani. *The Globalization Paradox: Democracy and the Future of the World Economy*. New York: Norton, 2011.

Roiser, Martin and Carla Willing. "The Strange Death of the Authoritarian Personality: 50 Years of Psychological and Political Debate." *History of the Human Sciences* 15 (2002): 71–96.

Rosener, Judy B. "Ways Women Lead." *Harvard Business Review* 68 (November–December 1980): 119–25.

Ross, Jan-Michael and Dmitry Sharapov. "When the Leader Follows: Dethronement through Imitation." *Academy of Management Journal* 58 (June 2015): 658–79.

Rost, Joseph C. *Leadership for the Twenty-First Century.* New York: Praeger, 1991.

Rost, Joseph C. "Leadership: A Discussion about Ethics." *Business Ethics Quarterly* 5 (1995): 129–42.

Rost, Katja, Emil Inauen, Margit Osterloh, and Bruno S. Frey. "The Corporate Governance of Benedictine Abbeys: What Can Stock Companies Learn from Monasteries?" *Journal of Management History* 16 (2010): 90–115.

Rousseau, Denise M. "Is There Such a Thing as 'Evidence-Based Management'?" *Academy of Management Review* 31 (2006): 256–69.

Rowlinson, Michael, Roy Stager Jaques, and Charles Booth. "Critical Management and Organizational History." In *The Oxford Handbook of Critical Management Studies,* edited by Mats Alvesson, Todd Bridgman, and Hugh Willmott, 286–303. New York: Oxford University Press, 2011.

Rowntree, Benjamin Seebohm. *The Human Factor in Business: Experiments in Industrial Democracy.* London: Longmans, Green, 1921.

Sage Reference. "Glass Ceiling." *Encyclopedia of Race, Ethnicity, and Society,* 2008. Accessed at www.sagepub.com/northouse6e/study/materials/reference/reference14.1.2008.

Salancik, Gerald R. and James R. Meindl. "Corporate Attributions as Strategic Illusions of Management Control." *Administrative Science Quarterly* 29 (1984): 238–54.

Salas-Lopez, Debbie, Lynn M. Deitrick, Erica T. Mahandy, Eric J. Gertner, and Judith N. Sabino. "Women Leaders: Challenges, Success, and Other Insights from the Top." *Journal of Leadership Studies* 5 (2011): 34–42.

Salpukas, Agis. "Young Workers Disrupt Key GM Plant." *New York Times,* January 23, 1972: 1, 35.

Sandberg, Sheryl. *Lean In: Women, Work, and the Will to Lead.* New York: Alfred A. Knopf, 2014.

Santos, José. "Strategy Lessons from Left Field." *Harvard Business Review* 85 (April 2007): 20–21.

Sattler, Jerome M. "Racial 'Experimenter Effects' in Experimentation, Testing, Interviewing, and Psychotherapy." *Psychological Bulletin* 73 (1970): 137–60.

Savitz, Andrew W. *The Triple Bottom Line.* San Francisco: Wiley, 2006.

Schapiro, J. Salwyn. "Thomas Carlyle, Prophet of Fascism." *Journal of Modern History* 17 (June 1945): 97–115.

Schein, Edgar H. *Organizational Culture and Leadership.* San Francisco: Jossey-Bass, 1985.

Schein, Edgar H. *The Corporate Culture Survival Guide: Sense and Nonsense about Culture Change.* San Francisco: Jossey-Bass, 1999.

Schein, Virginia E. "The Relationship between Sex Role Stereotypes and Requisite Management Characteristics." *Journal of Applied Psychology* 57 (1973): 95–100.

Schein, Virginia E. "The Relationship between Sex Role Stereotypes and Requisite Management Characteristics among Female Managers." *Journal of Applied Psychology* 60 (1975): 340–44.

Schein, Virginia E. "Sex Role Stereotypes and Requisite Management Characteristics, Past, Present and Future." Western Ontario: National Centre for Management Research and Development, Working Paper NC 89-26 (November 1989).

Schein, Virginia E. "A Global Look at Psychological Barriers to Women's Progress in Management." *Journal of Social Issues* 37 (2001): 675–88.

Schein, Virginia E. and Ruediger Mueller. "Sex Role Stereotyping and Requisite Managerial Characteristics: A Cross Cultural Look." *Journal of Organizational Behavior* 13 (1992): 439–47.

Schendel, Dan. "On Strategic Leadership." *Strategic Management Journal* 10 (1989): 1–3.

Schlesinger, Arthur M., Jr., *The Age of Jackson*. Boston: Little, Brown, 1945.

Schmidt, Warren H. and Robert Tannenbaum. "Management of Differences." *Harvard Business Review* 38 (1960): 107–15.

Schoemaker, Paul J.H., Steve Krupp, and Samantha Howland. "Strategic Leadership: The Essential Skills." *Harvard Business Review* 91 (January–February 2013): 131–4.

Schulman, Bruce J. *The Seventies: The Great Shift in American Culture, Society, and Politics*. New York: Free Press, 2001.

Schwartz, Felice N. "Management Women and the New Facts of Life." *Harvard Business Review* 67 (January–February 1989): 65–76.

Schyns, Birgit and Jan Schilling. "How Bad Are the Effects of Bad Leaders? A Meta-analysis of Destructive Leadership and Its Outcomes." *Leadership Quarterly* 24 (2013): 138–58.

Scott, Cynthia D. and Dennis T. Jaffe. *Empowerment: Building a Committed Workforce*. London: Kogan Page, 1991.

Seligman, Adam B. "Charisma and the Transformation of Grace in the Early Modern Era." *Social Research* 58, no. 3 (Fall 1991): 591–620.

Selznick, Philip. *Leadership in Administration: A Sociological Interpretation*. New York: Harper & Row, 1957.

Semler, Ricardo. *Maverick: The Success Story behind the World's Most Unusual Workplace*. New York: Warner Books, 1993.

Senge, Peter M. *The Fifth Discipline: The Art and Practice of the Learning Organization*. New York: Doubleday, 1990.

Shallenberger, David. "Professional and Openly Gay." *Journal of Management Inquiry* 3 (1994): 119–42.

Shartle, Carroll L. "Early Years of the Ohio State University Leadership Studies." *Journal of Management* 5 (1979): 127–34.

Shartle, Carroll L and Beatrice J. Dvorak. "Organizational Analysis Activities in the War Manpower Commission." *Psychological Bulletin* 40 (1943): 701–13.

Shaw, James B., Anthony Erickson, and Michael Harvey. "A Method for Measuring Destructive Behavior and Identifying Types of Destructive Leaders in Organization." *Leadership Quarterly* 22 (2011): 575–90.

Shelby, Tommie. "Race." In *The Oxford Handbook of Political Philosophy*, edited by David Estlund, 336–53. New York: Oxford University Press, 2012.

Shills, Edward. "Ideology and Civility: On the Politics of the Intellectual." *Sewanee Review* 66 (1958): 450–80.

Silverman, David. *The Theory of Organizations*. London: Heinemann, 1970.

Simon, Barbara Levy. *The Empowerment Tradition in American Social Work: A History*. New York: Columbia University Press, 1994.

Simpson, Ruth. "Presenteeism, Power and Organizational Change: Long Hours as a Career Barrier and the Impact on the Working Lives of Women Managers." *British Journal of Management* 9 (1998): 37–50.

Sirota, David and J. Michael Greenwood. "Understand Your Overseas Work Force." *Harvard Business Review* 49 (January–February 1971): 53–60.

Slipp, Samuel. *The Freudian Mystique: Freud, Women, and Feminism.* New York: New York University Press, 1993.

Sloan, Alfred P. *My Years with General Motors.* New York: Doubleday, 1964.

Smircich, Linda. "Concepts of Culture and Organizational Analysis." *Administrative Science Quarterly* 28 (1983): 339–58.

Smith, Miriam. "Diversity and Identity in the Non-profit Sector: Lessons from LGBT Organizing in Toronto." *Social Policy & Administration* 39 (October 2005): 463–80.

Smith, Peter B. *"Culture's Consequences:* Something Old and Something New." *Human Relations* 55 (2002): 119–35.

Smith, Steven G. "Historical Meaningfulness in Shared Action." *History and Theory* 48 (February 2009): 1–19.

Smith, Wendy K. and Marianne W. Lewis. "Toward a Theory of Paradox: A Dynamic Equilibrium Model of Organizing." *Academy of Management Review* 36 (2011): 381–403.

Smock, Charles D. "The Influence of Psychological Stress on the 'Intolerance of Ambiguity.'" *Journal of Abnormal Psychology* 50 (1955): 177–82.

Snow, Bradford. "Experience and the Passage of Time." *Philosophical Perspectives* 25 (2011): 359–87.

Sobel, Robert. *The Age of Giant Corporations: A Microeconomic History of American Business, 1914–1994.* Westport: Greenwood Press, 1993.

Solomon, Barbara B. *Black Empowerment: Social Work in Oppressed Communities.* New York: Columbia University Press, 1976.

Søndergaard, Mikael. "Research Note: Hofstede's Consequences: A Study of Reviews, Citations, and Replications." *Organization Studies* 15 (1994): 447–56.

Southgate, Beverley. "Replacing the Past with Disobedience." *Rethinking History: The Journal of Theory and Practice* 17 (2013): 222–34.

Spector, Bert A. "Transformational Leadership: The New Challenge for U.S. Unions." *Human Resource Management* 26 (1987): 3–16.

Spector, Bert A. "Business Responsibilities in a Divided World: The Cold War Roots of the Corporate Social Responsibility Movement." *Enterprise and Society* 9 (June 2008): 314–36.

Spector, Bert A. *Implementing Organizational Change: Theory into Practice.* Upper Saddle River: Pearson, 2013.

Spector, Bert A. "Using History Ahistorically: Presentism and the Tranquility Fallacy." *Management & Organizational History* 9 (2014): 305–13.

Spector, Bert A. and Paul Lawrence, "General Motors and the United Auto Workers." In *Human Resource Management: A General Manager's Perspective,* edited by Michael Beer, Bert Spector, Paul R. Lawrence, D. Quinn Mills and Richard Walton, 683–710. New York: Free Press, 1985.

Spencer, Herbert. *The Study of Sociology*. Ann Arbor: University of Michigan Press, 1873/1961.

Standiford, Les. *Meet You in Hell: Andrew Carnegie, Henry Clay Frick, and the Bitter Partnership That Transformed America*. New York: Crown, 2005.

Stanley, David. "Role Conflict: Leaders and Managers." *Nursing Management* 13 (2006): 31–37.

Starch, Daniel. *How to Develop Your Executive Ability*. New York: Harper, 1943.

Staw, Barry M., Pamela L. McKechnie, and Sheila M. Puffer. "The Justification of Organizational Performance." *Administrative Science Quarterly* 28 (1983): 582–600.

Stein, Judith. *Pivotal Decade: How the United States Traded Factories for Finance in the Seventies*. New Haven: Yale University Press, 2010.

Steinweis, Arthur. "Hitler and Carlyle's 'Historical Greatness.'" *History Today* 45 (1995): 33–39.

Stets, Jan E. and Peter J. Burke. "Femininity/Masculinity." In *Encyclopedia of Sociology*, edited by Edgar F. Borgatta and Rhonda J.V. Montgomery, 997–1005. New York: Macmillan, 2000.

Stogdill, Ralph M. "Personal Factors Associated with Leadership: A Survey of the Literature." *Journal of Psychology* 25 (1948): 35–71.

Stogdill, Ralph M. *Handbook of Leadership: A Survey of Theory and Research*. New York: Free Press, 1974.

Stojanović, Svetozar. "From Ideology to Pragmatism." *Society* 25 (May–June 1988): 24–27.

Stone, Pamela. *Opting Out? Why Women Really Quit Careers and Head Home*. Berkeley: University of California Press, 2007.

Stouffer, Samuel A., Edward A. Suchman, Leland C. DeVinney, Shirley A. Star, and Robin M. Williams, Jr. *The American Soldier: Adjustment during Army Life, Vol. I*. Princeton: Princeton University Press, 1949.

Stout, Lynn. *The Shareholder Value Myth: How Putting Shareholders First Harms Investors, Corporations, and the Public*. San Francisco: Berrett-Koehler Publishers, 2012.

Strozier, Charles B., Daniel Offer, and Oliger Abdyli, eds. *The Leader: Psychological Essays*. New York: Springer, 2011.

Strum, Daniel. *The Sugar Trade: Brazil, Portugal and the Netherlands, 1595–1630*. Stanford: Stanford University Press, 2013.

Strumpf, Dan. "Stock Buybacks Hit New Records." *Wall Street Journal* (May 7, 2015). Accessed at http://blogs.wsj.com/moneybeat/2015/05/07/stock-buybacks-hit-new-records.

Stuller, John. "Lee Iacocca and an America That's Back on Its Feet." *Saturday Evening Post* (October 1984): 46, 104–105.

Sullivan, Daniel. "Measuring the Degree of Internationalization of the Firm." *Journal of International Business Studies* 25 (1994): 325–42.

Sutton, Charlotte Decker and Kris K. Moore. "Executive Women – 20 Years Later." *Harvard Business Review* 63 (September–October 1985): 42–66.

Tai, An-Ju R. and Randi L. Sims. "The Perception of the Glass Ceiling in High Technology Companies." *Journal of Leadership and Organizational Studies* 12 (2005): 16–22.

Takaki, Ronald. *A Different Mirror: A History of Multicultural America.* Boston: Little, Brown, 1993.

Tang, Hua, Tom Quertermous, Beatriz Rodriguez, Sharon L.R. Kardia, Xiaofeng Zhu, Andrew Brown, James S. Pankow, Michael A. Province, Steven C. Hunt, Eric Boerwinkle, Nicholas Schork, and Neil J. Risch. "Genetic Structure, Self-Identified Race/Ethnicity, and Confounding in Case-Control Association Studies." *American Journal of Human Genetics* 76 (2005): 268–75.

Tannenbaum, Robert and Fred Massarik. "Leadership: A Frame of Reference." *Management Science* 4 (1957): 1–19.

Tannenbaum, Robert and Warren H. Schmidt. "How to Choose a Leadership Pattern." *Harvard Business Review* 36 (March–April 1958): 85–101.

Taussig, F.W. and C.S. Joslyn. *American Business Leaders.* New York: Macmillan, 1932.

Taylor, Frederick Winslow. *A Piece-Rate System.* New York: American Society of Mechanical Engineers, 1895.

Taylor, Frederick Winslow. *Shop Management.* New York: Harper & Brothers, 1903.

Taylor, Frederick Winslow. *The Principles of Scientific Management.* New York: Harper & Brothers, 1911.

Taylor, George R. *The Turner Thesis: Concerning the Role of the Frontier in American History.* Lexington: Heath, 1971.

Taylor, Paul C. *Race: A Philosophical Introduction.* Cambridge: Polity, 2004.

Terman, Lewis M. "The Use of Intelligence Tests in the Army." *Psychological Bulletin* 15 (1918): 177–87.

Terman, Lewis M. and Catherine C. Miles. *Sex and Personality.* New York: McGraw-Hill, 1936.

Thomas, David A. "The Impact of Race on Managers' Experiences of Developmental Relationships (Mentoring and Sponsorship): An Intra-organizational Study." *Journal of Organizational Behavior* 11 (1990): 479–92.

Thomas, David A. "Racial Dynamics in Cross-Race Developmental Relationships." *Administrative Science Quarterly* 38 (June 1993): 169–94.

Thomas, David A. "The Truth about Mentoring Minorities: Race Matters." *Harvard Business Review* 79 (April 2001): 98–107.

Thomas, David A. and John J. Gabarro. *Breaking Through: The Making of Minority Executives in Corporate America.* Boston: Harvard Business School Press, 1999.

Thompson, James B. *Organizations in Action: Social Science Bases of Administrative Theory.* New York: McGraw-Hill, 1967.

Thoroughgood, Christian N., Art Padilla, Samuel T. Hunter, and Brian W. Tate. "The Susceptible Circle: Taxonomy of Followers Associated with Destructive Leadership." *Leadership Quarterly* 23 (2012): 897–917.

Thorpe, Judie M. "Lee Iacocca and the Generation of Myth in the Spokesman Advertising Campaign for Chrysler from 1980–1984." *Journal of American Culture* 11 (1998): 41–45.

Tichy, Noel M. and David O. Ulrich. "SMR Forum: The Leadership Challenge – A Call for the Transformational Leader." *Sloan Management Review* 26 (Fall 1984): 59–68.

Tilles, Seymour. "The Manager's Job: A Systems Approach." *Harvard Business Review* 41 (January/February 1963): 73–81.

Tilles, Seymour. "How to Evaluate Corporate Strategy." *Harvard Business Review* 41 (July/August 1963): 111–21.

Tillman, Linda C. "African American Principals and the Legacy of *Brown*." *Review of Research in Education* 28 (2004): 101–46.

Tourish, Dennis. *The Dark Side of Transformational Leadership: A Critical Perspective*. London: Routledge, 2013.

Tourish, Dennis. "'Evidence Based Management' or 'Evidence Oriented Organizing'? A Critical Realist Perspective." *Organization* 20 (March 2013): 173–92.

Trachtenberg, Marc. *The Craft of International History: A Guide to Method*. Princeton: Princeton University Press, 2006.

Treece, James B. "The Mood at Lordstown Changed from Confrontation to Cooperation." *Automotive News* (October 31, 2011): 15.

Treynor, Jack T. "The Financial Objective in the Widely Held Corporation." *Financial Analysts Journal* 37 (1981): 68–71.

Tupes, Ernest and Raymond Christal. *Recurrent Personality Factors Based on Trait Ratings*. Washington, D.C.: United States Air Force, 1961.

Turner, Barry A. *Exploring the Industrial Subculture*. London: Macmillan, 1971.

Turner, Frederick J. *The Frontier in American History*. New York: H. Holt, 1920.

Turner, Henry Ashby, Jr. *General Motors and the Nazis: The Struggle for Control of Opel, Europe's Biggest Carmaker*. New Haven: Yale University Press, 2005.

Uhl-Bien, Mary and Russ Marion. "Complexity Leadership in Bureaucratic Forms of Organizing: A Meso Model." *Leadership Quarterly* 20 (2009): 631–50.

Uhl-Bien, Mary and Rajnandini Pillai. "The Romance of Leadership and the Social Construction of Followership." In *Follower-Centered Perspectives on Leadership: A Tribute to the Memory of James R. Meindl*, edited by Boas Shamir, Rajnandini Pillai, Mary Bligh, and Mary Uhl-Bien, 187–210. Charlotte: Information Age Publishers, 2007.

Uhl-Bien, Mary, Ronald E. Riggio, Kevin B. Lowe, and Melissa K. Carsten. "Followership Theory: A Review and Research Agenda." *Leadership Quarterly* 25 (2014): 83–104.

United Nations Conference on Trade and Development. *The Universe of the Largest Transnational Corporations*. New York: United Nations, 2007.

United States Department of Justice Civil Rights Division. *Investigation of the Ferguson Police Department*. Washington, D.C.: Department of Justice, March 4, 2015.

Uyterhoeven, Hugo E.R. "General Managers in the Middle." *Harvard Business Review* 50 (March–April 1972): 75–85.

Van der Toorn, Jojanneke, Tom R. Tyler, and John T. Jost. "More than Air: Outcome Dependence, System Justification, and the Perceived Legitimacy of Authority Figures." *Journal of Experimental Social Psychology* 47 (2011): 127–38.

Van Knippenberg Daan and Michael Hogg, eds. *Leadership and Power: Identity Processes in Groups and Organizations*. London: Sage, 2003.

Van Knippenberg Daan and Sim B. Sitkin. "A Critical Assessment of Charismatic-Transformational Leadership Research: Back to the Drawing Board?" *Academy of Management Annals* 7 (2013): 1–60.

Vogel, David. "The Books That Shaped the Public's View of Business." *Business & Society Review* 6 (September 1973): 58–63.

Vogel, Ezra F. *Japan as Number One: Lessons for America.* Cambridge: Harvard University Press, 1979.

Vroom, Victor H. and Phillip Yetton. *Leadership and Decision Making.* Pittsburgh: University of Pittsburgh Press, 1973.

Vugt, Mark van and Anjana Ahuja. *Naturally Selected: Why Some People Lead, Others Follow, and Why It Matters.* New York: Harper, 2011.

Wade, Peter. *Race, Nature and Culture: An Anthropological Perspective.* London: Pluto Press, 2002.

Waller, James E. "The Social Sciences." In *The Oxford Handbook of Holocaust Studies, edited* by P. Hayes and J.K. Roth, 667–79. New York: Oxford University Press, 2010.

Wallman, Steven M.H. "The Proper Interpretation of Corporate Constituency Statutes and Formulation of Director Duties." *Stetson Law Review* 21 (1991): 163–96.

Walton, Richard E. "How to Counter Alienation in the Plant." *Harvard Business Review* 50 (November–December 1972): 70–81.

Walton, Richard E. "From Control to Commitment in the Workplace." *Harvard Business Review* 63 (March–April 1985): 77–84.

Watkins, Michael D. "Seven Transitions Good Leaders Must Make: Moving from a Functional Leader to a General Manager." *IMD: Tomorrow's Challenges* 1 (June 2012): 1–4.

Watson, John. "Psychology as the Behavioralist Views It." *Psychological Review* 20 (1913): 158–77.

Watson, Tony J. "Group Ideologies and Organizational Change." *Journal of Management Studies* 19 (1982): 259–75.

Waxman, Chaim I. *The End of Ideology Debate.* New York: Funk & Wagnalls, 1969.

Weber, Max. *The Protestant Ethic and the Spirit of Capitalism.* New York: Norton, 1905/2009.

Weber, Max. *The Theory of Social and Economic Organizations.* New York: Oxford University Press, 1947.

Weber, Max. *The Methodology of the Social Sciences.* New York: Free Press, 1949.

Weber, Max. *Economy and Society: An Outline of Interpretive Sociology,* Vols. 1–2, edited by Guenther Roth and Claus Wittich. Berkeley: University of California Press, 1978.

Weinryb, Elizar. "The Justification of a Causal Thesis: An Analysis of the Controversies over the Theses of Pirenne, Turner, and Weber." *History and Theory* 14 (February 1975): 32–56.

Weiss, Richard M. *Managerial Ideology and the Social Control of Deviance.* New York: Praeger, 1986.

Weiss, Richard M. and Lynn E. Miller. "The Concept of Ideology in Organizational Analysis: The Sociology of Knowledge or the Social Psychology of Beliefs?" *Academy of Management Review* 12 (1987): 104–16.

White, Hayden. *Metahistory: The Historical Imagination in Nineteenth-Century Europe*. Baltimore: John Hopkins University Press, 1973.

White, Hayden. "The Historical Text as Literary Artifact." In *The Writing of History: Literary Form and Historical Understanding*, edited by Robert Canary and Henry Kozicki, 41–62. Madison: University of Wisconsin Press, 1978.

White, Hayden. *The Content of the Form: Narrative Discourse and Historical Representation*. Baltimore: Johns Hopkins University Press, 1987.

White, Hayden. "Response to Arthur Marwick." *Journal of Contemporary History* 30 (April 1995): 233–46.

Whitman, Meg and Joan Hamilton. *The Power of Many: Values for Success in Business and Life*. New York: Crown, 2010.

Whittington, Richard and Michael Meyer. *The European Corporation: Strategy, Structure and Social Science*. Oxford: Oxford University Press, 2000.

Whyte, William H. "Groupthink." *Fortune* (March 1952): 114–17, 142, 146.

Wieviorka, Michel. "An Old Theme Revisited: Sociology and Ideology." *Comparative Sociology* 2 (2003): 510–21.

Wilkins, Mira. "Multinational Enterprises and the Varieties of Capitalism." *Business History Review* 84 (2010): 638–48.

Williams, Joan C. and Rachel Dempsey. *What Works for Women at Work: Four Patterns Working Women Need to Know*. New York: New York University Press, 2014.

Williams, Joan C., Mary Blair-Loy, and Jennifer L. Berdahl. "Cultural Schemas, Social Class, and the Flexibility Stigma." *Journal of Social Issues* 69 (2013): 209–34.

Williams, John E. and Deborah L. Best. *Measuring Sex Stereotypes: A Multination Study*. Newbury Park: Sage, 1990.

Williams, Tara. *Inventing Womanhood: Gender and Language in Later Middle English Writing*. Columbus: Ohio State University Press, 2011.

Williamson, Oliver E. *Markets and Hierarchies: Analysis and Antitrust Implications*. New York: Free Press, 1975.

Wilson, Howard. "Changing Patterns of Supervisory Leadership." *Industrial Management* 13 (November 1971): 11–12.

Winfrey, Oprah and Joan Barthel. *Oprah*. New York: Knopf, 1998.

Witzel, Morgen. *Builders and Dreamers: The Making and Meaning of Management*. London: Financial Times Prentice-Hall, 2002.

Witzel, Morgen. "Monks and Multinationals: Business Models of the Middle Ages." *European Business Forum* 18 (Summer 2004): 74–76.

Witzel, Morgen. *A History of Management Thought*. London: Routledge, 2012.

Witzel, Morgen. "The Leadership Philosophy of Han Fei." *Asia Pacific Business Review* 18 (2012): 489–503.

Wolf, Theta H. "The Emergence of Binet's Concepts and Measurement of Intelligence: A Case History of the Creative Process, Part II." *Journal of the History of the Behavioral Sciences* 5 (1969): 207–37.

Wolfers, Justin. "Fewer Women Run Big Companies than Men Named John." *New York Times* (March 2, 2015): A3.

Wong, Leonard, Paul Bliesce and Dennis McGurk. "Military Leadership: A Context-Specific Review." *Leadership Quarterly* 14 (2003): 657–69.

Wren, Daniel A. and Arthur G. Bedeian. *The Evolution of Management Thought*, 6th edition. San Francisco: Wiley, 2009.

Wyatt, Frederick and Hans Lukas Teuber. "German Psychology under the Nazi System: 1933–1940." *Psychological Review* 51 (1944): 229–47.

Yarrow, Andrew L. "The Big Postwar Story." *Journalism History* 32 (2006): 58–76.

Yeadon, John David. *Herbert Spencer: The Evolution of a Sociologist*. New York: Basic Books, 1971.

Yerkes, Robert M. "Man-Power and Military Effectiveness: The Case for Human Engineering." *Journal of Consulting Psychology* 5 (1941): 205–9.

Yukl, Gary. "Managerial Leadership: A Review of Theory and Research." *Journal of Management* 15 (1989): 251–89.

Yukl, Gary. *Leadership in Organizations*, 8th edition. Boston: Pearson, 2013.

Zaleznik, Abraham. *Human Dimensions of Leadership*. New York: Harper & Row, 1966.

Zaleznik, Abraham. "Managers and Leaders: Are They Different?" *Harvard Business Review* 55 (May–June 1977): 67–78.

Zaleznik, Abraham. *The Managerial Mystique: Restoring Leadership in Business*. New York: Harper & Row, 1989.

Zerubavel, Eviater. "Social Memories: Steps to a Sociology of the Past." *Qualitative Sociology* 19 (1996): 283–99.

Zimbardo, Philip G. and Ken Musen. *Quiet Rage: The Stanford Prison Study*. Stanford: Stanford University Press, 2003.

Index

ABB, 200
Abernathy, William, 170–71, 237
Academy of Management Annals, 248
Academy of Management Review, 27, 133
Achilles, Edith, 40
Achilles, Paul, 40
Acker, Joan, 125, 233
Ackroyd, Stephen, 83
Adams, Fred, 214
Adler, Nancy, 127, 195, 241
Administration Industrielle et Generale (Fayol), 161
administrators, 165
Adorno, Theodor, 41, 225
African American women, 132, 139–40
African slaves, 98
agency theory, 6, 104–06
agentic characteristics, 171
Ageton, Arthur, 36
Agho, Augustine, 84
Agnew, Spiro, 169, 234
agreeableness, 42
Ahuja, Anjana, 28
Aizawa, Ken, 214
Al-Farabi, 49
alienation, 73
Allaire, Yvan, 78
Allport, Gordon, 42
Altman, Steven, 194–95
Alvesson, Mats, 155
"Ambiguity of Leadership" (Pfeffer), 27, 32
American Anthropological Association, 133
American Historical Association, 112
American Management Association, 153
American Psychological Association, 38, 39
American Soldier, The (Stouffer), 224–25
Anastakis, Dimitry, 189
Ancien Régime, 20
Anderson, Cameron, 136, 150

Andrews, Kenneth, 163
Ankersmit, Frank, 5, 8
Ansbacher, L.H., 40–41
Anshen, Melvin, 12
Ansoff, H. Igor, 34, 49, 50, 163, 236, 250
Antonakis, John, 188
Anuja, Anjana, 28, 247
Appelbaum, Jerome, 24
"Are Women Executives People?" (Bowman et al.), 125–28, 145, 222, 229
Arendt, Hannah, 89
Argyris, Chris, 84–85
Armistice Day, 40
army leader, 34–35
Arrigo, Jean Maria, 38
Art of Japanese Management, The (Pascale and Athos), 78
Art of War (Sun Tzu), 35
Asch, Solomon, 122
Ashby, W. Ross, 51
AT&T, 43
Athos, Anthony, 78
Atkinson, Rick, 37
Attanucci, Jane, 145
Authoritarian Personality (Adorno), 41, 225
authority structure, 181
automobile industry, 174–76
Avolio, Bruce, 92

Babcock, Linda, 147
Bachrach, Peter, 93
Bailey, Beth, 143, 169
Baker, Christopher, 121
"banality of evil" (Arendt), 89
Bandsuch, Mark, 110
Baratz, Morton, 93
Baritz, Loren, 46, 227
Barnard, Chester, 83, 161, 193, 223
Barthel, Joan, 33
Barthes, Roland, 8

298

314   Index

Printed in the United States
By Bookmasters